# VALUE MANAGEMENT IN PROFESSIONS

## About the Editors

**Nalin K. Shastree** has been a practitioner of higher education for almost three decades and has significantly contributed for understanding of changing shades of the discipline at the conceptual level. Apart from being a Professor of Botany (presently he is on leave), he has served in various managerial capacities in institutions of higher learning, including the positions of Principal, Co-ordinator, College Development Council and Registrar in institutions like Vaish College, Rohtak, J.V.B. Institute, Ladnun, Magadh University, Bodhgaya, Babasaheb Bhimrao Ambedkar University, Lucknow and Guru Gobind Singh Indraprastha University, Delhi. He has three books, twenty seven research papers and more than a dozen articles on various dimensions of educational management to his credit.

**B.R. Dugar** is an Associate Professor and Head of the Department of Non-violence and Peace in J.V.B. Institute (Deemed University), Ladnun. Trained in Indian Philosophy, Dr. Dugar has done his doctoral work on various facets of super sensuous knowledge and human consciousness. He has published more than six dozen articles and four books.

**J.P.N. Mishra** is an Associate Professor of the Science of Living, Preksha Meditation and Yoga in J.V.B. Institute (Deemed University), Ladnun. Trained as a life-scientist, Dr. Mishra has chosen an area of research which deals with the effects of meditation on the human physiology. He has published twenty research papers in journals of repute and has two books to his credit.

**Anil Dhar** is an Assistant Lecturer in the Department of Non-violence and Peace, J.V.B. Institute (Deemed University), Ladnun. He has extensively worked on meditation and value education and has published sixteen research papers in journals of repute.

# VALUE MANAGEMENT IN PROFESSIONS

## Present Scenario, Future Strategies

*Edited by*
**Nalin K. Shastree**
**B.R. Dugar**
**J.P.N. Mishra**
**A.K. Dhar**

**CONCEPT PUBLISHING COMPANY, NEW DELHI-110059**

**Cataloging in Publication Data—DK**
*Courtesy:* D.K. Agencies (P) Ltd. <docinfo@dkagencies.com>

**Value management in professions :** present scenario, future strategies / edited by Nalin K. Shastree ... [et al.].
p. cm.
In Indian context.
Includes bibliographical references.
Includes index.
ISBN 8180693414

1. Social values—India. 2. Teaching—Moral and ethical aspects—India. 3. Business ethics—India. 4. Professional ethics—India. I. Shastree, Nalin K., 1955-

DDC 174 22



ISBN : 81-8069-341-4

First Published 2006



*Published and Printed by*
Ashok Kumar Mittal
**Concept Publishing Company**
A/15-16, Commercial Block, Mohan Garden
New Delhi-110059 (INDIA)

*Phones* : 25351460, 25351794
*Fax* : 091-11-25357103
*Email* : publishing@conceptpub.com

# Blessings

The people's concern for the erosion of values all over the world is a very big challenge before all human beings for ensuring a sustainable social structure. The challenge to ensure the human development is massive and no worthwhile achievement is possible without an upsurge of ethical values, of cleanliness of public life, ending prevailing cynicism and corruption and developing a commitment to respect the cultural wealth and imbibe the value system by all the people, all over the globe.

Values are our beliefs about one ought or ought not to behave or about some state of existence worth or not worth attaining. These are the abstract ideals, positive or negative, which represent a person's belief about ideal modes of conduct and ideal terminal goals for ensuring a just and fair social order. We need to see values like a yardstick, we need to guide thc actions, attitudes, comparisons, evaluations and justifications of ourselves and others. The value spectrum has both subjective as well as objective dimensions. Sometimes, we speak of the value as meaning the individual's experience of satisfaction and sometimes values refer to the quality of an object or of an act. This happens in appreciation of the relationship between an organism and an object, although, we can not ever be sure just how much each contributes to the interrelationship.

Increase of violence has increased the magnitude of corruption also. The societal disregard for non-violence, morality, interdependence, sympathetic feelings and collective consciousness has adversely affected the creative potential of the people in general. This may be viewed that a relationship between creativity and values is an integral and important part of a forward looking, just and fair social order, since values stand as an intrinsic part of the human personality, which reflects in attitudes, beliefs, faith and in various other societal as well as individual's domain. Creativity is the basic mantra of societal progress and therefore, all creative persons should be virtuous; although all virtuous persons may not be having all creative ability. Some of the human values work as motivators for human beings, some help the individuals to decide as how to use their creative thinking or develop as an object in the wider interest of the mankind, whereas by the virtue of certain ethical, moral and social values, teachers, parents and administrators may be made motivated to inspire the creative talents to nurture and enhance the creative potential through activating various steps like commitment, preparedness and actualization. One should not forget the great values of justice, liberty and equality as seen in Plato's republic.

Value affirmation aims at modification and purification of behaviour, which improves the psychological behaviourism. Disciplining the self is the key to success because it moulds the individual's character and also determines individuals reactions and responses to other values and society at large. Self-discipline is the maintenance of orderliness and obedience through autosuggestions and strengthening the human consciousness.

Development of values is a life long process. It is not something that is completed by the early childhood. As the world changes, we do change and as we strive to change, the world again changes. The overemphasized importance on creation, possession and enjoyment of material wealth and the search for organic satisfactions is to be re-looked into through sensitizing the people for appreciation of a value-based system of living, irrespective of their religious faith, their caste and creed oriented background and making them aware that satisfaction lying beyond the sensate level of life is of immense importance and people need to experience the spiritual freedom and integrity.

Present Book entitled "Value Management in Professions" is a composite effort of Prof. Nalin K. Shastree, Dr. B.R. Dugar, Dr. J.P.N. Mishra and Dr. Anil K. Dhar, which is a commendable exercise in view of the fact that the editors have tried to address related contemporary issues pertaining to the crisis of values in all walks of life and they have focused an aim to find out some solutions, too. The editorial approach is an elaboration of the pioneer efforts made under the leadership of Ganadhipati Tulsi, who strived hard for making a value-based social structure through his Anuvrat movement by way of making an understanding of the basics of the Science of Living and deviced practicing the Preksha meditation. I hope the present intellectual exercise activated by various scholars shall bring some positive changes in the societal perceptions and shall reaffirm people's faith in the value-based society. I wish the present effort all the success.

**Acharya Mahaprajna**

# Foreword

I consider it a privilege to welcome and foreword "Value Management in Professions" edited by Professor Nalin K. Shastree and others. The book is a valuable resource input in emerging knowledge society leavened by the enlightened editorial approach of Prof. Shastree and his editorial colleagues and contributors. The book has the blessings of Acharya Mahaprajn who is, by common consent, a great moral force and ethical loadstar of our times.

Professor Nalin K. Shastree and his editorial colleagues have endeavoured to explore ways and means of developing and broad consensus on fostering Value affirmation in different professions with a particular focus on Value Management. The book has chosen a comprehensive thematic range covering Values in Social Life, in Teaching Profession, Education and in Business Management. It is my considered view that knowledge society without Values would be a wasteland. On the other hand, emphasis on Value Management in Professions would turn social, cultural and business life into an oasis. Values are essentially country-specific, culture-specific, and time-specific, but there is a common thread of human sensitivity and ethical responsibility, which runs through all the beads of the rosary of values. In the prefatory chapter on editorial approach, it is stated that Indian culture is rooted deeply into spiritual values and those values must necessarily find their way into the life of every member of their society. The editors are conscious of the unique grandeur and continuity of India's cultural heritage in which the importance of life comprises values of truth and compassion. The editors have endeavoured to initiate a multicultural exploration towards the understanding of Values and Management of Value realization in society. In this exploration, the book marks the most important milestones of sincerity, simplicity, gentleness, modesty, compassion, humility, courtesy, cooperation, fair-play, self-reliance, self-control, truthfulness, non-violence and patriotism on the path of secular and spiritual solidarity beyond caste and creed. Professor Nalin K. Shastree and his colleagues travel that path of exploration and identify the many dimensions of Values, which are aptly described as the abode of humanity. The concept of Values is explained and annotated in various contributions with great lucidity and conventional grooves of thoughts are interrogated and a purposeful attempt is made to emancipate our professions and our life from narrow and conventional shackles of thoughts and prejudice. The contributions in the book shows a remarkable commitment to contribute to the global ethics of human enlightenment rooted in reciprocity and harmonious human transformation. Professions have the power and the responsibility to assist in that transformation if only there is an implicit commitment to the ethical values in each and every profession. The book seeks to answer the challenges before the learned professions in the world and the answer to those challenges is the quintessential meaning of Dharma which is synonymous with duty and which alone can contribute to progress and prosperity in every walk of life.

I believe that Value Management in the Profession has much to do with excellence. To achieve excellence, a group, organization, or a country has to have the will, the determination, the honesty, and the sincerity and rectitude, in short an internalized and assimilated value system and a mindset dedicated to excellence, as well as a critical apparatus of excellence as the touchstone and a resource base as well as a methodology earmarked to achieve excellence. As an ancient Vedic hymn reminds us "The holy hymns desire, bless and fulfil only those who are awake." To be awake is, I believe, is to be cognizant of the value system.

The world has been in the business of engineering and reengineering mindsets at every step of human civilization and at every turn and twist of human experience. That is what Philosophy, Religion, Culture, Art, Science, Technology, Law, Linguistics, Sociology, Leadership, and Management are all about. In an address to Symbiosis at Pune, a few years ago, I had occasion to reflect on the concept of excellence and its intimate relationship with Management and I had pointed out that it is in the minds of men, women, and children that the pursuit of excellence begins. Indeed it is in the minds of men, women, and children that we have to build the foundations of excellence, of human values and of discipline, of creativity and of leadership.

With all the telescoped advances in knowledge, we still do not know enough of the ways in which the human mind works. We do know however that there are billions and trillions of cells in the human brain; we do know that the physical brain acts as the hardware for the versatile software of our conscious mind; we also do know that our ancestors had intuitively delineated the outline of the science of consciousness of which yoga, the science of concentration is the best known branch. Excellence in Action in Yoga, says our tradition. Yoga is the science of consciousness. I believe that the science of consciousness is the key to incremental and exponential excellence and to the unlimited potential, adaptability, and versatility of the human mind.

Excellence is a relative term. It is a hallmark of quality. It denotes a very high grade in qualitative evaluation generally in relation to a person or a product or an organization. The pursuit of excellence may also be an integral part of a value system. It could be a cultural or national characteristic. It could also be a credo or a standard of quality as an aspect of running an organization or of manufacturing or marketing policy. It is a ubiquitous yardstick in every walk of life. Of course, it is not an absolute or static concept. Nor is it an entirely abstract concept. It is both objective and subjective. It is both comparative and competitive. It has to be constantly and consistently cultivated. There are no quick fix recipes for instant and improvised excellence. It calls for dedication and integrity to create a symbiotic conjunction of the various internal and external components and concomitants of excellence. Most of the time, it is possible to see and recognize excellence objectively in a person or a product or an organization.

Personal excellence is the basic building block. It depends primarily on the inborn, acquired and cultivated qualities of the individual. An individual has to be strongly motivated to achieve personal excellence. He or she has to have a strong sense of self-confidence and a commitment to the pursuit of excellence, a pursuit which is often handicapped and equally often encouraged and assisted by situations, opportunities and reactions of superiors, colleagues and followers. Personal Excellence paves the way for Organizational Excellence, which in turn ensures the Excellence of the Product. Whatever that product may be. Excellence is a catalyst and a bridge between charismatic leaders and their followers, a hyphen that joins them and the buckle that binds them.

Not every leader at every stratum of life has that charismatic excellence which inspires and transforms the society or the organization. Nor is charisma a substitute for work -aday pragmatism. We need both Charismatic transformational leadership as well as operationally practical transactional leadership. Charismatic leadership fires the imagination of the people who can acquire an uncanny capacity for a quantum jump and a long leap forward. Transactional leadership sustains and keeps the group, the community, or the organization going. There are some rare individuals who have the ability to transform their followers and have at the same time the competence to transact on behalf of their followers the twists and turn in their lives while negotiating with their rivals and adversaries. That rare combination was found for example in our nation's political life in Mahatma Gandhi who shaped leaders out of common clay, who never lost the common touch and never lost the ability to transact, negotiate and deal with the concerns of the common people hold the view that a combination of both transformational and transformational leadership in the right proportion is essential in public life as well as in the management of all public affairs and private business. Ideally, both transformational leadership and transactional leadership have to be guided by considerations of public interest and the spirit of public service. A demagogue's unbridled and unprincipled transformational mass leadership endangers society by reckless populism and leads it to the orgies and the abyss of self-destruction, tension, conflict, and hatred. Unbridled and unprincipled transactional leadership easily turns into anti-social, corrupt, and self-serving wheeling-dealing. Neither of those distortions are conducive to excellence or to social well-being.

I recall that David Neidert in his book Four Seasons of Leadership (1999) tells us that hard work, action and perseverance are the only fairy dust that would fulfil our dreams in the cycle of life. According to him, winter is the time of reflection and self-introspection leading to a clear perception of the mission and goals of leadership, Spring is the time of renewal, growth and commitment; Summer is the time for exploring and nurturing core values; and Autumn is the time of transition, transaction and transformation, a time for living leadership in the workplace and community. To fulfil the responsibility of leadership, we must understand Reality fully and Contextually and to weave the threads of values in these mosaic of Reality. This is what Professor Nalin K. Shastree and his colleagues invite us to do through Value Management in Professions and particularly through Values in Educations and Teaching Profession, Values in Social Life, and Values in Business Management. I am sure that this book will prove to be a harbinger of meaningful academic reflection which will restore the centrality of the Value system in the professions and in our daily life.

**Dr. L.M. Singhvi**

# Contents

*Blessings from* ***Acharya Mahaprajna*** v

*Foreword by* ***Dr. L.M. Singhvi*** *vii*

*List of the Contributors* *xv*

*The Editorial Approach* *xix*

SECTION I
**VALUES IN SOCIAL LIFE**

1. Value Realization Eternal Code of Ethics 3
*Upadhyay 108 Gyan Sagar Ji Maharaj*

2. Values: Ultimate Destiny of Humanity 11
*Nalin K. Shastree*

3. Value Education for Secular Society 35
*Kireet Joshi*

4. The Declaration on Global Ethics in the Light of Modern Physics 42
*Sampooran Singh*

5. Values in the Tradition of Indian Thinking and Values Relevant to Our Contemporary Needs 52
*S.P. Banerjee*

6. Purposeful Living 63
*K. Rama Rao*

7. Developing Values for Self Development (Teacher-based Activities for Professional Growth) 72
*M.R. Chilana*

8. Value Management and Police Administration 81
*Shri Ram Arun*

9. Economic Development and Values 85
*N.M.P. Verma*

10. Ethics in Dental Profession: An Overview 103
*Nimish Nimeya*


---

## SECTION II
## VALUES IN TEACHING PROFESSION AND EDUCATION

---


11. Education in Human Values for Human Excellence Amidst Diversity 115
*Bhoomitra Dev*

12. Trends in Value Education 118
*B.R. Duggar*

13. Moral Values and Education 133
*S.R. Bhatt*

14. Good Education 137
*R.P. Singh*

15. Value Education: A New Dimension 142
*T. Vasantakumar*

16. Values for University Teachers: Need of the Hour 148
*P. N. Muthiah*

17. Modernity vs. Value Oriented Education 153
*J.P.N. Mishra and Anil Dhar*

18. Valuing Professional Growth Image, Intent and Initiatives 160
*Mulk Raj Chilana*

19. Typologies of Values for Teachers 164
*Shyamanand Singh*

20. Teacher's Attitude Towards Children 172
*V.K. Sabharwal*

21. Value Orientation and Self Understanding in Teacher Education 182
*Arti Sen*

22. Values in University Teaching 191
*Madhulika Paul and V. K. Gupta*

23. Values in Higher Education: A Sociological Appraisal 196
*Raj Singh and M.L. Sharma*

24. Towards Value Based Management in University Education 202
*A.K. Pandey*

25. Value Education Based on Ethics in University Leadership with a Special Reference to the Indian Tradition 215
*R.R. Verma*

26. Restructuring Teacher Education for Value Orientation 222
*V. Usha Sri*

---

SECTION III

## VALUES IN BUSINESS MANAGEMENT

---

27. Managing Value Based Ethical Behaviour in Business and Governance 241
*Shailendra Singh and Kumud Singh*

28. Values and Managerial Excellence in the Changing Business Environment 259
*Swami Prasad and Shalini Nigam*

29. Values for Business Managers 266
*V.K. Gupta and Madhulika Paul*

30. Role of Business Managers 272
*Shalini Nigam, Swami Prasad and Puneet Mathur*

31. Values for Business Managers: An Integrated Approach 282
*D.N. Kapoor and Niraj Gupta*

32. Managerial Value System in Internationalised Business Environment 291
*A.K. Satsangi and S.P. Kaushik*

33. Relational Values of Managers: A Key to Successful Training and Development Programme 299
*Pravin Saxena and Swami Prasad*

34. Values in Management and the Labour in the Perspectives of Globalisation 304
*I.C. Awasthi*

35. Whither 'Humane' Governance? Searching for Values in Public Administration in India 312
*P. Raghu Ram*

36. Values in Public Services 325
*Marina R. Pinto*

37. HR-Management: A Holistic Value-based Approach 343
*B.P. Singh, A.K. Singh and K.K. Goel*

38. Ethics in Advertising 358
*Amish Ameya*

*Index* 374

## List of the Contributors

**A.K. Pandey,** Assistant Registrar, Babasaheb Bhimrao Ambedkar University, Lucknow-226 025.

**A.K. Satsangi,** Reader, Dayalbagh Educational Institute, Agra.

**A.K. Singh,** Reader, Department of Commerce, Delhi School of Economics, University of Delhi, Delhi-110 007.

**Amish Ameya,** Assistant Manager, Times Response, The Times of India, 7, Bahadur Shah Zafar Marg, New Delhi-110 002.

**Anil K. Dhar,** Department of Non-violence, Anuvrat and Peace Studies, J.V.B. Institute, Ladnun-341 306 (Rajasthan).

**Arti Sen,** C/o Dr. B.R. Dugar, J.V.B. Institute, Ladnun-341 306 (Rajasthan).

**B.P. Singh,** Former Professor, Head and Dean, Faculty of Commerce and Business, Delhi School of Economics, University of Delhi, New Delhi-110 007.

**B.R. Dugar,** Head, Department of Non-violence, Anuvrat and Peace Studies, J.V.B. Institute, Ladnun-341 306 (Rajasthan).

**Bhoomitra Dev,** Former Vice Chancellor, Deen Dayal Upadhyaya Gorakhpur University and Rohilkhand University, Bareilly, Plot No. 53, Shakti Nagar, Lucknow-226 016.

**D.N. Kapoor,** Dean, Faculty of Commerce, Dayalbagh Educational Institute, Dayalbagh, Agra.

**I.C. Awasthi,** Institute of Applied Manpower Research, New Delhi.

**J.P.N. Mishra,** Head, Department of Science of Living, Preksha Meditation and Yoga, J.V.B. Institute, Ladnun-341 306.

**K.K. Goel,** Director, Delhi School of Professional Studies and Research, D-30, N.D.S.E. Part-1, New Delhi.

**Kireet Joshi,** Chairman, Value Education Centre, Ex Member-Secretary, Indian Council of Philosophical Research, Former Secretary, Ministry of Human Resource Development, Government of India, New Delhi.

**Kumud Singh,** Associate Professor, Krishi Gyan Kendra, Acharya Narendra Dev University of Agriculture & Technology, Barabanki (U.P.).

**M.L. Sharma,** C.C.S. Haryana Agriculture University, Hissar-125 001.

**Madhulika Paul,** Department of Economics, Dayalbagh Educational Institute, Dayalbagh, Agra.

**Marina R. Pinto,** C/o Indian Institute of Public Administration, I.P. Estate, New Delhi-110 002.

**Mulkraj Chilana,** Former Professor, National Council of Educational Research and Training, Aurbindo Marg, New Delhi.

**Nalin K. Shastree,** H-7, Type V, Delhi Government Officer's Flats. Model Town II, Near Alpana Cinema, Delhi-110 009.

**Nilmani Prasad Verma,** Reader and Head, Department of Economics. Babasaheb Bhimrao Ambedkar University, Lucknow-226 025.

**Nimish Nimeya,** Junior Dental Surgeon, Department of Dental Sciences, Dr. N.C. Joshi Memorial Hospital, Karol Bagh, Delhi.

**P. Raghuram,** Assistant Professor, School of Legal Studies, Babasaheb Bhimrao Ambedkar University, Lucknow-226 025.

**P.N. Muthuiah,** Department of Education, Madurai Kamraj University, Madurai-625 021.

**Pravin Saxena,** Department of Law and Accountancy, Faculty of Commerce, Dayalbagh Educational Institute, Dayalbagh, Agra.

**R.P. Singh,** Former Professor of Education, N.C.E.R.T., Pocket-A-4/206, Kalkaji Extension, New Delhi-110 019.

**R.R. Verma,** Assistant Registrar(SG), Indian Institute of Technology, Kanpur.

**Raj Singh,** Department of Sociology, C.C.S. Haryana Agriculture University, Hissar.

**S.K. Agarwal,** Department of Hindi, L.N. Mithila University, Darbhanga.

**S.P. Banerjee,** Professor of Mental and Moral Philosophy, University of Calcutta, Kolkata.

**S.P. Kaushik,** Reader, Dayalbagh Educational Institute, Dayalbagh, Agra.

**Sampooran Singh,** House No. 580, Sector 10 D, Chandigarh.

**Shailendra Singh,** Professor, Human Resource Management Group, Indian Institute of Management, Lucknow.

**Shalini Nigam,** Department of Business Administration, Dayalbagh Educational Institute, Dayalbagh, Agra.

**Shri Ram Arun,** Chairman, U.P. SC & ST Commission, Lucknow.

**Shyamanand Singh,** Associate Professor, Department of Political Science, M.D.S. University, Ajmer.

**Swami Prasad,** Department of Applied Business Economics, Faculty of Commerce, Dayalbagh Educational Institute, Dayalbagh.

**T. Vasantha Kumar,** Professor & Head, Department of Kannada, University of Bombay, Vidyanagari, Santacruz (East), Mumbai-400 098

**Upadyaya 108 Shree Gyansagar Jee Maharaj,** (A Digamber Jain Saint), C/o Shrut Samvardhan Sansthan, 247, Delhi Road, Meerut.

**V. Usha S.,** Department of Psychology, Sri Sarda College of Education, Salem (Tamil Nadu).

**V.K. Gupta,** Department of Accountancy and Law, Dayalbagh Educational Institute, Dayalbagh, Agra.

**V.K. Sabharwal,** Professor, Department of Education, University of Delhi, Delhi-110 007.

# The Editorial Approach

Values are not only the right or the wrong, something symbolic and abstract, but also a vector for psychic development and to ensure eternal bliss and lead to a state of consciousness. The being of values is independent of things; they do not change in varying circumstances. In words of Kant, the essence of values may be perceived as, "We must do unto others as we would have them do unto us. So act that you could wish the maxim of your action to become a universal law of conduct. This value affirmation also leads to ensure the social fabric intact by way of ensuring an ethically sound society."

Values, which bear normative overtones, exhibit a preference and ensure quality in action, irrespective of the sanctions that go with social norms. Values standardise different modes of behaviour along a continuum—from the most desired to the least desired and also the undesired, which may be explicit or implicit and there may be a significant gap between the ultimate and the proximate values. In proximate terms the choices may be situational and pragmatic, although they may be at variance from the ultimate desired action that may continue to be articulated and cherished and form a part of the cognitive universe and encompass within them universal as well as evaluative elements. Some values may be universal to a society, others may be specific to particular groups and categories. For a country of India's cultural heterogeneity, social complexity, economic inequalities, and ideological differentiation, unanimity in respect of all values is neither possible, nor perhaps desirable. Values rooted in personal belief can be left out of consideration so long as they do not clash with national and social values that need to be promoted. The autonomous individual is an active individual. The consciousness of individuals should be extended to enable them to critically examine the goings on in a society and to judge the rights and wrongs of what is happening. The fact has to be appreciated that individually held values get directly or indirectly, consciously or subconsciously, projected in their respective walks of life. Therefore, a consensus is needed regarding some premises and in respect of some core socio-political as well as academic values so that in various professions, minimized economic disparity and cultural deprivation can lead to enhance the equality of creative expression and realization of genuine freedom with an aim to achieve optimum ethical standards in various professions.

Knowledge has to be considered at the core of technology development. Several kinds/forms of knowledge, including technical knowledge, knowledge of attributes (especially quality), knowledge pertaining to context, knowing how to learn and knowing how to marshal knowledge for all, by way of ensuring a faith in social justice would be required to be integrated for initiating and maintaining reforms and would also necessitate debunking all discriminatory practices based on ethnicity or caste/creed/religion/region or gender. The gospel of egalitarianism shall mean much more than mouthing some high-minded slogans—an attitude of caring for and sharing with the deprived and the under-privileged. If one accepts democracy, secularism and social justice as an important defining social value, one will have to learn to be appalled by the enormity of injustice meted out to large sections and categories of the community. The acceptance of these core values should be judged not by their formal enunciation, but by the praxis they generate. This has to be realized in a context specific situation which witnesses knowledge as not a neutral object, rather is socially constructed where every living social component contributes in its generation and spread education, the teaching-learning process must aim at sharpening the problem solving capabilities of the learners. Socially useful knowledge will, therefore, involve coming to grips with the pressing problems of the day as well as their multi-dimensional cause analysis and identification of possible pathways for finding an appropriate solution. Application orientation will have to be accepted as an important value to be reflected in all dimensions of professions, if the ideal of creative teaching is accepted.

A propitious climate for true academic growth shall require freedom of enquiry. The operating culture of academic life, when burdened with authoritarian management and bureaucratic procedures, inhibits the growth of ideas and corrodes the cultivation of excellence, which is the central value of intellectual growth. At the same time the freedom cannot divert itself from social responsibility. Great spurts in knowledge require concentration of ideas and collaboration of efforts. The contribution of lone workers has not been insignificant but major breakthroughs in the present state of knowledge will be possible if and when teams pursue problems in a challenging but harmonious working relationship. This shall bring in the society a synthesis of two important values—one of freedom of enquiry, and the second of fostering a true team spirit for the attainment of not only the stipulated scientific values but also a sense of contentment and satisfaction in the professional life. This will also facilitate the knowledge workers to transmit the heritage with full of social consciousness and would also be able to illuminate the pathways to social action. This will make a value addition to the professionalism.

In times to come, the world would be facing problems out of dehumanization as a result of technical changes. One of the essential messages has to be taken into account that education must enable every person to solve his own problems, make his own decisions and shoulder his responsibilities. All the changes in society, particularly on account of the fantastic development of the power of the media have accentuated this fear and given even greater legitimacy to the imperative that stems from it. In this century these phenomena may look even larger. If we decide at this point of time to affirm values in the social structure the problems will, then no longer be, so much complex to prepare children for a given society where every one is equipped with the powers and intellectual reference points needed for understanding the world around, and behaving responsibly and fairly.

This is not simply an individualistic imperative. Recent experiences show that what might appear to be only an individual's way of defending himself or herself against an alienating system, or one that is perceived as hostile, sometimes offers societies, too, the best chance of progress. The diversity of people's personalities, their independence and initiative and even the desire to provoke—are all safeguards of creativity and innovation. To reduce violence and combat the various ills afflicting society, new methods born of experience have to be examined which may prove to be extremely effective.

Present Book is an effort to explore various possibilities which can contribute in developing a consensus for realizing value affirmation in different professions in three sections. In order to address the theme of 'Value Management in Professions', chosen for the discussion in this monograph, which has now come to the fore and in conceiving the contents of value education, it has been envisaged to examine the multifacetal, professional and social context of which our wellbeing is today an important and crucial element. In such a broad framework of the theme of value education it has been thought to present an exclusive reading material and practical guideline, up to certain extent, on the subject of values in different professions in terms of its necessity, present state and possible future strategies. In order to strengthen the conceptual theme, the book has been divided into three sections:

I. Values in Social Life,
II. Values in Teaching Profession and Education,
III. Values in Business Management.

Section I has been addressed by ten authors around the theme "Values in Social Life". Indian Culture is rooted deeply in her spiritual values and unless these values find their way into the life of every member of the society. The complex growth of the psycho-social phenomena responsible for the evolution of a value system has to develop a sense of unity and equality through cooperation, solidarity, cutting across religious, caste and cultural barriers so that the basic virtues like sincerity, simplicity, gentleness, modesty, compassion, humility, courtesy, cooperation, fair-play, self-reliance, self-control, truthfulness, non-violence, patriotism etc. can grow in the whole of the society. The dialogue has been initiated under the ambit of multidimensional exploration towards value realization through eternal code of ethics by a famous Jain saint, Upadhyaya 108 Gyan Sagar Ji (Value Realization: Eternal Code of Ethics) who has emphasized on the unique greatness and continuity of the Indian culture which can be traced to her imparalleled experimentation, discovery and achievement in the ocean of spirituality. Underlining the importance of love, compassion, non-violence, truth, equality etc., he has focused his ideas on the purification of the thought processes through the innovative technique of *Anekant* which puts a healing touch at the root of the human psyche and through a constructive process of conflict resolution, tries to stop the war or blood shed. It has successfully propounded it as a core societal value as it makes all absolutes in the field of the thought irrelevant and naive and imparts maturity to the thought process and introduces flexibility and accommodation by way of strengthening the originality to the human mind, which in turn helps the individual, society and the nations to become conflict-free. He has ended with a unique formulation of limitation of desires, through illustrating five sins. He views the vow of partial limitation of possession or abstention from major possessions, which are endless as the desires are endless, as not only a spirit of generosity but also the key of contentment and optimizing balance in the social structure.

The second article, contributed by one of the editors (Nalin K. Shastree), has been aimed to search various dimensions in the value domain which is the abode of the humanity. He has made a sketch for identifying a common ground in values, beliefs and commitments in our quest to mature the idea of holism in education, which would be needed to have a sense of the transcendence amidst the ocean of knowledge explosion. In addition to spot the polarization phenomena of values, he has identified the functions of intellect, judgment, reasoning and decision-making reflecting in various definitions propounded by a variety of thinkers in addition to identify a starting point to look within and where the convergence of individual values into institutionalization of the said values can be traced, both in the western thought process and in the Indian ethos. He has ended up with a synthetic approach for making out an optimum understanding of the values by way of presenting a fusion of intellect and emotion.

Secularism should aim at bringing about unity of religions on the basis of the unity of moral and spiritual values and stands for life, affirms ideals of growth and aims at the maximum possible perfection of life. Kireet Joshi has questioned dogmatism, ignorance and superstition through affirming the ideals of truth and scientific temper aiming at progressive and comprehensive knowledge in order to combat the authority and privileges of the selected few (Value Education for Secular Society). He has recognized the growth of love, compassion, fraternity as the central issue of our age and has underlined that development of science should be supplemented by enormous development of human goodness in order to strengthen a secular social structure.

The Declaration on Global Ethics in the Light of Modern Physics is an exploration to unfold the mystery of tension between science and human consciousness with a conviction that man's evolution is not biological but psychological. Mind looking at mind, or atoms with consciousness looking at atoms with consciousness are the theoretical suppositions developed by Sampooran Singh who emphasizes these experiences of wonder and mystery when he looks at the universe. He elaborates further that in the world of the quantum, it is both the awareness and the creation of experience through a fusion of ontology, epistemology and psychology. His value perception underlines the need of a quantum jump from successive consciousness to simultaneous consciousness and coins a new term of humanist technology which will redefine the radical transformation of human psyche.

The Indian tradition, which is out and out spiritual in nature has remained disrespectful of material progress and affluence and all that matters is the progress in the realm of consciousness and spirit and not in physical and the surrounding material/natural environment. S.P. Banerjee has explored various dimensions of the Indian tradition in regard of the conception of the ultimate values of life (Values in the Tradition of Indian Thinking and Values Relevant to our Contemporary Needs). He has emphasized for the need to take recourse to the basic cultural framework of harmoniously synthesizing the spiritual grounding with the material needs/scientific attitude, persistence with dynamism.

Dedication to some ideal, or universal and eternal values in relation to lay down the foundation of a purposeful living has been conceptualized by K. Rama Rao. His concern reflects in his quest to find out the components of unity in the midst of diversities—most particularly among the major religions in their ethnic contexts. He has also laid down an action programme of teaching the young minds so that they can understand the essence of unity of all religions by way of ignoring the minor ethnic differences and strengthening the spirit of enquiry focused towards the search of truth.

Talking about values may not be all sufficient and the most important and desirable activity is to plunge into a positive action plan. M.R. Chilana has formulated TBINSET (Teacher-based in-service education and training) which envisages to explain the ways and means to elaborate the activities which a teacher may undertake in promoting their own self-development, in his article entitled "Developing Values for Self Development". He hopes that the said programme shall assure an existence of a healthy atmosphere in the professions to have continuous and critical evaluation of all educational inputs to achieve the noble goals of educating the children and the youth and to improve the conditions as felt by the persons on the job. He expects that the programme may, possibly, at one hand afford the best opportunity to capitalize upon the individual strengths and ambitions of the teachers and use as its basis and the intrinsic motivational factors of the individual, whereas, on the other hand, it may serve a profitable support and supplement to in-service educational activities.

Police, an integral and important organ of governance are supposed to be polite, obedient, loyal, intelligent, courteous and efficient, reflect the working of an institution which has been vested with the responsibilities of maintaining high standard of discipline, faithful performance of duties in accordance with law, obedience of lawful orders, not committing any misconduct, refraining from falsehood, not indulging in corrupt or improper practices or abuse of authority, not to do an act adversely affecting the unity of the force by creating divisions on grounds of religion, caste or community and not to do anything which adversely affects the integrity and repute of the country and to maintain absolute integrity (Value Management and Police). Sri Ram Arun (a former DGP) opines that values are tested during crisis and disasters and has stressed the doctrine of the maximum good of the maximum number as an efficient strategy to maintain a value system in the Police organization.

What ought to be good or bad as the prerequisite of a sound value management and rationality around has moved as a guiding factor in the domain of positive, normative and welfare economics by N.M.P. Verma in his article on "Values and economics: Exploring an Interface". While developing out a comprehensive understanding of the facets of nationalism, values and globalization in the context of the realities of traditional social values and inequalities, the author has emphasized that the socio-economic and political transformations in the economy can take place only with the ethical values. Addressing the interface he has focused on the utility theory, rational expectation, social welfare, normative economics, gender values, inequalities and through highlighting a caution he has indicated about the dangers of a valueless educational economy. More than ever education's essential role seems to be to give people the freedom of thought, judgment, feeling and imagination they need in order to develop their talents and remain as much as possible in control of their lives. Education must contribute to the all-round development of an individual-mind and body, intelligence, sensitivity, aesthetic sense, personal responsibility and spiritual values. All human beings must be enabled to develop independent, critical thinking and form their own judgment, in order to determine for themselves what they believe they should do in different circumstances of life. That type of learning may be termed as real learning or education with values. The last article of this section addresses a new domain, dentistry, which is becoming popular day by day. Nimish Nimeya has discussed various ethical questions from a critical point of view in the overall societal context. He has developed a model for understanding the dynamics of ethical decision making and has also discussed the same in the legal context. His objective analysis for making a perception of conflicts and emphasis on the exercise of choice throw a new light on the issues taken into consideration.

Education must provide a climate for the nurture of values, both as a personalized set of values, forming one's character and including necessarily social, cultural and national values, so as to have a context and meaning for actions and decisions, and in order to enable the persons to act with conviction and commitment. Values combine a person's thoughts, feelings and actions on a particular belief of issue and establish a harmonious relationship between them since 'head', 'heart' and 'hand' come into play in our everyday actions. It is this harmony that prevents us from being inhuman and sub-human in a society that is torn and fragmented by various forces and where the loss of treasured values becomes not only a personal loss, but leads to the degeneration and disintegration of the society. Therefore, the role of a teacher in shaping the character of students is of paramount importance since they emerge as the best model in the society and are having the responsibility to be the mentor of his students as gentlemen of character.

An academician with a rooted commitment for social consciousness can illuminate the pathways to social action. A social consciousness unafraid to imbibe the social criticism in the domain of knowledge has to be emphasized and valued. Knowledge is important in itself, but at some stage one has to ask the question: knowledge for what? Knowledge, thus, has to be socially relevant and useful. To invest a social purpose into education the teaching-learning process must aim at sharpening various dimensions of the faculty of learning. The teaching profession has a leadership function. It has to sensitize the masses and use its privileged position to produce generations that will attend the journey of growth of the Nation by way of becoming a committed architect. A balance has to be struck between the collective good and individual as well as group interests. Second section of this book is an attempt to crystallize the perceptions of values in teaching profession in specific and education in general.

The dialogue has been initiated (in the first article entitled Education in Human Values for Human Excellence and Amidst Diversity) by an educationist who has also been a Vice Chancellor twice (Bhoomitra Dev), in a core perception that we are living in an age of guided missiles and misguided men and our malleable conscience has created moral wastelands. He begins with emphasizing a need to underline the need of synthesizing emotions with logic so as to achieve a holistic and harmonized development as a result of the finest education in human values. In order to ensure a state of excellence and a peak level in human evolution, conceptualization of a triangle of fire, fuel and invocator has been advocated so as to optimize the level of instinct, intelligence and intuition, in addition to uphold the human dignity and a balance with the nature and valuing human sensitivities. He concludes with a trilogy of education in human values for human excellence amidst diversity through *Roop, Lila* and *Dham* in order to find a Niagara of happiness.

One of the editors of the Book, B.R. Dugar has explored in depth, various trends in Value Education with a conviction that values, which are the guiding principles of life are attributes that spring from the sublimity of soul and are influenced by the changing philosophical ideologies, sociological perspectives, social conditions and political doctrines. He also views that the erosion of values is now a national phenomena, so complex and gigantic that a more balanced academic curriculum, new learning materials and strategies and dedicated teachers having less prejudices and bias would be needed to address the issue. He has underlined the need to conceive an apparatus of structures, content and processes to transmit knowledge, by way of having much concern or commitment to respond to the task of communicating and inculcating values necessary for creating ideological climate congenial to appreciation of cultural heritage and taking pride in one's history and having confidence in human capabilities to overcome material, social, religious and spiritual problems of living. He has emphasized that education without vision is waste, education without value is crime and education without a mission is a burden. He is conscious of the India's rich heritage with its vast canvas of knowledge and enlightenment and philosophical commitment for value affirmation, which has been relegated to the backseat and materialistic desire-based behavioural pattern, which has taken over the front driving seat and therefore, he has suggested for a need of a reversal as a system approach. He has a strong belief in a changed globalized context of scientific and technological advancements that the entire system of education needs to be redefined, reorganized, reshaped and recharged with new energy—which he calls a second revolution—a revolution of values for which education would be the vehicle.

In order to explore an inter-relationship between moral values and education, S.R. Bhatt has explored an inter-relationship between moral values and education through psychoanalysis of the pathological cases of violation of norms, which include the impact of badness—madness, rashness and folly. He has laid down an emphasis on trueness of knowledge—the *samyak jnana* and has drawn an inference that wisdom or true knowledge is not devoid of action, that it consists in a practical sense of values, and that virtue being knowledge can be taught and acquired. He has underlined a need to train the individual in a proper way to know the good and to act up to it, which he has nomenclatured as the Education Theory of Goodness.

Good Education is the focal point of R.P. Singh, where he has initiated the dialogue that good education is a universally accepted goal of a society, although its nature is both vague and indefinite. He has concluded that the good education may be a desirable goal but it is difficult to offer. So long good education can be given outside one's self-interest and without competition, its desirability stands uncontested.

"Value Education—A New Dimension" is an article of T. Vasantakumar, where he has emphasized to create a value climate and has conceived the discipline of Axiology, which concentrates on the study of values and their nature. He has emphasized that values are not mere articulations of some nebulous, idealistic notions and should be perceived in their respective dimensions. He has systhesized western as well as eastern ethos—Smelser's Value Added Theory, which has been seen materializing in the events of *Yashodhar Charita*, where he has become successful in mapping the values under five heads, namely—spiritual, ethical, intellectual, moral and biological.

P.N. Muthiah has developed a synthetic view in his quest for a search for values for university teachers, with the core conviction that values reflect the culture of a society and are widely shared by the members of the cultural spectrum and become a goal when an individual tends to accept a value. While exploring his synthetic approach, he has categorized the university teachers as conformists, innovators, ritualists, retreatists and rebels. He has come across a conflict of objectivity *vs.* subjectivity, change *vs.* constant and the state of hierarchies, if any and has characterized values on itellectual, moral spiritual, aesthetic, economic, religious, and cultural plains and has emphasized the need to motivate teachers for inculcating values.

Modernity *vs.* value-oriented education is an article of other two editors of this Book, namely J.P.N. Mishra and Dr. Anil Dhar. They have underlined the common belief that modernization is responsible for the crisis in values to a larger extent, especially of a close knit small society, which demands cooperation, loyalty, dependence on relations, neighbours etc. They have established that in moral education indoctrination should be avoided and defects of value clarification and cognitive developmentalism should be removed by the educators. They have chalked out a positive strategy for inculcation of values through the system of the Science of Living and have come up with a definite curriculum design also.

Mulkraj Chilana has contributed on Teachers valuing Professional Growth through a combination of image, intent and initiative. He is of the view that a teacher has to play multi-dimensional roles and there is a need for a teacher to grow every moment and he/she is not supposed to be limited in the classroom only. A teacher is not merely an instructor, rather he is also a facilitator. For ensuring value affirmation and professional growth hand-in-hand, he has stressed for in service teacher education programme at micro and macro levels.

Shyamanand Singh has made an insight in the domain of values and has drafted typologies of values for teachers. Starting from the common concept of good and desirable, he has successfully emphasized for the importance of a normative and cognitive element associated with the doctrine of values. The quest of a society to survive and perpetuate leads to an adherence of values and around this philosophical conviction he has identified the typologies like scientific/secular, human/spiritual/moral/religious/political/authoritative/aesthetic/cultural type. He has emphasized that the value education attempts to prepare students for the job as well as provide spiritual knowledge for the peaceful life and an orderly social systems.

The task of developing proper attitude towards students provides a great challenge to the teacher education. The psychodynamics of developing genuine attitude transformation remain largely mysterious. Dr. Y.K. Sabharwal has explored the dynamics of these challenges and in order to change the "Teacher's attitude towards children" need for in-service trainings and orientations has been put forth, since he believes that nevertheless, the importance of appropriate human material, especially in terms of intelligence, attitudes and communication skills, remain of significant use.

Arti Sen, in her article entitled "Value Orientation and Self-understanding in Teacher Education" has emphasized for the need of emergence of a new set of values that may serve as a bridle to the self, since she is of the view that the problem is not to check the erosion of values but the same is in terms of rediscovering them in new forms. She has evaluated the theory that values are caught and not taught and has suggested that value development should take place in a very subtle way during the process of the individuals interaction with his/her environment both natural and social. Education should also develop compassion and fellow-feeling, finer aesthetic sensibility, moral zeal and compassion and fellow-feeling and control over one's own egoistic impulses and finally to a capability of feeling a sublime joy by re-establishing the lost harmony between the individual self and the larger world as the ultimate value of human life and Sen stresses that the practice of self-understanding is the first step in the achievement of these higher values in life.

"Values in University Teaching" has been explored by Madhulika Paul and V.K. Gupta with the bone of contention that the ethos of the teachers needs to be changed from those of the merchants to those of the *gurus* since the secret of teaching values is to inspire and kindle the quest among the students by means of one's own example of character and mastery of knowledge, which can be reflected in a Trimurti of Brahma (a creative thinker), Vishnu (as a teacher and sustainer of knowledge) and Mahesh (a scholar who reads widely and deeply), who revels in swimming in the ocean of knowledge, finding pearls and rubbles and making them accessible to his students.

Raj Singh and M.L. Sharma have made a sociological appraisal of Values in Higher Education, in view of the fact that sociological thoughts generally attribute strategic importance to moral values in the processes of institutionalization and social control. They have, therefore, underlined the necessity of channelizing the student's energies into meaningful and challenging pursuits and for that they have suggested for intensification of curricular programmes in addition to rich and varied programmes of co-curricular activities including yoga, meditation and science of living.

Stepping towards a "Value based management in the University Education" has been made by A.K. Pandey. Recognizing values as complex entities their conceptualization through the individual's socialization has been viewed as a dynamic process. He has outlined three guiding principles for value management with reference to university system, comprising of excellence, equity, justice and empowerment. While exploring the dynamics of value management he has tried to make a fusion of the core concepts of value engineering through the form of the conscious and systematic application of a set of techniques that identify the needed functions, establish values for them, develop the alternatives to perform these functions at minimum cost with desired reliability in assuring a value-based management in the university system; universities have to strive hard for maintaining a standard of learning in the context of a relatively less restrained or less structured form of educational arrangements.

Addressing the complex reality of the dominance of man over nature for material comforts, V. Usha Sri (Restructuring Teacher Education for Value Orientation) has underlined the need of a contemplation for readjustments in the educational curriculum, with a mission to change the mentalities. She has outlined a curriculum, which lays good emphasis on the integration of philosophy and psychology with education and values. She has also proposed a five year (after plus two) and a two year (after graduation) on the basis of innovative pedagogical ideas, which would be entirely, a new approach towards imparting value education.

R.R. Verma has focused on the "Value education based on Ethics in University Leadership with a Special Reference to the Indian Tradition", with the hope and presumption that in an open atmosphere of free exchange of ideas the leadership in the university will naturally seek to inculcate its own ethos in the minds of the teachers and students. Making *dharma* synonymous of duty, an avenue of ten-fold qualities comprising of *dana, sila, pariccaya, ajjava, maddava, tapa, akkoda, avihimssa, khanti,* and *avirodha,* have been emphasized as a quality of a good leader of the university.

In an ever-changing world in which social and economic innovation seems to be one of the main driving forces, a special place, should be given to the qualities of imagination and creativity, the clearest manifestations of human freedom, which may be at risk from a certain standardization of individual behaviour. The twenty-first century needs this variety of talents and personalities; it also needs the exceptional individuals, who are also essential in any civilization. It is therefore important to provide children and young people along with different professionals with every possible opportunity for discovery and experiment to aesthetic, artistic, sporting, scientific, cultural, social, spiritualistic and many more eternal values which it seems we have somewhere left behind. Every society creates a framework of norms, in order to ensure an orderly structure and avoid chaos. This codification exercise is as old as the human civilization.

Application of ethical standards in the commercial sphere is a difficult exercise because success in this area emphasizes the achievements of material objects and targets. Shailendra Singh and Kumud Singh (Managing Value based Ethical behaviour in Business and Governance) have identified four underlying principles for acceptance of values which comprise of test of universality, utilitarianism, rights and justice. With the help of these principles they have developed a behaviour—legal framework in which four outcomes have been recognized. In order to deal with ethical dilemmas and eroding values, a three-dimensional framework, comprising of three agencies individual, self-organization and the third Party to bring about a change in behaviour of two targets (individual self or organization) has been depicted in preventive or curative ways. Author's are conscious of the constant struggle for upholding value-based ethical behaviour in business organizations and therefore, have opined that their three-dimensional framework proposed to manage and transform individuals and organizations may work effectively and a synthesis of preventive and curative measures may be of great use.

Swami Prasad and Shalini Nigam have explored a relationship between the "Values and Managerial Excellence in the changing Business Environment", with the understanding that on one hand the declining moral standards in personal, behavioural and social life and the national ideological commitment affect adversely the values of democracy, socialism, secularism and modernization; on the other hand the need and importance of value orientation in every sphere of our life including business management and the managerial excellence cannot be ignored. In his effort to conceptualize the value system specifically for Business Managers, he has focused on four key areas including entrepreneurial, intellectual, interpersonal and socio-emotional values. The move towards privatization, liberalization and globalization, especially in the context of the recent GATT Agreement is leading towards creation of a new world order in overall commercial activities and have opened up new horizons of business opportunities. Therefore, the new manager has to anticipate and perceive the changes and has to mend himself towards an approach concentrating on flexibility, team work and learning as well as doing good work on inter-disciplinary grounds.

While analyzing "Values for Business Managers", V.K. Gupta and Madhulika Paul have crystallized the idea that ethics does not rest on feelings of approval or disapproval, rather it is based on hard core realities of businessmen, which should be concerned primarily with the relationship of business goals and techniques to human welfare. Authors have explored the complex inter-relationship of organizational and individuals values and have suggested that managerial ethos is connected with the character and values of managers as a professional group.

Managers have to take up social responsibilities and have also to think through the values, the beliefs, the commitments for their society and have to assume leadership responsibilities beyond the discharge of the specific and limited business philosophy of their institutions. While prioritizing the "Role of Business Managers" Shalini Nigam, Swami Prasad and Puneet Mathur have emphasized that in view of the fact that our society is becoming a society of organizations, all institutions, including business, will have to make fulfilment of basic social values and beliefs. They have further stressed for adoption of a strategy to avoid under-importance to materialism and accumulation of wealth by any means; fair or foul along with a commitment for sense of duty.

D.N. Kapoor and Neeraj Gupta have developed an integrated approach towards mapping values for business managers with the understanding that ignorance of systematic and profound philosophical foundations of Indian value-system has resulted in a skill-strong, values weak orientation, which with the blind imitation of western patterns and styles and creating a problem in facing the challenges is exposed by the recent changes. Being inspired from the karmayoga of Shrimadbhagvad Geeta, authors have suggested that B-schools should incorporate an integrated approach to value education based on Indian value system so that they can produce ethically sound, intellectually alert, socially involved and committed business leaders of the future and not just business managers.

In common parlance value are associated with the innate nature of an individual to perceive a thing in a particular manner which influences ultimately the organizational climate, in addition to develop and determine the selection of a corporate strategy which can predict the vision for the future. A.K. Satsangi and S.P. Kaushik have underlined the need of a specific value system in the era of openness, transparency, competitiveness, quality consciousness and globalization, so as to adjust comfortably in the changing environment, without affecting adversely the output value not only of the individual but also of the system. In his article entitled "Managerial Value System in International Business Environment" in terms of the value perception, they have conceptualized six categories of the executives, namely the theoretical, economic, aesthetic, social, political and the religious executives and have traced a relationship between values and international business environment.

The most effective managers are those who can best develop the human resources of an organization for the purpose of achieving organizational goals and objectives through training and development. Identifying "Relational Values of Managers: A Key to Successful Training and Development Programme", Pravin Saxena and Swami Prasad have emphasized the significance of values as part of manpower management development and also an important form of the organizational development. Training and development should basically aim at improving one's productive capacity for the betterment of both the trainee and the organization to which one belongs. Trainer is needed to understand and appreciate both the individual and the organizational environment in view of the fact that creating an organizational environment is a tough and challenging endeavour where conflicting and contradictory value systems are identified with a commitment to achieve an alignment among individuals as well as the organizational environment.

I.C. Awasthi, in his quest of underlining "Value in Management and the Labour in the Perspectives of Globalization" has analyzed the technological changes causing profound impact across enterprises and industries in terms of work organization, employment, skill profile, management industrial relations and labour standards because of which organizations are under constant pressure for increased productivity, quality and profitability against the background of shifting business perspectives, globalization and ever-increasing competition. These pressures are attending organizational options, not merely how to manage current business but looking beyond it through focusing on key skills, core competencies and flexibility to meet new challenges and circumstances posed by the external factors. In this complex scenario the author opines that the NGO's can give a fresh breath for a better community development and affirming a value based system.

With an objective to examine the role and significance of values in providing good governance to the people P. Raghuram has tried to make a search for the role of values in 'Public Administration'. He has emphasized that values form the basis of human behaviour and constitute an important dimension of social phenomenon and its understanding can provide a clue to understand how these societies or groups develop end transform themselves. They are like the laws of the land which one need more to protect the people from bad. Marina R. Pinto has analysed further the value system in the Public Administration and has explored the conflict between the public service with virtues and public service with evils of corruption, nepotism, power and money. He has emphasized on the strengthening of qualities of courage, fortitude, justice and prudence. In another effort the relevance of values and impact of moral values on the efficiency and effectiveness on management in today's dynamic and competitive world has been discussed by B.P. Singh, A.K. Singh and K.K. Goel, on the basis of some case studies. The authors have emphasized that there is a positive impact of high moral values on the efficiency and effectiveness of managers. An interesting discussion has been made by Amish Ameya on ethics in advertising, which is gaining importance due to glamour and money. addressing the positive as well as negative effects of advertising, the author has addressed the moral order to which advertising refers, because it writes on the hearts and embodies the human fulfilment. He has underlined the component of truthfulness, human dignity, social responsibility and has stressed on a rigorous respect for the moral, cultural and spiritual requirements based on the diginity of human beings. Ethical choices reflect objectively between right and wrong and underline the values such as fairness, justice, integrity and commitment as universal and eternal and involve empathy, fairness, compassion and love for the marginalized and have nots with a commitment to serve the larger interest of the society by way of laying down an inter-connection between the individual and the society. A value based system of governance not only deals with the widening gap between the promise and performance of those who govern, it also focuses on how best the correctives can be applied in the system.

In recent trends of thought we have been presented with the ideals of learning to be and learning to become. It is only where there is a right balance of the development of all our faculties, including learning as well as doing that we can reach and attain the state of self-possession and self-mastery. We can then experience our true being and discover the secret of our perceptual being. We need to emphasize, therefore, not only the education of various components of our being, viz. physical, vital, rational, aesthetic, moral and spiritual but also to implement that right type of education is given in our different walks of professional life. It is the need of hour to develop such a balanced and ideal society where every professional tends to address the call of related values and implement them in his or her life without any additional efforts.

Present book is a conglomerate of various approaches which aim to conceptualize a framework for ensuring a value based approach in all professions. The framework is not merely an ideological vision, rather it has gone far, remained critical as well as analytical and has culminated into a constructive approach for laying down strong foundations of a viable system which can remain not only workable but also sustainable over a period of time. We believe that the authors have suggested useful future strategies and programmes to be adopted for optimal benefit of individuals and society as well. Editors convey their sincere thanks to all authors who have contributed in this book. We also record our gratitude to the administration of Jain Vishwa Bharati Institute (Deemed University), Ladnun for activating a constructive dialogue on values in society. This book could not have been published without the sincere efforts of Sh. Ashok K. Mittal of M/s. Concept Publishing Company, who has taken personal interest in the publication of this book; we put on record our sincere gratitude for his efforts.

We hope that this present experiment will be of use for academicians, policy-makers, administrators and all those who believe that only an ethically sound society can ensure a sustainable growth.

**Nalin K. Shastree**
**B.R. Dugar**
**J.P.N. Mishra**
**Anil K. Dhar**

# SECTION I

## VALUES IN SOCIAL LIFE

# 1

# Value Realization

## *Eternal Code of Ethics*

UPADHYAY 108 GYAN SAGAR JI MAHARAJ

---

The nature of man is such as to urge him to participate in the fullness of life, to be receptive of the significant and to lie open to whatever has meaning and value. Fortunately, our country has a cultural heritage which is at least five thousand years old and quite a few of its elements have been widely appreciated and acclaimed. There is a common belief, that Indian tradition is out and out spiritual in nature.. And, the history of India would remain enigmatic, particularly, the remarkable phenomenon of the continuity of Indian culture through the millennia would remain a mystery, if we do not take into account the role that spirituality has played not only in determining the direction of her philosophical and cultural effort but also in replenishing the springs of creativity at every crucial hour in the long and often weary journey. It is true that spirituality has played a role in every civilization and that no culture can claim a monopoly for spirituality. And yet, it can safely be affirmed that the unique greatness and continuity of Indian culture can be traced to her unparalleled experimentation, discovery and achievement in the vast field of spirituality. Indian culture has recognised spirituality not only as the supreme occupation of man but also as his all integrating occupation. Ancient visionary seers and saints have expounded the universal and eternal values playing a role of beacon in the midst of darkness of ages and helps one to perform his mundane duties in harmony and attain, the highest goal prescribed for human being.

Thus, quest after values and the attainment thereof constitute the very core of human life. There is an innate necessity in man, caused by his finitude and imperfection to participate in the process of value-realization. That is why consciously or unconsciously value-concepts, value discrimination and value judgement feature prominently in his life. In fact, values occupy a pivotal role in human life. Values are described as the socially defined desires and goals that are internalised through the process of conditioning, learning and socialization. Values are goals set for achievements and they motivate, define and colour all our activities cognitive and effective. Eternal ideals and values propounded ages ago like, of non-violence, truth, non-stealing, chastity, non-possession, love, compassion, purity, simplicity etc. etc. are still relevant in the modern era. Out of these the first five are the basic of the foundation of **morality and value realization.**

The **principle of non-violence** is existent all over in Vedic, Jaina and **Buddhist scriptures**. It has been stressed by religious exponents, social reformers and political leaders, and above all it has been accepted as important from the point of view of one's ownself. Thus, it is religiously, ethically, socially, politically and psychologically important and necessary. The instinct of love, sympathy or '*Karuna*' (compassion) furnishes the basis of non-violence. In fact, it is essential for an individual as a member of a family, as a member of the society, as a member of a nation and as a member of the whole universe.

Schopenhaver has laid that non-violence is non-hate or absence of hatred that is in positive sense sympathy or love. Absence of hatred promotes love, which is the source of unification of different individuals. Further, it is a fact of common experience that hatred retards the common development of both the mind and the body of the individual, while love makes them bloom forth in their natural splendour in the lover. And, to this culture of hatred there is no antidote except the practice of love, compassion, equanimity etc.

There are certain peaks of development of the concept of non-violence, and can be traced from the Vedic times down to the time of Buddha, Mahavira and Gandhi, and its extreme form can be noticed in Jainism. The entire Jaina religious and philosophical system is founded on non-violence. The essence of knowledge, lies in non-killing which is the supreme principle said by the omniscients. The principle of non-violence is the principle of equality or '*samta*'; as has been pointed out, '*samta*' is the basic of all morality, philosophy and logic of Jaina thought and prevails all over system. *Samta* is that no one is inferior or superior, everybody has the potentiality to develop himself and can achieve the highest goal. One's behaviour should be such that it does not retard the development or injure the physical, mental, or intellectual vitality of life of others.

In the intellectual or the philosophical field too, Jainism propound the theory of '*Anekant*', which means that every judgement is relative. This theory in brief, expresses the view that every judgement reveals only one aspect of reality, and therefore every judgement is relative and subject to certain conditions. It is because one forgets this limitation and regards his own judgements as unconditionally true, that he indulges in number of conflicts and disagreements and thus hurts the feelings of those who have a different view of reality. '*Anekant*' purifies the thinking. It invites to do away evil thoughts and to cultivate good thoughts. The importance of this comprehensive synthesis of '*Anekant*' in day-to-day life is immense inasmuch as this doctrine supply a rational unification and synthesis of the manifold and rejects the assertions of bare absolutes. The moment one begins to consider the angle from which a contrary viewpoint is put forward, one begins to develop tolerance, which is basic requirement of the practice of non-violence. Origin of all bloody war fought on the surface of this earth can be traced to the war of ideas and beliefs. '*Anekant*' puts healing touch at the root of human psyche and tries to stop the war of bloodshed. It makes all absolutes in the field of the thought quite irrelevant and naive, imparts maturity to the thought process and supplies flexibility and originality to human mind, which in return helps the individual, society, nation to become conflict-free. And, only in this type of environment and atmosphere a person can use his potentiality to attain the supreme goal.

The term 'truth' has got varied implications. It is derived from '*sat*' and '*sat*' is more often understood in the sense of ultimate Reality. It is that which is never destroyed or destroyable. But sometimes '*sat*' also means a general objective goodness, virtue and chastity; beside this, it means genuine, honest, sincere and faithful etc. It is considered that the true essence of the whole universe is even more profound than the ocean and more stable than Mt. Meru. This, as is apparent, is the metaphysical truth understood as highly important in the Jaina scriptures. As a moral principle also it is considered very significant.

Truth, it is said, does not only pertain to our faculty of speech but to mind and body as well. Only that truth in speech is called truth which is coherent with body and mind, as it is sometimes said that the origin of truth lies not in the mouth but in the heart. Truth, in the systems of Indian philosophy is one of the top ranking tenents of morality.

Though it is the most abstract principle, it furnishes the ground the most concrete tenets of morality. Its validity and universality can be realized as a basic principle of life.

In the modern era, Gandhiji is one of the biggest exponents of truth. The remarkable thing about him is his application of truth, not only in his personal life, but in political life too with great success, which is his unique contribution. The concept of '*satyagraha*' is Gandhi's contribution to international politics, which means to holding or sticking to the principle of truth. About the results of this programme of '*satyagraha*', which Gandhi applied against the untruthful regime of British, nothing is needed to be said as everything is well known. Today even, this application of the principle of truth has an extreme potentiality in itself, for the cultivation of which certain basic defects such as fear, selfishness, greed and cowardice are needed to be checked.

The ethical principle of non-stealing is actually based on the first and foremost principle of non-violence. Whether stealing is understood in the sense of a crime or in the sense of a sin, the virtue of non-stealing fundamentally originates in non-violence either in the positive sense of maintenance of social order or in the negative sense of abstinence from hurting others by way of depriving them of their property or other necessary belongings. But it is only limited or restricted non-violence pertaining to human beings and not to all living creatures. One who observes this precept has a very strong or healthy feeling of social welfare (which is rooted in non-violence, love and sympathy); it is therefore not only negative but positive as well.

Its importance has been pronounced by all major schools of thoughts for the all aspects of life, in this life and the lives beyond. In Jainism the principle of non-stealing is a moral principle only because it vindicates the principle of non-violence. Stealing is also violence, because it hurts both apparent and real vitalities of the person whose wealth is stolen, which maintains the mental as well as physical equipoise of him. Anything taken ungiven with attachment or inadvertence is stealing. Abstinence from this is non-stealing. It has been laid down that, "if you really want to obtain spiritual happiness and to preserve your moral life, fame and character, and above all want to attain the supreme happiness in this life, and the life after, never get entangled in the net of stealing. One, who really desires riddance from this embroilment, never takes anything ungiven."

For understanding properly the precept of non-stealing in practical conditions, five major transgressions are mentioned in the scriptures.

These are: (i) Buying a stolen article or property, (ii) imparting instruction on the method of committing a theft, or engaging thieves, (iii) evading the civil laws and political laws, (iv) adulteration and selling impure commodities and deceiving the customer and (v) keeping false weights and measures. In these five heads come all the modern businessmen's tacts of wrong sampling, reducing the quality of the product, getting involved in smuggling markets, buying smuggled goods, helping the smugglers etc. It can be said that non-stealing (stealing either taken in the sense or a crime or a sin) has been regarded as an important virtue in Indian tradition ever since the time of Vedas, and is one of the most accepted moral tenents of all civilization, in a certain sense it is made more important than non-violence because it directly deals with social morality.

One of the significant moral precepts is sexual or sensual restraint. This value of divine deed is prevalent in entire Indian religious system. The terms '*brahmacarya*' however, is most popular. The reason for its popularity lies in its very connotation and literal meaning which is comprehensive enough to include in itself all allied moral principles, primary and secondary. '*Brahmacarya*', as it is known, means control or complete renunciation of sexual or sensual desires but this is only what it conventionally means. It is a combination of two terms '*Brahman*' and '*carya*'. '*Brahman*' in brief means the ultimate reality, the supreme being, the ultimate or the final truth in the sense of the highest good or ideal and '*carya*' means code of conduct or way of living. The combined term '*Brahmacarya*' thus means code of conduct, actions, or movement in quest of true '*Brahman*' or the ultimate truth. The ideal of '*brahmacarya*' is, therefore, the attainment of the final goal of ultimate truth by eradicating wrong and superficial notions or ideas and avoiding wrong actions. In this sense, it has a close relationship with the principle of truth as a moral and metaphysical principle as sexual or sensual desire becomes a hindrance to the achievement of final goal. It is an established fact that sex restraint would give power and energy to a person which can be applied to various other projects.

In Jainism, the term of '*brahmacarya*' indicates all relevant virtues which are auxiliary to liberation. In general, therefore, it means the means of liberation; but as a precept its field has been restricted to abstention from sexual indulgence, since sex is considered a major hindrance to liberation because like other vows, this vow of '*brahmacarya*' too is dependent on the vow of non-violence. It is asserted in various texts that the vow is rooted in the vow of non-violence, and sex desire and sex indulgence are also explained as an act of violence. 'The vow is therefore a corollary of the vow of non-violence; though the value of '*brahmacarya*' is much emphasized because the very institution of asceticism is dependent on it, asceticism is futile in itself without the implementation of celibacy. Actually there are only two strong tenents of asceticism, viz. non-violence and celibacy. With this concept of '*brahmacarya*' based on non-violence, its glory is pronounced in the scriptures in various places. It is said that all gods, demons and satans, etc., show respect for him who observes '*brahmacarya*', which is very severe and painstaking.

However, the institution of marriage occupies an important place in the whole of Indian culture and religion, though it may appear as contrary to the principle of '*brahmacarya*'. But, an historical account of the institution of marriage, its aim and development, is very necessary and important in the sense that it gives an idea of relative social habits in different times and cultures, and also an idea of different ethical standards in different times. Marriage in itself is not an instinct, but an institution based on an instinct or the need to mate. It is a symbol of development of the advanced human make up, which manifests the fulfilment of the basic desire of sex in a controlled and channelized form and stoppage of anti-social outburst of this desire and where 'the adjustment of two personalities to a common way of life is full of delights and difficulties, reconciliations and disagreements. A person is supposed to be faithful to his own wife both physically and mentally, he should not think of any other women. It is said that "if you speak to a woman, do it with pureness of heart.... say to yourself, placed in this sinful world, let me be a spotless lily, unsoiled by the mire in which it grows, is she old, regard her as your mother, is she honourable as your sister, is she of small account as your younger sister; is she a child, treat her with reverence and politeness." In this age of free-sex, the demographical problems, several diseases like AIDS etc. etc., this concept of chastity or controlled chastity plays a role of light tower to the passionate and lustful persons and restless world.

The fifth significant value of 'non-possession' is one of the basic values propounded in the traditional Indian system and has the equal importance in the different schools of thought. 'Non-possession' which is usually translated as '*aparighraha*'. The term '*parigraha*' is the opposite of the '*aparigraha*', and is constituted of two terms, i.e. '*pari*' and '*graha*'. '*Graha*' is rooted in '*grahana*' which means to take hold of, taking or accepting or receiving something, '*pari*' means round or round about abundantly, richly, but it is usually used to express fullness or high degree. Thus, *parigraha* means acceptance, or taking or receiving gifts or other worldly possessions. '*Aparigraha*' means abstention from taking possession of, refusal to master or overpower. The concept relates to renunciation and refers to the absence of desire to keep possessions. Basically, real *parigraha* arouses from within, it pertains more to thoughts and attitude than to objects and thus is inseparably associated with violence. It is said that one who has attachment to land and other objects, money, gold and silver, cattle and horses, servants, wife and other relatives, and is obstructed by such desires is to face the dangerous calamities just as a boat with a small hole in it is ultimately to face disasters.

But, it is non-practical for one to abstain himself from the possessions, as he has to make sure of his maintenances, for the maintenance of his family and for a normal living in the society. Even though, it is very much possible for him to observe this value in part in his daily life. The duty of the householder lies in limiting all his possessions and consequently controlling his limitless desire to possess more and more. It is in this sense of limitation of possessions that it is called the vow of partial limitation of possession or abstention from major possessions which are endless as the desires are endless. The laity's vow of '*aparigraha*' thus can be referred such as smaller vow of non-possession, limitation of possessions, abstention from major kinds of possession and as Gandhi said, limitation of desires which implies both a limitation of desires as well as a spirit of generosity.

To conclude, it is necessary to say that behind the limitation of desires—the essential quality of *aparigraha*—there works a self-imposed socialistic spirit. Though it makes room for the fulfilment of the needs, it requires desires to be controlled. Here an apparent resemblance can be discovered between '*aprigraha*' and the communist belief that every one should be equal economically, and that one should be given according to ones needs and not according to one's desires; for the staunch communists this ideal of economic equality is to be achieved by a bloody revolution. However, the two ideologies (least '*parigraha*' and economic equality) cannot be assimilated to a great extent, but it can be said at the outset that the former would function in a definitely better way than the latter if applied at all, because voluntariness always works better than force. But, at the same time one can very well imagine the picture of the new society, which would certainly be different from that of the present society. Here, as the precept declares, the ideal of the householder is to curtail his desires, limit his possessions and try to remain satisfied with what he has and not always to strike for newer and newer achievements in terms of physical, social, economic and industrial development. For the moral way of living in society, partial vow of non-possessions of the laity is inevitable and necessary. Even from social point of view in the modern world partial non-possession or limited possessions would be a great blessing, specially in developing or underdeveloped countries like India. These moral principles, which have been guiding human behaviour for thousands of years, may still remain useful to the man of the modern era in the present conditions.

# 2

# Values: Ultimate Destiny of Humanity

NALIN K. SHASTREE

---

> *"What a chimera is man! What a confused chaos! What a subject of contradiction! A professed judge of all things and yet a feeble worm of the earth! The great depository and guardian of truth and yet a mere huddle of uncertainty! The glory and scandal of the universe!"*
>
> —*Blaise Pascal*

## Countless Errors of Humanity: Introduction

Homo sapiens stand poised between a collapsing past and an indeterminate future, where the established landmarks of the humanism and the value system have started disappearing, one by one, and we seem to be adrift on a boundless ocean of contradictions, impelling all aspects of life on the planet, stretching in all directions towards the horizon of uncertainties. Humanity, at crossroads, is addressing the most difficult and crucial question—how to survive; how to grasp the immensity and propensity of multidimensional transitions and how to promote a quantum jump in human consciousness by way of re-formulating the human perceptions and understandings, where the man's destiny is lying in the hands of politics amidst the explosion in various fields of science and technology, which are redefining the whole of perceptions in the domain of the value system.

## The Vision of Truth

The origin of the modern age may be seen in the phenomenal intellectual growth, which is continuing without any slackening of pace, and changes in our understanding in the years ahead which may well be greater than these that we have seen in our own lifetime. The effects of the new knowledge have been particularly noticeable in the economic sphere. Technical improvements have made possible a mechanisation of labour that has resulted in mass production, the rapid growth in per capita productivity, and an increasing division of labour. The increase in the integration of policy making has revolutionised the system of transportation, communication, business, public administration, health care system, education etc. Cosmopolitan criteria of personal association is replacing gradually the restraints imposed by race, creed, family and caste. The former divisions between peasants, townspeople, and aristocrats have given way to a more homogeneous society in which one's position depends more on individual achievement than on inherited status. This complex and interrelated series of changes in man's way of life has become a part of the universal experience and in many respects it is one that holds great hope for the welfare of mankind; although, in many respects the destructive processes have emerged as more powerful and effective—they have destroyed traditional patterns of life which through the centuries had evolved many human values and had ensured a cohesive social system. The onslaught of technology, and its effects on society and industry is an ongoing phenomenon and galloping advances in science and technology have resulted into changes of not only tools, the infrastructure and work related activities, but also in the socio-political organisational structures, demographic profiles and even the concepts associated with the national identity and sovereignty; ultimately threatening to destroy the finer fabrics of our society. In exchange for the old, it has created a mass society where privacy, individualism, and quality tend to be submerged by standards of taste and administrative processes, in which the expediency of public affair get pronounced but simultaneously witness the degeneration of those human values which were evolved through the centuries.

## Education: The Prime Instrument

Not only in the passage of traditions, but also in modern times education is the prime instrument—a liberal instrument in the creation of man and also in shaping of his destiny. Shils and Anderson (1966) indicate that the role of education plays in inculcating a sense of national loyalty and in creating skills and attitudes essential for technological innovation. However, Anderson (1966) opines that education itself is not adequate and appropriate, social environment for education is also critical. That is why formal as well as informal methods of learning and acquiring new skills and attitudes, generate their importance in a variety of manners. The tension between a pragmatic view of education, as the means to political and economic ends, and a contrasting vision of learning, as the continuous refinement of meaning has also to be addressed with a focus on the fact that education is not just related to stacking packets of information in the memory chamber of the learner or to add some dimensions in the thinking powers of the learners, rather it is concerned with the development of the whole personalities. This holistic treatment of education enables us to seek educational questions as merely, part of a much vaster range of psychological, sociological, political and ecological problems and concerns, and to seek balance in our understanding and appreciation of human needs and potentials by way of making reference to their global context and significance. There is much common ground to be explored in values, beliefs and commitments in our quest to mature the idea of holism in education, which would be needed to have a sense of the transcendence. The component of spirituality is also important in order to identify the efforts to reclaim the wholeness and holiness of education, and indeed of meeting the civilisation. The spiritual faculty generates a knowledge, not of causes and explanations, but of meanings and purposes which can inspire, reconcile and unite values and interests enabling education to contribute fruitfully to the exploration not only of the intellectuals, but also of the effective and spiritual dimensions of human experience, which culminate into the holism of education and make the man complete.

**Polarising Values**

Values are basic beliefs that underpin the way we think, feel and respond to things happening in the outer world. They are basic orientations to the way things are or should be; they reflect preferences for outcomes and are accepted as most desirable and right option exercised. As values enable a link to be established between society, culture and the individual, it can be said that people's value systems are formed and shaped to a large extent by the prevailing cultural norms and values in society at large. Culture influences the organisation of social activities by affecting meaning to changing technology and economic activities, while values themselves tend to remain stable at the core of cultural foundations (Brown and Chatterjee, 1999).

Values are regarded as standards and patterns of choice which one feels/considers important and develops as a positive conviction that guide persons and serve as the authorities in the name of which choices are made and actions are taken for getting satisfaction, fulfilment and meaning. A value is just like other developments, a state of mind, a mental deposition, an attitude or an emotionalised state of the mind towards some idea, thing or tradition carrying positive and negative charges within itself (Rani, 2000). Values may also be described as a system of personality traits which are in harmony with the inner nature of an individual and which are in accordance with the values approved by the society (Shetty and Pushpanadham, 2000). The value domain, however, depends not only on the choice of modes of actions adopted in order to attain the ultimate goals and objectives through developing means like co-ordination, linkages, networking, preferences and appreciations culminating into conceptualisations in the form of do's and don'ts. Therefore, defining values although is difficult, but may help in crystallising the conceptions for polarising values.

## Defining Values: Identifying the Functions of Intellect, Judgement, Reasoning and Decision Making

Values have been variously viewed. Perceptions have been developed with respect of preferences, criteria, objects, possessions of intellect, and/or state of mind. In order to develop a multidimensional approval in respect of understanding the concept of 'value' some definitions are being quoted here, in which the said domain has been addressed from various points of views.

*Kulckon* (1951) has emphasised on delving into the framework of the value domain and opines: "Value is a conception, explicit or implicit, distinctive of an individual or characteristic of a group, of these desirable, which influences the selection from available modes and ends of action."

*Borsodi* (1965) has taken into consideration of variations in the value areas and choices by way of visualising that "Every human action is the reflection of an individual value; and every human institution is the outgrowth of a social value."

*Konapka* (1973) has viewed the implications of various processes contributing in the formation of values and has identified the steps involved, which are as follows:

(i) value formation within the individual is a developmental phenomenon,
(ii) it is a constant, never-ending process through the total life span, but with a peak in adolescence,
(iii) it is an intellectual as well as emotional process, finally,
(iv) outside the early childhood years, it is an active process; the person interacting with the external stimuli.

*Havighurst* (1953) has put an emphasis on the processes contributing towards acquisition of values. He defines value as "an object or state of affairs which is desired. These processes are as follows:

(a) through satisfaction of physiological drive,
(b) through satisfaction of emotional experience,
(c) through concrete reward and punishment,
(d) through associations of something with the love or approval of persons, whose love and appreciation is desired,
(e) through inclusion of someone in authority, and lastly,
(f) through reasoning or reflective thinking.

*Raths et al.* (1966) has opined in regard of concerns of acquisition of values and has theoretised his views as "Value-clarification approach". He states that, "one arrives at values by an intelligent process of choosing freely; choosing from alternatives; choosing after careful consideration of consequences of each alternative; prizing or cherishing, publicly affirming; and finally acting upon the value regularly.

*Thompson* (1952) has viewed the process of value development as internalization or interiorization. He holds the view that, "Children are born in a society where norms and values are established, but the process of interiorizing them is such that it is not exactly certain how children acquire the fairly stable value systems existing among adults".

*Good* (1959) has also recognised the importance of internalization and describes it, "as an acceptance by the individual of the attitudes, codes principles or sanctions that become part of himself in forming value judgements or in determining his conduct. Thus, internalization refers to the process by which an individual acquires the values of his culture".

*Cole* (1987) stressing on the need of value judgements opines that, "Value judgements are inescapable demands of life; ... however, every man finds himself inextricably entangled in a web of values on which his very life depends."

*Piaget* (1932) while elaborating on the process of learning of values in children has viewed, "value development and moral judgement on the basis of value development. Moral judgement was considered by him as a gradual developmental process involving not the learning of rules, but a kind of cognitive restructuring, a natural cognitive enfoldment contingent upon child's growing ability to cooperate with others, their experience, relationships with peers and members of the society, cooperative activities with mutual understanding between peers and freedom from constrains imposed by authority. Conventional and rational are the two ways, two stages of cognitive development involved in children's learning of values. Learning of values is a process of maturation, development and cognitive restructuring." These findings have also been verified by Morris (1958) and Loughram (1967).

*Kohlberg* (1969) has viewed the theory of values which includes moral development as an expression of individual ethical behaviour. Approach is although very common, but may not prove to be always correct. Details of his concept are presented in the table as under:

**Classification of Moral Judgement**

| *Level* | *Basis of Moral Judgement* | | *Stage of Development* |
|---|---|---|---|
| I. | Moral value resides in external quasi-physical happenings, in bad acts or in quasi-physical needs, rather than in persons and standards. | 1. | Obedience and punishment orientation egocentric deference to superior power or prestige, or trouble-avoiding set. Objective responsibility. |
| | | 2. | Naively egoistic orientation. Rigid action is that which instrumentally satisfies the self's needs and occasionally of other's. Awareness of. |

(*Contd.*)

| *Level* | *Basis of Moral Judgement* | | *Stage of Development* |
|---|---|---|---|
| | | | relativism of value to each actor's needs and perspectives. |
| II. | Moral value resides in performing good or right roles, in maintaining the conventional order and the expectancies of others. | 3. | 'Good boy' orientation. Orientation to seek approval, and to please and help others. Conformity to stereotypical images of majority of natural role behaviour, and judgement by inventions. |
| | | 4. | Orientation to doing duty showing respect for authority, and maintaining the social order for its own sake. Regard for earned expectations of others. |
| III. | Moral values resides in conformity by the self to shared or shareable standards, rights or duties. | 5. | Contractual legalistic orientation. Recognition of an arbitrary element or starting point in rules of expectations for the sake of agreement. Duty defined in terms of contract, general avoidance of violation of the will or rights of others, and majority will and welfare. |
| | | 6. | Conscience of principle orientation. Orientation not only to ordained social rules, but also to principles of choice involving appeal to logical universality and consistency. Orientation to conscience as a directing agent and to mutual respect and trust. |

*Source*: After Kohlberg (1969), in D.A. Wetten and K.S. Cameron, Developing Management Skills (Harper Collins, New York, 2nd ed., pp. 61).

The Kohlberg's concept elaborates a gradual development of the value system and is near to the Indian doctrine of *nishkamkarma* which lays an emphasis on the purity of mind. He has postulated three stages in the development of values; each with a different kind of motivation for acting morally. He has identified these stages as under:

(a) "Pre-moral stage, involving two sub-stages at which the first motive for acting, morally, is obedience to adult authority and second motive is individual's own need satisfaction;
(b) Conventional stage, involving the two sub-stages at which the first motive for acting morally is the desire to seek approval from others and the second motive in respect for authority and social order; and
(c) Autonomy stage, at which the first motive for acting morally in respect for the rights of other people and the second motive is one's own conscience or rational principles and universal rules constituting fundamental values. Reasoning is considered by him to be the solid ground on which learning of values must rest."

*Eysenck* (1960, 1964) while emphasising for a learning theory approach he has opined that "all values are learned behaviours and conditioned responses."

*Band and Walters* (1963) *and Bronfen Brenner* (1970) have an agreement in common that value development is directly linked with imitation and modelling processes. They have demonstrated that "children learn values not only from what they are told to do by adults, but also from what they see adults doing. Symbolic models in films, television or in books also have similar effects. Children learn values as they observe around in the society, as they are rewarded or punished in the society.

*Gupta* (1986) while considering for cultural tenets in terms of a codification defines in philosophical contexts and views values as "those standards or a code of conduct for conduct conditioned by one's cultural tenets and guided by conscience, according to which human being is supposed to conduct himself and shape his life patterns by integrating his beliefs, ideas and attitudes to realise cherished ideals and aims of life."

*Wucholin* (1957) views value as "a conception, explicit or implicit, distinctive of an individual or characteristic of a groups of these desirable traits which influence the selection from available modes and ends of action."

*Chakraborty* (1991) has viewed in relation to human sentiments and emotions. According to him values may be the emotional distillation which provide a firm establishing insights enabling derivations of decisions from choices. These are commitments often shared with others because of their power to guide interaction, and again, will come to be so exercised emotionally rather than intellectually. He further views that the objectivity of the value paradigm may also be viewed in terms of shared emotions.

*Jacob et al.* (1962) have treated values as universal belief systems that guide action across a variety of human situations. Thus, they observe values as broadly based preferences which individuals hold in relation to perceived appropriate courses of action directed as desired outcomes. They reflex the psyche of the operating person in terms of right or wrong in the light of certain given parameters under particular circumstances.

*Rokeach* (1973) has conceptualized values, when they are expressed as actions and often include respect for rights in terms of allowing others to hold values different from our own perceptions. He has, broadly, put human values in two categories—terminal values and instrumental values. Terminal values are those which reflect in a person's preference for the outcomes desired or the ends to be achieved. In other words they are akin goals a person is seeking during his lifetime. Whereas, instrument values are those which direct human behaviour towards achieving the goals of terminal values. He opines "Values as an enduring belief, a specific mode of conduct or end state existence along a continuum of relative importance."

*Allport* (1932) has categorised six broad areas of the value system, namely theoretical, economic, aesthetic, social, political and religious. They are, of course, broad headings for a generalised view of how rational thinking, practical application and interest groups could influence people's behaviour.

*Lester et al.* (1988) have developed the idea to view values as a prototype, which offer a frame of reference for behaviour. This view strengthens adopting a purely analytical point of view.

*R.P. Singh* (1993) has worked out the typologies of values which is as under:

1. *Scientific/Secular Values*: Where religion interferes with intellectual and social development, like objectivity,

rationality, integrity, impartiality and overall excellence in all walks of life.

2. *Spiritual/Moral/Religious Values*: Although, sometimes, religion becomes intolerant but its bone of contention carries brotherhood, tolerance, accommodation, compassion, firmness of principles and conscience. Religion primarily helps an individual to derive some solace in life during time of adversity and gives a way to maintain a socially cohesive life.
3. *Political Values*: Political systems imbibe various values like dictatorship, democracy, secularism, equality, fraternity, fundamentalism etc.
4. *Aesthetic Values*: These are related to the social life, and for advancing intellectual pursuits. They represent the consumption of knowledge as the supreme form of beauty, truth and goodness. This has been discerned in Indian philosophy which underlined the ultimate goal of "*Satyam*, *Shivam* and *Sundaram*". These values have also been subjected to various shades of struggle in the passage of time. In some societies these values reflect the panorama of virtues, idealism, reality and sometimes they depict the differences of opinion; raise protest against system and suggest viable alternatives.

## Searching for the Starting Point

In the ocean of humanity, where we confront with countless errors—all contributing to inhumanity, let us try to recognise the vision of truth that has inspired so many thinkers, saints, artists, writers, statesmen who recognised value affirmation as a unifying purpose to life (Jaki, 1978; Capra, 1983) and association of which with all walks of life has not only emerged as an element of hope but also a starting point of regeneration in the whole of system. While making an effort for polarising values in the domain of human consciousness we may recognise them as relatively stable choices or preferences about our behavioural dimensions and also relate to the objectives, goals and concerns of education. Value positions may be adopted unreflectingly and thus prejudices/biases may intercept them or they may also be the product of rational and experiential enquiry leading to or from deeply-held beliefs. Values are thus, meaningful for the understanding of human behaviour. The ground upon which we hold values may be referred to as beliefs, which can of course refer to any significant area of human experience; especially related to human consciousness. This emphasises for underlining the importance of spiritual values. Grimmitt (1987) suggests that spiritual values, however, have a distinct nature; human spirituality is not merely a core value among others but is the source of the human capacity to value, because most of our actions are the results of value assumptions rather than deliberate decisions. Values or belief's may also refer to any significant area of experience which lead to the knowledge possessed by the entire being that humanity is neither the sole nor the original possessor of consciousness. This awareness, although, can be established scientifically or empirically but gets evolved sufficiently as to be relatively consistent over time and establishes an understandable correlation between human intellect, rationality and wisdom under the umbrella of human consciousness.

Plunkett (1985), while recognising the dimension of spirituality has recognised the dichotomy in the perception of values, by way of distinguishing timely (those concerned with immediate aims pervading everyday life) from timeless (reflecting belief in absoluteness) values. There may emerge contradictions, they may apply different assumptions, they may provide different meanings to words and develop different perceptions.

## Looking Within

An acceptance of the role of values as imperative appears as implicit with the conceptualisation that positive values will guide the overall professional behaviour. The concepts and practices of all collective human endeavours towards value affirmation have to be viewed in the background of various definitions given, which emphasise that individual values are the primary ingredients that create and organise the collective value system in order to establish a civil and humane society. The convergence of individual values into institutionalisation of the value system can be viewed by the notion that psychological states relate to action-orientation and mental disposition as reflected in the separation of harmonising enlightenment on one hand by *Sattwa* and *Rajas* and *Tamas* on the other. The psychological energy-force of *Sattwa*, as the transmutation of action into a restorative psychological state providing understanding and illumination, holds a special relevance. The *Guna* separation of *rajas* as a kinetic force in which conflict is unresolved, effort is dissipated and values are characterised by individualistic notions of self-centred ambition. This course of transition has been well elaborated by Chakraborty (1997) who nomenclatures it as *Guna* Theory, which may be viewed as under:

**The Guna Theory Values in Human Personality**

| *Guna* | *Leading to* | *Value* |
|---|---|---|
| | *Sattwa* | |
| Equilibrium translating into harmony | | Psychological illumination, poise, severity, positive attitude, contentment, forbearance, forgiveness |
| | *Rajas* | |
| A force of kinesis leading to struggle, effort, passion and action | | Dynamism, fluctuating moods, anger, envy, crookedness, vindictiveness, vanity |
| | *Tamas* | |
| Inconsequence and inertia resulting in obscurity, incapacity and inaction | | Laziness, confusion, indecision |

The ethical codes of Indian tradition emphasise *sadhna* or self-cultivation and self-transformation so as to deliver a common good to the society, since the genesis of value determination triggers from individuals. Similarly, the dominant morality of ancient Chinese culture is also virtue centred, which gives a central place to the concept of common good to all members as a community. The common is made possible and is at least partially defined by a way of life in which all members cooperate to achieve it (Wong, 1986). The Japanese idea of *Kyoser* (the pursuit of happiness, prosperity and concern for community-based justice) is also very similar to this idea. The similarities of the Indian concept of an idealised social system (*Ramrajya*), where the virtue of the ruler becomes the key variable and Confucian teachings are alike. As Becker and Connor (1986) have pointed out, "the Confucian moral tradition stressed human-relatedness, rather than separateness of persons, as the essence of man's existence. The self of the human subject is explained rationally, as the occupant of social roles, not as an equal discrete entity. There can be no fulfilment for the individual in isolation from his fellow man. In the Confucian ethical system, being a person is something one, does not something one is." As in the Confucian social hierarchy, respect for tradition and an order of status based on relationship are predominantly contained, in the Indian tradition as well individual gain and self-determination are considered appropriate only in the complex context of adhering to established loyalties and principles. The central point of the Asian tradition is that it does not present truth-untruth or good-evil as dualities of objective measurability. The emphasis is on *dharma* (religion) and the efforts to emphasise *sadhana* or self-cultivation and self-transformation is culminated into the achievement of human consciousness. So, while value-centred morality may have its expression in a common good, the genesis of value determination itself rests with individuals. Values cause individuals to behave in an ethical way, ethics enable themselves to choose actions which serve a common good (Brown and Chatterjee, 1999).

**Mapping the Values Terrain : Western Approaches**

The domain of the value system can be viewed for three main perspectives, viz., the rationalist, the holistic and the spiritualist (Plunkett, 1985) and this has been illustrated in the figure. Categories A, B and C are although analytically separated and their independent existence is recognised. However, a variety of overlaps, linkages and synthetic approaches also emerge in categories D and G (Fig. 2.1).

A. *Rational (Pragmatic) Values*: The rationalist ideology perceives that market is the best mechanism for deciding choices and solutions, not just the economy. Industrialism was developed on a philosophy of utilitarianism, which contained a pragmatic idealism that greatest happiness should be assured for maximum people. This doctrine had rationality contained as the concept of best fit in terms of deriving individual's advantages in order to fulfil their materialistic, expectations. However, this does not take care of the societal interest. This value system privilege those who already control resources and attach blame to those who fail to survive in the market. The weaker members of the society are further marginalized and rise of unemployment and economic inactiveness fuels to crisis.
B. *Holistic (Intuitive) Values*: Value system, in this category, realises human beings as a part of an ever-changing global or

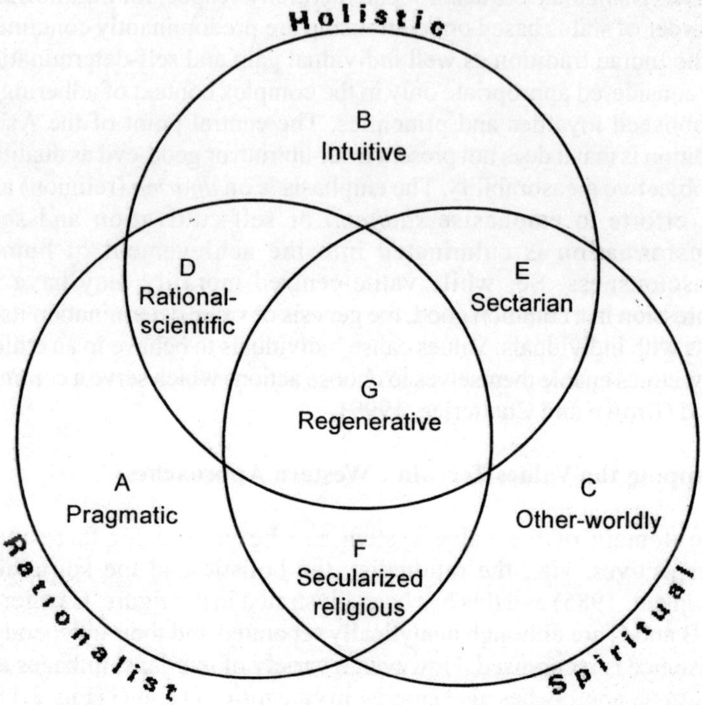


*The three main perspectives*
Rationalist values
Holistic values
Spiritual values

*Exclusive Forms*
A. Pragmatic values
B. Intuitive values
C. Other-worldly values

*Areas of linkage and synthesis*
D. Rational-scientific values
E. Sectarian values
F. Secularized religious values
G. Regenerative values

**Fig. 2.1:** Value System: Various Perspectives

cosmic reality and this entails an understanding of human beings as body, mind and feelings (Roszak, 1981; Bohm, 1981; Davies, 1984). This view makes an appreciation for the human needs and desires that go beyond rationality and searches for a space for subjective or intuitive awareness of our constantly evolving experience within totality that cannot be grasped either by mind or through the senses. This philosophy takes for emphasising the respect for human dignity/respect and leaves scope for flexibilities in order to understand varieties—culture, lifestyle, experience, emotions, scientific understandings, rationality and spiritual direction. The exactness and conceptual structure however, lacks.

C. *Spiritual (Other Worldly) Values*: Ideally spiritual value system is not a religious affirmation, nor it relates anywhere with the sectarian thoughts; rather it has a deep-rooted concern for interiorization, self-awakening and an overall human consciousness. The characteristic of such approach is the acceptance of both as inner self and beliefs in mysteries, such as of faith and eschatological hope, which are not amenable to rational analysis.

D. *Rational-holistic (Rational-scientific) Values*: This theory takes care of high moral grounds for its rational-scientific understanding of reality and covers comprehensive understandings of the mature and finality of humanity, society and education make a philosophical basis for this value system. Marxism (liberal, pluralist and humanist with holistic aspirations) is a good example which offers a total and definitive interpretation of human reality which is aesthetic, materialist and dialectical and based upon the continually renewal struggle of economic and political interests which are mutually exclusive. The moral element comes from the Marxist identification with the worker as the critical contributor to production. In contrast the liberal pluralist theories of reality are agnostic, individualistic and tied for their moral legitimacy to notions of human rights and respect for social contrasts. This value system underlines a rational, legal and constitutional approach which finds empirical political solutions under administrative centralisations.

E. *Holistic-spiritual (Sectarian) Value*: Spiritual holistic perspectives are apt to lead to a variety of dogmatic forms, such as sects or cults with a strong commitment for their propounded truth, illumination or mission. This value system ensures rigidity in its followers who develop their narrow boundaries and internal hierarchies. Such associations may be sometimes extremely creative and effective, whether in proselytising or in applying the energies of their adherents to assigned tasks. It is also not surprising that people can be swept away by the new synthetic teachings of cults combing, however, incongruously, religion, psychology, even behavioural psychology are emerging from heavy persuasion and indoctrination can also be viewed and methods for combating the same are not seen.

F. *Rational-spiritual (Secularised religious) Values*: This variant of the value system can be viewed as a synthetic approach between rationalist and spiritual or religious view-points, to the extent of a virtual conflation of faith and reason. In a situation, where rationalists and modern pragmatists consider spiritualism as a taboo area, an effort to institutionalise the religion is the rationale behind this value system. Religious leaders make the social system (political educational, business etc.) aware of the choices/priorities/ codes and efforts are made to assimilate them.

G. *Rational-holistic-spiritual (Regenerative Values)*: The three components (rational, holistic and spiritual) have been presented in the model at basic and also at intersecting positions and this value system involves their synthesis. A view of humanity which embraces mind, heart and spirit, requires a linking perspective, one which is not provided by any of the value positions. Rationalism has been very well emphasised and holism has also been appreciated as a viable alternative but spiritualism has been viewed with variations. Western concept has considered it as divine—a creator, universal force, independent of humanity outside space and time, a non-personal entity. This system develops a view to subordinate human reason to the divine since our individual wills, purposes and destinies are not completely of greater value and purpose than we could ourselves conceive. Ultimate reality and truth may not be ours to know, but what if they are known by, an infinite, all-knowing God?

**Values in the Indian Tradition**

Indian tradition does not respect much the material progress and affluence and all that matters is progress in the realm of consciousness and spirit and not in physical and surrounding material environment. India's cultural tradition has viewed two distinct cultural trends, e.g. spiritualistic (*atmavadi*) and materialistic (*anatmavadi* or *svabhavavadi*). Besides, the four *purusharthas—artha, kama, dharma* and *moksha*—have been valued for the maintenance of social life Philosophical systems accord value differently these four and accord priorities differently. As for example in a common sense, naturalistic trend of thinking (*Lokayate*) *artha* and *kama* will have preference to desires of others while in a system like *Advaita Vedanta*, *Moksha*, certainly is the highest value. But other values are not totally rejected or ignored. Since man has to play different roles at different occasions, the sense of balancing of harmony (*Samanvaya*) is one of the cardinal values in the Indian tradition, which has been more pronounced by the doctrine of *Anekanta* and technique of *syadvad* in the Jain tradition; the same is not only an act of balancing rather the same is also a powerful strategy to create dialogue and resolving the conflicts. In the *upanishadic* elaborations hierarchical ordering for creating harmony has been underlined as acceptance of *annamaya* (material), *pranamaya* (vital), *monomaya* (physical), *vigyanamaya* (intellectual) and *anandamaya* (blissful) stages. Sri Aurbindo has rightly remarked this as maintenance of harmony of spirit, mind and body.

The concept of harmony implies a very important value almost as its logical corollary, i.e. tolerance (Banerjee, 1993). Indian traditional context signifies the healthy attitude of mutual trust and respect and sincere attempt to understand the other's point of view without giving up one's own justified conviction which has been logically established through the technique of *syadvad*. This mental make-up has been, probably the background of the present day concept of secularism—which can be viewed as the acceptance of all positive religious values as equally good and not rejection of them simply because they are enshrined in different religions.

Dharma is another very important *purushartha*. It connotes different things but the English term religion is not an appropriate synonym of *dharma* (Banerjee, 1993). According to him, "*dharma*" comes from the root *dhr* (*dhr+man*) which means that which holds something up. *Dharma* etymologically implies the nature of something as has been defined accurately as "*Vastu Swabhavo Dhammo*" in the Jain tradition. *Dharma* may mean duty; it may function as natural or descriptive concept or as a moral or prescriptive concept (the way things are and the way they ought to be). Other view points see dharma as *svadharma*, *paradharma*, *yugadharma*, in addition to non-violence (*ahimsa*), truth (*satya*), non-acceptance of gifts (*aparigraha*) etc. The multidimensional concept of dharma, if not anything else, at least stands for a broad humanistic stand on life of an individual and in its private as well as social aspects. It pleads for a sense of a charitable balance and open-mindedness in all aspects of life.

*Artha* is necessary for social, individual and economic survival like *kama* which values bestowing proprietorial rights on individuals. In both the *purusharthas* an over-indulgence leads to disruption of the value system.

*Moksha* or *Nirvana* has been valued as the ultimate goal of human life. This is also viewed as all journeys come to a point of termination somewhere—this is the story of the processes and products. It is a solemn promise for those who have qualified for it through their modernisation, observance of social norms and performance of all necessary obligations (Singh, 1993).

*Ashtang Yoga* is another dimension of Indian Value System which was propounded by Patanjali—a great saint, which comprises of dimensions (Shankar, 1994), as follows:

**Five Yamas**

(i) *Non-violence (Ahimsa)*—Not to kill and not to perform any such act which creates a damage for others. The Jain tradition goes a step ahead and considers even not to conceive a thought to harm any organism under its ambit.

(ii) *Truth*—To say in exactness and as per correct perception.

(iii) *Non-Stealing (Asteya)*—Not to use anybody's thing without permission, not to take possession of anybody's articles.

(iv) *Celibacy (Brahmacharya)*—Control over sensuality and limited use of sex.

(v) *Aparigraha*—Not to collect goods/articles more than the legitimate use of the individual.

**Five Rules (Niyam)**

(i) *Cleanliness (Shauch)*—To clean not only the body and clothes but also the thoughts and to have right thinking—positive thinking.

(ii) *Contentment (Santosh)*—To remain contented and not to become impatient.

(iii) *Meditation (Tapa)*—To control the body, mind and spirit.

(iv) *Study (Swadhyaya)*—To study good literature regularly with a view to ensure concentration.

(v) *Worshipping the God (Ishwar Pranadidhan)*—To have faith in the God and daily worship with a view to purify mind and spirit.

*Self-awareness*—Another dimension of value doctrine: Knowing the self, knowing the emotional outbursts of one's psyche in the form of hate, love, anger, like, dislike, etc. are essential to perceive in order to know oneself since they also reflect about levels of our own consciousness (Sharma, 1993). According to Carlo Suares (1950), self-knowledge is action, immediate, powerful, concrete and the only action which can bring us out of our state of confusion. It is as urgent, real and practical as leaping into a life boat at the time of shipwreck. He, while elaborating the concepts of Krishnamurti, suggests that by virtue to self-knowledge, one leads into a sphere in which there are no words and thoughts become silent. With this we need to strengthen in us a state of mind which is keen observation and intense awareness, yet impartial, disinterested and simple, in the manner of a store-keeper looking after the registering of a swift coming and going of goods. Self-awareness is not a technique that one develops, cultivates and increases through time through sharpening (Krishnamurti, 1954). The process of self-awareness can be viewed as under:

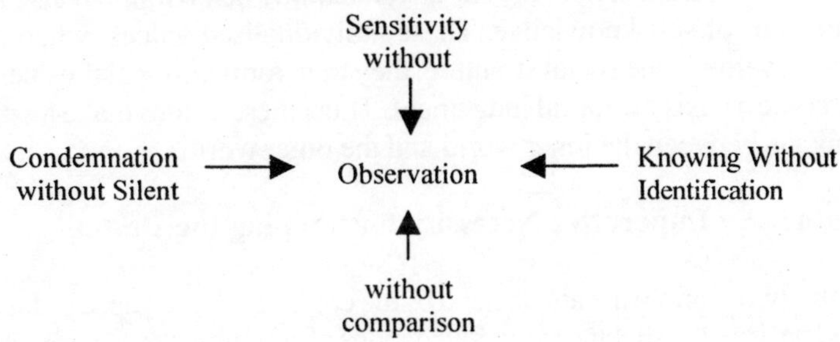

Rajnish (1984) has added in this the total alertness of mind and recognises a state of bliss as a result of the state of self-awareness.

## The Gandhian Value System

Gandhi, who had a tremendous faith in non-violence (*Ahimsa*) believed that all training without strengthening the spirit of culture is of no use. He emphasised for the value system which accords prime importance to the culture of heart and development of character, which he keeps above and also emphasised for the component of character building and opined that end of all education and all training should be man making. Gandhi appeared to be more influenced by the doctrine of right conduct emphasized in the jain tradition, where it has been said "Nanassa Saar Ma Yaro" (Essence of knowledge is the right conduct).

## Understanding Values: A Synthetic Approach

Conceiving the fact that human being is not only a biological entity developed from a protoplasmic mass, rather the same is a complex combination of body, mind, spirit, emotions, feelings etc, values may be perceived as those orientations/conceptions/beliefs, which emerge in the psychological domain of the total personality of a human being in the state of crystallization of a product of fusion of intellect and emotion. This fusion works for interconnectedness for establishing a vital link between society and individual through the cultural bonds in order to explore new vistas of human consciousness. The catalyzing force for this conceptualisation is the attitude of interiorization which results into the overall satisfaction of the psychological drive, which emerges into a prototype, in regards of decisions pertaining to choose the best alternatives as choices, either explicit or implicit, and ultimately develops into a frame or reference, not only for understanding behaviour but also as an indicator of self-knowledge. These individualised values, when grow and develop in the social structure, they transform into social values and become a basis for moral judgement. Thus, these values make a vibrant linkage between the inner world and the outer world.

## Value: An Imperative Necessity for Shaping the Destiny

After two world wars and the end of the cold war, the collapse of fascism and nazism, the shaking to the foundations of communism and colonialism and in the era of globalisation, privatization and liberalisation, humanity has entered a new phase of its history. The social disarray of the nations, the disregard for justice, which pushes citizens to margin, the anarchy overtaking our communities is eluding peace and bringing agony on the globe. The commitment for ensuring a culture of non-violence, respect, justice and peace and an affirmation that a common set of core values is essential in order to appreciate that we all are interdependent is such a truth which has to be lived in heart and action. There is a strong need to strive for a just, social and economic order, in which everyone has an equal chance to reach full potential as human being, where everybody can speak and act truthfully and with compassion, dealing fairly with all, by way of avoiding prejudice and hatred and strengthen a culture of solidarity and relatedness. The irrevocable, unconditional norms, which are most commonly found in the teachings of all world religions, for all areas of life, for families and communities, for all vocations and professions, for races, nations and religions make us to understand the whole humankind as our family and are, indeed, the prerequisite conditions for a sustainable world order. There exists a consensus among all religions, which can be the basis for a global value system—a minimal fundamental consensus concerning binding of all values which are, indeed, the irrevocable standards and fundamental moral attitudes. There is a need to emphasise for a value system in all walks of life, which can dismantle mutual arrogance, mistrust, prejudice, and even hostile images and can offer a fundamental sense of trust and prepare a ground of meaning ultimate standards of credibility and create a spiritual home. Every individual has an intrinsic dignity and inalienable rights, and each also has an inescapable responsibility for achieving a transformation in the human consciousness, because values are related to the state of mind and give a way of looking things which may develop into a pattern of behaviour of various shades of life and social conduct. As our decisions and deeds, even our omissions and failures have far reaching consequences, especially for awakening our spiritual powers through a technology of dialogue for better understanding and for ensuring socially beneficial peace-fostering earth-friendly ways of living.

The great foundations of richest value system of India, propounded by ancient sages, who relentlessly sought after the highest integral knowledge and perfection, have exhibited India's distinctiveness. Our culture has always stood for universality and common fraternity of the entire human race, and our aspirations are reflected especially in the educational field in creating, strengthening and developing a national system that should be geared to the highest ideals of universal peace, unity and harmony. Our rich value system has recognised education not only as a liberating force but also as an evolutionary force which enables the individual to rise from mere materiality to superior planes of intellectual and spiritual consciousness. Education, in Indian ethos, has emerged as a dialogue between the past, present and the future so that the coming generations receive the accumulated lessons of heritage and transmit it to future generations. We need to connect all humanised brain batteries into series which can work on multi-faceted dimensions, extend effortlessly cooperation for achieving development with less bias and prejudices and can have a self-awareness for peace and harmony not only with themselves but also with their environment in order to ensure the development of new faculties of consciousness. This value system would be the ultimate end of human bliss and would also ensure compassion and love for the mankind.

## REFERENCES

Allport, G., Vernon, P.E., and Lindzey, G., (1932). *Study of Values,* Houghton Niffin, Boston.

Bandura, A. and Walters, R.H., (1963). *Social Learning and Personality Development,* Holt Rinehart and Winston, New York.

Banerjee, S.P., (1993). 'Values in the Tradition of Indian thinking and values relevant to our contemporary needs'; *Tulsi Prajna,* JVBI, Ladnun; pp. 19-27.

Becker, B.W. and Connor, B.E., (1986). On the Status and Promise of Value Research, *Management Bibliographies and Reviews*, 12, pp. 3-17.

Bohm, D., (1981). *Wholeness and the Implicate Order*, Routledge & Kegan Paul, London.

Borsodi, R., (1965). The neglected science of values, *Journal of Human Relations,* 13(4), 433-45.

Bronfen Brenner, U., (1970). *Two Worlds of Childhood,* Russel Sage Foundation, New York.

Brown, M.I. and Chatterjee, S., (1999). The Relevance of the Guna Theory in the Congruence of Eastern Values and Western Management Practice, *Journal of Human Values*, 5; pp. 93-102.

Capra, F., (1983). *The Turning Point: Science, Society and the Rising Culture,* Fontana, London.

Chakraborty, S.K., (1997). Seminar Series: *Human Values in Management, Management Centre for Human Values*, Calcutta.

Cole, E.G., (1987). The Restless Quest of Modern Man, in the *Relevance of Value Education Today, Value Education: Today's Challenges,* Nirmala Convent, Mysore, p.3.

Davies, P., (1984). *God and the New Physics*; Penguin, Harmondsworth.

Eysenck, H.J., (1960). The Development of Moral Values in Children: The Contribution of Learning Theory; *British Journal of Education Psychology*.

Eysenck, (1964). *Crime and Personality*, Routledge and Kegan Paul, London.

Good, C.V., (1959). *Dictionary of Education*, McGraw Hill, New York.

Gupta, N.L., (1986). *Value Education: Theory and Practices;* Krishna Brothers, Ajmer.

Havighurst, R.J., (1953). *Human Development of Education*, Longman's Green & Co., New York.

Jacob P., Flink J. and Schuchman, H., (1962). Values and their Function in Decision Making: *American Behavioural Scientist*; 5, pp. 6-38.

Jaki, S., (1978). *The Road of Science and the Ways to God*, Scottish Academic Press, Edinburg.

Kluck Ohm, C., (1951). Values and Value Orientations in the Theory of Action. In Talcolt Parsons & Edward A. Shils *et al. Toward a General Theory of Action.* Cambridge, Mass: Harvard University Press, 409-10.

Kohlberg, L., (1969). Cognitive Development in Socialisation in Goslin's Handbook of Socialisation Theory and Research, pp. 61-65.

Konopka, G., (1973). Formation of values in the developing person. *American Journal of Orthopsychiatry*, 43(1), 86-96.

Krishnamurti, J., (1954). *The First and Last Freedom*, Victor Gollancz Ltd., London, pp. 95.

Loughram, R., (1967). A Pattern of Development in Moral Judgement Mode by Adolescents; *Educational Review.*

Morris, J.P., (1958). The Development of Adolescent Value Judgements, *British Journal of Education Psychology.*

Piaget, J., (1932). *The Moral Judgement of the Child,* Routledge and Kegan Paul, London.

Plunkett, D., (1985). The timeless and the timely in Souper, P.E.(ed.). *The Spiritual Dimension of Education*, University of Southampton, Southampton.

Rajneesh, (1984). *The Rajneesh Bible,* Vol. II, Rajnish Publications, Boulder, Colorado, USA, pp. 718.

Rani, Seema, (2000). *Approaches to Value Education and the Role of the School and the Curriculum; Education in India,* Association of Indian Universities, New Delhi, pp. 44-51.

Raths, L.E., Harmin, M. & Simon, S.B., (1966). *Values and Teaching; Working with Values in the Classroom.* Charles E. Merrill, Ohio.

Rokeach, M., (1973). *The Nature of Human Values*. Free Press, New York.

Rokeach, M., (1973). Value Education: Need of Present Generation; (quoted) Shettly *et al.* (2000); Value Education in India, Association of Indian Universities, New Delhi, pp. 74-79.

Roszak, T., (1981). Person/Planet: *The Creative Disintegration of Industrial Society:* Granada, London.

Shankar, G., (1994). *Shiksha Ki Drishti se Yam-Niyam Ka Mahatwa;* Importance of Environment and Values in Education System, Gurukul Kangri University, C.O.P., pp. 24-30.

Sharma, A.P., (1993). Developing Awareness in Teachers Towards Values; *Tulsi Prajna*, JVBI, Ladnun; pp. 50-57.

Sharma, R.P., (1993). Social Ethos and Education: Search for Basic Premises; *Tulsi Prajna*, JVBI, Ladnu; pp. 28-35.

Shetty, A. and Pushpanadham, K., (2000). *Valuing Values; Value Education in India;* Association of Indian Universities, New Delhi, pp. 95-100.

Shils, Edward & Anderson Arnold, (1966). On defining modernisation in *Modernisation: The Dynamics of Growth*, ed. Myron Weiner; Voice of America Forum Lectures.

Singh, R.P., (1993). Value Education for the Gandhian Perspective; *Tulsi Prajna*, JVBI, Ladnun, pp. 7-18.

Singh, R.P., (1993). Values for Education; *Tulsi Prajna*, JVBI, Ladnun, pp. 70-76.

Suares, C., (1950). *Krishnamurti and the University of Man*. Cheting Bombay. pp. 7-8.

Thompson, G.G., (1952). *Child Psychology*; Houghton-Niffin, Boston.

Wuchohn, (1957). Value Education: Need of Present Generation; (quoted) Shettly *et al.* (2000); *Value Education in India*, Association of Indian Universities, New Delhi, pp. 74-79.

3

# Value Education for Secular Society

KIREET JOSHI

The subject that is chosen for discussion is of great significance. For the theme of Value Education has now come to the fore, and in conceiving the contents of Value Education, we need to examine the social context of which secularism is today an important and major element.

At the outset, however, we may observe that secularism is ridden with ambiguities in our Indian situation; it is thus left to everyone to interpret it in anyway one thinks best. There is a view of secularism, which consists of equality before law irrespective of caste, religion or race. But this view often tends to become tainted in actual situations where there are unreasonable demands coming from religious groups, which insist on special provisions which tend to mitigate the idea of equality before law. There is also the idea of secularism which advocates that the state funds should not be utilised for the promotion of any religion. In practice, very often, this rule is employed even where there is a question of the promotion, not of any religion, but of ethical and spiritual values. There is a tolerant view of secularism, which aims at equal respect for all religions. Here, again, it has become difficult to create an ethos where equal respect for all religions could be practised, and no significant efforts have been made to create a climate where secularism understood in this sense can flourish. There is also a synthetic view of secularism, which aims at bringing about unity of religions on the basis of the unity of moral and spiritual values. This is an excellent idea, but here, again, no significant effort has been made to actualise this view in practice. A very powerful interpretation of secularism is the materialistic view which denies any justification for religion as such. This view tends to get an upper hand since it can be more convincingly made out that materialism is incontrovertibly secular. The net effect is that our country has tended to promote confused thought on this vital subject, and people are afraid to think on this subject with clarity and boldness. There is also a tendency to shut the doors even of those tendencies in religions and in spiritual planes which lie above religions, which, if consciously acknowledged and promoted, would heal the divisions of religions, bring about greater understanding among them, and, eventually enable us to cultivate the scientific body of spiritual knowledge. What we need today is a positive recognition of spirituality as distinct from religion; we need also to recognise that there exists a scientific body of spiritual knowledge, and that this needs to be promoted by the state. We may also note that this becomes all the more necessary when we find that the truth that lie behind democracy and socialism can be integrated and expressed effectively only when the ultimate spiritual aims are recognised and promoted.

In sum, the urgent need of India is to evolve a clear concept of secularism on the basis of a recognised body of spiritual knowledge which embraces all domains of human life—physical, emotional, vital, dynamic, intellectual, ethical and aesthetic.

Having said this, let us observe that secularism, in spite of its ambiguities, has several clear and distinguished features. It stands for life, it affirms ideals of growth, and it aims at the maximum possible perfection of life; it stands for liberty, it affirms the individuality of individuals, and it aims at ever-growing being and becoming; it questions dogmatism, ignorance and superstition, it affirms the ideal of truth, science and scientific temper, and it aims at progressive and comprehensive knowledge; finally, it combats authority and privileges of the select few, it affirms the right of the weak and the oppressed, it aims at universal emancipation.

Secularism is wedded to the conception of the right of all individuals as members of the society to full life and the full development of which they are individually capable. The master potency of this conception is so great that it is no longer possible to accept the theory that the many must necessarily remain for ever on the lower ranges of life and only a few climb into the free air and light. It is impossible for us to accept as an ideal any arrangement by which certain classes of society should arrogate development and full social fruition to themselves, while assigning a bare and barren function of service alone to others. Full development of all is the mark of secularism.

The second master idea that secularism would affirm is that the individual is not merely a social unit, but he is a soul, a being, who has to fulfil his or her own individual truth and law as well as his or her natural or his or her assigned part in the truth and law of the collective existence. It is for this reason that secularism insists on individual freedom, on individual initiative, individual thought, individual will, individual consciousness.

Application of these two conceptions has led to momentous experiments in democracy, socialism and democratic socialism. These experiments have not been entirely successful. It has been found that when liberty is assured, equality has suffered, and when equality is sought to be assured, liberty gets strangulated. In fact, democracy puts forward a trinity of values, liberty, equality and fraternity, and it appears now that the key to the fulfilment of the democratic ideal will depend upon the extent to which the value of fraternity will be applied to the disbalancements which are created in experiments of liberty and equality. A serious issue for secularism is to fathom deep into the heart of fraternity and to create conditions for the realization of the spirit and practice of universal brotherhood. As we said earlier, secularism affirms individualism. But at an early stage of the development of individualism, it was realised that the unrestrained use of individual judgement without an objective criterion of truth would mean a perilous experiment. A search was, therefore, instituted to discover a general standard of truth and also for some principle of social order. This search resulted in an answer provided by the discovery of physical science. This answer was two-fold: (1) Physics demonstrated a truth of things which depended upon no doubtful scripture or fallible authority, since that truth was written on the open book of nature which everybody can read, provided he had the patience to observe and intellectual honesty to judge; (2) Science provided a norm of knowledge and principles of verification to which all can freely and most rationally subscribe. This answer was the culminating point of the 19th century in Europe, which was preceded by two centuries of preparation. During these two centuries, the method of scientific induction was evolved, and a new scientific outlook on the world was developed. What we call today scientific temper is the result of this great endeavour. Since then, there is a widespread acceptance of the attitude which maintains that statements of facts should be based on observation, and not on unsupported authority.

It must, however, be observed that the victory of the physical science was largely due to its application, its technique and technology. Beginning with the discovery of gun powder and mariner's compass to the discoveries of electricity and telegraphy, and atomic power, we have a long story of mixed colours of good and evil, and we have today increasing number of sensitive and refined thinkers who have even come to equate science and technology with domination and violence. Some of them have fixed their attention on the way in which development is projected in India and elsewhere, and they have brought out quite vividly the peril of plunder, propaganda and violence to which masses of people are being subjected in the name of science and development. Promises of science have come to be questioned and there are increasing trends of thought which advocate limits to growth and the use of technology to control technology. The idea of the 'small is beautiful' has achieved a wide appeal. There is a growing awareness that all is not well with science and technology, that things cannot be allowed unchecked and unchallenged, and that fundamental issues of humanity's future need to be considered without any dogmatism, even if it implies questioning science itself.

We need, however, to draw up a more balanced evaluation of contribution of science, particularly when scientific progress has a great role to play in determining the directions of value education. Let us, first, underline that science has affirmed the virtues of impartiality, of ever-widening quest of knowledge. It has fought against ignorance and superstition, and it has enhanced the cause of education. Science has enlarged for good the intellectual horizons of human race, and raised, sharpened and intensified powerfully the general intellectual capacity of mankind. In its dispassionate movement, science pursues truth for the sake of truth and knowledge for the sake of knowledge. This is the highest right of the intellectual of humanity, and in this dispassionate functioning, there is perfect purity and satisfaction.

On the other hand, when science tries to apply its discoveries and functions to life, it becomes the play thing of forces over which it has little control. This is the reason why the balance sheet of science is a mixed one. While, on the one hand science has made discoveries which have promoted practical humanitarianism, it has, on the other hand, supplied monstrous weapons to egoism and mutual destruction; while, on the one hand, it has made a gigantic efficiency of organisation utilisable for economic and social amelioration of nations. It has, on the other hand, placed the same efficiency of organisation in the hand of national rivalries for mutual aggression, ruin and slaughter; while, on the one hand, it has given rise to a large rationalistic altruism, it has, on the other hand, justified monstrous egoism, vitalism, vulgar will to power and success; while on the one hand, it has drawn mankind together and given it a new hope, it has, on the other hand, crushed it with the burden of commercialism.

Science does not have within itself any inherent leverage by which it can prevent its exploitation by human impulses and passions, and since it can produce great results, its explication for evil can also be great. The modern civilisation, which is science-based, has to deal with an extremely difficult issue that it has created, namely, that of the emergence of dominant economic barbarism. This barbarism impels humanity to sink in mud of desire and hunger on a massive scale. It makes satisfaction of wants and desires and accumulation of possessions its standard and aim. It has conceived of the ideal individual in the image not of the cultured or noble or thoughtful or moral, or spiritual person, but of the successful person. It puts forward the opulent plutocrat and successful mammoth capitalist as images of achievement and fulfilment. It is this barbarism which assigns to them the actual power to rule the society. It prescribed pursuit of material, success, comfort and enjoyment for their own sake. It subordinates all other pursuits; it looks upon beauty as nuisance, art and poetry a frivolity or means of advertisement. Social respectability is its idea of morality; it uses politics as a door for markets and exploitation.

It is now increasingly recognised that the development of science should be supplemented by enormous development of human goodness. Bertrand Russell has pointed out that there are two ancient evils that science, unwisely used, may intensify: they are tyranny and war. In an important study of the theme of science and values, Bertrand Russell declared:

> "*There are certain things that our age needs, and certain things that it should avoid. It needs compassion and a wish that mankind should be happy; it needs the desire for knowledge and the determination to eschew pleasant myths; it needs above all courageous hope and the impulse to creativeness. The things that it must avoid, and that have brought it to the brink of catastrophe, are cruelty, envy, greed, competitiveness, search for irrational subjective certainty, and what Freudians call the death wish... The root of the matter is very simple and old fashioned thing... the thing I*

> *mean — please forgive me for mentioning it is love — Christian love, or compassion. If you feel this, you have a motive for existence, a guide in action, a reason for courage, an imperative necessity for intellectual honesty."*

We thus see that the central issue of our age is the growth of love, of compassion, of fraternity. This is the conclusion that is reinforced when we consider the issues of human unity and those of development. Global unity if necessitated by a number of factors, the growth of science which is universal in character, powerful means of communication and prospects of enormous economies if regions and continents can unite. But even when there are increasing reductions of armaments, there is a fear in mankind; for there are still enough nuclear warheads which can destroy the world several times over. Hence, there is a continuing need to build the defences of peace in the mind and hearts of men. Again, at a time when the world is shrinking, the gulf between the rich and the poor is widening. The sharp disparities of development and asymmetrical relations among nations are impelling disadvantagious countries to seek unattainable goals. The resulting vicious circle of dilemmas and predicaments can be broken, it seems, only if it is realised that development like peace is indivisible and that not by competition and exploitation, but by mutual help and cooperation can the goals of development be realised. Development of peace and development of cooperation seem to be indispensable for the modern society's future growth and advancement.

It is clear that if democracy and secularism are to survive, if science is to be utilised for stabilising society, if world unity is to be achieved, and if development of all nations is to be secured, we have to work vigorously on human beings. It is evident that present structures of society and human nature as they are today are incapable of taking us to the road to fulfilment. And it seems obvious that the systems and structures cannot be changed if human nature cannot be changed. And when we speak of the change of human nature, we speak of radical operations of the maladies of human nature. We need to create human beings who will feel spontaneous brotherhood with all; we need human beings who will effortlessly extend cooperation in tasks of development; we need human beings who will have peace with themselves so that they will radiate peace in their environment.

This goal that we need to seek is to be viewed in the context in which we find an irresistible drive towards totality and all comprehensiveness. The wheels of the world are spinning so fast today that we are obliged to overpass our limitations continuously and interminably. We are proceeding towards the future where a peculiar combination of wide comprehensiveness and effective specialisation will become imperative; they will have to be fused together.

This is further reinforced by the human crisis created by the need of the development of new faculties of consciousness. All this explains why we need value education and why we need integral education. In recent trends of thought, we have been presented with the ideal of learning to be and learning to become. It is only when there is a right balance of the development of all our faculties that we can reach and attain the state of self-possession and self-mastery. We can then experience our true being and discover the secret of our perpetual being. We need to put emphasis on the education of all our parts of being—physical, vital, rational, aesthetic, moral and spiritual. And the development of faculties and capacities of these parts of the being is closely connected with the question of the values that they seek. Values are the ultimate ends that personality seeks to embody, express and fulfil. Corresponding to each capacity, there are specific values. Our physical being seeks the value of health and strength; our vital being seeks the value of harmony, and heroism; our rational faculty seeks the value of truth and universality; our moral will seeks the good and the right; our aesthetic sensitivity seeks the value of beauty and joy; and our spiritual faculties seek experiences and realization of inalienable fraternity, unity and oneness. Integral education, therefore, is the same as integral value education.

This, we may say, is the broad framework of the theme of value education, and we stand in the need of clarifying and discussing implications of this framework. Much work has been done during the last three decades and more. But the issues are difficult. They involve questions of goals of education, contents of education, methods of education. They relate to the goals of society also, and therefore, the climate of the life at home, life in institutions, and life in general. There are also issues connected with parents and teachers, questión as to how we look upon the child, how the entire society gets involved in the process of learning and teaching. There is also the issue of developing secular society into learning society. It is for this reason that we need to think more and more rigorously, and to be engaged in the process of value education.

4

# The Declaration on Global Ethics in the Light of Modern Physics

SAMPOORAN SINGH

Physicists have come to see that all their theories of natural phenomena, including the "laws" they describe, are creations of the human mind; properties of our conceptual map of reality, rather than of reality itself, or in other words, parts of the map, not of the territory.[1] James Jeans emphasized that the new physics "Fell into the error of identifying appearance with reality",[2] and Eddington wrote, that "physical science is concerned with a world of shadows".[3] Scientific reason established the relative character of all objects experienced in the waking state, the limitations of the sensual world which are relativity, finitude, transitoriness and changeability, and also its concepts of time, space and causality.

Objective science by excluding subjectivity cannot, even in principle, deal with our thoughts, feelings and emotions, with subjective experience of any kind. It excludes "I". The exclusion is total. Our feelings—love, joy, ecstasy, pain, what not—are inherently incapable of unambiguous communication. There is no problem more mysterious than the mind-brain-body interaction, or our subjective experience. Modern science has not made it less intractable. On the other hand it has added a new urgency and also a new poignancy. During the last few years we explored the psychodynamics of the mind-brain system, or subjective nature of man.[4,5]

Maurice H. Wilkins highlights our failures in scientific education in words:

> "I agree with Einstein that the sort of scientific education we have now has produced a narrow-minded way of thinking

> amongst scientists, so that they give no proper attention to the moral and psychological dimensions... Science as it is today doesn't tell us very much about the real nature of human beings... Scientists don't pay attention to the need for moral values in science... Science is a human activity. How therefore can science, being a human activity, be separated from all virtues and values?"[6]

Erwin Schrodinger also echoed, "Scientific attitude would have to be rebuilt, science must be made anew. Care is needed."[7] Many scientists have also discussed restructuring of science.

The psychiatrist R.D. Laing emphatically reminds us: "Out go sight, sound, taste, touch and smell and along with them has since gone aesthetics and ethical sensibility, values, quality, form, all feelings, motives, intentions, soul, consciousness, spirit. Experience as such is cast out of the realm of scientific discourse".[8] According to Laing, hardly anything has changed our world more during the past four hundred years than the obsession of scientists with measurement and quantification.

Man's evolution is not biological but psychosocial. This involved accumulation and transmission of experience through his newly acquired powers of thought and speech communication. Man became extrovert and this led to the accelerative progress of science in the external field. This gave relative knowledge of the world of experience that is revealed through the senses. In the words of Eddington, science "gives us only knowledge of structural form and not knowledge of the content (in consciousness)".[9]

Never before, until now, has the tension between science and human conscience, between technology and ethics reached a point where it has become a threat to the world as a whole.[10] We do not perceive the threats hanging over our heads—the crisis of perception, the psychic disease—warning us of the pressing need for a radically new and universal ethical outlook on the future of present-day science and survival of mankind. We have to realise that peace and genuine human progress are not possible, and never will be, without a new ethical outlook.

## Nature of Value Systems

Broadly speaking, we may divide values under four heads for ease of understanding; virtues, social values, ethical values and spiritual values. A brief discussion is as under:

*Virtue*: It is a pattern of thought; it is 'what should be', virtue is a cultivation. Virtue may be true or false. One is caught in a back-and-forth movement and it has its role in the psychological activity of mind, in the psychological time. It has a material origin.

*Social Value*: These are facts or social uniformalities. These are moral norms or ideals that envisage ideal individuals and ideal social relationships. These arise from the conditioned mind, the psycho-physical activity of the brain; these have material origin. These are historically conditioned socio-political expressions of religion. These are local, parochial and temporary in application. They may change with the change of social circumstances. These are external relationships of the individual with society. If in social values, we bring in measurement, and comparison, the values lose their significance and become immoral.

*Ethical Value*: A mind that has set aside seeking in the future and has denied its past is an ethical mind. It refers to a non-dual frame of reference in the mind spectrum and it arises from the depth dimension of man. An ethical mind perceives the fact, the 'what is'; it is also called the "perception of the inner perceptual construct"; "direct perception of actual fact, an "inward perception (i.e. through the mind)", an "insight or intuition"; it gives "spontaneous response", which bestows the capacity to meet the present challenge.

True ethics means a movement from perception to perception. It implies self-expression of intelligence. Living ethically from moment, to moment is practical and concrete, not an abstract idea. Ethics or values arise from the depth dimension or from the spiritual dimension of man.

We define ethical value as the perception of the 'within' in man; it arises from the inner depth dimension of man; it bestows the capacity to see the false as the false and the true as the true; it is the key to the integration of man.

*Spiritual Value*: All knowledge is structured in consciousness. This recognizes that consciousness alone can be totally self-referral, so the pure mind or non-dual state of mind is presented as an object to pure consciousness, then it reveals itself; or in other words, the non-dual mind perceives the spiritual value. The ultimate ethical value is called spiritual value. Spiritual value is awareness of awareness itself.

## Values in the Light of Indian Philosophy

Swami Ranganathananda, a senior monk of the Ramakrishna order, in December 1966 stated, "Indian thought has always upheld the view that all values proceed not from matter but from the spirit of man... All ethical values are essentially spiritual values; they proceed from the trans-sensual dimension of the human personality. This dimension, which stimulates the ethical sense, is beyond the reach of animals and of such humans who, like animals, are content to live at the sensate level."[11] S.P. Kanal, wrote, "To teach children to value truth in life is to cultivate in them a commitment to scientific temper, that is, love for and use of scientific method in understanding and evaluating situations in life."[12]

The sensate man is essentially self-centred, and his love and concern for his neighbour is dictated by prudence, and expediency. This led Indian thought to insist that all rational ethical theories should derive their sanction not from any external source but from human nature itself. A rational theory of ethical values must be based on the perception of wholeness of man. All true ethics must be non-variable, so universal and global.

We reject the virtues and the social values of the outer socio-economic-political fields and uphold the ethical and spiritual values emerging from the trans-sensual dimension of human personality, from the depth potential of man, the inner nature of man, the wholeness of man.

## Values in the Waking State of Mind

In the Waking State of Mind or in the relative frame of reference, we have accumulated partial experience and fragmentary knowledge, and this is called the cultural belief structure. This structure spontaneously disintegrates and gives thoughts, feelings, emotions, and so on. In this state, the mind cuts itself into the object (atoms with consciousness) and the subject (atoms with consciousness). Richard Feynman talked about "atoms with consciousness" matter with curiosity?[13] Mind looking at mind, or "atoms with consciousness" looking at mind, or "atoms with consciousness" looking at "atoms with consciousness" give us the experience of wonder and mystery whenever we look at the universe. We are looking at ourselves. Consciousness performs a dual role in the universe. In the world of the quantum, it is both the awareness and the creation of experience. It is the being and the knowing of experience. It expresses itself at the hierarchical levels. With the stroke of the twentieth-century quantum eraser, the dividing line between ontology (theory of being) and epistemology (theory of knowing) is rubbed out. A fusion of ontology, epistemology and psychology is beginning to emerge.

Mind constructs a time-space matrix in the external field and this is the materialistic activity. This activity cannot give us ethical values. The symbolic-dualistic knowledge is devoid of all values. Bertrand Russell believed that wisdom becomes increasingly necessary with every advance in science and technology, and that although our age has surpassed all others in knowledge, it has not enjoyed a correlative increase in wisdom; and he called for a "new ethical outlook".

**Values Emerging from Non-dual Knowledge**

Great thinkers of science (...........) including Einstein, Schrodinger, Heisenberg, Eddington, and so on..... tell us today that what science gives us is only a conceptual, short-hand report of the time-space matrix of the universe; and recently they stumbled upon another mode of knowing, called intimate, or direct, or non-dual knowledge. This led to the understanding of life directly, instead of in the abstract, linear terms of representational thinking. Pere Teilhard de Chardin wrote that in man "the existence of a *within* can no longer be evaded, because it is the object of a direct intuition and the substance of all knowledge."[14] Einstein, in almost the last interview that he gave it to the international magazine *Life* said:

> "The mind can proceed only so far upon what it knows and can prove. There comes a point where the mind takes a leap—call it intuition or what you will and comes upon a higher plane of knowledge but can never prove how it got there. All great discoveries have involved such a leap."

Fritjof Capra concluded, "the rational part of research would, in fact, be useless if it were not complemented by the intuition that gives scientists new insights and make them creative".[15] All this suggests that mankind has to work through understanding the psychodynamics of his own mind-brain system called self-knowledge for a quantum jump from logical and scientific reason to intuitive wisdom, from sensate values to spiritual values.

We now explore the deepest connotation of intuitive wisdom. Victor F. Weisskopf wrote, "Chinese thinking emphasizes the intuitive component—the importance of inspiration in scientific thinking." [16] Erwin Schrodinger wrote, "The world is given to me only once, not one existing and one perceived.... Nothing is reflected. The original and the mirror-image are identical. The world extended in space and time is but our representation."[17] This state of mind is called the non-dual state or non frame of reference in the mind spectrum. The non-dual frame has the capacity to perceive the wholeness, which implies to perceive the truth, the fact. The perception of the fact involves knowing the values (the content in consciousness), and the time-space format (Knowledge of structural form).

The values self-express themselves: (a) when the symbolic-dualistic frame is transcended and the non-dual frame is activised, and (b) the non-dual frame has the capacity to perceive the wholeness, the truth, the fact. The values are defined as the implicate order of thought, the truth nature of thought, the content in the consciousness. A mind that has transcended the past and does not project in the future is an ethical mind. A mind that has transcended thought-time has the capacity to perceive the ethical values.

The universal values are open-mindedness and not abstraction, non-violence and not violence, peace and not war, creativeness and spontaneity and not repetitiveness, wisdom and not knowledge, intuition and not logical reason and intellectual gymnastics, freedom and not bondage, bliss and not pain and misery, truth and not falsehood, love and not hatred. The basic problem is that these absolute values cannot even be defined in words and cannot be taught in hourly lessons in schools/colleges/universities, these values self-express themselves when there is understanding of life direct. So the only challenge facing the human race is mutation of the human psyche which leads to a quantum jump from psychosocial evolution to spiritual evolution.

## The Oneness of Mankind

Schrodinger concluded, "Consciousness is never experienced in the plural, only in the singular ...... consciousness is a singular of which the plural is unknown."[18] He added, "Mind is by its very nature a *singulare tantum*. I should say: the overall number of minds is just one."[19] Gregory Bateson concluded, "There is larger mind of which the individual mind is only a subsystem".[20] Kurt Godel also emphasized that he believed that there is only one mind. D.S. Kothari called "the great Upanishadic formula"—"the different individual selves on the empirical plane are one and the same on the transcendental plane, *tat tvam asi*."[21]

We see that the symbolic-dualistic frame of reference represents the individual mind, while the non-dual frame of reference represents the one mind of the human race. As all ethical/spiritual values emerge from the non-dual frame, so values are beyond cause and effect, and are universal, or global, or these are shared by the human race.

**Humanist Technology**

Due to shortage of space, the humanist technology for mutation or radical transformation of human psyche is not discussed. A short summary has been published recently. [22]

When we see the nature of value systems, we conclude that virtues and social values are constructs of the relative frame of reference in the mind spectrum. The values are relative, finite, transitory, changing, and have causal connections: these cannot bring in mutation in the human psyche. Ethical values are synergistic to virtues and social values. These transcend the law of causation. These tend to minimize the matter content in the consciousness, so these lead to mutation of the human psyche. When one discovers the truth in life, the ethical and spiritual values self-express themselves. Truth and more truth, that is the way to happiness and welfare. The consummation of ethical values is spiritual values. Love, truth, joy are spiritual values. Love is not different from truth. Love is that state in which the thought process, as psychological time, has completely ceased. Where there is love, there is revolution, because love is transformation from moment to moment.

When living in the ethical and spiritual values is sustained for a long chronological time, then it becomes a normal state of consciousness. So living the values becomes spontaneous like inhaling and exhaling. This leads to a quantum jump from successive consciousness to simultaneous Consciousness (Global or Universal Consciousness). This results in a perception of globalization.[23] This ends all barriers between man and man, and between man and nature, and there is peace, harmony and beauty.

## The Declaration on Global Ethics or the Universal Declaration of Human Values

Thought expresses its objective nature as time-space matrix in the symbolic-dualistic frame of reference of the mind spectrum. It engages itself in logical and scientific reason or intellectual pursuits. Max Born at the third Pugwash conference stated, "clever, rational ways of thinking are not enough. The danger of mass slaughter .... can only be overcome by moral conviction, by a determination to replace national prides and prejudices with human love."[24] Bertrand Russell in England and Sorokin in USA have warned that modern civilisation cannot survive unless it is inspired by ethical and spiritual values. Among these values, the most important, which they stressed, was love. According to Einstein, the foundation of values must be independent of repetitive and mechanistic dynamics of the conditioned mind. Love, truth, freedom, peace, and so on are the spiritual values and these self-express themselves when thought-time is transcended, and intelligence is activised. Thought expresses its true subjective nature as values in a non-dual frame of reference. Values are the implicate order of thought, the true nature of thought, the content in consciousness.

The universal declaration on global ethics is that human mind has to make a quantum jump from symbolic-dualistic frame of reference to non-dual frame of reference in the mind spectrum; and non-dual frame will self-express itself as ethical values or global ethics. Global ethics is defined as the perception in a non-dual frame of reference of mind. And one who is wholly consecrated to Truth, who wants to live then Truth, serve the Truth, would know at each moment the ethical values; it would be a kind of intuition or revelation or insight which would make you know the truth, the global ethics at every moment. To perceive the ethical values or global ethics, man has to make a quantum jump from psychosocial evolution to spiritual evolution. The future of mankind is hinged on welding of Eastern Spirituality and Western Science, and out of that will emerge a new dimension of all-inclusive integral consciousness that leads to ending of all human crisis, pain and misery, and bestows freedom, peace and bliss on human life. This is the only vocation of the human race.

## Conclusion

Mankind has started living in a synthetic (symbolic-dualistic) world, which is a construct by the relative frame of reference in the mind spectrum, or waking state of consciousness. This frame of reference is engaged in an intellectual process, the observer operating on the thing observed, which leads to distortion of the fact, and this is called the crisis of perception. Every activity in this field is repetitive and mechanistic. It is aware of the time-space matrix and is totally devoid of all ethical and spiritual values. We have to realise that man divorced from nature cannot be happy and his power to resist nature is hopelessly funny.

The non-dual frame of reference has the capacity to perceive the wholeness, which implies perception of the fact, the truth. The perception of the fact involves self-expression of the values which are universal or global.

The value is defined as the implicate order of thought, the true nature of thought, the content in consciousness. It is only the mutation, the inner transformation, of the human psyche that has the capacity to resolve all psychological problems. This will ensure human survival along with all fauna and flora.

The challenge is addressed not only to the structure of education but to the nature and quality of man's mind and life. This approach—to understanding of life directly and to live in light of that feelingful understanding—breaks through frontiers of particular cultures and establishes an entirely new set of values, which in turn can create a new civilisation and a new society.

## REFERENCES

1. Fritjof Capra, (1988).The Tao of Physics, Bantam Books, Second Edition, pp. 147, 277.
2. James Jeans, in Commins and Linscott,(1969). *Man and the Universe, The Philosophers of Science*, New York: Washington Square Press, p. 384
3. *The Nature of the Physical World*, London: Cambridge University Press, Arthur Eddington, 1928
4. Sampooran Singh, (1988). Science and Spirituality Booklets; Taking the Quantum Jump; The Human Paradox: Non-violence and Relationship to Meet the Challenges to Mankind; Human Psyche and Contemporary Physics; The Future of Mankind? Faith Publishers, 586/10 D, Chandigarh, India, The Self and Its Mind-Brain Equipment, (1987) *Ibid.*
5. *Ibid.*, (a) A Renewed Look at the Wave-Particle Complentarity in the Light of Mind-Brain Interactions, Bulletin of the Theosophy Science Study

Group, India, June & August, 1988, Vol. 26 Nos. 3 & 4, pp. 35-37; (b) *The Unity in Mankind,* 15th International Human Unity Conference, November 11-15, 1988, Souvenir, pp. 71-72; (c) The Future of Humanity? Orissa: International Coloquium on the Future Humanity, November 6-9, 1988, Souvenir, pp. 1-9; (d) Holistic Perspective and Human Values, Holistic Science and Human Values, February 1989, Vol. 1, No. 1, pp. 9-14; (e) Humanist Technology, Holistic Science and Human Values, May 1989, Vol. 1, No. 2 pp. 43-48; (f) Kanwaljit and Sampooran Singh, Mind's War on Cancer and AIDS, *The Tribune*, July 16 1989; and (g) Kanwaljit and Sampooran Singh, Towards Full life, *The Tribune,* August 6, 1989.

6. Maurice H. Wilkins, (1988). *In Synthesis of Science and Religion*, Bombay: The Bhaktivedanta Institute, pp. 35, 37
7. Erwin Schrodinger, (1967). *What is Life? & Mind and Matter*, Cambridge University Press, pp. 132.
8. R.D. Laing, (1982). *The Voice of Experience,* New York: Pantheon,
9. Arhur Eddington, *Space, Time and Gravitation,* pp. 200-201
10. Federico Mayor Zaragoza, A New Ethical Outlook, *The Courier*, May 1988.
11. Swami Ranganathananda, *Ethical and Spiritual Values*, The Institute of Culture: The Ramakrishna Mission, Calcutta, 1967.
12. S.P. Kanal, (1993). *Value Education for a Secular Society,* University of Delhi: Department of Philosophy.
13. Richard Feyman, (1981). In Fred Alan Wolf, *Taking the Quantum Leap,* Harper & Row, pp. 227-28.
14. Pere Telhard de Chardin, (1959). *The Phenomenon of Man,* London: Collins, pp. 55.
15. Frigjof Capra, *op. cit.*, p. 18.
16. Victor F. Weisskopf, (1973). In Hideki Yukawa, *Creativity and Intuition,* Tokyo: Kodansha International Ltd., Introduction, pp. 8.
17. Erwin Schrodinger, *op. cit.,* pp. 137, 146.
18. *Ibid.,* pp. 94, 95.
19. *Ibid.,* p. 145.
20. Gregory Bateson, (1988). In Larry Dossey, *Medical Science and Non-violence,* New Delhi: Gandhi Peace Foundation, pp. 12-13.
21. *Ibid.,* pp. 13-14.
22. Sampooran Singh, (1993), The Human Survival: The Emergence of a New Global Civilisation, *op. cit.*, pp. 90-110.
23. *Ibid.,* pp. 76-85.
24. Max Born, (1973) in Hideki Yukawa, *op. cit.,* pp. 189-90.

5

# Values in the Tradition of Indian Thinking and Values Relevant to our Contemporary Needs

S.P. BANERJEE

Every community or country tries to reassess its value-frame periodically in its attempt to sustain itself, if possible, with dignity. The need of such reappraisal is felt more acutely in the periods of crisis, supposed or genuine. There is a widespread feeling in our contemporary society that the present state of affairs in our society is far from normal and symptoms of a disease are manifesting themselves through degeneration and decadence in all fields of our social and cultural life. The political arena shows shameless corruption and gross violation of minimum norms of decency and decorum in all fields of our social and cultural life. Academic field is showing signs of utter frustration as shown through rampant malpractices in examination and careless teaching; the religious attitude is becoming more and more fundamentalist and intolerant and above all, there is lack of mutual trust and respect. Consumerism in the economic field, gross hedonism in moral life and cynicism and scepticism about the political authority or any sort of value-structure are resulting in ultimate frustration and despair and most serious of all, in failing out of the vitality of the nation as expressed through a lack of innovativeness and creativity.

To the discerning section of the society this is high time that we take a close look at our cultural roots and find out if the ills stem out therefrom. Fortunately or unfortunately our country has a cultural heritage which is at least five thousand years old and quite a few of its elements have been widely appreciated and acclaimed. But that should not lead us to complacence and need not blind us to the dead lock in our cultural heritage which is irrelevant to the needs of our society today. It is, therefore, proper that we reassess our cultural heritage in order to determine what is to be retained, what is to be rejected and what is to be modified and readjusted to the conditions of a free, multilingual, multireligious society with inevitable ethnic pluralism. A very significant historical reality to which we must pay our serious attention is the comprehensive attack on our cultural moorings by the colonizers of the recent past who planned to throw the community totally out of its keel in order to implant new, alien structures to facilitate and retain their political and financial stranglehold on the country. However, it will again be going to the other extreme if one thinks that whatever has come from the foreign colonizers who ruled the country immediately before our achievement of political freedom, is all bad and injurious to our culture. What is being suggested is that the concerted effort of the foreign rulers to denigrate our cultural moorings including all the important institutions like family, education, religion and policy had devising effect on these institutions and our present ills might have some of the causes in this phenomenon. And before this, the loss of political independence since around 1000 A.D. with the advent of the Muslim invasion with its strong unilinear culture and did also affect the character of the practice born out of the traditional culture.

## II

There is a common belief, reinforced by eminent writers like S. Radhakrishnan, that Indian tradition is in and out spiritual in nature. Indian tradition is disrespectful of material progress and affluence and all that matters is progress in the realm of consciousness and spirit and not in physical and the surrounding material/nature environment. This monolithic view of Indian cultural tradition is not correct. There are, as is evident from a general look at Indian cultural history, at least two clear trends in our cultural tradition, e.g. *atmavadi* (Spiritualistic) and *anatmavadi* or *svabhavavadi* (materialistic). The conception of the ultimate values or summum bonum of life does also bear out this contention. Four *purusarthas* or basic values are mentioned—*artha, kama, dharma* and *moksha.* It depends on the nature of the philosophical system as to how these values are ordered and priority accorded to them. As for example, in a common sense naturalistic trend of thinking (*lokayata*) *artha* and *kama* will have preference to or desired of others while in a system like Advaita Vedanta *moksha* certainly is the highest value. But other values are not totally rejected or ignored. For the practical life of a man they also have their respective roles to play. And this sense of balancing of harmony (*Samanvaya*) is one of the cardinal values in the Indian tradition. Harmony does imply a gradation a hierarchy. A good harmonious life requires all aspects of life to be kept together. In the Upanishadic thinking also one finds this hierarchical ordering, not rejection, of the need of all of the stages in man's march towards his goal even in spiritualism, e.g. as in the acceptance of *annamaya* (material), *pranamaya* (vital), *manomaya* (physical), *vijanamaya* (intellectual) and *anandamaya* (blissful) stage. Sri Aurobindo, the great sage and savant of modern India, very aptly remarks[1]: "A true happiness in this world is the right terrestrial aim of man, and true happiness lies in the finding and maintenance of natural harmony of spirit, mind and body. A culture is to be valued to the extent to which it has discovered the right key of this harmony and organised its expressive motives and movements. And a civilization must be judged by the manner in which all its principles, ideas, forms, ways of living work to bring that harmony out, manage its rhythmic play and secure its continuance or the development of its motives."

The concept of harmony implies a very important value almost as its logical corollary, i.e., *tolerance.* There is no exact Sanskrit synonym for this English word, but the suggestion and its bearing is clearly manifested even in the life of an ordinary Indian of yesterdays. It does not connote the dictionary meaning of the term 'tolerance' which has a negative sense—tolerating the intolerable. In the Indian traditional context it would rather signify the healthy attitude of mutual trust and respect and sincere attempt of understanding the other's point of view without giving up ones own justified conviction. But there would also be readiness not only to tolerate but also to accept the others point of view if it is rationally superior and is of higher moral virtue. Tolerance would rather mean to give up any claim of exclusive truth or superiority for ones own religion or point of view and accept that other views/ religions can be equally true or valid. This mental makeup may be the proper background of the modern fashionable concept of secularism—acceptance of all *positive religious values* as equally good and not rejection of all of them simply because they are enshrined in different religions. Though it sounds quite impractical, we find in Sri Ramakrishna's teaching a grand example of this sort of acceptance.

A very important *purusartha* is *dharma.* It connotes different things but the English term 'religion' should not be taken as the synonym of *dharma.* The word '*dharma*' comes from the root *dhr* (*dhr+man*) which means that which holds something up. Dharma etymologically implies the nature of something, e.g., it is the *dharma* or nature of water to flow downwards. But *dharma* also means duty. In the *Mahabharata,* specially in the Gita, we come across different uses of the term *dharma* in one of which it comes nearest to the English term religion as in *'Sarvadharman parityajya mamekam saranam vraja'. Dharma* may function as a natural or descriptive concept or as a moral or prescriptive concept (the way things are and the way they ought to be). It is thus easy to confuse between the two uses—descriptive and prescriptive—that which happens to be the way of something and that which is commendable. According to some, this confusion is at the root for justifying caste system in its present form. The system if justified on the ground that it is a part of the *varnasrama dharma*, the implication being that the inequalities inherent in the hierarchical system ought to be there (*dharma* in the prescriptive sense) for no better reason than that they happen to be there (*dharma* in the prescriptive sense) for no better reason than that they happen to be there (*dharma* as natural). However, it has to be mentioned in this context that in the Hindu tradition the moral use of the term '*dharma*' is a derivative of its nature use, and ultimately something ought to be so because that will be the fulfilment of its nature. One point should be noted in passing, though we may have some discussion later on this subject, that there is general misunderstanding about *varnasrama dharma* as *varna* is usually understood as a synonym for *jati* (caste). It is not so *varna* is a functional distinction as distinguished from *jati.* It is based on the recognition of, what is described in present day fashionable phrase, difference in aptitudes and innate capacity to do some sort of work rather than the other.

In *sastras* and *puranas* a number of dharmas have been mentioned. *Svadharma, paradharma, yugadharma*, etc. are well-known. *Ahimsa* (non-violence), *Satya* (truth) *Aparigraha* (non-acceptance of gifts) etc. have been mentioned as *dharma* in the *sastras*. These are cardinal values/virtues for any human community.

Be that as it may, it may be noted that a comprehensive and balanced outlook about human life has permeated the traditional Hindu thinking. Hinduism does not discourage earning money. There are hundreds of *nitisatakas*, the *Itihasa Puranas, Srutis* which urge man to work hard and become prosperous. It has even been said that without money *dharma* is not possible. *Udyama, sahasa* and *yatna* are encouraged for becoming prosperous. But what is not approved of is prosperity without proper effort for acquiring it or amassing too much of wealth, by depriving others. Money has great value but only as a means and not as an end in itself. It is a means to promote moral life through its proper utilization in charity and sharing with others. Accumulation of wealth without limit and continued effort to multiply it is called avarice (*lobha*) and in Hindu ethics this is most despicable. This is a hindrance to man's proper activity—trying to realize himself through contemplation. Restraint and proper control of all avenues of enjoyment to live a balanced life directed towards achieving the highest goal in freedom or *ananda* has been the basic tenet in the Hindu ethos. Life must be full and of quality. The *atmavadi* tradition would prescribe for it a march in the depth of consciousness (this is proper yoga) to arouse oneself to his/her fullness. The Mahabharata mentions the good and learned Brahmana who lived by *unchhavrtti* (sila on natural bounty of the Indian forests) with his family in Kurukshetra, who in his poverty, contentment, independence and spirit of sacrifice was even greater than the great virtuous emperor Yudhisthira. The virtuous butcher of Mithila, the upright shopkeeper *Tuladhara* of Benaras, though poor and of low profession, were great people who could teach the Brahmanas about Brahmanism. The Harmonious character with piety and contentment was adored as the shining jewel. The basic attitude is relativistic—accommodative rather than of exclusiveness as in either-or attitude. It is an attitude of all plus—not rejecting or having outside any positive moral value received from any quarters.

It is never claimed that ancient Hindu attitude was an epitome of all positive values in its best. But it is difficult, if not otherwise motivated, to miss the lofty, open minded attitude, respectful of all other views, when there was no direct challenge to this and an attempt to utilize this broadness to wipe it out of existence. The multi-dimensional concept of *dharma* if not anything else, at least stands for a broad humanistic stand on the life of the individual in its private and social aspects. It pleads for a sense of charitable balance and open-mindedness in all aspects of life.

## III

The description given above is of a period of at least one thousand years from now—when the *sastric* injunctions were the highest. We have a vivid, detailed discussion of all these things in the *dharma sastras*, Mahabharata and specially Kautilya's *Arthasastra. Arthasastra* shows that despite the somewhat loose pluralistic social structure of the Hindu culture and its decentralized functioning, a well-planned and highly efficient central apparatus could be devised to see to the smooth functioning of this structure. It did not interfere with the basic *varnasrama* dharma and the centralised governmental powers to deal with anything contrary to the political authority. There are also reasons to believe that ownership of land in ancient times was communal of which practice the *jajmani* idea that even when one owned land one was obliged to give various shares of the produce of the land to the people who worked on it and even allocate some land to them. So, it appears that the fashionable cliché of modern times—socialism and social justice were not only known but were also actually practised in the society.

Inroads were made first around 1000 A.D. by the Islamic invasion and settlement. Islamic assumptions were absolutistic which found Hindu culture with its relativistic pluralistic-polytheistic religious and social practices a source of great irritation and so tried to break them down. Sir Henry Maine[2] Points out that even Hindu law was not recognized by Islam for which it was mandatory to introduce Islamic law within its dominions. As Maine says, the government of the day behaved as if the laws did not exist. And this was a great change from the rude shock to the Hindu assumption that the *dharma* of the government was to protect and further the righteous social order instituted by the sacred Hindu law. So, the atmosphere was unfavourable, if not hostile, to the growth and sustenance of Hindu culture. Signs of decadence were visible and in its attempt to survive Hindu ethos underwent a radical change for the worse—from openness to narrowness, from accommodation to rejection, from catholicism to conservation. Wrong application of certain moral values made them offensive and the original practice of hierarchy based on quality and action turned into a rigid caste system with oppressive practices on the so-called *Sudras*. The Hindu society also failed to absorb the tribals into its folds which resulted either in their being converted to Muslims or later, in a large number during the British days, into Christians.

The worst attack came from the Britishers. While Islam was generally intolerant of Hindu laws, practices and culture, it somehow was integrated in the cultural milieu creating a new sort of compositive culture. But the Britishers were alien in all sense of the term and tried not only after branding the existing rich culture as barbarous and primitive and destroying it to its core and marrow. The foreign rulers not only spread an image of superman about themselves but took all apins to prove the inferiority of the traditional culture and establish in converting many Hindus to Christianity but also to culturally alienate the English-education elite to subvert Indian culture through their westernized mentality.

Swami Vivekananda, an English-educated Indian, was one of the few pioneers who fathomed the depth of the danger and a life-long teacher tried to uphold the superiority of the traditional culture in eloquent and argumentative way. He gave a new focus and direction to the *Advaita Vedanta*, usually scoffed off as totally inapplicable to worldly affairs, in a strongly action-oriented pattern for the benefit of the man in the street in his ordinary way of living. He tried his best to generate a new hope through reasserting our faith in our humanistic, noble culture and resurgence of patriotism. This was a direct confrontation between the culture of the conqueror and that of the conquered. Sir John Woodroffe, a sincere admirer of Indian tradition and culture, sensed a peril Indian culture was running in the broad perspective of the conflict between European and Asiatic cultures and expressed his deep concern for the preservation of Indian culture as its destruction, in his estimate, would be a disaster for the entire human community. Another great personality to visualize the impending danger attempted to be created through the lure of material prosperity and Macaulization of the indigenous system of education was Sri Aurobindo, the great revolutionary turned a yogi in the wider and deeper interest of the country for spiritual revitalization. He warned about seven decades ago that 'material comfort', 'material progress' and 'material efficiency' become the 'gods of worship'. He observed that the cultural dominative of the alien colonizers did tend not only to dominate but also to ruin the rich cultural heritage of India. Sri Aurobindo writes[3]: "Already she (India) has been largely affected by European culture and the peril is far from over, on the contrary it will be greater, more insistent, more imperatively violent in the immediate future". How much true is it today. In my own experience I have come to see, while touring the length and breadth of the country along with the National Commission on Teachers (1983), that "English-medium Schools" have mushroomed even in remote villages and even the poor, the simple tribal tries to send his ward to these or missionary schools in the hope of securing a white-collar job for his wards when grown up. This tendency exposes the cultural confusion that exists in the mind of the "educated" power-elite which has not been able to get over the colonial hang over. Almost in every educational cupboard Macaulay's ghosts are discovered. The elite has tried to pass it off as a conflict between "tradition and modernity" and squarely places the blame on the "illiterate" mass of common people. But the reality is that the common man is ready to accept the benefit of all scientific and technological innovations provided in his native wisdom he is convinced of its efficacy. But it is the elite who suffers from the conflict as he cannot totally get rid of the cultural moorings nor can he avoid the effects of his education. For him "modernization" is a synonym for "westernization", a senseless aping of the western culture. "Modernity" can never be achieved by trying to ape or graft another alien life-style on our own. It has to well up from our own cultural moorings and traditions. Nobody can jump out of his skin however profitable it might be to do so. The material affluence of the western society need not drive us off our rails as material prosperity is not the last word in human civilization. We do certainly need new techniques and science to harness nature and produce more for our bio-physical existence. But that cannot be the sole aim of the human community. Modernity has to come from within, integrated with our life-style and with our humanistic cultural parameters. Creation of 'scientific temperament' is certainly very necessary as it implies freedom from superstition and readiness to accept facts as they are. While accepting this attitude judiciously and opening ourselves up to the "advanced world", we need not give up our relativistic-pluralistic-synthetic outlook and choose the analytic-abstract and exclusive attitude of European culture. Rationality is very valuable but not at the cost of reasonableness. Material progress is certainly necessary, food has to be found for the millions of our countrymen, but the solution of the problem does not need throwing our humanistic foundation overboard. Our resurgent march in science and technology, medicine and other practical sciences can be most meaningful it can be integrated with our broad cultural framework. The framework, of course, needs reassessment to identify what is living and relevant to our present needs and what has become totally irrelevant with the passage of time. The height of progress that was achieved in Astronomy, Geometry, Ayurveda, Satyavidya and such other sciences can be integrated with the new developments in this fields in modern times. While we have to worship science and technology, we need not make a fetish of them and give up our spiritual grounding in the hope of attaining material affluence.

We may now clearly state the points made above. We have noted that the traditional Indian culture which is atleast 5000 years old has many laudable features in it. It is broadly humanistic, catholic and accommodative. One of its basic elements is an attempt at harmony (*samanvaya*) which results in tolerance in the positive sense of the term. *Dharma* in its multidimensional use characterizes the tradition. Though the tradition is not averse to *artha* and *kama* (it rather encourages their proper and judicious role), it directs itself to a higher level of spiritual ideal in which alone man finds his fulfilment.

However, we have also to note that some of the important aspects have become quite irrelevant or repugnant and therefore, discardable. As the original ideal of *Varnasrama dharma* has been lost and it has degenerated into rigid caste system, it is better for us the sooner it is totally rejected. So also is the case with the barbarous practice of untouchability. It is obnoxious and cruel and cannot be accommodated within the broad humanistic perspective of our culture. While spiritual base of our culture has to be retained, the practice need not be totally antimaterialistic and body-despising. The robust, health outlook of a full life and life of quality has to be rejuvinated. The concept of social justice and fairness which was not absent in the tradition has to be reinforced. Our newly acquired form of polity—the democratic structure of the society—has to be solidly founded. There are certain inherent values/virtues in the democratic form of government, e.g., liberty, equability justice and fairness, equality before the law which are to be properly inculcated to build up a proper egalitarian society. Of course, these values were not unknown to our tradition. The Gupta period and Asoka's rule can exemplify the existence of these values and their implementation in practice. One virtue which appears most important today is the revival of respect for our tradition and deep love for our motherland. Both have started disappearing, paradoxically enough, after the achievement of our political freedom. Our deepest crisis lies in this gradual feeding out of love and respect for our humanistic tradition, its resurgent power and genuine cosmopolitanism arising out of patriotism. As Sri Aurobindo says: "Either India will be rationalised and industrialized out of all recognition and she will be the leader in a new world-phase, aid by her example and cultural infiltration the new tendencies of the West and spiritualise the human race. That is the one radical and poignant question at issue."

As we have noted above, a 'rational' attitude is certainly constitutive of the scientific temperament. But if it is bereft of the human qualities, it becomes mechanical and dehumanizing. So we would rather prefer "reasonable" outlook—rationality plus humaneness—rather than a rigid, analytic, abstract, exclusive and mechanical atmosphere of rationality.

India is at cross-roads today. She has to decide upon her course of action in accordance with the value-structure she chooses. If the rationalistic-atomistic model of European culture with its triumphant march to material progress through tremendous progress in science and technology is our choice, we have to initiate whole-heartedly a fundamental chance in our culture totally removed from, if not opposed to our spiritualistic-organic-synthetic cultural framework. But is it possible or desirable? Should we substitute reasonableness for rationality, accommodation for exclusion, spiritualism for materialism? And why, after all, should we try to jump out of our skin?

If the warnings of our greatest teachers and transvaluers of values like Swami Vivekananda, Sri Aurobindo, Rabindranath Tagore and Gandhiji are to be heeded, India will commit suicide if she tries to change her cultural mooring and foundation. While we must be open to receive all information and knowledge for the material betterment and prosperity of our county, we need not abandon our synthetic-humanistic-spiritualistic attitude and feel apologetic for our lack of material affluence. We must remember that:

> "There is behind our imperfect cultural figures a permanent spirit to which we must cling and which will remain permanent even hereafter; there are certain fundamental motives or essential idea-forces which cannot be thrown aside, because they are part of the vital principle of our being and of the aim of nature in us, our *Svadharma*".[5] We have also to remember that along with this permanent nature, *Svadharma,* there is also the law of mutation as contained in *Yugadharma*—which is possible only on the background of *Svadharma.* Becoming needs being on which it rests. Sri Aurobindo, the seer, has the vision. "The race must obey this double principle of persistence and mutation or bear the penalty of a decay and deterioration that may taint even its living centre."[6]

The crying need of the hour is taking recourse to the basic cultural framework of harmoniously synthesising the spiritual grounding with the material needs/scientific attitude, persistence with dynamism. A community need not become an exclusive worshipper of material progress for affluence. The Indian cultural traditional has withstood the ravages of time not certainly through a materialistic world view. A proper synthesis between spiritualism and materialism is possible and India's genius can achieve it as prophesied by the great modern seer Sri Aurobindo.

The greatest single factor other than the sincere political will to rejuvenate the country and preserve its democratic egalitarian structure is *education.* Education is nothing if it is not value-education. Through the system itself, through the example of the teacher some basic human values, e.g., fellow-feeling, sharing with others, discerning of the right and wrong and practising the right, not encroaching upon other's rights, spirit of tolerance and mutual understanding can be generated. The ultimate goal is achievement of human freedom, political, economic and cultural, which manifests itself in creativity.

It is not a little interesting to note that Karl Marx, advocating and upholding the theory of dialectical materialism, has in the end of the journey through violent revolution, reached a fully spiritualistic conception of man-free from alienation and contradiction-returning to him through creativity actualizing all his potentialities and becoming a Complete Man. Interestingly again, Rabindranath Tagore, through a completely different route, e.g., that of the Indian tradition, reaches the same man, creative and always "exceeding himself through the "surplus" in him and becoming the Universal Man. So the ideal is there and it is beaconing us to proper action.

Whatever be the challenges of the present times, our motherland with its tradition and readjustment of the traditional values to the contemporary needs will be able to face up to them and retain its own perspective. Darkness is the deepest just before the dawn. And that glorious dawn has been signalled by our greatest modern teachers and revolutionaries like Swami Vivekananda, Sri Aurobindo, Rabindranath and Gandhi.

## REFERENCES

1. Sri Aurobindo (1985) *The Foundations of Indian Culture*, Sri Aurobindo Ashram, Pondicherry, Fifth Impression, p. 2.
2. Quoted by William Adam in his *Law and Custom of Slavery in British India.*
3. Sri Aurobindo, *The Foundations of Indian Culture*, p. 6.
4. *Ibid.* p. 11.
5. *Ibid.* p. 32.
6. *Ibid.* p. 32.

# 6
# Purposeful Living

K. RAMA RAO

Purposeful living is a living with dedication to some cause. It could be a dedication to some ideal, or universal and eternal values, a life of self-sacrifice to a worthy cause or something similar to these. Such a life cannot be lived without an awareness of its worthwhileness, early in one's life, even from childhood. It needs planning. In the beginning, the planning is done by one's parents, sometimes even by the school or teacher or well-wisher of the child. But later on the planning may undergo changes, partially or completely, as desired by the agent himself/herself. However the initial stage of planning is the stage of carefully preparing the individual physically, intellectually and emotionally so that the final goal of life could be decided by the individual himself/herself as one attains maturity. Two examples, namely, of J. Krishnamurthy and Aurobindo Ghosh may be mentioned here — planned for some goal but later on changed by the agent himself.

At the moment, all over India, education is getting more and more competitive due to greedy and selfish parents at one end, though this is still limited to a minority and illiterate and ignorant parents at the other end who are unaware of any worthy purpose of education except to prepare their children for Government jobs or to become doctors or engineers. To quote from Socrates (who lived more than two thousand years ago):

> *"Fellow citizens, why do you turn and scrap every stone to gather wealth and so little care for your children, to whom, one day, must relinquish it all?"*

This applies to India and many other countries of the world even today. Why and how to educate children is the most important question that should face parents, teachers and all responsible citizens.

In human life three things are certain, i.e., birth, death and a living in between. Even though the same is true of plants and animals also, they do not possess any control over how they can shape their future. It is left to man alone, in spite of all the odds one may face in the process. It is this capacity of man that has changed the face of the world and has kept the process going. To enable children to become aware of and to put this power into operation is itself an important aspect of education and self-education—which could mean in its metaphysical aspect as well. But confining to the simple pragmatic sense, how one can change the face of the world for the better, is the object of this paper.

But what do we understand by 'the face of the world'. It could mean differently for different individuals. An individual's world could be narrow or broad as one conceives it, when 'Narrow', it is limited to himself and his immediate surroundings, when 'Broad' it could mean the entire world, its flora and fauna and all the people inhabiting there. An individual's world could also be any where between these limits such as the family, the society, the state or nation. These differences arise because of limitations in one's thinking and imagination and the type of education one has received. Should man be narrow-minded and selfish or should he be broad-minded and altruistic with a consideration for others? We have the answer from our ancient seers and sages who said:

> *ayam nijah paro vetti ganana laghu cetasam undara caritanantu vasudhaiva kutumbakam.*

It is only the petty minded that discriminate, saying 'mine and other'; for the benevolent the entire world is one family. This understanding is crucial for self-education even in its materialistic sense. To live with a spirit of sacrifice—*yajna*—dedicating to serve because the whole universe is ever engaged in an act of sacrifice and going against that current by getting narrow minded and selfish is unbecoming of humans, is basic to purposeful living. To live for *'shreyas'* and not for *'preyas'* should be the motto. The spirit of self-sacrifice cannot be gained unless one has respect for and practises *'dignity of labour'* and does not aspire for cheap popularity, quick money and mere soft collared jobs.

Looking at the world, we see that everyone is working as if, for himself/herself. This seems to be true of all from labourer and farmers upto the engineer, doctor or a professor. A closer examination, however, will reveal, that barring a few in each category, the majority work for others as well. What prompts them work for others? Is it not the love of their job/profession, a sense of satisfaction gained by the work/ service rendered to fellow beings? It is this attitude to work, which is vanishing of late, that education must develop in children. This should remind us of the great saying in the Zoarastrism scripture *'Yasna'*.

> "Happiness comes to him from
> Whom happiness goes to others".

In support of this, it is pertinent to quote Dr. Einstein also, the great physicist of the twentieth century. He says:

> "How strange is the lot of us, mortals? Each one of us is there for a brief sojourn for what purpose he knows not, though he sometimes thinks he senses it. But without deeper reflection, one knows from daily life, that one exists for other people. A hundred times everyday I remind myself that my inner and outer life, are based on the labours of other men, living and dead, and that I must exert myself in order to give in the same measure as I have received and am still receiving.... I regard class distinction as unjustified in the last resort based on force. I also believe that simple and un-assuming life is good for everybody, physically and mentally.
>
> The ideals which have lighted my way and time after time, given me new courage to face life cheerfully have been *truth, kindness and beauty* .... The trite objects of human efforts, possessions, out-success, and luxury have all seemed to me contemptible."

In spite of repeated efforts to establish a morally pure, peaceful and happy society, evils creep in and steps are necessary to prevent/ eradicate evil influences of the negative attitudes and habits, such as, dishonesty, anger, selfishness, hatred, jealousy, sluggishness, etc. in children. While many believe that a faith in God can help in eradicating these negative traits and attitudes, it is also necessary to remember that a faith in one's ownself or self-confidence is essential; this is because a blind-faith in God turns out to be a faith in fate and many people resign themselves to it and remain in active, thinking that their future is already decided and nothing can be done by them to change it. While one should not expect miracles to happen, one should avoid being pessimistic and lazy. Hard work and self-confidence can alone bring success and joy to anyone. To quote a Sanskrit sloka:

> *Udyoginam purushasimham upaiti Laxmih*
> *daivene deyam iti kapurusha vadanti*
> *daivam nihatya kuru paurusham atmashaktya*
> *yatne krute yadi na sidhyati kotradoshah*
>
> (It is only the industrious that can gain wealth; worthless people say that God/Fate brings wealth. Kill the fate and work like a lion aiming men. There is nothing lost if you do not succeed; try again.)

The great Jnanapeeth awardee of Karnataka Dr. K.V. Puttappa says:

> *eshtu devara neeneshtu nambidodenu*
> *ondishtu nee nambadire ninna neenu*
> *nathu savira janaru suttaliddodamana*
> *Chitia hatyake yaru tadeya kattuvarayya*
>
> (Of what use is it if one has faith in countless gods but has no faith in one-self? How can ten thousand around help you prevent killing your own consciousness?)

Besides creating self-confidence, an attitude for being industrious and serviceable to others, education must strive to inculcate in children certain universal and eternal values. These could be truth, love and beauty as advocated by the great sages of India and endorsed by the great modern scientist Dr. Einstein. Many thinkers in this field, of late, have advocated cultivation of several virtues. A few years back even the NCERT has recommended the cultivation of about eighty- four virtues. In this connection, it must be pointed out that values are the ends to attain which, virtues happen to be the means. To illustrate this point the virtue of being honest to oneself and to others leads one to the value truth-speaking and to the more abstract value 'Truth'. This virtue is basic for a morally pure life—individually, family-wise, socially and nationally. A host of other essential values like democratic spirit, egalitarianism, scientific temper, liberty, fraternity, etc. have been placed before us by political and social philosophers. Education must include all these for preparing dutiful and useful citizens.

People normally believe that conscience is a sure guide for anybody's right living. But this is not found to be correct. Because a fanatic—be he religious, political or any other—thinks that his religion, political philosophy or other way of thinking is the most correct way, because it is approved by his conscience. If conscience were to be a sure guide for our actions, there should be no difference in thinking among people on any moral issues. People who are capable of reflecting upon the existing moral standards have always suggested superior moral standards. They have condemned the existing low moral standards, fought against them, themselves undergoing much suffering and indignity during the course of such fights. A study of such examples will educate and train children to think of better moral standards than the existing customs and traditions and keep morality of the human race always dynamic. Teachers should be aware of this and educate children to become capable of better moral standards.

It is not merely for the individual that better moral standards are necessary but also for the family, society, nation and the whole world. Sometimes we follow double standards of morality. In this context it is pertinent to remember the words of Gandhiji. He says—"One and the same set of moral laws and values should guide and regulate the various activities of man in all the different spheres of life. One cannot be truthful in one's personal and social life and yet untruthful in one's economic and political conduct... The politician, the lawyer, the merchant and people in various other walks of life make the same distinction between their professional morality and their social or personal morality. Though otherwise honest people they do not mind indulging in fraud and force in their professional lives... This is because we do not consider life an integral whole. We have expediently devised different moral codes for different aspects of our lives......unless humanity realizes that human life is an indivisible whole and the moral law applies equally to all aspects and spheres of life, there can be no peace in the world."

Finally, what is the purpose of a value based life or morally pure life? It should be to live and let others also live in and atmosphere of peace. Because without peace at all levels—individual, family, society, nation and the world—there can be no comfort or progress for people at any of these levels. This must have been the reason why the ancient seers of India always chanted shantimantras before they began any social or family function. One such is

*sahanavhavatu sahanau bhunattu*
*sahaveeryam karavavahai tejasvina vadhitamastu ma vidwishavahai*
*om shantishanti shantih*

Besides living causing no embarrassment to others and disturbing their peace, one should realize 'how one lives' is more important than 'how long', one lives?

India is a country of people with diversities of several types who are still in the process of training themselves to become a nation. The most vulnerable point of their diversity consists in the different religions followed by different sections of its people. To bring unity and harmony among these, there is only one method and that is by understanding the basic principles of other religions in order to realize the unity of all religions.

It is of no use merely giving precepts. One should also show the way to live a purposeful life. Let us remember the saying:

*No moralist was made so in a day*
*Nor any one of them was a born moralist*

A purposeful life cannot be lived without following moral principles. One should realise that the physical and the intellectual development stop for all humans at about the age of twenty, whereas moral development can go on as long as one lives a morally better life.

Foundation for a purposeful living must be laid even when children are young. At the Kinder Garden stage and at the elementary school level children should practice living purposefully. Besides helping them to acquire good manners, they should be kept engaged in activities basic to environmental cleanliness—its negative and positive aspects and practising as many virtues as they possibly can. Besides they should commit to memory certain rhymes and poems, in their own mother tongue. These should be carefully selected, newly composed, if already not available.

Such verses should be composed to contain a knowledge of worthwhile manners, habits, environmental protection, dangers from evil habits, the benefits of a virtuous life, the purpose of human life—individual and social—and any other worthwhile object. As many of these as can be possible may be memorised by children.

Indian children should be engaged in activities which help in realizing the goals mentioned in the foregoing. A few activities could be suggested: seed or sapling planting, maintaining the school garden, cleaning school campus—inside and outside, cultural activities such as singing—chorus and solo, chanting prayer, music—vocal and instrumental, drawing and painting, visit to places of worship of different religious faiths and reciting/listening to the particular prayers and knowing their meanings, role playing, enacting dramas based on good, purposeful living and few other similar activities.

Children could be exposed to stories conveying struggles between virtuous and vicious beings—humans or animals. These could be folk tales, fairy tales, short stories, simply anecdotes from real life or epics, or history or the lives of great personages. Related moral principles underlying these lives/stories/anecdotes have to be spelt out then and there. There could be other methods and activities too.

For the pre-adolescent and the adolescent whatever methods are introduced must be based on thinking, reasoning and discussion. Leading a life dedicated to certain universal and eternal values demands continuous and consistent practice. It is possible to discern in this process three phases—awareness, faith and practice of any chosen ideal or value. These three could go almost simultaneously. The danger of anyone or all of these vanishing from the individual temporarily or for ever is always there. Hence, *dharma, shraddha* or moral earnestness and *apramada* or moral watchfulness, should always be cultivated. This stage being a formative stage in the life of every individual, it should be fully made use of by parents and teachers to enable children to choose the right path by themselves and not forcing them to follow what the adults think to be right; yet, adults should intelligently, sympathetically and patiently guide the children to help them select the right path. An awareness created on such things will lay the foundation for a better human society and can reduce exploitation of have-nots by the more powerful.

Children could be exposed to the lives of great men and women—past and present, native and foreign—so that they can identify themselves with some of them for emulation. The craze for emulating the silver screen and video screen heroes should be replaced with real heroes in life, who lived for what they said. This is the sure and successful method by which many have become great. No country and no part of the world is wanting in such examples. A disciplined life devoted to an idea/ideals and values is what is necessary for a developing child and the lives of great men and women from different walks of life, social, religious, political, can inspire children to decide to live a better life. It is futile to expect school children to read big books on biographies. Smaller books in simpler language—mother tongue of the children—is the need of the hour.

Children could be enabled to think and discuss over the meaning of the words—virtue, value, ideal, moral, dharma and many others. They could exercise their mind on the purpose of individual and collective life—at different levels and discern the basic unity underlying all life. The causes of disunity, hatred, etc. among individuals, families/nations and the causes of the destruction of the human population, such as, wars and natural upheavels and the causes of destruction of natural sources of wealth and power, the causes of pollution of the essential requirements of life of all kinds could be known by them. Awareness created in them of the foregoing can lay a foundation in their minds for a better and safer human life. One can expect minimised exploitation of the have-nots by the more powerful.

Character building is a slow process and needs continuous effort by the agent. Teachers and parents should place before children several examples/models and situations involving moral conflict and moral issues. These can be served to some extent by exposing children to good literature—which they can easily understand and follow—such as elicts, prose pieces, poems, short stories, parables and other such forms. The language should be the one familiar to children and children should be provided the meaning of different words, if any, in the poem or passage.

Real life-situations, culled out through personal observation, newspapers and journals, could form the basis for discussions on moral issues concerning human societies. During these discussions it is not so important that a decision should be arrived at, right or wrong, as to enlighten (the group about the issue involved, enable them to do moral thinking and help them learn the art of group discussion through healthy participation without offending others, and contributing one's ideas finding the principles and applying them to situations, says Norman J. Bull:

> *"It is the application of the principle to the situation, and above all the derivation of the principle from situations, that must be the basis of effective moral education".*

A very rich and inexhausive source of lessons in value education is Sanskrit literature—more particularly the slokas of *Hitopdesa* and the *Niti Sataka* of Bharthruhari. Those who have even an elementary knowledge of Sanskrit can make use of these to carry home to children the concept of good character and human values.

Indian children must learn to find unity in the midst of diversities—most particularly among the major religions, in their ethnic aspects. This can be done in giving children a knowledge of the biography of great religious founders—how they lived a life of love for all and sacrificed all their belongings and pleasure in the search for truth and spreading the message of truth. In these lessons, it is necessary to highlight the common points among all religions—the basic truth—God or no God, living must be morally pure, and what one sows one reaps—the common spiritual exercises prescribed by all religions, such as, cleanliness of body and mind, prayer, *japa*, meditation and an austere living. The basic unity of all religions should be the goal of these lessons, ignoring the ethnic differences.

It is possible to do some justice to the foregoing procedures through the existing subjects and the co-curricular activities. But at least a few of these lessons must be set apart for some of the foregoing ideas/ concepts as also for creating an awareness of certain immediately demanding issues, such as environmental pollution, ecological balance, afforestation, prevention of evil habits, eradication of false values, such as children as a source of wealth, untouchability, preference for male children and racial or caste superiority.

# 7

# Developing Values for Self Development

*(Teacher-based Activities for Professional Growth)*

M.R. CHILANA

Education undoubtedly is the most important means for the development of a society. The quality of education needs to be promoted with many fold approaches like preparation of good curricula, revision of ample physical facilities, support of professional guidance and research findings which may lead to better teaching learning process. But most important step in this direction is the preparation of the teacher. No other effort will bring any fruit unless the teacher contributes to the transaction of quality education in the classroom. The programme of teacher preparation requires continuous professional learning by teacher. There have been numerous ways to promote better learning through external agencies. These programmes include activities of the Extension Service Centres and Centres of Continuing Education. There have also been attempts to organise summer courses and sporadic refresher courses for teacher development. All these activities require absence of the teacher from his school. This also results in lesser opportunities for the professional growth of teachers. It is, therefore, necessary that teachers develop the value of promoting their own professional growth. This is helpful not only in making the teacher more effective in the classroom but this also helps in any improvement of the personality of the teacher. So may be more satisfying to the teachers as persons as well. For participation in this programme, a teacher appreciates value of his own growth and continuous development and as such he undertake activities which may lead not only to intellectual understanding of his professional needs but also they may help the teacher to improve his attitude and abilities to impart more effective instructions. Since main thrust in the programme is self-effort of the teacher to undertake desired activities, the programme may be termed as teacher-based in-service education and training—'TBINSET'. Here we envisage to explain the ways and means to elaborate on the activities which teacher may undertake in promoting their own self development.

It is pertinent to highlight that it is obligatory for all workers to continue gaining fresh knowledge throughout their periods of employment. But the need for such provision is much more for teachers in the schools. Teaching is one of the most dynamic professions. The fast developing contours of knowledge in this throbbing world of change, innovation development and progress have great many implications for the school curriculum. Teachers must be kept abreast of the latest developments in the society so that it may be possible for them to adjust the school curricula and gear the school programmes to the emerging socio-economic, political and cultural needs of the community. The necessity for providing effective in-service education to teachers increases especially because of the fact that education is a key force for all development and teacher is the linchpin of the educational structure. The quality of the teacher determines the quality of schools. Only a good teacher can make the school good and thus help to produce strong and effective persons in society. It is, therefore, very important, in the modem context, that adequate procedures should be developed for the in-service education of teachers. In this regard self-biased activities are very significant.

## 'TBINSET' Implies

In order to help the teacher grow in his professional skills, there is need to have a variety of organizational provisions and to involve all possible agencies like teacher training institutions, supervisory staff, university staff, curriculum development centres, teachers' associations and even the community at large. These attempts will cover the institutional contribution for in-service education of teachers. But the individual medium signifies a very useful approach with distinct advantages of its own. It implies self-efforts and voluntary participation of the individual to grow in the profession. It underlines the intrinsic motivation on behalf of the teacher. It assumes that every one accepts the responsibility of solving the day-to-day problems of teaching. It highlights the desire on behalf of each of the members of the teaching fraternity to work at personal level to upgrade the status of the teaching profession. It gives an evidence of the personal concern of an individual teacher to make all education endeavours relevant to the social needs and individual requirements. In short, it assures existence of a very healthy atmosphere in the profession to have continuous and critical evaluation of all educational inputs to achieve the noble goals of educating the children and the youth and to improve the conditions as felt by the persons on-the-job.

**Various Ways**

There are many personal in-service mediums which have the potential to lead to the professional growth of a teacher. Some of them selected for discussion here are independent reading, original writing, self-evaluation and action research.

*Independent Reading*: Independent reading is perhaps the easiest possible approach for the teacher to follow because of the availability of library facilities in almost all the schools. Also, it is in no way less important if not the most significant avenue to lead to the professional development of the teacher. Books bring to us the rich minds from all disciplines. And how easy it becomes to establish the contact. Wide and varied reading helps in expanding the vision and broadening the perspectives of the reader. Our goal is to have the teacher with regular reading habit. "Reading make a full man", is a well-known maxim. What should the teacher read? It would be ridiculous to suggest that the teacher should be reading books and journals only on education. In fact, his field is much broader. He has to read about philosophy as much as about sociology, science, technology and psychology, etc. Reading of the daily newspapers and general magazines is also necessary for the teacher to know the trends in the society. All this will help him to relate education to life needs.

The habit of independent reading is not only an important means of professional growth but it is also the basis for all other activities of in-service education. One cannot take to writing unless one has profound reading habit. Similarly self-evaluation techniques and action research are possible only if one develops sufficient background through self-study. Again, in-service mediums for groups like seminars and workshops can attain their objectives optimally only when its members acquire sufficient knowledge beforehand through the study of the related literature.

*Original Writing*: Writing is definitely a difficult task and unfortunately, so far, professional writing has remained predominantly restricted to the college teachers and researchers in education. It is, however, very much desirable that school teachers also take to this approach. It would have a double advantage. First, we would understand the teacher's way of working, his problems and his plans to improve things. Secondly, this exercise will do the teacher more good than to the readers of his writings. The value of the writing to the writer lies in the fact that he understands more fully what he has been doing. In this process, he may perhaps discover the inadequacies of his actions. In proposing his new plans in his write-ups, the teacher is likely to deepen his sensitivity about different aspects of the problem or an approach. That is why, it is said, "writing makes a man perfect".

Our goal is to have teachers who are able to write about their experiences and procedures adopted by them in their work. We should look to reading what their problems are and how in their opinion they can solve them. They should come forward to state their opinions about different educational facets and significant issues like student indiscipline, politics and education, curriculum and examination procedures etc. Their views should also be solicited on some of the important social issues. It requires a great mental discipline and well-structured thinking in order to reduce one's thoughts to writing symbols. These qualities will be a great deal of asset to the teacher. This approach will, therefore, serve well the purpose of his professional growth.

*Self Evaluation*: This concept embodies the idea that a teacher should accept the responsibility to improve the quality of his own work. He should be able to evaluate his own work as objectively as possible. He would grow professionally by knowing his strong points and weaknesses so as to strengthen the former and remove the latter. He will at least be able to think about better techniques to strengthen his methods of work. In this way, he will become his own supervisor.

There can be several devices for the teacher himself to evaluate his work. He may introspectively visualize how far he has been successful in achieving his objectives of a particular activity. Students may also help him in this regard. He can seek their opinion or ratings on different points. Another simple device will be that the teacher may do an exercise to write down what he would expect of another teacher to do for performing a particular task. He may later on compare how far he did the work according to the description made by him. This procedure will definitely help the teacher to be more rational, apart from its affording him an opportunity of self-analysis. This would by all means, lead to his professional development.

*Action Research*: The teacher, as a practitioner, is faced with many problems, solutions to which can be best discovered by him alone. Research can prove a great help to the teacher in this regard. It is unfortunate that research—has so far been understood as too sophisticated an approach to be undertaken by a teacher. This erroneous concept has to be wiped out. Research implies application of a scientific method to know the truth, to understand cause and effect relationship and to make accurate predication. Defined in a simple way, it means asking a question and finding the answer, based on objective evidence. It helps the teacher to apply objective methods to analyse any situation and to adopt unbiased approach to solve the problems coming in his way. Action research signifies the participation of person on-the-job to undertake research methods.

Teachers can become more effective in their work by adapting methods of action research to improve their work. This will also afford an important opportunity to the researcher to grow professionally. He would develop an attitude of enquiry and keenness to expand knowledge.

These are essential conditions for learning. He would also learn through such experience how to identify problems and to take initiative to tackle the same, to apply objective methods to understand the phenomenon, to interpret the data in an unbiased way and to recognize his own mistakes. Above all, it will imply high motivation on behalf of the teacher to solve his difficulties and to understand his atmosphere. All these processes serve to lead the teacher to professional growth in an ample measure.

*Many More*: The avenues suggested above are by no means exhaustive of the potentialities for profitable in-service mediums. Based on these broad approaches, a teacher may develop in-service vehicles of his own. However, the major theme, reverberating through all these activities, is the genuine desire of the teacher to be able to become a better professional. These approaches substantially contribute to the stimulation of professional interests, development of confidence in work and an understanding of professional requirements. Above all, they imply proper motivation on behalf of the teacher to become more effective in his work.

## Own Satisfaction

An important consideration underlying the pursuit of individual avenues to professional growth is the personal thrust of the teacher which means his being concerned about the professional matters. In order that a teacher may involve his personal interests and identify his ambitions to this task, it is necessary that he should realise its rewards in terms of his personal satisfaction. Here we are concerned with the intrinsic motivation of the teacher and arousal of his inner desire to improve himself. Intrinsic motivation is the best condition: to seek wholehearted devotion from an individual. This is like the inner drive of hunger or thirst, with its biological or organic basis, which gives rise to activity with full force. Similarly, psychological needs, which tend to spurt the individual to action, are needs for acceptance, independence, recognition, fulfilment and maximum achievement in socially approved ways. In order that the teacher may follow individual avenues to his professional development with his full potential, he has to recognize among others the value following internal incentives:

- — Personal satisfaction in being able to do one's work better.
- — An opportunity to develop personal and professional capacities.
- — Satisfaction from gaining new knowledge.
- — Satisfaction coming from wcrking on modern approaches in his work.
- — Chances which these avenues afford to make education as a potential force for social development.
- — Desire to make original contribution to his field of work.
- — Drive to build up a professional library.
- — Feeling that his contribution is appreciated.
- — Ambition that he is raising the status of the profession by his personal efforts.

## Motivating Factors

It is also pertinent to visualize the general atmosphere necessary in the profession to guide the individual teacher to adopt ways and means to grow professionally. It covers the area of extrinsic motivation. Since teacher grows and lives in the society, it does matter to him how others feel about him. Thus, praise, lecognidori and acceptance from higher officials serve as external incentives. Social values like, status, prestige, money, reputation and achievement in terms of higher status may also be used to achieve desirable action or behaviour from the teacher.

Given below are some of such conditions which will provide external incentives to the teacher to follow the methods and techniques of professional growth at his own level:

— Promotion in status or rank for being an innovative teacher.
— Recruitment of all or a large portion of the higher posts on the basis of direct competition rather than seniority being the only criterion.
— Increase in salary for undertaking research or for writing original papers and articles.
— Award of appreciation certificates for doing good work.
— Expression of oral appreciation on behalf of higher educational authorities for good work of the teacher.
— Opportunities for teachers to publish their views on educational and social issues.
— Reduced pricing of publication and educational journals for teachers.
— Liberal policy to permit teachers to participate in in-service education programmes of institutions leading to higher degrees/diplomas.
— Study leave for teacher to undertake higher studies.
— Travel grants for teachers to see educational institutions.
— Grants for books and contingencies to help teachers to take up action research.
— Appreciation of teachers adopting innovative approaches in their work rather than insisting on traditional and routine for guidance.
— Requiring the teacher to state in his annual self-evaluation proforma the books and articles read, papers contributed, self-supervision, procedures applied and action researches undertaken.

There are also some negative aspects of the extrinsic motivation. For example, sometimes criticism also motivates people, even if the teacher would consider it derogatory and unreasonable. It is, therefore, desirable that positive factors should be emphasized.

**Possible Effect**

The approach to appreciate and develop individual avenues to in-service education provides a great potential for achieving the quality education. On the one hand, it affords the best opportunity to capitalize upon the individual strengths and ambitions of the teachers and uses as its basis, the intrinsic motivational factors of the individual. On the other hand, it serves profitable support and supplement to in-service educational activities teacher training colleges, supervisory staff and other such institutions. A teacher, who is continuously engaged in reading and writing action research activities and adopts self-evaluation techniques in his work, will definitely devote himself more wholeheartedly when he is participating in such type of in-service activities of all types more realistic and related to the actual problems of the schools and the felt needs of the teachers. It is also a useful means to help the teacher to gain deeper personal insight into his problems and develop self-understanding of his weaknesses and deficiencies as well as also to formulate action point to remedy the same. This will substantially contribute in moving our schools from the routine drudgery of yesterday into the vibrating and lively atmospheres of tomorrow.

**Shared Responsibility**

Major responsibility for following the individual avenues to professional growth, undoubtedly, rests personally with the teachers and other educational workers including the principals and supervisors. Each of them has to realize the significance of adopting such means to professional growth and draw greater satisfaction for thus having been able to do their work better. But other agencies can also make useful contribution in this direction. The pre-service courses should serve to prepare the teacher to learn throughout their service periods as a compelling necessity of the profession they have chosen to work in. This would require developing in the teacher under training abilities and skills to continue gaining more and more knowledge, greater understanding and better techniques to do their jobs in a more efficient way. The supervisory staff have even greater responsibility to appreciate teachers' attempt to be continuously learning. The Departments of education may have to adopt policies and procedures which do not impede such efforts of the teachers. In turn, they have to build conducive incentives which can produce such an educational atmosphere where the teacher who continues to read, write, think and experiment is amply rewarded to keep up his motivation for professional growth. To train the school teachers in the process of self-education self-responsibilities lie with the pre-service teacher training institutions as well as special in-service teacher education departments/centres. The teacher under training should not only understand the importance of this programme, but it is also desired that conscious efforts are put forth to develop in the prospective teacher habit and to learn the skills to undertake related-activities. Teacher educators at both pre-service and in-service levels should adopt practical techniques and demonstrate actual gains of each other. Resource persons in the continuing Education Centres may also evaluate the impact of reading, writing and action research at the mid-term as well as in final evaluation at the conclusion of each programme. Ultimately, however, the effect of these activities is to be gauged after the teachers return to work in their classroom situations. Of course, the real impact of teacher learning should ultimately be visible on student behaviour. The acid test of TBINSET will be how far children have learnt to use the tools of self-education. Thus, the emphasis of schools will shift from teaching to learning, and from learning to self-learning.

**Conclusion**

TBINSET seeks to meet the applications of the National Policy on Education to seek participation of teachers in all education processes including their own professional growth. This strategy is supplementary and complimentary to all INSET programmes. Teachers participating effectively in TBINSET will contribute more in programmes organised by colleges of education and other external agencies. In School-Based INSET programmes, their role will be immense because of all pervassive nature of activities. SBINSET and TBINSET will undoubtedly result in innovative schools, creative teachers and fast developing educational practices. This mode of teacher development, therefore, has a great promise to help education contribute to Human Resource Development.

# 8

# Value Management and Police Administration

SHRI RAM ARUN

Values play very important role in shaping the human beings, society, organisations, countries etc. Good values imbibed in and followed by the majority help in excelling in various fields and lack of them leads to degeneration. Universally accepted human values, generally cutting across the geographical, religious, spiritual and social barriers etc. have always been the guiding factors of management of the affairs of the nations and governments. This vision was also reflected by Pandit Jawaharlal Nehru, in his speech on 14th August, 1947 on the eve of India's independence saying that "at this solemn moment we take the pledge of dedication to the service of India and her people and to the still larger cause of humanity—freedom and power bring responsibility— the service of India means the service of millions who suffer....It means the ending of poverty and ignorance and disease and inequality of opportunity....as long as there are tears and suffering our work will not be over." To translate this vision into practice we adopted *The Constitution of India,* the preamble of which mentions that 'we the people of India, solemnly resolved to constitute India into a *sovereign, socialist, secular, democratic, republic* and to secure to all its citizens:

> *Justice, social, economic and political,*
> *Liberty of thought expression, belief, faith and worship, Equality of status and of opportunity*

and to promote among them all,

*Fraternity assuring the dignity of the individual and the unity and the integrity of the nation*

These goals could be achieved only by managing the country's affairs by honestly following the set values of our composite culture and spiritual faculty. The unfortunate part is that economic development and mad race for physical comforts has given rise to many ills and the 'values' and morality have been the worst casualties giving rise to materialism and economic offences.

Police, an integral and important organ of governance, are to do their best in helping the nation building. It is expected of 'Police' that they will not only be epitomes of goodness but will also be the guiding force in implementing various values, legal, moral etc. in society. Every letter of the word 'POLICE' expects them to be 'polite', 'obedient', 'loyal', 'intelligent', 'courteous' and 'efficient'. Thus value based management of police becomes very very difficult task as to meet the expectations of 'goodness' but at the same time fulfil the undue pressures of the powers that be.

Police in our country and also abroad have not been enjoying healthy reputation and public opinion has generally been against them. They are regarded as partisans, disobedient and disloyal, lethargic and negligent, inefficient and immoral, cruel and dishonest. A value based code of conduct had been evolved for the police in our country. It includes maintaining a high standard of discipline, faithful performance of duties in accordance with the law, obedience of lawful orders, not committing any misconduct, refraining from falsehood, not indulging in corrupt or improper practices or abuse of authority, not to do an act adversely affecting the unity of the force by creating divisions on grounds of religion, caste or community and not to do anything which adversely affects the integrity and repute of the country and to maintain absolute integrity. They are also bound by the 'Government Servants' Conduct Rules' which are generally value based.

The fundamental basis for any criminal justice system is the law of the land, specially in a democratic society. The very process of law in a democratic society ensures a measure of public sanction expressed in legislatures through their elected representatives. The credibility of the system depends on the strength or weakness of the laws framed and their proper implementation by agencies responsible. Police, prosecutors, advocates, judges, jails and correctional services are the distinct organised wings of this system. The ultimate object of the system is to ensure peace and order in society. The role, duties, powers and responsibilities of the police with special reference to prevention and control of crime and the maintenance of public order has to be fitted into the overall requirements of the criminal justice system as a whole. Police role in maintaining public order has greater limitations. Maintenance of order implies a certain measure of peace and avoidance of violence of any kind. Outbreak of violence in any noticeable form implies breakdown of order. The characteristic features of the existing social structure in India are: (1) inter-group conflicts may be due to caste, religion, language etc., (2) majority population being of restless youth, (3) increasing unemployment giving rise to various problems including commission of crimes, (4) increasing pressure of poverty, (5) gradual increase in concentration in urban areas, (6) increasing awareness of the poor and the destitute to become 'haves' and the increasing terrorist activities all factors contributing to breakdown of law and order.

The role of police is to maintain law and order but it has no say in making of 'laws' or the expected 'order'. Police must faithfully implement the laws framed by the legislature and take action against the offenders without any fear or favour. It must act against the violators and maintain the order in society to avoid chaos. In doing so they are accountable to courts of law, government of the time and ultimately the people. The management of all this and the department itself is becoming very complex and difficult day by day as the values are getting eroded and interests of the politicians in power are generally in conflict with the established norms and good values and they expect police to be partisan and party and individual friendly rather than people friendly. Those police personnel who follow the set values and the rules are at times made to suffer forcing the fence sitters to think twice before following the right path.

'Truth' has always occupied a respectable and important place not only in one's life but also in management of various affairs including administration. Policemen should also be trusted but the Indian Evidence Act, 1872, makes the confession made before them inadmissible, whatever be the rank and status of the policeperson before whom the confession is made. Policemen at times concoct evidence in the interest of the case so that the evidence adduced convinces the court in securing conviction. Such law is not value based and therefore, management of police on this count becomes difficult. Such law needs a change.

Values are tested during crisis and disasters. People are supposed to come out to help the victims on humanitarian grounds. The experience shows that, but for few good people, the persons who happen to be at the site, may be natural disaster like earthquake or manmade disaster like train accident, usually indulge in removing belongings of the dead and injured. This is inhuman and devoid of values. Police are expected to act immediately and efficiently in handling such situations and in providing relief to victims. They are also supposed to mobilise the people in rendering selfless service. Management of police and others on such occasions becomes very difficult task hence human values of service before self need to be deeply embedded in everybody.

'The maximum good of the maximum number' is the ultimate goal of good governance. The administration by elected representatives and beaurocracy including police over years has gradually deteriorated. The values are getting eroded and those who matter are interested in results and not in means. Our Constitution expects all of us to be above prejudices of caste, religion and sex and do ones best in achieving the goals mentioned in the preamble of the Constitution. If police perform their duties properly, honestly, sincerely and efficiently, they will be doing great service to the nation by creating climate of peace and harmony thus paving the way for planned development. Let the political and beaurocratic masters and the police officers themselves manage the police according to value based norms and not to use it as a tool for fulfilment of individual needs and greed. 'Jai Hind', the slogan of police, exhorts them to work for the betterment of our motherland. This could be achieved only by enforcing value system. The need now is to improve ourselves and the organs of governance including police and let everybody follow the long cherished values.

9

# Economic Development and Values

N.M.P. VERMA

## Introduction

Value is the conception or ethical belief of consumers, producers, sellers and various other economic agents about 'what ought to be good or bad' which is based on both economic and non-economic factors. Every discipline has a set of value. In economics, however, term 'value' is frequently used in a couple of ways. Firstly, in initial discussions value is related to subjective ideas and opinions. For instance, in the theory of consumer behaviour subjective value has been observed superior to objective value. The reason of superiority of subjective value over objective value is because of the fact that measurability of utility in cardinal manner is unrealistic. The marginal utility theory of demand assumes that utility can be measured by applying objectivity and thus can be measured in quantitative terms. In other words, utility is cardinally measurable. For example, utilities of consumer can be shown in numerical terms like 0, 1, 2 , 3, 4 and so on. If a consumer receives no utility then it can be denoted by 0, if a consumer obtains one unit of utility then it can be indicated by 1 and likewise for other digits. Identifying utility numerically may differ from consumer to consumer and from person to person because of the difference in subjective feeling and psychological behaviour feeling which is dependent on level of consumer's satisfaction. Therefore, it is not wise to denote derivation of utility in digits. It may, however, be ranked in preferential order. This ranking may facilitate the consumer to compare one set of performances to another set derived from other consumption bundle.

That is the reason that Marshallian analysis of objective value judgement of consumer has been found inferior to Hicksian analysis of subjective value judgement in the initial version of consumer theory.

**Rationality and Value Judgement**

The prerequisite of sound value management is having a rational behaviour. Rational thinking and rational acting can lead to rational preference ordering (Samuelson, Arrow). It may not be possible to think of development with natural face with irrational attitude. Preference ordering based on irrational behaviour may be misleading and, may not yield a scientific result. It may not be possible to adopt the rank ordering of the utility of a drunken consumer or a mad man or a sad person. Naturally in this process of revealing values congenial environment plays its own role.

Revealing values by a rational consumer under uncongenial environment may not yield a desired result. It may not be possible for a rational person to behave rationally all the time. The constraints under given environment play its own role in the decision making process. A rational consumer may reveal his value irrationally under in-congenial environment. Nevertheless the same rational consumer can reveal value correctly under suitable atmosphere. Therefore, it is constraints of environment which also play a pivotal role in the whole value management process, that is why, in the whole consumer theory a rational behaviour of the consumer has been assumed. What further needs to be added in the theory is congenial environment during which rational acting and reacting is feasible. In the analysis of Marshall, Hicks, Alien and Samuelson congenial environment as prerequisite for a rational consumer must be incorporated for subjective value arrangement and ordering. In other words, proper atmosphere for revealing subjective value ought to be assumed in ordinal utility analysis, indifference curve analysis and revealed preference analysis. For proper value management of the consumer, conducive market without any imperfections, is warranted.

**Value and Social Welfare**

Once we shift from the theory of consumer behaviour to welfare economic theory then again value judgement becomes very significant. Noted economist like Robbins asserted that value management in economic analysis would be making the subject unscientific. Therefore, there is a dire need to properly manage various value judgements. Some of the modern economists are of the opinion that a consensus should grow on the basis of value judgements which may be helpful for the economy and the society. Prof. Streeten was of the opinion that economists cannot and should not refrain from making value judgments if their studies are to be more than a purely formal technique of reasoning. In any case, if the value judgment of individuals coincide with each other then it may be termed as the 'social value judgment' because it represents the whole group. The same social value judgment' may become the law in practice because the majority of society has followed the same taste. Thus, once social value judgments have been obtained which are based on subjectivity, it becomes the objective value judgement. The management of such social value judgement which becomes the objective value judgment must also be done on the basis of decisions of the group. The study of welfare economics is imperative for making various policy recommendations to promote social welfare. In order to fulfil this objective ethical norms based on various value management is essential. However, sometimes it may not be possible to associate ethical value management with social value management.

Truly speaking, economics studies a vital part of welfare of society because as Marshall, a noted economist, said that economics is a study of mankind in the ordinary business of life and examines that part of individual and social action which is connected with material requisites of well being. Professor Boulding was critical of this definition. He opined that economics is virtually a study of human valuation and choice. To him this spirit of economics may be treated in a wider sense. If it is so then the conception of value management has to be explored in at least three branches of economics:

(a) Positive Economics
(b) Normative Economics
(c) Welfare Economics

The way of value management differs in these three branches of economics. According to noted economist J.M. Keynes a positive science may be defined as a body of systematized knowledge concerning 'what is,' normative science or a regulative science is a body of systematized knowledge relating to criteria of what ought to be and concerned with the ideal as distinguished from the actual....The objective of a positive science is the establishment of uniformities of a normative science, the determination of ideals. Thus in positive economics we derive propositions, theories and laws following central rules of logic. These theories, laws and propositions explain the cause and effect relationship between economic variables. Management of values or value judgment, therefore, seems more exposed to normative economics. In normative economics value is meant the conceptions of the people about the feeling—good feeling or bad feeling. For example, a policy maker puts the target on the basis of normative economics, e.g. there should be 5 per cent rate of growth in the economy. It may also be called 'expected value' as quoted by Harrod in his growth theory. The positive economics shows actual values that have been obtained after observing the economic phenomenon. Here value is not exposed. Thus these areas of economics are not on the same side of coin rather both are different sides of a coin. For planning, normative economics comes first as it is based on values, positive economics comes next where forthcoming values are properly examined for performance appraisal. The difference between positive and normative economic values is due to lack of economic policy and planning. For this special efforts need to be done. In other way it may be scientific to say that the non-realisation of values in normative economics may be compensated through other welfare measures. Normative side of economics is concerned with welfare propositions because the tastes of having delicious or non-delicious ultimately depends upon its effect on welfare as per the individual and societal values. In this sense welfare economics is different from positive economics. According to Prof. Graft "the normal way of testing a theory in positive economics is to test the conclusions, the normal way of testing welfare values is to test the assumption.... In positive economics the proof of the pudding is indeed in the eating. The welfare cake on the other hand is hard to taste that, we must sample the ingredients before baking."

## Nationalism, Values and Globalization

The noted classical economist Adam Smith about whom people said that he was, both Adam and Smith of scientific and systematic economics, happened to be a Professor of Moral Philosophy. He said: "it is not from the benevolence of the butcher, the brewer or the baker, that we expect our dinner, but from their regard to their own interest. We address ourselves not to their humanity but to their self-love. Therefore, it is individual values which is both necessary and desirable for an 'efficient' economic system. The traditional Indian values based on restraint (*Nivriti*) is still preferable to intelligence (*Pravriti*). The utility of one individual may affect the welfare of the masses. That is why, in earlier days it was suggested to have limited wants, meaning thereby, limited values.

Fortunately or unfortunately, to curtail wants in order to downsize the values are rarely observed at the macro level. After economic reform, liberalization and global interactions of various countries and societies, limited wants of consumer and the people are a distant dream. Producers base their values on the growth of consumption and prices. That is why, there is a crystal clear contradiction between traditional economic values and modern economic values. The difference between the two values can be minimized once human moral values come into picture. The Japanese believe in nationalism so far as the question of economic growth is concerned. Their values and traditions have been used to perform the objective of modernizing the economy for socio-economic progress. Their values are based on the belief that the end of business is not money making only. The purpose of business is also to satisfy the customer through service. In Kautilya *Arthashastra* there are indications of three types of business values, namely *arjana, vardhan* and *rakshana*, meaning thereby, to create, to augment and to protect respectively. In modern economics also there are three values before an earner for expenditure purposes, i.e. transaction based values, precautionary values and speculative based values. Meaning thereby, a spender or businessmen keeps money for day to day expenditure, for making the casualties, calamities and other social needs and lastly for making more money out of the available money. Thus there is hardly much difference between primitive Kautilya economics and Keynesian economics. However after global competition among various business groups and in the market 'human values' are loosing the ground. There ought to be development with human face for which satisfaction of consumer, producer and factors of production is imperative. This has to be brought in the new global market and as evidenced by Japan's experience. Nowadays multinationals are often facing moral dilemmas because of market competition. Therefore, for managing managerial values following Ethics Litmus Test is imperative (Reddy and Srinath):

1. Does the cause of action you plan to follow seem logical and unreasonable? Or it makes sense to you, regardless of what others may comment, it is probably right.

2. Does it pass test of sportsmanship? If everyone followed the same course of action, would the result be beneficial for all?
3. Where will your plan of action lead? How will it affect others?
4. Will you think well of yourself when you look back at what you have done?
5. Try to look the problem objectively.
6. Hold up the final decision in the glaring light of publicity.

## Gender Values and Empowerment

The term "empowerment" received considerable attention in the 1960s in United States during its war against poverty, focusing on the empowerment of the low-income groups. Its usage is found in the American Black Radicalism of this time. The term also received popularity among various groups, from academicians to policy makers, planners, funders, social reformers and social workers seeking solutions to social problems. Among those who augmented to popularity of this term were those who worked with some particular under-privileged section of the society such as African-Americans and the Latinos who were accessed with less power and participation in social milieu. Virtually, the understanding of empowerment is closely linked to the understanding of development. The basic concept of development does not merely imply a cluster of benefits doled to people in need, rather it is a process under which a populance acquires a greater mastery over its own destiny by itself. The development is seen not only as a means to control over a large quantity of material benefits and resources, exercised by individuals, groups and committees, but also an essential ability to make choices and direct one's own and society's future course of life. There is a psychological construct in development, experts all over the world in recent days particularly in response to new ideas of welfare and development put forth, in this understanding of development where the emphasis shifts to effect the quality of the prescriptions of the individuals, groups and communities. The non-economic and non-material needs such as self-respect, self-worth, self-determination, self-reliance, freedom of expression, participation in decisions and a sense of purpose in life and work are some crucial elements of the development which has its epicenter towards people. An acceptance and popularity of this kind of understanding of the concept of development has been rising and well received (Tripathi, 2000).

Gender empowerment values have been one of the areas of concern for academicians in the late 20th century and in the beginning of the 21st century. Empowering women world-wide is virtually a very hard but most essential task. This is simply because of the fact that indicators of empowerment indicate a very sad picture about women. According to United Nations Development Programme (UNDP) following are the Gender Empowerment Measures (GEMs):

(A) Percentage of seats held in parliament by women.
(B) Percentage of Administrators and Managers.
(C) Percentage of professional and technical women workers.
(D) Percentage share in earned income by women.

**Table 9.1:** Gender Empowerment Measure: All Countries

| *Countries* | *A* | *B* | *C* | *D* | *GEM Value* |
|---|---|---|---|---|---|
| 1. All developing | 12.7 | 10.0 | 36.7 | 30.0 | 0.367 |
| 2. Industrial countries | 13.6 | 27.4 | 47.8 | 40.0 | 0.586 |
| 3. World | 12.9 | 14.1 | 39.3 | 30.0 | 0.418 |
| 4. India (138) | 7.3 | 2.3 | 20.5 | 26.0 | 0.228 |
| 5. Norway (1) | 39.4 | 30.9 | 57.5 | 42.0 | 0.795 |
| 6. USA (7) | 11.2 | 42.0 | 52.7 | 41.0 | 0.671 |

*Note*: Figures in brackets show GEM Rank.
*Source*: Human Development Report, 1997, UNDP.

According to the Human Development Report (GEM) value Norway ranks first, USA ranks 7th and India ranks 138th. In Norway 39.4 per cent of seats of parliament are held by women whereas in India it is 7.3 per cent which is lower than the average of all developing countries and that of USA. The percentage of administrators and managers in India is just 2.3 per cent (lower than all developing countries) whereas in Norway it is 30 per cent and in USA it is 42 per cent .

As regards percentage of professional and technical women is concerned in India there are 20.5 per cent such women. Whereas in Norway the related figure is 57.5 per cent and for USA 52.7 per cent. Lastly, the percentage share in earned income for women is 26 per cent for India and 42 per cent for Norway. Even in USA the related figure is 41 per cent.

Thus, although women population is about 50 per cent at the global level their share of seats in Parliament is just 12.9 per cent, the percentage of administrators and managers is 14 per cent, the percentage of professional and technical women workers is 39.3 per cent and the percentage share in earned income is about 30 per cent. These figures show that there is enough to be done for women in general and *dalit adivasi* and backward women in particular. There are discriminations—gender and caste based discriminations in the pre and post-markets such as in education, training, employment, wage, human capital, capital and other non-pecuniary benefits. In addition to this, there are social discriminations in the pre and post-markets. In addition to this there are social discriminations on the basis of race in several other countries like USA, South Africa etc. The marginalised dalit women are facing economic and social hindrances particularly in India. Farm and non-farm women workers are facing several socio-economic problems. There has been segregation of job which are not conducive for womens' development. Even in several Asian and other countries such situations are prevalent.

About 85 per cent of women workers are in agriculture compared to about 70 per cent of men in India. But few women own or control land. This is especially true for economically poor women who are landless mainly. This handicaps them in warding off poverty for themselves. Therefore ownership and control over landed and non-landed property will title them to secure production opportunities, increase their bargaining power and provide mortgageable assets or saleable assets for time of crises. Surveys of household consumption expenditure in many countries show the incidence of income poverty to be high among female headed households. Although in Asia, China has made enormous progress in gender equality and empowerment but it is still the girls who are more deprived in poor families. There are also instances of anti-feminine development in developing nations with reference to life expectancy at birth, adult literacy rate and drop-out ratio in education (UNDP, 1997).

## Traditional Social Values and Inequality

The orthodox society has a closed value system because of the dominance of caste, sex and religious factors. This value gave rise to caste dominated hierarchy with structured social differences. This type of social values based on caste was so deep-rooted in the organic composition that it persisted throughout especially in Indian history.

Every social value develops a tendency to exist, perpetuate and continue through several techniques.

In the caste dominated society Brahmin, a superior caste, used to guide the society. They created holy texts and social laws, which governed the subject matter of education and culture. It disseminated purity and religious and civic disabilities and privileges of various castes, restriction, social interaction and choice of occupation. All this was ultimately meant to produce uncritical subscriber of Hindu religion and caste ideology. Since imparting of education was highly restricted, the lower castes were excluded on the ground of untouchability and the choice of occupation was restricted. Similarly the people of lower castes were restricted to own land and agriculture. The four-fold division of social values into Brahmin, Kshatriya, Vaishyas and Shudra came into existence and these were designated as Varnas. Within Varna, castes were according to their occupation, within this framework of Varna and caste, class formations also took place, like landlords, peasants and agriculture labourer and as well as artisans.

In a few parts of India, a parallel non-orthodox stream of thought through the emergence of Upanishads and Buddhist literature also developed which became a challenge to Vedic brahminical values. Buddha openly declared the varna system unreasonable because all human beings belong to a common human values. He opined that one cannot be considered superior just because of birth or lineage. Buddhism was the greatest challenge to priestly elite. Many kings found Buddhism more suitable. The priestly elite were quite conscious of all these forces. It was clear from that the ancient Vedic religion could not be revived in its earlier form. So many old Aryan practices have therefore to be outrightly rejected and non-Aryan values found entry into the revived religion.

For restoration of Varna hierarchy the backbone of traditional Indian social values, Smritis came into existence and Sanskara became operational in an effective manner. Manu-Smriti was the first attempt of the priestly elites. Armed with the ancient myth of creation and various sacraments, together with the doctrine of karma, Manu tried to revive the ancient values of Varna hierarchy and also tried to assign each and every ethnic group a specific place in varna system according to his own criteria and thus in Smriti era, once again Brahman ensured unquestionably the supreme position for themselves and Shudras were given lowest social value. In any case they were not allowed to receive any asset and have to serve to the higher Varna. Manu took no cognizance of the doctrine forwarded by Buddha that the people of all Varnas belong to one human value. Caste not only remains salient feature of social theory.

As British rule prospered, rationality became broader and more powerful. Some notion of equality was implicit in various colonial institutional values. Gandhiji started national movement against colonialism but also against the vested economic interest and untouchability. Ambedkar fought against prevailing discriminations against the lower strata of the society particularly the have-nots. As a result many benefits like reservation in services and position in power structure could be made available to the deprived class through constitutional obligation (Singh, 2000).

Even after 50 years of independence we could not reduce inequalities substantially. Today about 35 per cent population lives under poverty, a condition of life so characterized by malnutrition. Illiteracy has to be beneath the reasonable definition of human decency. The style of economic development has been under the control of power structure of the society so change in the power structure can bring a lot of metamorphosis in economic development also. In India caste dominance has the element of numeric strength, economic and political power, education and modern occupational segregation.

In the case of Gandhian non-movements, the recent emphasis is on decentralized planning for people's self-government. The Panchayati Raj Institution could not succeed. A joint front called the national front for Tribal Rule, succeeded in bringing tribal people from all over the country on one platform, on the vital issues of tribal self-rule. Among the struggles that employ the strategy of armed revolt are the "insurgency" struggles in the North-East, Kashmir and the militant struggles of the 'Naxalites' in the forest of Andhra Pradesh, Madhya Pradesh, Maharashtra and Orissa. The shrinking of the welfare functions by state and its promotion of global market-driven 'development' at the expense of marginalized groups and their rights, forms the backbone of present social values. The stereo type of an activist is changing from that of a "khadi-clads, jhola on the shoulder and hawai chappals in feet" type to one of sporting a "cellular phone", working on a laptop and operating on e-mail and internet". The image and operations seem to subscribe to a mindset "act globally, think locally" which seems to be a reverse of the earlier dictum "think globally, act locally" (Singh, 2000).

The socio-economic and political transformations in the economy can take place with ethical values. Realistically, people start from where they are, with what is possible, thus "mini transformation" in the structure and relationships in people's immediate environment will prepare them for wide systemic changes. As we are concerned with the employment of marginalized target groups who are affected not only by the system but also by oppression in their immediate environment, one has to consider seriously the area of mini-transformation, without a sense of achievement, control and confidence to tackle the smaller issues one cannot target for a change at larger level. Changes in the immediate environment should become the "identity oriented" paradigm (Cohen, 1982: cf. Panda and Sharma, 1996). One of the issues that are of concern to most activities is the lack of values in their endeavours. Lack of value leads to a lack of moral commitment towards economy and society. Hence there is a dire need to rework the development models giving them value orientation.

Valueless politics, even through powerful coalitions, is not enough. There is an increasing need for political participation by intellectuals in the electoral sphere. The electoral arena must reveal sobriety for social development. Empowerment of intelligentsia should be distinguished from state sponsored, valueless participative agenda. Transformation of social relations, which is at the core of an empowerment agenda, is seldom and intrinsic principle of a programme perspective or its early stages in the process of empowerment (Singh, 2000).

However, it has been realized that empowerment should also be value-based. Virtually it may be determined for the economy and the society. Needless to highlight the lack of values among planners. Planned development in India has widened the gap at regional level. There is a hiatus in rural and urban area. The percentage share of rural sector in national income has declined. The per capita income in rural sector has risen by more than 135 per cent. Just an increase in GDP does not mean any real welfare of all people. Poverty alleviation programmes could not reduce number of poors. Reforms are like old wine in a new bottle. Substantial reduction of absolute poverty is a distant dream. Therefore, rational reallocation of public resources are required. This can be done by increased spending on social sector where the spending has been minimum. An efficient social delivery system is the only ethical value to save the poor. The average per capita expenditure among major states on social sector was only Rs. 211 in 1997-98. And a significant portion of this was spent on salaries of staff. Virtually value education can play a vital role in poverty alleviation. Rural demand is the prime mover of the economy in all the budget which needs thrust along with commerce, industry and telecommunication. During one decade of reform, subsidies and expenditure on social sector reduced. As a result annual growth rate in agriculture has come down.

Our poverty has originated from historical process, pro-urban policies and socio-political structures while history cannot be reversed, policies can be changed and new future can be built with equitable distribution of social benefits particularly the "assets" without which reforms cannot have any social justice in India. The last decade witnessed an increase in caste mobilization in politics and all social groups are becoming more aggressive and the question of social justice is becoming more important now (Singh, 2000). Thus value generation, dissemination and diffusion is the *sine qua non* of the present.

**Value Education and Development Scenario**

Value education is one of the key components of socio-economic transformation. It helps build human capabilities. It also generates various opportunities. Meaningful education has potentiality to develop a sustainable society. South Asian development planners and also planners of African and Latin American countries must realize the role of value education for sustainable economic development. The classical economists such as Adam Smith, J.S. Mill, Karl Marx and Alfred Marshall have fully recognized the role of value education, and the same has been reasserted by Schultz, Becker and Sen.

The economies that have acquired the relevant knowledge and skills can compete successfully in global markets. Thus has been the experience of Japan, the East Asian industrializing economies like South Korea, Hong Kong, Singapore, Malaysia, Thailand, Indonesia and China. By combining their low wages and relevant education and skills, they converted their poverty into an asset and captured the global markets through rising labour productivity.

According to the theories of Schultz and Becker education provides people with the skills that allow them to be more productive in their work, thereby creating for them the opportunity to earn higher wages in the labour market. Human capital is defined as the stock of useful, valuable and relevant knowledge built up in the process of education and training. Investment in human capital, through schooling, increases the productivity of labour. Higher wages in the labour market are, therefore a reward for the higher productivity of workers with a greater stock of human capital. This is the most widely accepted economic explanation for educated workers receiving higher rewards in the labour market (Becker, 1993 and Schultz).

Empirical evidence have also provided strong support for this hypothesis (Knight and Sabot, 1990). For example, the average salary in Bangladesh of a Secondary School educated woman is as much as seven times higher than that of a woman with no education (World Bank, 1993b). Another survey in Bangladesh revealed that skilled workers in the construction industry receive double the wages of unskilled workers. Yet another study by Jamison and Lau (1982) shows that four years of schooling, on an average, increases the output of farmers by about 8 per cent. In Pakistan, the greatest increase (2.7%) in agricultural productivity was associated with a ten per cent increase in male literacy (Resegrant and Evenson, 1993). In addition to increasing the productivity of the educated worker, education also raises the productivity of neighbouring labourers by providing an important role model. A study found that over a five-year period, the profits of Indian farmers with no schooling were 4 per cent higher, if their neighbour had completed primary schooling than if he had not. Farmers with more schooled neighbours also adopted new seeds earlier (Foster and Rosenzweing, 1995).

Powerful arguments in favour of the "human capital" school have recently been presented in two World Bank studies (1993b and 1995a). Analysing the experience of 192 countries, the World Bank comes to the conclusion that as much as two-thirds of the wealth of nations consists of human and social capital (Social Capital signifies sound institutions and good governance which, in turn, depend largely on the coverage of value education). In some countries, such as Japan, that lacked a good natural resource base, human and social capital are estimated to have contributed 85 per cent to the total national wealth, while physical capital (machinery, buildings and physical infrastructure) 14 per cent and natural capital only 1 per cent. The inescapable conclusion is that a dearth of natural resources can be compensated for by building up human capital through value education (as in Japan) but that the dearth of human capital cannot be overcome through natural wealth. For example, oil resources are plentiful in the OPEC nations, but there has been limited development of human resources. A summary of the contribution of human and social capital to the total wealth of various regions is given in Table 9.2.

**Table 9.2:** Contribution of Human Capital: (Per cent Share)

| *Region* | *Natural capital* | *Physical capital* | *Human and social capital* |
|---|---|---|---|
| Sub-Saharan Africa | 52 | 17 | 31 |
| East Asia and Pacific | 12 | 13 | 75 |
| South Asia | 9 | 15 | 76 |
| Latin America and Caribbean | 35 | 15 | 50 |
| Middle East and North Africa | 32 | 29 | 39 |
| Eastern Europe | 43 | 16 | 41 |
| High Income Countries | 17 | 16 | 67 |
| Primary Good Exporters | 44 | 20 | 36 |
| Other Developing Countries | 28 | 16 | 56 |
| World | 20 | 16 | 64 |

*Source*: World Bank, 1995c.

The East Asian experience shows the importance of basic and technical education in building a stock of valuable and relevant human capital. Empirical evidence shows further that there is no industrial society today with an adult literacy rate of less than 80 per cent. No illiterate society has ever become an industrial tiger. As regards rate of return to education, the human capital hypothesis suggests that investment in education is conceptually identical to an investment in development by calculating the rate of return to such investment. Technically, the rate of return to expenditure on education is that discount rate which equates the future stream of benefits with the present stream of costs.

The private rate of return measures the relationship between the cost and benefits of education for a particular individual. It is generally calculated in terms of financial costs and benefits to an individual. The social rate of return, however is a broader and much more relevant concept. It includes all the cost borne by society as a whole, for example fees, scholarships and administrative expenditure borne by the state instead of the individual. More pertinently, it includes social benefits all the 'externalities' generated by an increase in the level of education, such as improved standards of hygiene, lower rates of infant and child mortality, reduced rates of population growth, raised civic consciousness, greater political participation, and an improved sense of national unity. Education is generally heavily subsidized at all levels by the state, and many social benefits cannot be fully measured. Nevertheless, the social rate of return is a more relevant concept (Kumar, 2001).

The studies based on rate of return show that social returns to investment in education are among the highest in a society. For instance, a 1988 study in Nepal (World Bank, 1994; Kumar, 2001) found the following social rates of return: a 100 per cent on investment in primary education; 29.1 per cent to lower secondary; 15.0 per cent to secondary and 21.7 per cent returns to investment in Bachelor's degree. Girl's education normally has a higher overall return than boys' education, with the maximum differential at the secondary level. Table 9.2A shows the results of some empirical studies on rates of return to education.

**Table 9.2A:** Social Returns Investment in Education

| *By region* | *Primary* | *Secondary* | *Higher* |
|---|---|---|---|
| Asia | 19.9 | 13.3 | 11.7 |
| Sub-Saharan Africa | 24.3 | 18.2 | 11.2 |
| Latin America and Caribbean | 35 | 15 | 50 |
| Industrial Countries | 14.4 | 10.2 | 8.7 |
| World | 18.4 | 10.9 | 10.9 |
| By Income Group—Low Income | 23.4 | 15.2 | 10.6 |
| Lower middle Income | 18.2 | 13.4 | 11.4 |
| Upper middle Income | 14.3 | 10.6 | 9.5 |
| High Income | NA | 10.3 | 8.2 |

*Source*: Psacharopoulos, 1994.

The Key results of various studies are summarized below:

— Primary education has the highest social rate of return followed by secondary education.

— As National Income increases, the returns to all levels of education decline, but primary education still has the highest return.

— South Asia and Sub-Saharan Africa show the highest rates of return on investment in primary education.

Overall, there are two important conclusions that emerge from rate of return studies. First, the overwhelming priority for investment in basic education, particularly in low-income countries, second, investments in improving the quality of the education system also yields high returns (Behrman and Birdsall, 1983). This is a very important conclusion for enhancing value education.

The most powerful evidence for the role that education has played in achieving and maintaining high rates of economic growth comes from the experience of Japan and the East Asian industrializing countries (see Table 9.3). Overall 60 to 90 per cent of their growth is explained by the accumulation of physical and human capital. Primary education emerges as the most significant contributor to predicted growth. While the East Asian 'miracle' was based on many factors, all analysts agree on the central role that the spread of basic education played in shaping this miracle. Therefore, value education at the primary level itself is very important.

**Table 9.3:** Contribution of Primary Education to East Asian Growth

| *Country* | *Per cent of Predicted Growth Attributed to Primary Education* |
|---|---|
| Thailand | 87 |
| Hong Kong | 86 |
| Indonesia | 79 |
| Singapore | 75 |
| Malaysia | 73 |
| Taiwan, China | 69 |
| South Korea | 67 |
| Japan | 58 |

*Note:* Predicted growth is the share of the actual growth predicted by the variables in a cross-country long run growth regression (from 1960-85): the variable includes enrolment rates, the population growth rate, average investment and geographical dummy variables.

*Source:* World Bank, 1993.

The low contribution of education to economic growth in certain countries, such as Nicaragua, Cuba, Sri Lanka, and Indian state of Kerala, is because the complementary economic and social policies that are necessary to ensure sustainable human development are often missing. Education with inadequate, remunerative and productive jobs rarely leads to sustainable economic growth. Alongside job creation and credit for the poor, improvements in childrens' nutrition are essential to ensure that educational performance is not hampered by poor health. In short, it is necessary for value education to be part of a wider human development strategy. Such complimentary policies can also reinforce educational progress, for instance, if a country with a 50 per cent illiteracy rate doubled its GDP per person, it could expect illiteracy to fall to 27.3 per cent (Anand and Ravallion, 1993).

**Table 9.4:** Contribution of Education to Economic Growth: Selected Countries and Regions

| *Country* | *Growth Rate Explained by Education* |
|---|---|
| Canada | 25.0 |
| Ghana | 23.3 |
| India* | 27.0 |
| Argentina | 16.5 |
| Nigeria | 16.5 |
| United States | 15.0 |
| Belgium | 14.0 |
| Kenya | 12.4 |
| *Region* | |
| Africa | 17.2 |
| Asia | 11.1 |
| North America and Europe | 8.6' |
| Latin America | 5.1 |

* From Loh,1995.

*Source*: World Bank,1995c and Loh, 1995.

From the synthesis of theoretical and empirical studies which link education and economic growth, it is very clear that no educated economy remains underdeveloped for long, while no illiterate valueless economy can achieve sustained rates of economic growth.

## Conclusion

To conclude, the present paper addressed to several issues which relate to value in education. It addressed the interface to focus on utility theory, rational expectation, social welfare, normative economics, ethical values, globalization, gender values, inequality and future of a valueless educational economy. The issues raised are pertinent in order to making an alternative arrangements for a decaying society. Various national and international agencies, the state, the electorate, teachers and students must be reminded with various ways of value education required for the nation in a global context. The least developed countries/less developed countries must recognize the symptoms of a valueless economy and counter the same. However, the job is unmanageable. Moral teaching and preaching is required along with sincere efforts for practising it.

## REFERENCES

Bergson, A., (1954). On the concept of Social Welfare, *Quarterly Journal of Economics.*

Boulding, Kenneth E., (1970). *Economics as a Science,* Tata McGraw Hill.

Graft, J.De.V., (1998). Theoretical Welfare Economics, (*OUP*).

Kothari, R.,: Elections and Democracy: Growing Depoliticisation, *Lokayan Bulletin* 12(6), 5-10.

Kumar, Anuj, (2001). *Literacy Led Human Development Among Social Groups*, M.Phil Dissertation, BBAU, Lucknow.

Little, I.M.D., (1957). *A Critique of Welfare Economics.*

Oomen, T.K.,: *Protest and Change-Studies in Social Movements,* New Delhi, Sage Publications

Panda, A.C. and Sharma A.K., (1996). Reconstructing Theory of Social Movements in India. *Social Action*, 46(3), 111-21.

Singh, Yasvir, (2000). *People's Empowerment: Issues for Social Justice*, Seminar Paper, IIPA, Delhi.

Stormquest, N.; Women's Education in Development from Welfare to Empowerment, *Convergence*, 21 (4), 5-17.

Strectum, Paul, (1950). Economics and Value Judgment, *OUP*, Quarterly Journal of Economics.

Hick, J.R., (1991). Value and Capital, (*ELBs*).

Pigou, A.C., (1932). *Economics of Welfare*, Macmillan.

Rao, Nitya, (2000). Education: Quality with Quantity, *Economic and Political Weekly,* Vol. 25.

Reddy, N. Ramakrishna, *et al.* (1997). Globalization, Management and Human Values in Atmanand (ed.) *Globalization and Dimensions of Management in India,* Shipra, New Delhi.

Robbins, L., (1938). *Nature and Significance of Economic Science*, Macmillan, London.

Sachan, Geeta, (1999). *Impact of Female Literacy on Economic Development* (A Case Study of Slums of Lucknow City) M.Phil Dissertation, BBAU, Lucknow.

Tripathi, V.P., *et al.* (2000). *People's Empowerment: Issues for Social Justice,* Seminar Paper, IIPA, Delhi

Verma, N.M.P., (2001). Planning and Literacy Status of the Scheduled Castes, *Ambedkar Journal of Social Development and Justice,* Vol. IX.

# 10

# Ethics in Dental Profession: An Overview

NIMISH NIMEYA

*The metaphysical reality or the truth of logical coherence must remain merely a theoretical possibility unless it is translated into good of life through right living.*

## Introduction

Indian philosophy in general ascribes the supreme place, of all, to ethics. The word ethics is derived from "ηθos" meaning character, and "ηθos" is derived from "εθos" meaning custom or habit. The term "moral" is closely associated with ethics, comes from the Latin word "mores", which primarily stands for "custom" or "habit" and secondarily means character. In general, it deals with the concepts and principles of morality. Ethics has various fields and sub fields of application including dental ethics. Dental ethics applies to moral principles and virtues to the practice of dentistry.

### *Ethics in Health Care*

Modern society has changed quiet a lot in the last few decades with the rapid technological advances in every sphere of life including health care and newer things are added everyday. We see that people are better informed and demand more and better services from the health care professionals, which are their right, and it is the duty of the health care professionals to provide it. On the other hand, strains of contradictory value system run through out the society. Large segments of society are becoming more materialistic, more self-serving, less reflective and less concerned for the welfare of the community. Ethical standard in modern society are in a time of rapid flux and show the contraction that characteristically attend such changes. Health care professionals in our society always enjoyed a supreme position but with the advancement of the technology several ethical issues such as female feticide, organ transplantation, cloning etc. have surfaced up which indicate that there is something seriously wrong with our health care system. In order to improve our health care system we need solid ethical foundation.

## Ethical Questions in Dentistry

Ethics are critical to being a professional, ethics in dental profession is focused mainly on the quality of care and the need to maintain public trust. Generally, ethical questions in general dental practice depend upon correct evaluations regarding diagnosis and treatment planning which has both the component, the diagnosis & treatment can either be right or wrong but the problem arises when a choice has to be made between good and better or between lesser of the two evils. In some cases evaluation has to be made on the basis of esthetics and personal preferences of the patient thereby putting the dentist in a state of dilemma whether the treatment he/she is carrying out is ethical or not. Ethical issues in dental profession are derived mainly from the rapid technological advances. Costly innovations like CAD/CAM'S, RVG'S, OPG'S, Intra oral cameras along with the increasing use of implants, lasers and newer and improved dental materials has indeed improved the quality of care but also made care more inaccessible to less affluent people.

*Dummett* in his encyclopedia of bio-ethics has described the ethical issues, which are faced by a dentist. To these are added other individual contributions appearing in the published literature along with a survey of issue done by me. These issues are:

### *Quality of Care*

One of the most frequent expressions of concern is for quality of care. Care might be inadequate if it involves the delivery of substandard care without the patient's knowledge, without consideration of the patient's wishes, without justification by virtue of special circumstances, and motivated solely by financial gains.

*Access to Dental Care*

Dentistry should be available, within reason, to all seeking treatment. A dentist should normally be available to address potentially health-threatening dental conditions and to ease pain and suffering. Although, under special circumstances a dentist can refrain from providing treatment i.e., he/she does not have the expertise or capability, patient's inability to pay, impaired professional ability but it is the duty of the dentist to refer the patient to the most appropriate place.

*Patient Autonomy*

This is major ethical issue in practice of dentistry. The ethical consideration imposes:

(a) Comprehensive knowledge on the past of the practitioner;
(b) Uncompromising veracity;
(c) Unbiased presentation of all reasonable alternatives and consequences, including cost and the probability of outcomes;
(d) Clear cut communication, so that he/she is fully understood by the patient.

*Advertising*

This is also emerging as major ethical issue. Growing competition and influence of the market-oriented thinking is responsible for this. A dentist should never misrepresent /mispropagate his/her competence in any way that would be false or misleading. Advertising by a dentist must not:

(a) Misrepresent facts,
(b) Mislead or deceive by partial disclosure,
(c) Create false expectations of favourable results,
(d) Misrepresent fees,
(e) Imply or guarantee atypical results,
(f) Compare professional ability of other practitioners,
(g) Refrain from aggressive marketing practice like discounting ploys, which diminish the profession in the public eyes.

*Abuse of Prescriptions by Patients*

The dentist must be aware of patient's legitimate needs for prescription drugs. The dentist should confront patients in case of suspicion because he/she has an ethical obligation to avoid becoming an enabler.

*Conflicts with the Patients*

This is a multidimensional problem as both the dentist as well as the patient can be the precipitator. The conflicts should be carefully addressed as they might have medico legal complications.

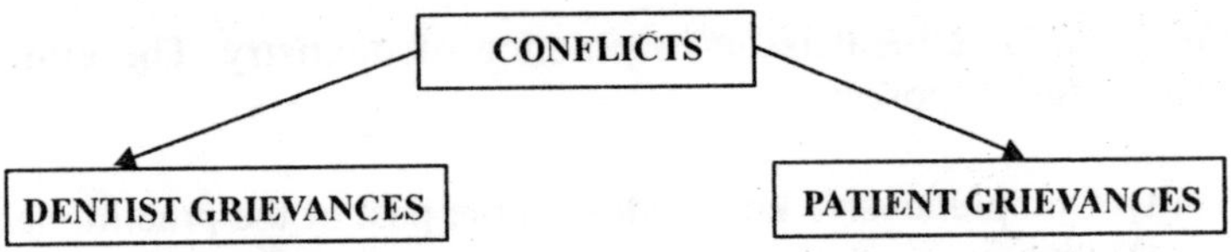


1. Patient not following pre/post treatment instructions
2. Non cooperation from patient
3. Expectation of miraculous results instantly
4. Non payment/underpayment

Substandard result
Failure of treatment
Medications
Fees

Proper communication with the patient in a way that he/she can comprehend properly is key to success in practice of dentistry.

*Community Programmes*

This is also a debatable ethical issue. It is very true that a dentist has certain obligation towards the community but it should be left to the dental practitioner himself/herself to decide the extent of participation in such programmes. One thing we must always remember is that participation in such programmes boosts the image of the profession in the public eye.

*Intra Professional Relationships*

Intra Professional relationship is another ethical issue, which should be managed very carefully. It is most ethical for the dentist to refrain from criticizing another colleague so as to build up ones own clientele. This helps to maintain the dignity of the profession.

*Relationship with the Patient*

It is ethical and as well as absolutely essential for dentist to have a thorough professional relationship with the patient. He/she should not use their position of influence to solicit or develop romantic relationships with patients. Dentist should avoid creating perceptions of inappropriate behaviour.

*Oversupply of Dentists*

This is a different problem but is related to ethics in every way. Over supply of dentists has a direct implication on the quality of care. Too many dentists could lead to too few patients and an increase in the possibility of over treatment. This may also lead to bitter intra professional relationship and can result in unhealthy practices.

*Curbs on the Practice by Quacks*

This is another major ethical issue in our country. It is the duty of the dental community to raise their voice against unqualified practitioners so that the quality of treatment is not compromised and the profession's image is not diminished in public eye.

**Values and Principles in Clinical Dental Ethics**

The basic values and principles in clinical dental practice are autonomy, non maleficence and beneficence. Ethical decision-making also involves both judging and choosing. Emotional state, incompetence, physical and mental disorders and other condition may adversely affect a dentist's decision-making capability. So it is very important that every Judgment and decision in clinical practice should reflect dentist's responsibility towards the patient. Ethical decision-making by dentist's can be simple and at times be quiet Complex. ***Ozar et al, 1988*** published a report that identifies all the key decision elements in clinical dental practice. They are :

1. Life and health
2. Appropriate and pain free oral functioning
3. Patient autonomy
4. Preferred pracfice values

5. Esthetic values
6. Cost
7. Other external factors

To this I would like add another element, which is:
***Examining the process of decision making***

*Life and Health*

The sustaining of life promotion of overall health should be the prime concern of all practitioners. Under no circumstances, dentist should undertake treatment that may put the life or health of a patient at risk. Occasionally, as in an example given by Ozar *et al*, a man suffering from malignant hyperthermia with serious facial trauma required general anesthesia to be administered but he was treated under local anesthesia in spite of limited working condition under local anesthesia.

*Appropriate and Pain Free Oral Functioning*

This involves the basics of disease prevention and maintenance of oral health in the most appropriate way. Pain free functioning should be of prime concern to the dentist and every treatment should be aimed at restoring the proper oral functioning.

*Patient Autonomy*

Patient autonomy refers to the ability of competent patient to make his or her own health care decisions. For e.g. if a patient wants tooth to be extracted whereas the dentist considers it otherwise, in this situation the dentist should explain the pros and cons of extraction and even if the patient still persists, his wish should be granted.

*Preferred Practice Values*

Preferred practice values are basically the lesser aspects of profession, which should be kept in mind. This involves things such as:

(a) **Employment of Auxiliaries in Dental Office:** A dentist should be careful in appointing auxiliaries in his office. He/

she should be confident about his/her ability and care must be taken before delegating duties to them. Duties should not be delegated at the expense of quality.

(b) **Relationship with the Staff:** The superior - subordinate relationship should be very professional. The Dentist must avoid conditions or action that promotes harassment or abuse of staff, patients or other related parties. The Dentist must maintain a good healthy professional relationship within the office.

(c) **Constant Up-gradation of One's Own Skills:** It is absolutely essential for the dentist to upgrade his/her own skill for the benefit of the patients. This includes attending seminars, conferences and providing the patients with best and safest treatment.

*Esthetic Values*

Esthetics is of prime concern in the practice of dentistry. Most of the treatment undertaken is due to esthetic reasons. A dentist should always consider the esthetic factors but it should never compromise pain free oral functioning.

*Costs*

Before deciding upon the treatment plan a dentist should consider the cost factor keeping in mind the patient's financial restrictions. The patient should be informed about all the available options regarding costs.

*External Factors*

There are many external factors, which influence the dentist's decision-making process; these include social factors such as the society, cultural factors, public welfare in general and even the dentist's own personal preferences.

*Examining the Process of Decision Making*

The process of ethical decision-making by dentists may be simple at times or quite complex. There are so many conditions, which may affect the dentist's decision-making process so it is required on the dentist's part to examine the whole process of decision-making. This involves considering the following decision-making elements:

1. Good ethics begins with good facts; before coming to a conclusion a dentist should consider all the relevant facts so that the problem is identified properly.
2. One should always consider all the available options and alternatives available. Ethical decision requires imagination and creativity to discern options not envisioned before.
3. One should always take the patient in confidence and should see that he is fully involved in the decision-making process. No decision should as far as possible should be taken unilaterally.
4. In crunch situation, one must not hesitate to take help from colleagues, teachers, journals, and books and also from organizations such as IDA etc. to resolve the issue.
5. Before coming to a conclusion one should rank all the possible outcomes and take the most suitable decision that resolves the issue. Every decision taken by the dentist should reflect his /her integrity and commitment to the noble profession of dentistry.

**Ethical Decision Making Model**

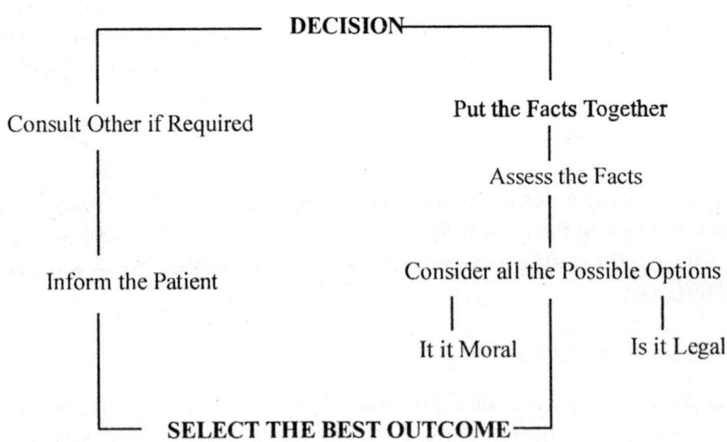

## Ethical *versus* Legal

One must view law as a guide for providing treatment that is in the best interest of the patients. Generally, we view the law preventively, in the sense of avoiding malpractice. As a result, law and ethics must be observed for their differences rather than their similarities. For example, it may be legal for a general dental practitioner to provide orthodontic care but unethical to do so without adequate training.

Most laws and regulations that govern dentistry do not normally prompt ethical conflicts, but in case of a conflict it is our moral obligation to follow the law of the land.

## Conclusion

A true dental professional is one who uses his special skills with the ethical considerations in order to benefit the society, regardless of personal gains. This quality should be consistently reflected in the decisions and actions of the dentist.

Although, sometimes the competitive internal dynamics of the profession can create inducement to unethical behaviour but one thing that every dental practitioner should remember is long term basis for success in the profession depends on the ability of adapting these ethical values and ensuring their fine weaving irretrievably into day to day life.

## REFERENCES

American Dental Association. *Ethics Handbook for Dentists*, Vol. 1.1, 2002-2003.

Beauchamp TL, Walters L, eds. *Contemporary Issues in Bioethics*. 3rd ed. Belmont, Calif: Wadworth; 1982: 655.

Cole LA. *Dentistry and Ethics: A call for attention*. J Am Dent Assoc, 1984; 109: 559-561.

Dummett CO. Ethical Issues in Dentistry. In: Reich W, ed *Encyclopedia of Bioethics*, New York : The Free Press.

*Encyclopedia of Philosophy* : McMillan Pub.

Gurley, John E. *The Evolution of Professional Ethics in Dentistry*. St. Louis, American College of Dentists, 1961.

Holloway JA, Mcneal Dr. Lotzar S. *Ethical Problems in Dental Practice*. J Am Coil Dent 1985; 52: 12-16.

McCullough Lb. Erthical Issues in Dentistry. In: *Cark's Clinical Dentistry.* Pliadelphia. Pa: JB Lippincot; 1988: l-17.

Ozar, David T. and Sokol, David J. *Dental Ethics at Chair Side: Professional Principles and Practice Applications*. St. Louis, Mosby. 1994.

Odom Jg. *The Status of Dental Ethics Instruction.* J Dent Edu 1988: 52: 306-308.

# SECTION II

## VALUES IN TEACHING PROFESSION AND EDUCATION

# 11

# Education in Human Values for Human Excellence Amidst Diversity

BHOOMITRA DEV

---

We are living in an age of guided missiles and misguided men. Our malleable conscience has created moral wastelands.

> *"Ehle khirad ne ye din dikhaye,*
> *Ghat gaye insan badh gaye saye."*

In the lines of Dinkar:

> *"Jhar gayee punchh Hemant jhare,*
> *Pashuta ka jharna baki hai,*
> *Upar-upar tan sanwar chuka,*
> *Man abhi sanwarna baki hai."*

Nature prefers diversity. Each person is like a unique genomic letter, kind of whom never existed in the past, can nowhere else be seen at present in the world, and shall, barring cloning, never visit the plant again. This has led to amazing levels of functional indeterminacy of human brain.

> *"Ekoham dwitiyonasti, na bhuto na bhavishyati."*

It is our congenital right that "the letter" is read early and fully.

Left half of our brain is more concerned with reason and logic, while the right dominates in emotion, arts and music etc. Principle of "use or fuse" guides its development. When we take adequate care of both the parts, uniqueness unfolds fully. Both $I_Q$ and $E_Q$ develop. Such a holistic and harmonised development is the result of the finest education in human values. It is a pity that many of us die much before realising our full potential. When we integrate our thought, speech and action, live our true nature (*Sahaj*), inward flowering may ensue. Such a glorious "return to our ownself" (*Swaroop*) further improves our quality of life.

"*Vidyaya, Vapusha, Vaacha, Vastrena Vinayaen cha.*"

We then epitomise—"*Atma deepo bhav*", "*Amritasya putrah*"—Children of immortality; and represent "*Satyam, Shivam, Sundaram*". We may also realise : "*Zindagi asl hai, khwab hai aur tarzae ada bhi*".

Excellence and simplicity often go together. With an open mind, noble thoughts are welcomed from all over the world. At such a peak level of human evolution, we epitomise the sanctified fire, fuel and the invocator— three in one. Levels of instinct, intelligence and intuition are crossed. We stand on the twilight zone of the known and the unknown. A tiny intuitive spark may widen our mental horizon, and the resulting break-through transgresses time. Such an excellent state of mind is attained when the doer merges with his aim. When somebody asked Picasso how he could, while painting, stand for so long without twitching an extraneous muscle, he told that he had left his body outside the chamber just as a Muslim leaves his shoes outside a mosque.

There are a few most essential human values, we need to acquire in the modern world today. First and the foremost is to uphold human dignity itself. While Gandhi distinguished between need and greed, he used what was usable because he wanted to salute the man who had spent a part of his life in producing it. Secondly, while he sang "... *Jane peer parai re*", he valued human sensitivity.

We are living in an "ICE-age"—age of information, communication and entertainment. Information is power. Faster the information flow, lesser the poverty. In the past, necessity was the mother of invention. With the paradigm shift, invention has now become the mother of necessity. With "death of distance", geography is history. Strong mind-benders have unleashed war for mindscape. World war has changed into word war. An anecdote from Israel explains the change. A physicist under spell had become a frog. He could again become a human if a beautiful girl kissed him. The frog spoke of the curse when two girls passed by. One of the girls picked it up and put it in her purse. Her friend asked her, "Won't you kiss him?" She replied, "No, I would not kiss it, because a speaking frog is more precious than a physicist". In order to curb such a high tide of insensitivity, there is a crying need for human values today.

Faith has been eroded. Divisiveness is on the rise. We have to learn the art of conflict resolution to reduce attrition. Shall we realise that mud thrown is ground lost. Excellence can be achieved by cooperation only.

We should not be anthropocentric. Planet Earth is on lease-hold, and not free-hold. Let us remember Voltaire, who said : "The bee was superior to human beings because one of their secretions is useful. Nothing that a human secretes is useful". We should extend the innate right of uniqueness to the biome also. Reckless industrialisation brings in conformity. We produce fumes of progress, and effluents of affluence. Global affluenza has to be controlled. When the environment deteriorates, the best flowers of our culture and civilisation wilt and wither first. We should allow mother Nature to choose her own dress more often, as in an Ashram, with its variety of foliage, flowers, fruits and seeds, with rain-bow colours, shape, size and fragrance. We should cultivate the art of appreciation of earth's beauty, and strive to leave the world better than we found it.

Lastly, we should learn to maintain eco balance between getting and giving. Ego lives by getting and forgetting, while love lives by giving and forgiving. This alone can maintain the Niagra of happiness.

*Jeevane yavadadanam syatpradanam tatodhikam,*
*Ityesha prathnasmakam bhagvan paripuryatam.*
*Pashbaddhah sada jivah*
*Pashmuktah sada shivah*

May I quote the words from an emblem : *Shastre Shaastre cha Kaushalam*. This alone can form a valuable triology of education in human values for human excellence amidst diversity, the triology of *Roop, Lila, Dham* indeed!

12

# Trends in Value Education

B.R. DUGGAR

---

We have arrived in twenty-first century. The nations of the world are striving utmost to bring into the lives of their people the marvels of science and technology. Undoubtedly, human life on this planet has been greatly enriched with the incredible scientific advance. We are living in a rapid changing world, ever stricken with fear of war and annihilation. Contemporary Indian situation witnesses ambivalence if not complete confusion of values. The character of the people has degenerated to such an extent that our social workers, enlightened citizens, statesmen and educationists who are concerned about the future of our country have been given alarm signals and calling for immediate remedial measures. Such warnings and exhortations do not seem to have much impact on our efforts to take urgent steps to improve our character and build a new India.

All values and norms are being cast to the winds in pursuit of self and power. There is a widespread spectrum of anomalies, dissension and conflict, misery, corruption, sensuality, falsehood, hypocrisy and degradation of mind, morals and relationship. Late Prime Minister Mrs. Indira Gandhi said, "Never in our lifetime have there been so many difficulties nationally or internationally, never so many dangers, shortages and crises" and added that there was an urgent and immediate need to foster character and discipline among the young generation. The youth of today is living in a more complex society, full of paradoxes and contradictions. On one hand they have experienced man on moon phenomenon made possible by advanced technology and on the other hand they have witnessed racial riots, wars, poverty and ecological imbalance. To them the institutions are no longer sacred shrines or temples of wisdom.

As education is not merely acquiring knowledge, gathering and correlating facts, it is to see the significance of life as a whole. Education means self-culture and self-improvement. This is the perennial source of illumination of various walks of life. That is why education is called the third eye, an insight to prove into visible as well as invisible world and to show the right path. The greatest saint of the age Mahatma Gandhi has also said, "Strength by itself is in main, skill by itself is in vain, they have value only when they are used for human welfare." Therefore the value education would not be intended to create values but to awaken them to rich tradition of values, they have already in their blood and to regulate their intelligence, inclinations and imaginations in consonance with those values. A society can survive even if beliefs are various but unless there is a common system of values it cannot cohere more over proliferation of beliefs. In the absence of unifying cord of common values it leads to total anarchy and societal disintegration. Values are considered potent determinants of human behaviour. They set the tone of behaviour patterns and help to make sense out of discrete human behaviour. Values are influenced by the changing philosophical ideologies, sociological perspectives, social conditions and political doctrinaires. In modern India there has been a revolutionary change in the field of values due to many factors in addition to the influence of the western culture, industrialisation, modernisation, urbanisation and other traditional values. However a conflict between traditional values and modern values is inevitable. It is also necessary to make efforts to present a new scheme of values in a clear and complete form. One of the chief tasks of the contemporary Indian society is to bring about a synthesis of the traditional social values with the modern social values.

The present situation in India demands such a system of education which apart from strengthening national unit must strengthen social solidarity through meaningful and purposeful constructive value education by adopting the interdisciplinary approach. Life will then be no more a mess or hell. To live in a blissful consciousness let us join our hand to create the value-oriented climate so that the values can be acquired and the interests of our scientists, scholars and students are awakened, their enthusiasm is fired to transverse the vast unknown region of the inner, no less than outer world.

Values are attributes that spring from the sublimity of soul. They are sentiments, like love, that involve mind, feeling and will, which are strong, deep and enduring. They are like truth, reflections of reality that are not obstructed by any kind of prejudice. They are attitudes that confer on man humanism and peace. Values in short, the moral personality of an individual. They enhance the finer side of his potential. They act as the conscience of the community which when kindled with torch of learning would make him realise the responsibility he owes to the society. Values are concepts that conserve life, that comfort life, that promote life and protect life. They foster peace, order, dignity, beauty, grace and delight. Values in one word are the divine side of man.

'True Education means building of character', Mahatma Gandhi said. And in the words of Einstein—"The most important human endeavour is the striving for morality in our actions. Our inner balance and even our very existence depend on it. Only morality in our actions can give beauty and dignity to life.

The values can be taught through lectures, text books, epics and several co-curricular activities and the young mind does catch them. But when he finds elders and leaders in the society the other way, he suffers from moral conflicts. There conflicts may turn him into a morally debased person or a hypocrite who bears the façade of morality and does everything immoral. Still others may justify immorality vehemently. Very few may come out as crusaders for establishment of moral values. They suffer, and in their suffering they are condemned as 'maladjusted'. Evidently the blame should laid on the elders and leaders of society, for they not provide good examples to the youngsters when they try to test the tenets of their moral values. At least here example is better than percept. If morality cannot be caught, it also cannot be taught.

Values not only help a man in self-evaluation, but also in self-drive. An educated man without values has thought which never flow into action. Values impart significance to life and meaning to death without values, life becomes a series of meaningless events, and death a shattering experience.

Education is inseparable from value oriented education. Such an education consists of four main features. It is a man-making and character-building process; it is the training of mind, body and soul; it is the quest for those nobler aims that integrate culture and technology, it is the hunt for that goal which liberates man from fear, inertia, ignorance and superstition. Real education should combine science and ethics. It should excite a passionate hunger for truth. It should aim at perfection and excellence. It should become an instrument of social change and national development. It should move towards humanism, liberalism and universalism. It should cut across all narrow barriers that divide man and man. It should help man reach his destiny, which is aristocracy of intellect and sublimity of soul.

Education is an extremely delicate subject, and long term planning in education requires utilisation of the results of decades of thought and experimentation. One of the abiding concerns in the field of education is that of value education. All though it is talked about much, there is little that is done about it. History and culture confirms that the individual, the social and the religious groups always pass on to the young their values and views about what is right and what is wrong. It is impossible for families and human groups to function as effective and progressive units without this transmission of morals. The vital connection among people, societies and world as a whole would be severed without the education of the moral and human values. To sustain the universal relationship man has valued with great importance the education of values to the young.

Values are norms for living whether social or individual. No one not even a thief or a dacoit can possibly live without values. The choice among value could be between accepting values or not. The acceptance by the individuals of values can be adjudged only against the social acceptance. Since societies are rarely uniform, the values would also differ accordingly. The question of value crisis is as old as human race itself.

One of the challenges in this field is how to make value education effective and interesting to the modern youth. Present days curriculum is full of content of techno informative data, consisting of facts, figures, theories and laws etc. The present day youth with its potential and goodwill to learn, concentrates on learning only the academic subjects. This poses a challenge to those concerned with the all-round development of the pupil through education.

The teacher and the taught represent the two most significant components of the educational subsystem. Over the decades the class base of both has changed. The teachers in increasing numbers, are drawn from groups which do not have a tradition of literacy and learning. The social background and cultural orientations of the learners and their instructors pose a new set of problems to the educational process.

With all the complexities of life, society and education, the question rising in our minds is— "Are we educating for life, for reality or merely for awards of marks and certificates?" Education, in other words, must initiate a life long process of developmental exploration, within its two dimensions, one of the self and the second of the community and the wider society. This emphasises the need for value education.

At the other end of the pendulum, there is a strong and persistent view that one of the worst crises of our times is the crisis of character and that since character is built largely during childhood and youth, it should be a special responsibility of schools and colleges to provide education for character building. In recent times, value education has also come to be advocated for increased cultivation of values, morals and ethics among students.

There are also deeper considerations which call for value education. The ideal of liberty, equality and fraternity have come to be acknowledged as the ideals of rational society. These ideals have also come to be accepted in the constitutions of various nations. In India, these ideals have been explicitly stated in the preamble of the Constitution. In addition, the Indian Constitution had declared under Art. 51A certain fundamental duties, which underline among other things, the pursuit of noble ideas which inspired our national struggle for freedom, promotion of harmony and the spirit of common brotherhood, and the development of the scientific temper, humanism, spirit of enquiry and reform, and striving towards excellence in all spheres of individual and collective activity.

## Value Education – Past and Present

In the history of human civilisation, India has been subjected to lot of transformation as a result of many foreign invasions. Many cultural sub-groups changed the ways of living, thought and values of India. A glance of philosophical, historical, political and social aspects revealed that there was a major shift of value orientation from ancient past to present modern day.

### *Past*

Ancient India was rich in its spiritual and intellectual attainment. The main objective of education, in the past, was to equip the child for spiritual and moral life. In spite of many differences among different schools of Indian philosophy, all of them realised the man's many-sided nature and viewed man basically as a spiritual being. Indian educational thought has been considered to be not only intellectual pursuit but also a practical aid to show the right way of living. Ancient Indian educational thought helped man to understand the values and ideal of life and also made him to live in accordance with them.

### *The Present*

As a result of scientific and technological development, man has shifted his way of living from spiritual to materialistic approach. This shift has taken place gradually consequent to alien cultural influence. Gone are the days of gurukulas, where education was mostly spiritual and pupil belonged to teacher but not to an institution or school. But in modern days pupil belong to a school where teacher teaches pupils by classes and not as individuals with their uniqueness and differences.

With this backdrop here arises the need to know the meaning of values, importance of values in education, the need of value based education so that accordingly plans, proposals and methodologies can be widely developed and adopted by the educationists who have a deep concern towards this serious problem which is taking a critical shape day by day.

### What are Values?

Value literally means something that has a price, something precious, dear and worthwhile, hence something one is ready to suffer and sacrifice for. In other words values are a set of principles or standards of behaviour. In the words of John Dewey, "The value means primarily to prize, to esteem, to appraise and to estimate. It means the act of achieving something, holding it and also the act of passing judgement upon the nature and amounts of values as compared with something else."

Values are regarded desirable, important and held in high esteem by a particular society in which a person lives. Thus values give meaning and strength to a person's character by occupying a central place in his life. Values reflect one's personal attitudes and judgements, decisions and choices, behaviour and relationships, dreams and vision. They influence our thoughts, feelings and actions. They guide us to do the right things.

Values are the guiding principles of life which are conducive to all-round development. They give direction and firmness to life and bring joy, satisfaction and peace to life. Values are like the rails that keep a train on the track and help it move smoothly, quickly and with direction. They bring quality to life.

People, especially the young, are confused about their values and value system. They are facing value conflicts and dilemmas. This is mainly due to the dramatic and far reaching socio-cultural and political changes that are taking place in our country and in other parts of the world. Besides these, there is a breakdown of traditional values without proper replacement, lack of adequate role models, conflicting ideologies and double standards practised by people in position of power and influence. At the same time there is awareness among people about human dignity and rights, a greater concern for the poor and the oppressed, the sick and the old.

In the light of all these it is but natural that people are confused about proper and sound values. Many young people openly reject some of the traditional values and question dogmatic beliefs held sacred for centuries. Often it happens that such people do not find replacements for the traditional values and hence a kind of vacuum is created in their life. This is not desirable because in the absence of values, they have no principle or foundation on the basis of which they can face life situations, make choices and decisions. A life without proper values will become chaotic and disastrous. It will be a boat without rudder. To guide our life in the right path and to embellish our behaviour with good qualities, we need values.

From the above discussion, a broad and simple working concept of value could be evolved. Any human activity, thought or idea, feeling, sentiment or emotion which could promote self-development of the individual in all its dimensions could be said to constitute a value. The other complementary function of a value is that it should also contribute to the welfare of the larger social units such as the family, the community and the nation of which the individual is a member.

## Condition of the Present Society

We are creating generation of youth who are neither Indian nor western, with the result that they find themselves caught in a dilemma. We are building a purely economic society which seeks security in money and not in concern for social harmony and social well-being. This has become so widespread that it is at the root of many other evils like injustice, exploitation and violence.

It is a fact that religious fundamentalism, language and regional chauvinism, caste and communal feelings are raising their ugly heads and threatening the very existence of our nation.

Religion when practised in its true spirit makes for high character. But we have allowed it to make us selfish and negligent. We can see evidence of this even when people go to temples to offer worship. They would readily break a queue to have 'darshan' of the deity and create chaos.

We try our best to build private property and protect but we have little regard for public property which in fact is the property of all of us. This is the hallmark of a person whose conduct is not based on an appreciation of values. The primary values we have to develop to promote the strength and greatness of our society, our country, is to show an abiding concern for others.

Increasing concern is expressed everyday about the general deterioration in values in contemporary social life. It is always the acts of immorality that have shown the signs of unhappiness, hatred, jealously, enmity in the society. The same immorality is exhibited in the form of mass copying, indiscipline and turmoil in the educational institutions. There is a need for appropriate educational action to meet these challenges. The National Educational Policy (1986) has started "The growing concern over the erosion of essential values and an increasing cynicism in society has brought to focus the need for readjustments in the curriculum in order to make education a forceful tool for the cultivation of the social and moral values."

Education is supposed to be a powerful instruments of change and progressive improvement of human behaviour, but in local practice, it is doing very little to cultivate moral and spiritual values in our youths and to promote national consciousness in the country.

The instances of deteriorating standards of human conduct and neglect of social concern are quite numerous in the recent history of our country in all walks of national life, and the prevailing crisis of character has stirred nationwide interest of people a critical appraisal of the school practices and our educational programme. The quality of teachers and teaching methods and school products has now become a subject of the deepest national concern.

In the aforesaid context of the National situation, the formal and informal agencies of Education-School and Home in particular, assure the position of supreme significance. It is the schools and homes where the primary attitudes and value towards social relationships and personal conduct get fixed and carried all through life. Unless the values we cherish are clearly defined and strongly and assiduously developed by all the agencies of Education, any educational system, no matter how elaborate or expensive, will fail in its purpose. A vigorous programme of value oriented education, therefore is the need of the hour.

An educationist has rightly observed : "The erosion of values is now a national phenomenon, so complex and gigantic that a more balanced school curriculum, new learning materials and competent teachers alone can do very little. The task of national development is massive and urgent and no worthwhile achievement is possible without an upsurge of ethical values, of cleanliness, of public life instead of the prevailing cynicism and corruption and genuine practice of moral and spiritual values by all sections of our society."

**Values in the Present Educational System**

The present educational system, however through its mechanistic approach has added to human psychological problems which through its formal and non-formal agencies has developed an apparatus of structures, content and processes to transmit knowledge without much concern or commitment to respond to the task of communicating and inculcating values necessary for creating ideological climate congenial to appreciation of cultural heritage and taking pride in one's history and having confidence in human capabilities to overcome material, social, religious and spiritual problems of living.

Our educational institutions at all levels are struggling hard for their survival and continuance under serious problems and it is felt that such problems as exist in these institutions, are a reflection of common problems in the community. The students of today have been deprived of their roots with the result that they have failed, by and large, to identify themselves with the community.

The dismal picture of our educational institutions and of social living within them and outside, makes it obligatory to redefine the role of education and employ it for building up an hierarchy of attitudes, values and moral standards.

Education does not consist merely in the imparting of text book knowledge or preparing the child for a career, however important these goals are. The moral and spiritual foundation on which we structure our educational system alone can mould the future destiny of India. As

Swami Vivekananda said, "We need a man making and nation building education."

In present circumstances we are passing through a period of value crisis. Truly speaking, the present life pattern in India is full of discontent and frustration due to prevalent designs of corruption, exploitation, hypocrisy and what not. It is due to loss of human values. Our former Prime Minister, Indira Gandhi had rightly remarked that we must stop the erosion of values here and now in order to build a strong nation, our teachers can play a vital role in this. The researcher is of the opinion that the teacher is not to be regarded as a merely communicator of knowledge, he has to be a director of learning, a transmitter of culture and values, a social engineer and an architect of the future society.

The report of a joint study on moral education conducted by the UNESCO and the National Institute for Educational Research, Japan has clearly indicated that the future of mankind depends largely upon the kind of education children are receiving all over the world today. Besides, making them better informed and more skilled, education must endeavour to help them become better human beings. In addition to education for knowing and education for doing children shall also receive education for becoming.

This is high time to take into consideration the deteriorating conditions of value system in order to inculcate basic human values such as truth, justice, peace, love, cooperation, law, non-violence, etc. in younger generation. Science and Technology have brought about vast and fast changes in all aspects of human life. We must not lose our bearing in this fast current. We must stand on our own and try to gear our educational system to cater to the vital needs of growing children specially in the area of values.

An educational system, if it really aims at making human life peaceful and happy, ought to pay undeviated attention, special care and constant focus on thoughts, motives, attitudes, actions and finally values in the life of human beings.

The present educational system, with all its complexities and intricacies has proved to be deficient in so far as it neglects, or does not give the deserving importance to values in human life. Thus, human sufferings and sorrows are for ever on the increase in spite of the phenomenal explosion of knowledge. Values have become the neglected lot in the current educational system and consequently has almost lost its value.

"Education without vision is waste; education without value is crime; education without mission is burden." Education in our life enables us to become comfortable and to look after our family well. But so far as the social progress is concerned, value based education is an unavoidable necessity. "A nation with atomic power is not a strong nation, but a nation with people with strong character is indeed a strong nation. If a nation is to be strong, then the character of the people needs to be elevated. For this purpose, value based education is an indispensable device."

Education has become a highly explosive subject to evoke general criticism. In theory, education is supposed to be a powerful instrument of change and progressive improvement of human behaviour, but in actual practice, it is doing very little to cultivate moral and spiritual values in our youths and to promote national consciousness in the country. The gulf between the content and purposes of education continues to be as wide as before despite several attempts in the past to reform the system and strengthen our new democracy.

The instances of deteriorating standards of human conduct and neglect of social concern are quite numerous in the recent history of our country in all walks of national life, and the prevailing crisis of character has stirred nation-wide interest of people for a critical appraisal of the school practices and our educational programme. The quality of teachers and teaching schools and school products has now become a subject of the deepest national concern.

## Higher Education and Values

Education is an extremely delicate subject, and long term planning in education requires utilisation of the results of decades of thought and experimentation. What will be the nature of the problems of higher education in the coming years and how we shall deal with these problems deserves utmost consideration of all those who have devoted themselves to the promotion of education and welfare of the youth.

Among various issues in higher education, the issue of value education is perhaps the most difficult. The main reason is that there is a doubt prevalent whether there is at all good case for value education, and whether value education is relevant to higher education. There is a trend of thought according to which, values are relative and subjective in character. It is therefore argued that individuals should be left to themselves to determine their own value systems and that educational institutions should confine themselves only to those studies where objective knowledge is determinable. There is also a view that value systems stem from religious beliefs and since these beliefs are dogmatic in character, they conflict with the demands of reason and hence they should have no place in education, where one of the chief objective is to cultivate among students pursuit of rational and scientific temper. According to some educationists, values, even if they are determinable, cannot be taught, and for this reason also, it is argued that there is no rationale to bring value education within the purview of schools and universities.

At the other end, there is a strong and persistent view that one of the worst crisis of our times is the crisis of character and since character is built largely during childhood and youth, it should be a special responsibility of schools and colleges to provide education for character building. According to some, education is incomplete, if it ignores the development of character. It is even argued that education is mis-education if it does not inspire commitment to values. In recent times, value education has also come to be advocated by those who are troubled by the prospects of nuclear war and eventual annihilation of the human race. They want education where the value of peace is enhanced. There are also thinkers who maintain that the contemporary world is moving rapidly towards the growing interchange and oneness and that this, in turn, demands increasing cultivation of the values of cooperation, mutuality and harmony which can be best fostered through education. Harmony of man and nature is also being recently emphasised in the context of the global concern for the protection of environment. The recent disturbing trend of increasing drug addiction among the youth also tends to retreat the necessity of education that promotes among youth the values of self control, discipline and right habits of thought and conduct. There is also universal declaration of human rights, and we have now a recent declaration of the right of a child search for perfection is too, becoming more and insistent, and this entails increasing stress on the dimension of values and value education.

At a still deeper level, there is a feeling that human life is becoming more and more complex and that this complexity can be controlled and mastered only if there is a radical change of human nature, which, in turn, implies certain attention to the issues of moral and spiritual transformation. True education, as it is affirmed, is man making education, and this implies that education should have essentially not only a dimension of value education but all its aspects should stem from and aim at value education.

## Present Trends in Value Education

The educational system of a country is the product of a vạriety of factors that characterise the life of a people value education in the form of character development is a potent force to be combined within the field of education. The impact of value education as an integral part of the educational system of a country is so profound that it can be conceived as an effective tool, by which the "Culture Pattern" of people is preserved and their national destiny is achieved.

The story of Indian education is as old as the story of Indian civilisation which can be traced back to four thousand years or more during which period India evolved different systems of education is accordance with the changing needs of the times.

Value oriented education assumes special significance in the Indian context today, where young men and women are passing through a crisis of character.

The world we live in has reached a point of moral and spiritual inability. We have to face the problem of how to acquire the new spiritual energies needed to remake the world and all the individuals must put their concerted efforts in this direction. Through education we have stuffed our children's minds with facts and neglected to teach them how to live. The kind of unpleasant incidents happenings daily in our institutions reveal the utter failure and futility of those values we preach. It would be more effective if the teachers explored less and acted more realistically and consistently. Values are better demonstrated by living them than by preaching them.

There are several values quite implicit in our educational institutions providing higher education which require a good deal of rethinking. The stress that is given to competition, the importance given to winning prizes, standing first in class, defeating others, are all trends that may create a lot of frustration within and aggressiveness towards others, making people selfish. There is a need for replacing these values with those which upheld, "The good of one as the good of all." Achievement should not bring about, as it does today, a feeling of competency that one is superior and the others are inferior. We see double standards in behaviour at all levels. What we preach we seldom practice.

The variety and diversities we see in caste, creed, colour and culture in a vast and complex nation like India, demands a new sense of commitment on the part of the institutions and teachers in developing the right kind of teaching-learning programmes that will help students learn and grow to be mature and responsible adults who can be the assets in the nation building process.

Since moral education is the preparation of individuals for participation and acceptance of social responsibilities and obligations, morality of constraints and acceptance of social responsibilities and obligations, morality of constraints and inhibitions is not productive. In the context of the socio-political climate prevalent in the country, we need a system of education which besides strengthening democracy, national unity and solidarity should further strengthen democracy as a form of government and a way of life. The roots of life are nourished in the soil of moral and spiritual values. There can perhaps never be a time when one can take for granted the moral and spiritual well being of a nation. It has to be promoted through a conscious and deliberate educational effort in the field of moral and spiritual values.

## Why is Value Education Indispensable?

One of the abiding concerns in the field of education is that of value education. Although it is talked about much, there is little that is done about it. In a fast changing society due to powerful materialistic influences on life, revolution brought out by science and technology and hunger for power, we find that eternal human values like freedom, justice, peace, dignity of human being, sacrifice, brotherhood, duty consciousness, worship of work, non-violence, peaceful co-existence etc. have been reined day by day. Mistrust, injustice, exploitation, selfishness, hatred due to caste, creed, race and religion, chauvinism, nationalism, just for positions, property and power are presently wrecking the society. Total social fibre is cracking. The world is divided into the poor and the rich, powerful and powerless, exploited and exploiters, criminals and law abiding, high caste and low caste and so on.

Surprisingly, value adoring humble people are thrown out in a race by the fast growing valueless individuals, groups, communities and even nations. Another change that is observed at the end of this century that people or groups who still cherish value based conduct or behaviour are thrown in oblivion. New generation is rapidly loosing faith in the values which are considered, throughout ages, necessary for self-attainment, meaningful for life, peaceful for existence and development or progress through mutual cooperation. For immediate gains, material pleasures and individual greed, all human values are sacrificed without a smallest scar on the consciousness of man. In other words, the society, at the end of the century, is entering into a jungle law by adopting the newly established value system, i.e. survival of the fittest with political instability, social insecurity and economic uncertainty, what we see the development of mental slums in various sections of the society.

Amongst all the living, human life is the most evolved creation in the universe. The excellency or superiority of human life as compared to other living beings can be easily identified. A man's life has to possess some meaning beyond mere self preservation for existence. In case of other creatures their life is manipulated by man in his own interest. Man is the only such unique creation in this universe who is under certain parameters free to make his own destiny. Now if man has to make his destiny, the question of values comes up. He has, naturally, to think what are to be the guiding stars of his life process. Values (the guiding stars) for man, which provide the prime motivating force behind his thought, emotion and action, have to be moral and spiritual life of man, has to be such as brings peace, progress and welfare of both, the individual and the society. And this is probably why the modern society is worried about what is called value-deterioration or value crisis from which they are suffering.

## Challenge Before Education

Now it has become necessary to change objectives and content of education at levels right from pre-primary to university, giving due weightage to value systems. India's rich heritage, with vast canvas of knowledge and enlightenment and philosophy of values, have been relegated to the backseat and materialistic desire based behaviour pattern has taken driver's seat. This order needs to be reversed. In a changed context of scientific and technological advancements, entire system of education needs to be redefined, reorganised, reshaped and recharged. Now at the threshold of the new millennium, it is a challenge before educationists to draw a programme to prepare a student to understand, adopt and hire the values for rich, satisfactory and meaningful individual and social life. Mere worldly knowledge will make his mind rich, but soul still remains poor. We, therefore, have to plan for making a full man. This become more essential in the era of liberalisation with additional dimension of human rights.

"Now India needs second revolution, a revolution of values and education has to be the vehicles of this revolution."

13

# Moral Values and Education

S.R. BHATT

The quest for values and the attainment thereof constitute the very core of human life. There is an innate necessity in man, caused by his finitude and imperfection, to participate in the process of value-realization. That is why consciously or unconsciously value-concepts, value discriminations and value judgements feature prominently in his life.

The nature of man is such as to urge him to participate in the fullness of life, to be receptive of the significant and to lie open to whatever has meaning and value. But the question is, how can he know what is valuable in life and how can he realise the same? Any process of value-realization presupposes knowledge, will, effort and appropriate resources. And it is not an easy task, though not an impossible one, to acquire all the four. That is why, more often than not, value-aspirations and value-pursuits remain mere utopian dreams. This is the travesty of human life that he is mostly ignorant of this *summum bonum* and even if he may know what he ought to aspire for, he is circumscribed and handicapped in realising the same.

II

The present day world is passing through value-crisis which has pervaded all the spheres of value-realization. This is more alarming in the moral sphere. A deeper penetration into the problem may reveal the fact that the present day tendency of value-negativism is a resultant phenomenon of the loss of faith in the moral order. The inevitable consequence of such a circumstance has been the disappearance of moral virtues and spread of vices. In order to resolve the value crisis both prevention and cure are to be employed simultaneously. For this purpose the system of education, which is the most important and foundation at sphere of value-realization, needs to be given serious and meaningful attention.

## III

A psychological analysis of the pathological cases of norm-violation may bring home to us as to why vice is due to. There seems to be four main types of factor which occasion vice, viz., badness, madness, rashness and folly, we may explain each of these as follows:

(i) In some individuals vices are innate and intrinsic. They possess some such psycho-ontological qualities of 'tamas' that they cannot do otherwise except evil. Like Nero they may rejoice in doing evil or, like Duryodhana they may possess the ability to recognise evil and yet may not desist from doing it. They may know the good and yet may lack the will to do it.

(ii) In some cases man's evil deeds result from some sort of mental disease. Such people are not bad but only mad. They do not have the discriminating capacity and the power to foresee the consequences.

(iii) Some people, who are neither bad nor mad, tend to do evil not voluntarily, but because they are compelled to do so by the circumstances.

(iv) But in most cases evil is due to ignorance or folly. Socrates has rightly opined that virtue is knowledge and vice is ignorance. The Upanisads also aver the same, '*Avidyaya mrtyumtirtva vidyaya amrtmasnute*'. The evil doer does not know the evilness of his act, otherwise he would not have acted that way. So it is the lack of knowledge, and not voluntary sinfulness that issues in bad conduct.

The ratio of the first group is quite negligible and these people can be checked only by constant vigilance and can be deterred by strict punishment. It is difficult to reform them through education or legislation. Those who fall under the second group should be sent to reformatories and treated psychologically. The people coming under the third category can be brought on the track by proper training and by improving their lot. The fourth group, which as we have said, is the largest one, definitely requires a moral and spiritual training. The last three groups provide the rationale for moral and spiritual instruction.

Here, it may be argued that the sinner knows that it is bad to commit sin and yet he does it. So it is not ignorance but wilfulness which is the cause of evil. But in such a view the connotation of knowledge is misconceived. By knowledge we do not mean mere intellectual awareness. It stands for wisdom which consists in a practical sense of values. This is the purport of the poet saint Kabirdas when he laments, *"pothi padhi padhi jagda mua pandita bhaya na koya"*. So a true knowledge must tell upon one's behaviour. There is no gap between genuine knowing and its doing. When the Gita declares that *'yoga karmasu kaushlam'* or the Mahabharat reasserts that *'yah kriyavan sa panditah'*, it is contended that there should be a conjunction of true knowledge and goodwill. One who knows the good cannot stop exercising it. When Duryodhana boasted that he knows the dharma his knowledge was only superficial and not genuine. To know good and not to act upto it is a psychological impossibility. A true knowledge of the good must stir the whole being of man. It must be noetic or illuminating. This is what the Jaina thinkers have declared when they said that *samyak jnana* inevitably leads to *samyak caritra*. Socrates and Jesus Christ also meant the same when they said that 'the sinner does not really know what the good is'.

From the above it is evident that wisdom or true knowledge is not devoid of action, that it consists in a practical sense of values, and that virtue being knowledge can be taught and acquired. What is needed is to train the individual in a proper way to know the good and to act upto it. And here comes the role of education. This is what is called the education theory of goodness.

The Indian seers were all the while conscious of this fact that a man devoid of wisdom can never be noble. '*Dhiya vihino nahi yati dhanyatam*'. So the task of education must be to inculcate in him wisdom or a practical sense of values. The words *samskara*, *samskrti*, *dvija*, *sattva-samshuddhi*, *visuddhatma*, *nididhyasan* etc. used for education which was imparted in those days. The famous convocation address in the Taittiriya Upanisad starts with "*Satyam Vada*," "*Dharmam cara*" etc. All this emphasises that wisdom can be acquired by him alone who has moral and spiritual qualifications. At present under the western influence we concentrate only on the measures (*pramanas*) of knowledge and do not take into consideration the most significant part played by the measure of knowledge (*premature*). The various instruments of knowledge like sound sense organs, sharp intellect, adequate methodology, etc. do play their role in the acquisition of knowledge, but more important is the knower who uses these instruments. The moral and spiritual character of the knower influence his capacity of acquiring the truth. The five-fold gradation of knowledge in the Jain epistemology, the *sadhama catustaya* of the Advaita Vedanta, the *sadhana saptaka* of Ramanuja's philosophy etc. all evince the more certain is knowledge.

The upshot of the above consideration is that the prime need of the day is a re-orientation of our nature of education. Instead of being mere job-oriented let it also be character-oriented. If our system of education fails to turn over a man into a man it has outlived its utility and is more than a dead weight.

# 14

# Good Education

R.P. SINGH

Universally people would like to offer to their children 'good' education. But what this 'good' is defied precise definition. In fact the concept and nature of this 'good' is so complex that one is afraid to attempt giving its precise meaning. We all know that all concepts have relative meanings. This relativity is such that no sooner do we start talking about any degree of precision it tends to degenerate into either even more relative or an individual standpoint. Therefore, it is no surprise that what we call 'good' here is also a very relative term. What one may regard as his 'good' may turn out to be another's non-good.

We shall therefore attempt here to illustrate the point. Let us say that A regards teaching of a scripture 'good'. But then scriptures differ and so do their definitions. The logic of religious faith is beyond discussion. Consequently one has no hope of even arriving at a universally acceptable religious definition of either good or not-so good. We could not apply this logic to teaching a secular subject like political, science or history. We come across here too similar difficulties as we had encountered in the case of defining a 'good' scripture. The 'good of all' which is a major political philosophy remains vague in asmuch as that neither do we know that 'good' is nor do understand the meaning of 'all'. This term 'all' covers normally 'all healthy, intelligent and honest citizens'. But the society does not consist of only healthy, intelligent and honest people. We shall face a very difficult situation if we prescribed the same regimen for the healthy and the unhealthy alike or for the intelligent and the unintelligent etc. The problem shall get further complicated if we made certain adjustments in the regimen to suit basic individual requirements. This would mean that the term 'all' needs certain modifications. The question then shall arise who is entitled to making these modifications. Is it an individual, a select group of individuals or the state. We shall be hard put to stating anyone of the above is beyond reproach or question. None has the ability whether in a group or as an individual to define such requirements. Because those who may have the ability may not be asked to do so and the one's who are not so competent may always be in a position to define these requirements.

Let us come back to stating that while 'good' education is a universally accepted goal of a society, its nature is both vague and indefinite. We must agree that to achieve something vague or indefinite is decidedly not the best way of going about attempting to bringing it about. We like to have precise definitions of concepts. Unfortunately this precision is elusive.

Why do we then say that 'good' education is a desirable goal if we are not able to define it? Is 'good' an idea, an aggregate of 'ideas' or the idealisation of something very real. It would appear that good is an idea. But it is an idea which is generally cherished by at least majority of people they may not know it in its exactness but they are aware that it is something positive as opposed to something negative. Indeed as an opposite of the absolutely undersirable 'bad', this 'good' is a positive and very desirable goal. In its contrast the 'good' shines against the 'bad'. It seems to have the splendour of the refulgent sun in whose warmth and light one may want to bathe during chilly, wintry days. Therefore the 'good' is what is not 'bad' but since both terms are equally vague, we are no wiser now than we were before.

In concrete terms a school run by Dr. Higgins for pickpockets may fall under the category of 'bad' education. It is bad because our laws do not allow such a school to flourish and even if a degree were granted by such a school, no one will really recognize that degree for the fear of social disapproval. Yet, surprisingly there are candidates willing to seek admission in Dr. Higgins school. This school may not offer a degree for recognition whether social or otherwise, but this education is decidedly very useful and comes in hardly for an individual's requirement. Pick-pocketing as a trade or skill may make us raise our eyebrows of disapproval together with a school on our face, but as a vocation it can be a worthwhile pursuit because besides the deftness of fingers it calls up on one's talent to distinguish a moneyed man from a pauper, a foolish person from a clever one, a gullible and less sharp from its very opposite. These powers of discrimination indeed are very desirable attributes and if this power alone distinguishes a man then a philosopher and a pickpocket are alike or at par in this ability. In other words even for a pickpocket which as a trade may be reprehensible and socially unwelcome, the attributes like that of the sense of discrimination, deftness of fingers, sharpness of vision, an ability to identify the source of profit, etc. are as desirable here as in any other vocation, be it law or medicine or judiciary. Even in the worse of trades therefore there are possibilities of training an individual in the best of the desirable attributes.

This then is not all. If all have a right to education then each individual has a right to choose the trade or vocation provided it is offered somewhere. If a school on the main road is good, no one could say that school in the interior of a bylane is bad only because of its location or situation. A physical location is not the only criterion of a 'desirable' school or an institution. If a trade offers the possibilities of earning one's livelihood, pickpocketing could also be a trade even though not socially recognised. It is socially disapproved because it contravenes a law. But then if non-contravention of the law alone is a single criterion of a desirable trade then do we not have doctors and lawyers who are as good pickpockets as any other. They use their skills to trick the gullible, foolish, and needy people to pocket their money for the job neglected or not done at all. The society may appoint a body of lawyers or doctors to oversee such behaviour and then such professionals out of their vocations. I personally find the trade of a lawyer or a doctor or a pickpocket alike in so many ways and unless caught they could all pass as gentlemen. What distinguishes 'good' from bad in such a case is that unless the law puts one in a spot, on the face of it all these practices are above board.

Surely very few will agree with the logic I have put forward. But 'bad' and 'good' are terms which are not the subjects of 'logic' but of axiology and ethics. Therefore, even if no one catches me, I should be able to catch myself; even if no one reproaches me, I should reproach myself; even if no one corrects me, I should correct myself. In other words the definition of 'good' is as much external, society-dependent and value-laden as it is personal, conscience-dependent and self-activating. What is perhaps being meant by 'good' is that education which develops a sense of discrimination, a recognition of the good of all, and by doing all that which promotes social well-being and also which helps control one's greed and selfishness in the interest of others. This kind of education is really meant for one's own moral development and this morality is to be adjudged on the single criterion of public good. An upright individual is a welcome addition to any society and if numerically they were to exceed the others, a society as a whole will become better suited to live in.

Howsoever welcome this sort of conclusion may be and despite all the logic which goes in its favour, it is difficult to establish that moral development is a necessary condition of education. If all the educated (i.e., degree or diploma holders) people were also morally developed, that is, they were conscientious, considerable and well-meaning, most of the advanced societies would be free of vices they are currently infested with. There shall be peace and harmony all around us. The fact is otherwise. Highly learned societies where technology and science have reached unparalleled heights are not exactly models living. In certain cases it would appear that for their own prosperity such societies do not seem to hesitate to steal each others secrets, information, knowledge, skill etc. and would not find it morally reprehensible to sow seeds of dissension in such societies which appear to be developing or appear to be competing with them. In fact some of the most developed societies are known to justify their own 'good' as the 'good of all'. They sell wars so that their 'war' industries may run, they consume more so that they are estimated to be more developed, they preach a lifestyle which helps them market their wares. In brief, their education is 'good' education because it helps them remain at the top of economic ladder and it is of no consequence to them if they are not on top of the world in moral judgement and the well-being of the mankind.

Similarly, orthodox societies when they decided that what they believe in is the only good of all, and in their judgement it is their function to spread their message of peace and convince others of their basic depravity and ungodliness, acquire the same status as the most developed societies and their attitudes to a very large extent become identical. Just as the developed societies are convinced of their correctness, the orthodox societies feel equally justified in teaching the heathens a moral lesson or two. If in one society consumerism and exploitation of the weak appears desirable, in the other conversion or teaching a lesson to the unbelievers becomes their *raison d'etre.*

Surprisingly education *per se* does not promote one or the other view. Education is neutral to morality and helps no one to form any type of judgement unless curricula is so designed. When history starts glorifying national achievements or culture, when ones standard of living gets undue attention, the colouring of vision starts which when consolidated starts orchestrating a 'desirable' national goal. Moral education may be good education but decidedly no curricula seems to have been designed to achieve this goal and even if it were possible we will not find teachers for it or a state to curb its competitiveness, greed or self-justifying tendencies. The moral people do not appear to be either assertive or aggressive whereas both secular and non-secular people are. The aggression is part of one's desire to uphold one's point of view and also to see that others find that standpoint justified. The tragedy of moral man is that he/she is not really proselytising.

'Good' education may be a desirable goal but it is difficult to offer it and even if offered, it does not seem likely to make an individual moral or morality a saleable commodity. If one can be moral without any education the vehemence of propagation of morality through education is considerably chastened. So long 'good' education can be given outside of one's self-interest and without competition its desirability stands uncontested. The sovereignty of 'good' is vitiated no sooner our vision gets clouded by either self-interest or our righteousness to the utter exclusion of other's point of view. The self-interest could be qualified by one's status whether monetary or political or caste and therefore it tends to restrict the value of 'good'.

# 15

# Value Education: A New Dimension

T. VASANTAKUMAR

"Should institutions and enlightened individuals not get into an in-depth analysis to ensure that universally accepted values and norms continue to guide the path of younger generation?"

The question put forward by one of the eminent educationists deserves sharp focus in the present "Value Climate".

'Axiology' is the branch of knowledge which concentrates on the study of "values" and their nature.

In general, values are socially defined as desires and goals that are internalised through the process of conditioning, learning and socialising. It means the act of cherishing something, holding it dear and also the act of passing judgement upon the nature and amounts of values as compared with something else.

Actually they are the guiding principles of life which are conducive to one's physical, social and mental health. They influence our selection from available models, means and ends of action. In other words a well defined value system is a social end or goal in itself, a set of values accepted by an individual as the member of a group. The individual prizes that set of values and directs one's activities towards achieving it. It consists of well structured ethical code, moral commitment, spiritual conduct, philosophical foundation, social accountability, upward mobility of ideals and sense of belongingness. These values clearly differentiate '*Purusha*' from '*Pashu*'. These human values could be defined as follows:

> "Righteous conduct at physical level, Truth at the intellectual arena, Peace at emotional plane, Love at psychological stage and Tolerance at social interaction."

Values are not mere articulations of same nebulous, idealistic notions. They should be perceived in their respective dimensions. The fast process of Westernisation and psuedomodernisation compel our youth to ignore these value dimensions. This phenomenon has been resulted in the proliferation of negative values. The modern society clearly shows a growing tendency towards 'agnotism', that is ignorance of human values. In this context we encounter with the question "how to manage this hostile value climate?

In the words of Gautama Buddha, "All that is necessary for the evil to triumph is that noble men should do nothing." One has to introspect. Have we, the so called Academicians, consider this aspect of our profession seriously? Have we worked out modalities to infuse excellent value system in the society in our own way? Have we ever thought that the concepts like *Lokasangraha* or *Lokakalyana* could be patronised by way of teaching and learning process in the classroom situation? Is there any systematic attempt made to achieve this goal?

In the words of Vivekananda, "Education is the manifestation of the divine perfection already existing in man". In the process of such manifestation one has to consider certain constituent factors.

Smelser's "Values Added Theory" identifies six factors responsible for the modification in the collective behaviour. They are:

1. Structural conduciveness.
2. Structural strain.
3. Growth and spread of a generalised belief.
4. Precipitating factors.
5. Mobilisation of participants for actions.
6. Operation of social control.

This backdrop stresses that concern for the community and value education cannot be treated in isolation as we normally do.

As Radhakrishnan Commission Report on education puts it "What we need is not the imparting of instruction but the transmitting of instruction and also of vitality, the civilization of human heart. Our institutions should have simplicity and an atmosphere of concentration that permanently influences life."

Gandhiji meant the same when he made a mention of Education of head, heart and hand.

The New Education Policy (1986) envisages, "growing concern over the erosion of the essential values and increasing cynicism in society has brought to focus the need for the cultivation of social and moral values." This problem is considered in the larger and National background. Therefore it is further observed that in a "culturally plural society, education should foster universal and eternal values oriented towards the unity and integration of our people. Value Education should help eliminated obscurantism, religious fanaticism, violence and superstition".

It is also true that this end cannot be achieved by introducing new policies, new institutions or new courses.

As the very word "University" implies a sort of collective spirit, its collective responsibility to nurture the moral and ethical constitution of the future generation is well pronounced.

It is said that the "Values cannot be taught but caught from the environment". Is it possible to inculcate positive values in the present generation through University Education? Do we really subscribe to the opinion "Universities are the major controllers of the values system of any society?" We have to concentrate on exploring the possibilities of a university teacher of literature in inculcating a strong value structure in the minds of the students through the analysis and interpretation of a given text.

With this objective, *Yashodhara Charitta* by Janna (l2th Cent. A.D.) a work in Kannada, is identified as source material, to work out a model. The episode of Yashodhara is portrayed in our classical literature, with a number of deviations and variations. The work of Janna is based on *Yashodhara Charita* by Vadiraja in Sanskrit. Janna's work is not just Kannada version of the original, but it is an artistic recreation of the same. One can look into the text from two different angles. One is the relationship between Yashodhara and Amritamati and other is the purification of the 'Atmas' of Yashodhara and Chandramati by a rigorous process of undergoing a series of rebirths. The two major concepts involved here are infidelity and violence. The concepts of fidelity and non-violence are rated very high in Jain Dharma, as we are well aware of.

The content of the work in short, is as follows:

Yashodhara is the King of Ujjaini, Amritamati is his Queen. They are leading a very happy and contented life. The disaster comes in the form of a melodious voice. The sweet songs sung by a Mahut, fall on the ears of Queen Amritamati. She falls in love with that person. She fails to control her impulse and develops extra marital relationship with him. His name itself is Ashtavanka and his personality deserves that name. This physical *Vakrata* highly symbolises the *Manasika Vikriti* of Ashtavanka.

King Yashodhara comes to know the infidelity of Amritamati. He goes to his mother Chandramati. Being unable to reveal the flaw of Amritamati, he tells her that he had a very bad dream on the previous night. She insists on offering a cock made out of flour to Chankika Devi to pacify the bad spirits.

Yashodhara reluctantly obeys mother's order. When he cuts the head of that 'cock', a 'vyantara' comes out of it and crows harshly like a live cock. Yashodhara's confidence gets shattered due to these two incidents. He decides to go to exile and seek salvation.

Amritamati offers a send-off party to Chandramati and Yashodhara. Under this guise she feeds them with poisoned *laddoos* and eventually kills them.

The *Sankalpa Himsa* committed by the mother and son makes them sinners and by way of *Prayaschitt*a they undergo a number of births and sufferings. After this process of purification they bom in *Ishana Kalpa.*

It is inferred from the story that the "Value Map" of the text plots the following values:

1. Spiritual .................................. Non-violence.
2. Ethical ..................................... Fidelity
3. Intellectual ............................... *Dhriti.*
4. Moral ....................................... Nobility.
5. Biological ................................. Instincts.

The text contains certain negative values as well. It shows the value conflict, role conflict, value distortion and value devaluation.

## University Education and Values

As we know, teaching in a university set up does not follow any specific pedagogy or strategy. It utilises either lecture method *in toto* or in combination with discussion method. This phenomenon restores high level of responsibility on teachers. The age of the students is another feature of university education. A university student normally belongs to the age group of 19-24 years. The fact that the student acquires the maturity by this time implies that he or she possesses a well developed cognitive structure. This factor makes the teacher's task difficult one on the one hand, and sensitive one on the other.

The concept of non-violence is of utmost value in the present violence ridden society. The academic system should help our youth to develop an integrated personality which enables them to establish human connection with the society. In this context, a teacher can highlight the far-reaching effects of violence on human being.

In the text, Yashodhara and Chandramati commit neither any act of violence nor do harm to any living organ. But the purity of the spirit is lost since they are consciously involved in the act of violence. This 'passive participation' itself makes the rigorous process of purification inevitable for them. The teacher can utilise verbal communication techniques to illuminate the value of observing Ahimsa in real life situation in all the three spheres, *Kaya, Vacha* and *Manasa.*

This context provides with an opportunity for the teacher to encourage the students to have a comparative outlook towards the collapse of any value at the mental level. We encounter with a similar incident in the episode of Renuka in Mahabharata. Renuka does not commit any sin at the physical level, but wishes to have conjugal relationship with Kartaveeryarjuna who is not her husband. This mere thought deprives her of *Pativratya* and she is accused of disloyalty to her husband, Jamadgani. She is beheaded for this breach of trust. This need not be elaborated further since all of us are familiar with this episode.

Amritamati's context cannot be fitted into the framework of such a simple structured interpretation.

The teacher has to keep his bias at bay in order to deal with such a complex and sensitive theme. The total objectivity would be lost if the teacher allows even the slightest domination of chauvinism—either of sex or of caste.

Janna allows *Sahrdayas* to have their own parameters of value judgement. Amritamati would not be at fault if one looks at her with purely humanitarian perception. If one rates universal values like sacrifice, collective spirit, moral bondage, sense of responsibility and understanding very highly, her flaw becomes grave in nature. In that case it does not deserve any sort of excuse. The teacher can leave the question open end, paving the way for 'n' number of interpretations in the minds of the students.

One would like to emphasise two aspects here. First one is how a teacher can deal with the negative values in a class-room situation without passing value judgement or without constructing a normative value design. Second one is how to nurture the value cognition of a target group, achieving the change in its behaviour in a desired way.

So in conclusion, the paradigm of value judgement is to be decided upon, by the content of the given text irrespective of its nature. In spite of the presence of subjective element, certain degree of objectivity is to be maintained in the process of value judgement. Otherwise the concept of "*Sadharaneekarana*" will not have any propriety in a work of art, because "*Sambandha Vishesha Sweekara* or *Parihara*" is to be distanced with to have "*Rasanubhuti*".

16

# Values for University Teachers: *Need of the Hour*

P. N. MUTHIAH

## Values—A Synthetic View

From time to time the universities are charged with failure to teach moral and ethical values. Some people believe that absence of moral teachings in educational institutions is the major cause for the erosion of social values.

No educational institution could operate for a day without attention to moral values. The teachers inevitably must be concerned about conveying to students concept of honesty, honour, truth, loyalty, charity, law and order and of all other virtues and characteristics upon which a civilized society depends. They are disseminated to the students by explanation, illustration, discussion of history, current affairs, literature and by the handling of behaviour problems and human relations. Values of the good, the true, and beautiful are more likely to be accepted and adopted by students if they have teachers who are motivated by those values and whom they like and respect.

Values motivate behaviour toward others. In other words the values the person holds affect his relationships. Teaching develops a multitude of situations in which students decide on the basis of their values how to behave towards each other. Teaching provides so well and so frequently for interpersonal and intergroup action.

When teachers think about values that govern their personal and professional lives, they must consider the following principles.

Values are that which an individual or community believe to be good or worthwhile. They may be objects, qualities or ideas. Values are motivating forces. They give a sense of purpose and direction to life. The Indian teachers have a set of traditional secular values which are in doldrums now. Values which operate among university teachers give superior status to them.

In order to function effectively, the university must be cognizant of the values of society. Values are of importance to the university because they are the central beliefs of individuals and society which set the general limits of thoughts and behaviour. Values are beliefs about what is desirable and what is undesirable.

Values reflect the culture of a society and are widely shared by the members of the culture. If the individual accepts a value for him, it may become a goal for him.

The term value refers to anything that the members of a society consider worthwhile to pursue and attain. It can be a desirable object, state or condition. There are some value orientations that are shared by almost everyone. Most of us value freedom, democracy and individualism.

## Values and University Teachers Problems

Three aspects of value system among Indian University Teachers can be explored: Material success, Individualism and Work.

The Indians especially university teachers give profound emphasis on material success. They have a craze for limitless things, house, luxurious items, clothes for every occasion, electronic gadgets and appliances. They want more money to travel extensively and entertain extravagantly. In short, they define success in terms of materialistic terms. The teachers who do not achieve success in these terms are considered failures by both themselves and by other people.

The relationship between materialism and the problems in higher education can be analysed. It is a confirmed truth among academic circles that achievement of wealth and material success is a highly esteemed goal, but different teachers, because of their circumstances adopt different orientations to the goal. The university teachers can be classified as conformists, innovators, ritualists, retreatists and rebels.

*Conformists:* They have two basic qualities, such teachers accept the positive value on materialism and believe that it is good to be wealthy and affluent. Second they achieve material success using the approved means—hard work, publishing books, undertaking tuitions, wise investments in share markets and prudent savings. In a nutshell conformists accept materialism as a goal and use socially acceptable means to achieve it.

*Innovators*: Innovators accept positive value on material success but reject working hard. They choose their own method of achieving material success. In other words they use deviant means to achieve the legitimate ends. For instance, the teachers may evade income tax payment, gambling, betting on race horses, purchasing lottery tickets, undertaking projects with the sole aim of producing false vouchers etc. They seek innovative measures to achieve material success.

*Ritualists*: These teachers have lost the hope of achieving material success, but they continue to engage in teaching ritualistically, i.e. they are not inclined to acquire knowledge in the latest development in their disciplines. They adopt the traditional way of teaching. They are conservatives and tradition bound. They are endowed with outmoded fund of knowledge and disseminate them.

*Retreatists*: The teachers who belong to this category have also lost hope of achieving material success. In a sense they are like rutualists. These teachers no longer engage in goal oriented behaviour. They are in real sense academic drop-outs. They withdraw socially, are chronic smokers, drunkards, and have a tendency to switch over their jobs and institutions. In short they are least inclined in academic pursuits and they are totally indifferent towards their profession for the sake of salary.

*Rebels*: These teachers reject the concept of material success and rebel against very education system itself. As a result, it go against the norms and standards stipulated by the university. They are threat to the very educational system itself.

**Individualism**

Teachers too have self. The society strongly believes in individuals. Every teacher wants to be independent, responsible and self-respecting. In other words the teachers want to be academically free and thereby enhance their self. Unfortunately the university system which is inherently colonial oriented does not offer academic freedom which they want.

Their problems are left unnoticed and the administration fails to take into account the suitable remedial measures. Consequently the personality of the university teachers is disillusioned.

*Work*: From Indian cultural point of view teaching is a noble profession. Traditionally, the Teacher-Guru is placed next to God. But now because of industrialization, urbanization, cultural diffusion, and cultural integration the teachers are dedicated to work and most of the teachers perceive work as a means for buying higher standard of living. Many of the teachers have problems in their work. For instance, the university, being a higher centre for learning expects every teacher to be research oriented.

Beside research pursuits, a teacher is expected to be a good teacher with high academic calibre. Unfortunately many teachers are good in teaching and bad in research and *vice versa*. Because of lacunae in ideal blending of research and teaching, many teachers have role conflicts.

As a result the teachers experience job dissatisfaction. Their teaching is essentially routine and boring. So they suffer severe disillusionment when they realize that they will not be rated high and fail to get recognition.

The discussion of values centres round the three main issues:

1. Whether values are subjective or objective?
2. Whether they are changing or constant?
3. Whether there are hierarchies of values?

This article does not attempt to answer these questions. It is mainly concerned with the fact what types of values an university teacher should have?

Generally we can discern individual values and social values. There is a close correlation between individual and social values. Individual value differs from person to person and social value differs from society to society. Individual values reflect in society. The university teacher values may be summarised as follows. This list is only indicative and not exhaustive.

*Intellectual values*: The teacher should strive towards higher standards of attainments. He should be inspired by the spirit of inquiry and develop love for knowledge. He should fight against evils like intellectual passivity, ignorance and shallow knowledge.

*Moral values*: The teacher must create a desire for achievement of goodness. He should fight against moral and social evils. This can be done by being a model himself.

*Spiritual values*: The moral and spiritual values are often interlinked. High regard for academic freedom and civil liberty will be the spiritual ideas of a teacher who has confidence in shaping his destiny.

*Aesthetic values*: The appreciation of beauty reflects the aesthetic values. The teacher should have well developed tastes for what is beautiful. There are ideals of balance, harmony, and fitness which serve as values to be grown.

*Economic values*: Economic values may instil in person a sense of belongingness to the profession and will develop courage, honesty, truthfulness and perseverance.

*Religious value*: This value is real, relevant and socially important. India being a secular society, religious value poses a problem to a teacher. There is no harm if the teacher helps the students to acquire knowledge about religion so that he can reflect upon those ideals in classrooms.

*Cultural value*: The uniqueness of humankind is that it has culture. This culture is transmitted from generation to generation by parents and teachers. So the teacher's values get modified through cultural factors and education becomes instrument for cultural transmission. So the teacher should bring about improvements in what has been accepted by traditional culture. A teacher should have cultural identity.

## Conclusion

Now a question arises whether these values are to be taught or caught? The demotiovated teachers should be taught about the different values. This is called orientation. It cannot be said that, all the teachers are deviod of all values. Many university teachers have some values regarding culture, religion and economics. These teachers' values should be enhanced with conscious effort. Academic Staff Colleges can play a vital role in this regard. This is called integration.

In a nutshell a demand survey to identify the needs of the university teachers can be undertaken and their values can be surveyed and accordingly new values can be infused in them by means of lectures, providing experiences and exercises. This can be called integration of existing values into new ones.

17

# Modernity *vs* Value Oriented Education

J.P.N. MISHRA AND ANIL DHAR

Misconceptual notion of modernity and rapid growth of science and technology and subsequent industrialization have caused a great threat and danger to our morals and values. In the changed social set-up, our definitions of good morals' stand questioned. Old values seem to be lost but new are yet to be evolved and brought into practice and as such we can term the present era as 'transitional' one. According to W. Durent "These, then, are the varied causes of our moral change. It is in terms of their transit from farms and houses to factories and city streets, that we must understand the generation which so boisterously replace us. Their lives and problems are new and different. The Industrial Revolution has them in its grip and transforms their customs, their garb, their work, their religion, and their conduct; to judge them in terms of the old code is as unfair and unhistorical as to force upon them the corsets and bustles, the beards and boots of our ancient days."[1]

Several scientific inventions have also their role in challenging our old and traditional, but very useful values to a great extent. It is difficult to compile a list of changes brought about by these scientific inventions in our daily life. Similarly it is not easy to compile a comprehensive list of 'good' or bad actions of mankind—as moment after moment a man is confronted with new situations and problems. It is said that the actions, speech or thoughts which are motivated by or admixed with perverted emotions, called sex-lust, anger, greed, attachment, arrogance and sloth or lethargy (*Kama, Krodha, Lobha, Moha, Mada* and *Matsar*), called six sins, enemies of a man (*shadripu*).

Now-a-days newspapers, magazines and other news media are flooded with reports of crime, murder, agitation and eve-teasing. We read in newspapers of several such occurrences where the landlord and tenants have exchange of hot words leading to stabbing. Disputes between father and son, between wife and husband, between son-in-law and father-in-law are not rare. For want of endurance in one's dealings all family ties are broken, people leave homes for ever out of disgust and anger. All these occurrences indicate deterioration in our ethical standards, loss of our moral and social values accruing great loss to families, society and the nation at large.

It is widely believed that modernization is responsible for the crisis in values to a large extent. The reasons are not far to seek. Modernization involves industrialization, use of modern and advanced techniques in agriculture and all other spheres of life and work. With modernization comes better communication that bridge the gap not only between places but also between people. The result is that the traditional values of a small closely knit society which demands cooperation, loyalty, dependence on relations, neighbours get eroded and people tend to ignore these values. They become more self-reliant and self-centred which makes men more impersonal in their conduct. Had the modern society consciously tried to retain or imbibe the values of self-discipline in individuals. Self-discipline teaches one not only to value one's rights but to respect those of others equally.

Incidents of violence and destruction are increasingly reported. People take a certain irrational pleasure in discriminating between their faith and that of others and resort to communal riots. Strikes and lock-outs are becoming more and more common. Rarely does a man read a newspaper without coming across an item reporting strikes, lock-outs and crimes. What few people realise is that strikes and lock-outs hamper the economic development and advancement of society. The total loss which the people suffer due to such anti-social and anti-national movement runs into millions of rupees each year. The major cause of such incidents is the loss of self-discipline in the average human-being, who is taken in by antinationalistic elements and ignores his duty and harms the economy and thus society in general.

Lack of self-discipline has led to an ignorance of one's values and duty which has adversely affected the structure of the society in the modern day. Indian society has also been affected by this trend and the process of disintegration of our basic social infrastructure and system is discernible all-around. The hazards we now face are far more dimensional than we had ever imagined earlier. Nietzsche says "When a tree grows up to heaven, its roots reach down to hell." We must not therefore be overwhelmed by the failure of many individuals to maintain self-discipline. Instead, we must try to make them understand, as Dr. Radhakrishnan wrote that "Error is not crime, it is only youth, immaturity, which can be controlled and corrected with the right effort."

This process of disintegration of values would soon prove to be disastrous, unless a conscious effort is made to reverse this trend and to inculcate in one and all, a spirit of discipline of the self. This cannot be done by simple physical processes. The initiation of the spirit and the awakening of the mind are the two modes of efficiently implanting values such as discipline of the self in people in all walks of life. Whittier has written, "When faith is lost, when honour dies, the man is dead."

Thus any man can be called a man as long as he guards his values, as soon as they are gone, the very reason for his being called 'Human' vanishes and he is lowered to the level of animals. Let every man realise that his values are guarded by his conscience and that these are not derived by nature or from reason, but by custom.

They crying need of the modern society is to inculcate the spirit of self-discipline and the values that follows from it, in every individual, from his childhood, through proper education and training.

Without values, the world could not be a place worth living in and, unfortunately, it is heading towards this state due to the present crisis. If no person is interested in life, in the true sense of the word, then we can carry on without bothering at present. But it is obviously not so.

The trend towards modernity is being grossly misinterpreted to mean removal of values. We, witness very often, a total lack of regard for the values of others amongst people. Today, very few people care for or have respect for the age old values—like freedom, belief, sincerity and self-respect, the right to work and freely express one's views. While we cherish individually these vines for ourselves, we show a total disregard for similar values of others. Very rarely are people found making true sacrifices for the benefit of others, selfishness fills the atmosphere and corruption and other immoral acts reflect totally corrupted values. Individuals take pleasure in misleading the stranger. Most people today refrain from or at least avoid taking so-called 'unnecessary' responsibilities making themselves morally accountable for some particular things, whether done by one or the other. Very few people are disciplined enough to fulfil and do justice to such responsibilities and duties, though they heartfully partake of all benefits they can derive from taking that responsibility.

Man is gradually losing the sense of duty which played a prominent role in human behaviour until recently. Today all of us know that men not only ignore their duty, but also do just the opposite of what they are supposed to be doing. The glaring and repugnant example of the assassination of our Ex-P.M. Smt. Indira Gandhi, by two of her own body-guards, brings forth a reflection on the state of affairs. To be sure, no one could imagine earlier that two men could kill the Prime Minister, that too a lady, 66 years of age, whom they were paid to guard. Again, the spy-ring unearthed in the Prime Minister's Secretariat had been leaking out vital secrets to other nations. Such are the traitors who have been completely taken in by this crisis, the crisis of values. Hundreds of examples reflect this. A single day of observation of the pattern of life in any city would reflect this too. The prevalence of a crisis is confirmed. That it has spread to all spheres is indicated by incidents all around us.

India used to take pride in its rich traditions, art, culture, ideals and teachings of great personalities. But all these seem to be dormant and polluted to a large extent. Our media like cinema, T.V., Video etc. could not provide desired nourishment to our culture, on the contrary, due to commercial type of competition in gaining cheap popularity and material benefits, they have polluted our culture. Except a very few they could not provide healthy and nourishing environment to our culture. Because of this cultural pollution, our work-culture that have affected the sincerity and devotion to duty in various walks of life. That is why we have to come across with the incidents referred to above. Self-discipline and self-restraint lack very much in the society. Discipline is regarded as a check on one's liberty or ceiling on one's right. In these circumstances, it is crying need of the day that inner discipline is generated among the new generation. It should not be a sort of imposition. Moreover, it should be more and more practical. In education, therefore, we need a genuine faith in the existence of moral principles which are capable of effective application. This application requires to be in the social-settings. John Dewey, a noted educationist, has rightly remarked on this point. According to him, "To isolate the formal relationship of citizenship from the whole system of relations with which it is actually interwoven; to suppose that there is some one particular study or mode of treatment which can make the child a good citizen; to suppose, in other words, that a good citizen is anything more than a thoroughly efficient and serviceable member of society, one with all his powers of body and mind under control, is a hampering superstition which, it is hoped, may soon disappear from education discussion."[2]

Therefore, in moral education indoctrination should be avoided and defects of value clarification and cognitive developmentalism should be removed by the educators, before they plan any strategy of value-oriented education. It will be possible when the teacher avoids imposing his own judgements or ideals and approving or disapproving the moral judgement of the individuals under his or her charge.

Our, experiences have revealed that moralizing has not served the purpose in the past nor it is going to serve the purpose in the present. It becomes mechanical process, neither it touches heart nor provide any scope for intellectual exercise, on the contrary, it becomes problematic specially when the question of indoctrination is raised. As values are governed by meta-ethical relativism, moralizing appears to be a form of indoctrination. Therefore, the strategy of Value-oriented Education is a challenge for teachers, parents and the society at large.

Acharya Mahapragya, a Jain Saint, a great philosopher and thinker, has formulated a system of education, known as *Science of Living*. It may prove to be a successful way of value-oriented education.

## Science of Living: A Positive Strategy of Value Oriented Education

If it is true and comprehensive value orientation education, complete education, it must aim at enhancing and developing the positive attitudes and inhibiting and subduing the negative one's. Science of living is the synthesis of the ancient wisdom and modern scientific knowledge for developing integrated personality through attitudinal change and behavioural modification. It is a positive resolve for creating a healthy human society—healthy in all respects—physically, mentally and emotionally. It bears and cherish the values. Although it is a technique of training the people from all walks of life in awakening their innate powers, its widest and most useful application is in the field of schools, college and university education to impart the training of value education.

## The Curriculum

The science of living is a training course based on scientific principles. It comprises various branches of learning drawn from both modern and ancient sciences as well as humanities. The main emphasis is on practical training and regular practice. The theoretical studies, however, are also included in the programme mainly in order to comprehend the fundamental theories and hypotheses made use in the practical exercises. The main constituents of the programme are:

***A—Theory***

1. *Philosophy*—To give the philosophical background of the programme.
2. *Sociology*—To review the sociological link of ourselves.
3. *Education*—To understand the basic concepts of the education both ancient and modern.
4. *Human Anatomy and Physiology*—To brief about the basic structure and fundamental functions of our body systems.
5. *Psychology and Psychotherapy*—To acquire the first hand knowledge of normal and abnormal human psychology along with various methods of psychotherapies.
6. *Ecology*—To understand the fundamental principles of ecological coexistence of all living beings.
7. *Non-violence and Healing Techniques*—To acquaint with basic concepts of various ancient as well as modern non-invasive, non-violent healing techniques.
8. *Meditation and Yoga*—To understand basic principles of meditation and yoga.

***B—Practical***

1. *Yogic Exercises*—To give exercise to all muscles and external muscular organs.
2. *Yogic Asanas*—To give exercise to deep seated organs and to control their activity.
3. *Pranayama*—Conscious control and regulation of breath.
4. *Kayotsarga*—Relaxation with self-awareness, with the help of autosuggestion.
5. *Preksha Meditation*—It is based on the principle of concentration on perception, and that too of internal phenomenon of consciousness and not that of external objects.

It is a techniques of seeing one's inner self. It comprises the following components as in ascending order—

(i) Perception of breathing,
(ii) Internal Trip through Spinal cord,
(iii) Perception of body,
(iv) Perception of Psychic Centres,
(v) Perception of Psychic Colours,
(vi) Contemplation.

The moral and spiritual values may be inculcated by the regular practice of contemplation.

## REFERENCES

1. N.L. Gupta (1983). *Value Education: Theory and Practice*, and W. Durent: *The Mansions of Philosophy*, our Changing Morals.
2. J. Dewey (1959). *Moral Principles in Education*, Philosophical Library, New York.

18

# Valuing Professional Growth:

*Image, Intent and Initiatives*

MULK RAJ CHILANA

## Need for Today

The National Policy on Education (NPE, 1986) and the Programme of Action for educational development in the country has laid great stress on the need for an effective teacher. The policy has given predominant consideration to the social status of the teacher and the need for academic inputs to upgrade the quality of teacher education both at pre-service and in-service levels. In fact, the major national goal in education emerges to be improvement of quality in education. To achieve this avowed objective, the predominant wherewithal appears to be enhancing teacher effectiveness. Recommendations of the Pay Commission for Teachers resulting in implementation of the new pay scales have given enough consideration to this need. The new initiatives in teacher education have also taken ample care to ensure that professional growth of teachers is given due attention. The District Institutes of Education and Training (DIETs) are entrusted with the responsibility of providing multifarious services to elementary schools including in-service education and training of teachers. Likewise Colleges of Teacher Education (CTEs) and Institutes of Advance Study in Education (IASEs) will take care of secondary school teachers. The gigantic Programme for Massive Orientation of School Teachers (PMOST) has already taken care to communicate the major messages of the New Educational Policy in the country. The policy has also highlighted the need for teacher participation and decentralisation. Decentralisation of education implies more control to all types of institutions. Need for trying innovative approaches has also been given due emphasis. All these points of view need not only a competent teacher but a teacher who grows continuously as per needs of the different roles he is required to play.

## Not Teaching Alone

Another reason why there is a need for teachers to grow every moment is that the functions of a teacher today and in the time to come are not limited to merely teaching in the classroom. A teacher is now responsible more for arranging the learning opportunities and even for promoting learning to learn. Thus, besides being instructor, he is a facilitator. He has to take care that everything in the class environments is used for development and growth of children. He has also to play the role of a motivator because of significance of motivation in education of children. In order to effectively play his role, he must be possessing skills of a communicator. This skill will help him to discharge his function more effectively. He has also to perform the job of an organiser so that learning arrangements made by him have wholesome effect on the children. His role as manager extends the classroom situations as he is required to provide community-based experiences to the children. In the role of a developer, the teacher of today is concerned with having relevant curriculum for every child. He has also to develop appropriate teaching aids to have effective communication. As evaluator, his job is not only to evaluate learning of children but also, his own performance and indicate all plans and skills visualized to achieve the objectives.

## An Authoritative View

It would be pertinent to list the view of authorities in education on teacher efficiency, teacher competence and teacher effectiveness which are essential ingredients of a growing teacher. According to C. Wood, "The Teacher efficiency is the degree of success of a teacher in performing essential and other duties specified in his context and demand by the nature of his position". Biddle is of the view that "Teacher effectiveness points to the effect of a teacher in a given classroom situation." These experts view the role of a teacher in the classroom. His position in the classroom requires inculcation of understanding among the young children. The other duties of the teacher include helping the parents and society to realize the significance of educating the next generation. The teacher is also supposed to serve as a link between the children and school management including the 'Departments of Education' at different levels. Flanders and Simons view the task from another angle. "Teacher effectiveness is an area of research which is concerned with relationship between the characteristics of teachers, teaching acts and their effects on the educational outcomes of classroom teaching." According to Medley "Teacher Effectiveness refers to results of a teacher and the amount of progress of pupils in order to achieve the specified goal of education." Thus, teacher effectiveness concerns the abilities of teacher to promote learning in students. These points of view indicate different aspects of teacher effectiveness, for example, effects of teaching, competence in teaching, ability to communicate, leading pupils towards further progress, achieving better effects of teaching and achievements goals of education.

The above views of the acknowledged authorities indicate different types of qualities which a teacher should possess, such as, understanding of children, spirit of cooperation, kindness, width of experiences, interest in work, manners, sense of humour, spirit of impartiality and love for the profession. A good teacher must also have the quality of inspiring students. Their professional training must also equip teachers for democratic behaviour, ability to judge and competence to learn from all situations. This will help to provide conducive environments in the school for free exchange of experiences among staff members. Above all, this would highlight the need for understanding the significance of the worth of every individual. Effective teachers also show emotional stability, favourable attitude to environments, better adjustment in profession and democratic, attitude in their dealing. Physical health of the teacher is also important. Thus, a closer look at the qualities of teacher will show categories of teacher qualities like, personal qualities, professional qualities, instructional qualities and qualities of human relations.

## Enhancement Through INSET

The characteristics and qualities of growing teachers, as mentioned above, may be enhanced through their effective in-service education and training (INSET).

It would be helpful, if some of such qualities are inherited and innate among the teachers. But, in any case, these characteristics can be developed.

These learned behaviours, learned feelings and learned skills may be developed through appropriate in-service education and training programme. If these characteristics are inculcated during in-service education programme, they can continue to stay with teachers, if the school principals are successful in supporting and creating school ethos for their positive treatment The in-service teacher education programme at the level of District Institutes of Education and Training (DIETs), Colleges of Teacher Education (CTEs), and Institutes of Advance Study in Education (IASEs) may help in developing professional development programmes which may create better understanding of the profession. These programmes may also lead to content enrichment. Likewise pedagogic skills like instructional and communication abilities may also be developed. Another significant aspect which may help a teacher grow continuously is the area of human relations. This will also include creation of awareness for international cooperation. The area of personality development is perhaps the most important aspect because a teacher must know his weaknesses and strengths if he is interested in the development of his personality. So the in-service teacher education programme at all levels should devote themselves to this important aspect of personality development of the teacher.

19

# Typologies of Values for Teachers

SHYAMANAND SINGH

---

The 'value' refers in its most general sense to what is good, desirable, and worthwhile. In an objective sense, it refers to things, activities, persons or experiences of individuals or groups that are deemed good. In a more subjective sense, it refers to personal or group preferences from among a number of possibilities. The concept of values differs from knowledge in that it has a normative element (things and actions are judged according to some norm) in addition to a cognitive element. 'Value' is a broader term than 'morals' since it includes not only moral values (moral goodness and moral badness) but aesthetic, cultural, educational, political and economic aspects as well. No sharp distinction, however, should be made between moral values and these other values, since moral judgements are often included within aesthetic, educational, political and economic concerns. Values are also considered as ideology propounded by different philosophers in different time, place and context.

## The Concept of Values

Values are the concern of many academic disciplines. The longest and most sustained treatment of values has come from philosophers, beginning with Greek philosophy and extending to such modern philosophies as positivism, existentialism, phenomenology and Marxism. Early philosophies emphasised the objectivity of values as something established in the very nature of things. In addition, values were seen by some to be of transcendent origin, rooted in the very nature of God or in God's will. More recent philosophies have paid more attention to the subjective element in values, i.e. the role of persons and cultures in the creation of values. Facts from the social sciences have forced philosophers to deal with the relativity of values within and the across cultures.

An important philosophic distinction is made between instructional values (means values) and intrinsic values (ends values). The former are means to worthwhile ends, while the latter designate what appear to be the ultimate values of the majority of persons. Suggested as ends values are survival, health, happiness, friendship, wisdom, freedom, self-respect and a sense of meaning in life. For many individuals religious values such as love of God and love of others are considered the highest human values. Although people differ on the hierarchy and interrelationships of these values, it appears that such values are sought within and across cultures. It represents values of particular class at a particular point and viewing the things from particular position in a prevailing system of social relations.

Philosophers have proposed different theories of grounds for determining whether things are good, desirable and worthwhile. These theories tend to take one ultimate value and attempt to connect all other values with it. Hedonism contends the view that pleasure or happiness is the good, the goal of all persons, something all should strive for, and the ultimate criterion by which values are determined. Utilitarianism sees that of value which promotes the good of the greatest number of people or the greatest possible balance of good over evil. Liberationism judges the value of things ultimately by their capacity to promote the greatest amount of human freedom. J.S. Mill said that, 'Government interference starves the development of some portion of the bodily or mental faculties when it deprives one from doing what one is inclined to do or from acting according to one's judgement to what is desirable.' A social contractualism based on fairness judges all human arrangements and experiences in their capacity to foster a basic fairness in society. The socialists like Jai Prakash Narayan considered the values of socialist society, in which all are workers of a classless society. It is a society in which human labour is not a subject of explanation with interest of private property. On which all wealth is truly national or common wealth, in which there are no unearned incomes and no large income disparities in which human life and progress are planned and where all live for all.

The over values is centred in the issue of the relativity *versus* universality of values. Logical positivists have denied all meaning to propositions about values. Many psychologists espouse determinism by which what people value is determined by biological or environmental causes. While some social scientists adhere to a theory of a core or consensus of values that keeps a society together, others, especially Marxists, take it for granted that values are determined by class and economic factors. From many anthropologists has come the conclusion that all standards and values are relative to the culture from which they are derived. These and other viewpoints cast doubt both on the objectivity of value and on the power of individuals to make or choose their own values. It may have elements of false consciousness of an established ruling class. But it cannot be called pure illusion as Mannheim called it. It may have an important 'scientific and realistic element' which could be treated according to the objective criterion of human experience as an addition to human knowledge.

## Need of Values

Values are norms for living whether social or individual. No one not even a thief or a beggar, can possibly live without values. The choice among values could be between good values and bad values. The goodness or badness of values can be adjudged only against the social acceptance. Since societies are rarely uniform, the values would also differ accordingly. The question of value crisis is as old as the human race itself. Socrates was asked 'How come the good always suffer and the bad prosper?' The whole story of job in the Bible though put differently is a description of values—the ultimate value of choice between Evil and Good. Suffering is supposed to accompany the choice of a good value. Therefore, almost all religions promise that those who shall suffer on earth shall be duly compensated in heaven and others penalised. Therefore, in religions it has been thought possible that a bad man shall enjoy himself, but this enjoyment is limited to his life span for eternally he shall be penalised and made to suffer. For those who do not believe in life hereafter or have no concept of Hell or Heaven, the life itself is the Ultimate truth.

Lord Buddha examined the nature of the feeling of pain. He found the great truth of the right path by following which people can get rid of pain. It is the eightfold path (i) right belief, (ii) right aspirations, (iii) right space, (iv) right conduct, (v) right mode of livelihood, (vi) right mindedness, (vii) right effort, (viii) right rapture. These are the way to self-restraint instead of self-mortification, to right action instead of inactivity. In the same period Lord Mahavira innovated Jainism and preached if a man is overcome by violent passions such as anger, self-consist greed or blind love, his soul is permeated by matter which binds it with fetters. His three-evils principles (trirbra) are right faith, right knowledge and right conduct. The Islamic ontology is characterised by the following principles. The oneness of and supremacy of God, universalisms and egalitarianism, the brotherhood of mankind, and the ascendancy of the moral dimension.

The concept of Satan in the Bible, Hell in Islam or Hinduism are added as elements of fear so that Man may not stray from the socially accepted norms. Social myths have their own degrees of importance. It is difficult to appreciate truth unless we know its meaning. The language of myths is therefore deliberately made symbolic. Symbols clarify the hidden meaning though they also confuse. One has sometimes to go beyond these symbols to derive real meanings.

## Typologies of Values

Society adopts certain norms of behaviour because it wishes to survive and perpetuate. In cases of deviations from these norms social disapproval can be expressed in the form of social abstractization. But their deviations from the norms are quite common and then each society keeps on reminding its members about the problems arising out of these deviations. Indeed each society has found for itself that these norms have to be so designed that all aspects of human life are adequately covered. Therefore, we have both typologies of norms and their gradations made available to us. For convenience of implementation and execution of these norms each society has its own functionaries.

The typologies of values may be:

1. *Scientific/Secular values*: For those societies where religion interferes with intellectual and social development. A recognisable body of scientific values are: (i) objectivity, (ii) rationality, (iii) integrity, (iv) impartiality and (v) excellence in academic matters.
2. *Human/Spiritual/Moral/Religious values:* Human values are righteous conduct at physical truth, at intellectual actions and peace, at emotional love, at psychic and non-violent actions, and at understanding level. Brotherhood, tolerance,

accommodation, compassion, firmness of principles and conscience are the other dimensions of human values. Religion can help an individual to derive some solace in life during times of adversity. It can also help maintain a socially cohesive life on the other.

3. *Political/Authoritative values*: Each political system has different sets of values. For example, in a dictatorship the cherished values are: conformism, obedience, humility, etc. In a democracy the values would be equality, freedom of speech and thought and similar values. In primitive societies we see total participation of communities and conformism to the words of kings or priests. In most cases the temporal and religious positions are interchangeable. In modern theocracies we can find these combinations made legal through dictates. However, democratic values with attributes like equality before law, freedom of expression, etc. come on top in this category.
4. *Aesthetic/Cultural values:* The aesthetic or cultural values like art, drama, music, dance, etc. are extensions of these inherent values.

Aesthetic values also have a long history of struggle. These values have not been universally similar. For example, music and dance are not acceptable in some religions. Arts are symbolic in nature, therefore a few societies censor them. In totalitarian societies art forms are used as media of protest, therefore they are closely watched. In other societies arts are used to reflect either the reality or the ideal and therefore they make the difference clear between what is desirable and what is not. The pursuit of arts, a value by itself, has no relationship with any particular art form.

It should be interesting to analyse a few of those values which concern humanity. Indians believe that *Dharma, Artha, Kama* and *Moksha* describe four important values of human life. These values may easily be regarded as eternal values. Each life derives its sustenance from some form of dharma, it must have some economic activity to earn one's livelihood, indulge in sex to procreate life and aim at salvation eventually. In brief, the human cycle consists of these four basic values, or socially acceptable norms of behaviour. A deviant in each case would create a problem and thus result in social disequilibirium. Consequently, disapproval must accompany approval. There are other values too: Truth, Beauty and Goodness, i.e. *Satya, Shiva* and *Sundar*. These are commonly believed to be the eternal values in all time and societies.

Dharma is generally believed to mean more than a mere religion. It covers the entire gamut of human life. So what one lives by is one's Dharma. For example, the Dharma of a king is to rule, the Dharma of a teacher is to teach, the policemen to enforce law, etc. Each individual has its Dharma. This Dharma is inviolable. We could think of a Dharma which a wine-seller has, or a jeweller has. They have a job to do. A wine-seller's Dharma is to sell wines whether or not his action may lead to someone's physical decay or destruction. Involved here is the other aspect of Dharma too. Wine-selling is an economic activity (*artha*), therefore it cannot be condemned.

## Values for Teachers

In the Indian education (Vidya) tradition, Vidya is of two kinds—*Baahya Vidya* and *Brahma Vidya. Baahya Vidya* concentrates on knowledge about outside world, i.e. secular knowledge, *Brahma Vidya* relates to the spiritual knowledge. The first type of knowledge is for jobs and second for the state of self-realization. The values education attempts to prepare students for the job as well as provide spiritual knowledge for the peaceful life and social system. It is rightly said 'Religion without science is blind and science without religion is lame'.

Education from the earliest schools to university level should be directed to all round development of human personality. The advance in value education largely depends on the values, qualifications and ability of the teaching staff. Teachers have to play essential role in the education of young people in a spirit of peace, justice, freedom, mutual respect and understanding of the universal values of all religions as Ashoka in Rock Edict XII proclaims. "One who reverences one's own religion and disaparages that of another from devotion to one's own religion, and to glorify it over all other religions does injure one's own religion most certainly. It is verified concord of religions that is meritorious. This imagination of Ashoka highlighted by the teachers, it will make national unity wider stronger and more lasting. Our government is secular but our culture is rooted in spiritual values. Secularism here does not mean irreligion or atheism or even stress on material comforts.

The Kothari Commission (1964-66) desired that values should be taught to students. Therefore the NPE 1986 has included, in the Policy, the parameters of the values themselves. They are as follows:

> "The growing concern over the erosion of essential values and an increasing cynicism in society has brought to focus the need for re-adjustments in the curriculum in order to make education a forceful tool for the cultivation of social and moral values."

In our culturally plural society, education should foster universal and eternal values, oriented towards the unity and integration of our people. Such value education should help eliminate obscurantism, religious fanaticism, violence, superstition and fatalism. The entire teaching community have a responsibility to see that these values should be inculcated among the students.

In the present post-modern world, teacher cannot teach human value in the classroom but through example and demonstration develop habits of scientific temper along with values of peace, love, courage, integrity and tolerance among our students. The preamble of the UNESCO states 'since wars begin in the minds of men, it is in the minds of men that the defences of peace must be constructed'. Teachers from primary level up to university are dealing with the young minds and they have inculcated in their minds to be free from fanaticism, religions hatred. Religion is a transforming experience with spiritual consciousness, belief and conduct, rites and ceremonies, dogmas, and authorities are subordinate to the art of self-discovery and contact with the divine and it is not for hatred with the followers of other religion. In this context the spirit of rationalism is relevant to modern age which is characterised by freedom of thought and faith, spirit of enquiry and scientific attitude. It can be developed through critical enquiry and rational approach. Like Buddha, teachers have to ask his disciples not to accept his teaching as a dogma or gospel. In the words of Lord Buddha:

> "Do not accept anything, because it is rumoured so, because it is the traditional belief, because the majority hold so, because it is found in the scriptures, because it is product of metaphysical argument and speculation, because of a superficial investigation of faiths, because it confirms with

> one's inclinations, because it is authoritative or because of the prestige value of your teacher."

These words of Buddha is the essence for the goals of higher education which provides students opportunity to reflect on the critical social, economic and cultural, moral and spiritual issues facing humanity. Its emphasis should be on the development of human values which are eternal and universal in character.

# 20

# Teacher's Attitude Towards Children

V.K. SABHARWAL

We know it only too well that the process of education is concerned with the development of childrens' personality. Yet we often forget that children taught by the same teacher respond to teaching in different manners as well as different measures. One would like to know the roots of these differences. Very often one finds that even identical twins exposed to the nearly similar, if not same, set of stimuli and sharing the same environment develop as quite different persons. One may become an engineer while the other may find salesmanship a soul-satisfying career.

Personality research has recently presented impressive evidence about environmental contribution to personality development. One may even take a position that the development of a child's personality is not so much determined by the inborn characteristics or by social conditions but by the specific attitude which he or she has towards the world of the people and the world of things. Let us extend this to teaching and learning and analyse what makes a teacher stand out in the classroom and influence his students in an unexpected, yet extraordinary manner.

During my talks to teachers, I often ask them to shut their eyes and recall faces of three or four persons who have influenced them in the most positive manner and who they consider unforgettable characters in their lives. I have invariably been told that at least one of the faces so happily recalled in their memories was that of a teacher. The other faces were of those who had influenced them in a manner similar to that of an ideal teacher, the teacher of their dreams. When questioned further, the most frequently cited answer is, "I was influenced by and drawn towards this teacher because of his/her concern for me." Yes, 'concern' is the secret of such amazing, almost mysteriously profound influence. This 'concern' for the students is also a result of one's attitudes to children in general and to students in particular.

A teacher too is a human being and his personality is also a two-layer personality, viz., the outer personality which is visible to others, and the inner personality which reflects and is nourished by his inner self. The teacher who has concern for his students is guided by his inner self. What influences shape this inner self—has been a peripheral issue in the changing priorities of educational research. Nevertheless it is an issue that teases us for an answer. Azarov (1988) describes four basic types of relationship that develop a teacher's inner self. These are:—

(a) his attitude towards the world of objects, towards science, technology, culture, and towards pedagogies proper and the means he employs;
(b) his attitude towards people, towards children... to those around him and especially those in trouble and experiencing difficult times;
(c) his attitude towards nature; and
(d) his attitude towards himself, his consciousness of himself as a teacher.

You must have noted that according to Azarov, the entire development of the teachers' inner self hinges upon his attitudes. Attitudes can thus be compared to that mysterious soil which determines the direction(s) as well as the limits of the evolving human personality.

Let us now shift our focus to effective teaching and try to analyse it. Teaching is admittedly a very complex task and effective teaching is believed to be so complex, multi-faceted and creative that it defies analysis. Researchers have nevertheless attempted to analyse effective teaching and have listed its chief features. Ryan and his colleagues (1960) observed the classroom performance of effective teachers and listed the following three bi-polar factors:

1. Warm and understanding *vs.* cold and aloof.
2. Organized and business-like *vs.* unplanned and slipshod.
3. Stimulating and imaginative *vs.* dull and routine.

Effective teachers were found to perform at the positive pole of each factor. It is easy to demonstrate that each of these factors can be analysed at a deeper level in terms of attitudes. 'Warm and understanding' *vs.* 'cold and aloof is essentially the result of a teacher's attitudes to other persons, especially one's students. Likewise, 'organized and business like' *vs.* 'unplanned and slipshod' is born of one's attitude to the task of teaching. And finally, 'stimulating and imaginative' *vs.* 'dull and routine' can be easily traced to the teacher's attitude to his subject as well as himself.

Going by the analogy that the taste of pudding lies in eating it, one can reasonably expect effective teaching to result in relatively greater gains in pupils' achievement. Rosenshine and Furst (1973) reviewed various studies of effective teaching and identified five teacher characteristics consistently related with relatively greater gains in pupils' achievement. The co-relates of effective teaching are as under:

1. Teacher is enthusiastic.
2. Teacher is business-like task-oriented.
3. Teacher is clear when presenting instructional content.
4. Teacher uses a variety of instructional materials and procedures.
5. Teacher provides opportunities for pupils to learn the instructional content.

Here too, each of these correlates can be reduced to attitudes: to one's self, one's task, one's teaching subject, and to people, especially one's students.

Most educators consider indirect teaching to be a better form of teaching than direct teaching. It is sobering to note that Flanders (1970) lists four indicators of indirect teaching and all of these are derived from and reflect the teacher's attitudes towards his students. Flanders' indices of direct teaching are reproduced below:

1. Teacher asks questions.
2. Teacher accepts pupils' feelings.
3. Teacher acknowledge pupils' ideas.
4. Teacher praises and encourages pupils.

Wragg and Wood (1984) conducted a study on pupils' view of teacher's classroom performance and found that young students are capable not only of discerning teachers' concern for their students but also of valuing it. Wragg and Wood asked student to imagine that the best teacher in the world has been sent to teach at their school. They were asked to describe how, in their view, this teacher would introduce himself herself; how she would be dressed and how they would expect their very first lesson with this teacher to be. Majority of the students expected this best teacher to introduce himself/herself by telling his/her name and something about his/her interests and hobbies. Most students felt that it did not matter much whether this teacher was dressed smartly or casually. And most students were of the opinion that this very best teacher in his/her first lesson would be understanding, friendly and firm.

Even routine classroom teaching provides irrefutable evidence that students highly value personal attention from teachers especially during moments when they are at a loss to decide what to do and who to turn to for help. Dozens of my students who have become full-fledged teachers after completing their pro-service training where eloquent about how a brief act of genuine personal attention to a student who was in dire need of it brought almost a sea of change in his/her attitude not only to the teacher but also to life in general and to the concerned student's self in particular. And these genuine personal encounters are real priceless rewards of our profession; these rewards far out-weigh the oft-heard hazards of the teaching profession.

Educational research has established that feelings are seldom acknowledged verbally in the classroom. It is nevertheless important that the teacher should be alive and responsive to the significant emotional content of what pupils are saying and doing as they are to the significant cognitive statements made by them (the pupils). In fact, 'intellectual distinction' and 'sympathetic understanding of the young people' are two essential qualities good teachers are expected to possess. According to Hutchinson and Young (1967), "a teacher should have the sort of mind that retains a smack of radicalism through life. This will enable him to keep one foot firmly planted in the future where the test of his work will lie. At the same time he needs a great measure of human understanding and sense of responsibility which will enable him to play his part in forming the character of the young people." It would however be worthwhile to remember that a teacher's influence upon his students is largely determined by the quality of his interaction with them. Most textbooks of educational psychology treat the teaching-learning process as a purely cognitive one. They disregard the affective moorings of human cognitive behaviour. This restricted view of the teaching-learning process reminds me of a fun poem which reads as follows:

> If you put your nose to the grindstone rough
> And keep it there just long enough
> You'll soon forget there are such things.
> As brooks that babble and birds that sing.
> Three things shall all your world compose
> Just you, the grindstone and your poor old nose.

While the apparent purpose of this poem is to humour the reader, it nevertheless has a message, and quite a serious one at that. For teachers who restrict their vision to just what they and their students do or observe, teaching may degenerate into a never-ending nose-grinding. But they who occasionally try to have a wholistic glimpse of what is happening in the classroom and link it with the purpose of education and its social context, the teaching-learning process assumes a much larger significance. In teaching as a nose-grinding activity, one's focus is on mere academic performance and one loses sight of the main task of education, i.e., of educating the human being. The result of such restricted perspective is a myopic vision of education in which education is regarded as the by-product of the efficient teaching of specific subjects. Unless education is viewed as whole process in which the learner's mind, heart and body are involved in an integrated manner, the learner's, personality will not be developed.

When we look at the changes in contemporary society, we discover that almost all social institutions are under streets. This is true of 'family' as well. Due to structural and functional changes during the recent past, the family is no longer capable of providing the comforting assurance it once provided to its members. The school should obviously provide children with necessary psychological support if they are to live positively and happily. If children are not to have a feeling of being adrift, if they are not to have a loss of a sense of purpose, if they are not to feel lonely, alienated and bitter, but frustrated as well, they must have a caring, a loving social environment to breathe and grow up in. As a child comes to realise himself, he unconsciously formulates his personal attitudes to different kinds of experience. His sense of belonging to other people is closely connected with the balance between his desires and his fears and the ways in which he comes to protect himself. All these things are inseparable from the love that envelopes him and if that seems to be lacking, there is a gap in the emotional covering that he needs for security. As a result of this, his vulnerability increases, his imagination may lead him astray or there may be some closing of his feelings which may take shape as hardened personality with strong streaks of bitterness and inexpensiveness. Teachers would do well to remember that a child's personality is not his own wilful creation, it is the combined result of the heredity and environment interacting incessantly through the individual organism. Students who appear backward or difficult, violent or aggressive withdrawn or sullen, should not automatically be blamed for it. The teacher too is an important part of the learner's social environment. The younger the learner, more fundamental the level at which he assimilate personal experience. Experience assimilated in such a manner during early life, including schooling, helps define the very purpose and meaning of being alive. A child coming from a broken home would have his miseries compounded if bullied in the school and/or rejected by the teacher. Therefore, one cannot sufficiently emphasise the lasting effects of the socio-psychological environment in which the child perceives himself to be and the manner in which he interacts with others (persons as well as objects) through it.

All theories of personality provide strong moorings for desirable educational practices, be it Erikson's, Freud's, Adiers' or Maslow's. Education has essentially a facilitative function in an individual's life. Education should help an individual to evolve his personality optimally to facilitate its best blossoming. Erikson's theory of critical stages in human development provides a good example of how a theory can promote and justify sound educational practice. Erikson postulates that both education as well as personality development are life-long processes; both continue in early infancy and continue right upto the evening of human life. Erikson of course does not equate 'education' with 'schooling', though 'schooling' is a legitimate part of 'education'. According to Erikson, there are eight critical periods or stages in the development of human personality and each of these is characterised by positive learning if the learning tasks related to it are successfully mastered, or negative learning if they are not. These stages are as follows:

| | *Stage* (+) | *Learning* (–) |
|---|---|---|
| 1. | Early infancy | trust *vs.* mistrust |
| 2. | Late infancy | autonomy *vs.* shame & doubt |

| | | |
|---|---|---|
| 3. | Early childhood | initiative *vs.* guilt |
| 4. | Middle childhood | competence *vs.* inferiority |
| 5. | Adolescence | identity *vs.* role-confusion |
| 6. | Early adulthood | intimacy *vs.* isolation |
| 7. | Middle adulthood | generativity *vs.* stagnation |
| 8. | Late adulthood | self-acceptance *vs.* despair |

Awareness about characteristics, demands and the learning tasks peculiar to each stage should shape not only the role of the teacher in the education of the young but also his attitude to them. Each of these stages is a step on the ladder. One has to master the lower stage and develop oneself through successfully negotiating the tasks corresponding to it before one can go on to the next stage. Otherwise the substandard infrastructure of earlier stages of the personality pyramid would take its toll in the superstructure as well. The growth of 'initiative', for example, has obvious implications for the kind of education essential to it. "Assuming that we want to encourage this initiative, assuming that we want children to develop their sense of independence, assuming that we want them to grow in responsibility, and to be capable of taking decisions and using their imagination, then the school or play group must give them opportunities to do these things" (Fontana, 1978, 27). Above all, it means having the right kind of relationship with children.

According to Erikson, the personality is formed by the end of adolescence. If the individual is successful in the self-discovery, if he negotiates successfully the crises of adolescence, he will be able to develop a clear and well-defined 'self-identity'; otherwise 'role-confusion' will be the result. The teacher who is keen to promote the learner's identity will invariably be tolerant and at the same time present clear and consistent standards which help the adolescent learner to understand the limits that exist in the new grown-up world that he is about to enter. At the same time, the teacher would not expect the same level of obedience and dependency from his students he did earlier when they were younger. The teacher would also give his students every reasonable opportunity to develop and to demonstrate his growing ability to take adult responsibility.

According to Peck (1990), "it is our commitment after conception which transforms us from biological into psychological parents". If commitment is the hallmark, the *sine qua non* of parental relationship, it can be easily understood why it should be the indispensable condition for attaining ideal relationship between the teacher and his students. It is through their willingness to extend themselves and empathise with their students that teachers grow. After all, learning from as well with their students is the sure way to experience the unique joy that our profession offers; it is indeed a pity that only a few are able to drink deep at this inexhaustible fountain of bliss.

In this context, the experience of those who underwent insensitive schooling and were nevertheless able to grow out of it and become humanistic teachers can be singularly revealing.

Here, for example, is Donald Clark ruminating over his early schooling:

> "When I think about what could have been going on all of those years and the needless agonies that could have been avoided, I would like to bring suit against those people who called themselves my teachers. But what court hears that kind of a case? I know that those teachers, poor creatures, were nothing more and nothing less than the sad products of the same sad 'educational' process" (Clark, 1971).

Mercifully, there is no acrimony, no malice in this reflection; instead we have sympathy here for the teachers who became an instrument for perpetuating the system that had 'dehumanised' them. If we were to apply this criterion of 'authentic concern' for the student as the basis for allowing persons to become teachers, we would not have enough of them to keep the wheels of the system moving. So many people already in this profession are not worthy of the title of 'teacher'. In most societies, teaching is taken as a job and not as a profession. Most teachers are content to function as 'babysitting wage earners'. Our society reflects 'mistrust' rather than 'trust'. Parents mistrust their children; siblings mistrust each other; teachers do not trust their students who in turn do not trust their colleagues. And all this in spite of our awareness that the building of trust is indispensable to enhance the quality of social as well as personal life. Trust enables people to open up to each other, leading to genuine mutual understanding and appreciation. What is far more important, trust is an essential ingredient in the growing-up process. A growing child needs a lot of trust through reassuring relationship to enable him to reach out into the world and to develop initiative, identity and self-confidence.

The task of developing proper attitude towards students provides a great challenge to teacher education. It has so far remained its despair because it involves extremely complex psychological process. The psychodynamics of developing genuine, attitude transformation remain largely mysterious even today. The bulk of educational as well as psychological research in this area has remained confined to "measurement of attitudes" with a little spill over to what has come to be known as "cognitive dissonance". The best precaution that can be taken in this regard is to select candidates for pro-service teacher education courses who have desirable attitudes towards children, the teaching profession and also their own selves. Incidentally, whatever changes in attitudes have to be attempted through teacher-education programmes should be strived for through pro-service education programmes. In-service education programmes are of relatively shorter duration, and only theoretical orientation about the nature and importance of teacher's attitudes can be presented through these programmes. Besides, it has been estimated that the "evaporation period" for in-service education programmes is at the most six months; the effects of even excellent in-service education programme cease to be available to most participant-teachers after this period. On the contrary, pro-service teacher education programmes have a duration of one to two years and consequently hold greater promise. Nevertheless, the importance of appropriate human material, especially in terms of intelligence, attitudes and communication skills, remains. The variety of attitudes tests used for selecting candidates for admission to these courses seem to have failed us by and large. In some states, percentage of aggregate marks at the qualifying examination is the sole criterion for admission. A string of reservation categories in addition to this makes a complete non-sense of the otherwise valid academic considerations that justify the use of a selection test battery. When one keeps in mind yet another two considerations, one a reality and the other myth about the teaching profession, one is likely to lose hope for any meaningful improvement in teacher education in India. The reality is that for most persons the teaching profession constitutes a residual vocational priority; one thinks of becoming a teacher only when one has been denied entry to other more lucrative and glamorous professions or jobs. The myth is that teaching is considered to be one of the least demanding, and soft jobs in which the remuneration is highly disproportionate to the amount of effort put in. One often hears parents recommending the teaching profession for girls because it would leave them with lots of free time to do justice to their responsibilities as parents. Nothing could be farther from truth. This myth needs to be exploded systematically, effectively and at the earliest. So far as the content of pro-service teacher-education programmes is concerned adequate weighting should be given to humanistic psychology. The writings of Carl Rogers, Erik Erikson, Abraham Maslow and other like-minded psychologists who have linked humanistic psychology with education provide much-needed corrective texts to replace the existing texts based on behaviourism, especially conditioning and connectionism. Mechanistic conception of the teaching-learning process as a carefully selected and sequenced series of stimuli to which children make a string of desired responses in order to arrive at "the pro-determined destination of target or terminal objectives represented by a set of equally predetermined learning outcomes presents an extremely restricted and unimaginative view of education. In such a scheme of education, the child is always expected to react; he cannot act on his own. Such an education can only dehumanise students as well as teachers. All this has to be replaced by affirmative education, one that affirms and fosters the human potential awaiting blossom in every child. Unless teachers with appropriate attitudes take up this jolly cross and view carrying it as their life's mission, the present sad system of education will continue to produce many more generations of sad, narrow-minded young men and women. Every child has as much at stake as the society and the nation he belongs to. India certainly needs a better deal.

## REFERENCES

1. Azarov, Yuri, (1988). *Teaching: Calling & Skills*. Moscow; Progress publishers.
2. Clark, Donald H. & Kadis, Asya L., (1971). *Humanistic Teaching.* Columbus, Ohio: Charles E Men-ill.
3. Flanders, N.A., (1970). *Analyzing Teaching Behaviour*. Reading: Addison-Wesley.
4. Fontana, David, (1977). *Personality and Education*. London: Open Books.
5. Peck, M. Scott, (1990). *The Road Less Travelled.* London: Arrow Books.
6. Rosenshine, B. & Furst, A.F., (1973). The use of Direct Observation to Study Teaching. In R.M.W. Travers (ed.) *Second Handbook of Research on Teaching*. Chicago: Rand McNally.
7. Wragg E.C. & Wood E.K., (1984). Pupil Appraisals of Teaching. In E.C. Wragg (ed.) *Classroom Teaching Skills:* London: Croom Helm.

# 21

# Value Orientation and Self Understanding in Teacher Education

ARTI SEN

On the occasion of the presentation of the Statesman Awards for Rural Reporting in Calcutta (September, 1992), a panel discussion was organized on the topic "Is corruption accepted as a way of life?" The discussion was attended by a huge audience. The majority of which were from the student community. Renowned thinkers participated in the panel discussion and unaniomously opined, "Corruption—more than a way of life, a part of the psyche". They painfully agreed that there is corruption in politics, corruption in journalism and even the "family was becoming an agency instigating people into corruption".

The selection of the topic, the nature and size of the audience and the conclusions from the discussion—everything is an expression of our deep concern over the moral degradation our country has reached at. There is growing concern over the erosion of values in every sphere of life.

As has been pointed out by Norman C. Dowsett, a disciple of Sri Aurobindo, "There were perhaps only a hundred years ago, four main values by which man conducted his life, viz., religion, education, social standards and politics. All these four values have been eroded over the past fifty years so that today they hardly remain the same values. The spirit has gone out of religion; we no longer educe knowledge from the student but rather accumulate information and call that knowledge; unity has disappeared from social and family life and politics has become a dirty game because there are no statesman left in the world but only poor politicians."

Our country thus, is passing through a value crisis that may ultimately lead to the crisis of existence, to the path of disaster. Reasons are many. The world wars, the partition of India, the explosion of population during the second half of the present century, the poverty, the illiteracy, complete breakdown of the indigenous mass-education system during the British rule, the process of industrialization, urbanization and gradual decay of rural life and culture, the inequitable distribution of wealth and the ugly disparities in the living condition of the rich and the poor, regional disparities in development, communal tensions and so on.

Prior to the beginning of the process of industrialization, Indian society was predominantly an agriculture-based rural society in which certain fixed and traditional values in different spheres of life were cherished by society and were transmitted from generation to generation without question, without challenge. Thus, value development took place normally and smoothly and social balance was maintained. Every individual in society knew his social roles and responsibility, knew what virtue was and what vice was and acted in accordance with the accepted values.

With the advent of modernity based on scientific doubts, inquiry, discoveries and technological inventions, way of life was changed to such an extent that traditional values became non-functional. The roots of the faith on traditional value were shaken. In western countries where the industrial revolution took place as a result of certain phenomenal changes inside the country. So, at least at the public sector a new set of values developed. In Indian society, industrialization was imported from outside and hence, the corresponding set of public values remained uncultivated in the Indian mind under changed condition, the traditional values did not work any more, thus giving rise to value vacuum. Value crisis in our country is so extensive and all pervading that we can call it a crisis of existence.

Erosion of values, however, is not a feature of the Indian society alone. It has taken place all over the world. Dr. Henderson, the Chairman of the World Education Fellowship, has explained this feature in a very impressive way. His view is that values supply a bridle to the body-ego which is necessary for its direction and control. In punitive societies, such a bridle was constituted by customs and religion. The tremendous progress of science and technology made this bridle completely ineffective and people started thinking that the ego is the master of itself and the environment. This is a false and dangerous notion that gave rise to greed, consumerism, cynicism, purposelessness, insecurity and a deadly complication of abnormality. It is now time to discover a "New acceptable and globally valid bridle, not imposed from without but evolved from within".

**Viable Methodologies**

What we need, therefore, is the emergence of a new set of values that may serve as a bridle to the self. The problem is not to check the erosion of values but rediscovering them in new forms. Man is essentially a being who cannot live without the awareness of eternal values like truth, beauty and goodness. Merged in the midst of falsehood, he will cry for the light of truth, in the midst of ugliness he will be thirsty for the beautiful. Totally fallen in sin, he will appreciate and love the good. The modern mind that is "seemingly self-sufficient, intelligent, sceptical, yet a mind living in sin with the soul of an Abraham; thus he knows two things at once, and both with equal assurance; that there is no God, and that there must be God". This is really a painful state of affair. And 'every persistent pain', writes Amlan Datta, "is a kind of crying out of the soul for a readjustment hopefully at a higher level."

Although basic values are same in all places and in all times, there are instrumental values that may change according to the needs of the specific time and particular society. If we recognize the inevitability and necessity of the breakdowning in older human values and emergence of new ones, a new statement of education becomes essential. This new education should break the chains of old authorities, formulate new objectives and focus the need for a readjustment in the older curriculum and introduction of new subjects in it, in order to make education a powerful tool for development of such values.

It has been said that values are caught and not taught. It is also believed that values cannot be imposed from outside but should develop from within. Value development takes place in a very subtle way during the process of the individuals interaction with his environment both natural and social.

Still, teachers have a very important role to play as friend, philosopher and guide, in this process of value development. He should help the students in acquiring adequate value information, value analysis, value judgement and value decision. He should help them in understanding the nature of value dilemma and value crisis, in resolving value conflicts and in formulating and implementing practical measures to develop strong will and determination to stick to the value choice the individual pupil has made for himself after clarification value problems.

Thus, value orientation and related facts, knowledge, principles, policies, strategies and attitudes should be very important components of teacher education programme. In India, value orientation in education and therefore in teacher education, has been given very serious consideration during the present decade and it has been accepted that teachers play a very important role in this matter.

Who are the teachers of our country? What are their personal and professional backgrounds? To what extent are they aware of their professional roles and responsibilities and the limits of their ability to perform these responsibilities? What is the nature of their own value structure? These are some of the questions that naturally crop up in our mind in connection with teachers' role in value development.

Rabindranath Tagore said "If a teacher does not possess learning, how can he impart it to others? A lamp cannot put light into other lamps if it does not itself burn and sheds light?" The same analogy stands in the case of the teachers role in value development. A teacher can help his student best in this matter when he himself possesses the value and presents his own life and behaviour as an illustration of the same. Such teachers will be rare in present day society. Gone are those days when teachers were highly regarded in society for their dedication to duty, simple living and high thinking. Teachers of today, like other citizens of the country, are the products of the present society and hence, are the sufferers of the same value conflicts. In many cases, teachers of today have come to the teaching profession not as their first choice but as their last resort. Society may expect many noble qualities and character traits in them. But in reality, teachers at best are persons of second grade merit and average character. In many cases, they start their professional life with a considerable amount of frustration. They start with very little interest in and special preference for the teaching profession. They rarely have clarity of concepts regarding change in values in the context of changing social situation. Then, there is a wide gap between values at the conceptual and the behavioural level.

Children catch values from parents and other significant members of the family, from important persons in the neighbourhood, from peers, from admired heroes, from books, from the media and last but not least from the teachers. Teachers are supposed to be the conscious agents of value inculcation. Students learn values from the contents of the subject matter they teach and also from the examples of their way of life and their behaviour pattern. Society expects a lot from the teacher. If the teacher falls short of this social expectation and is unable to live in consistency with the values, that are essential for the survival of society, the meddling effects on students will be less, or even negative. What is the way out?

One of the concrete measures to be taken is to make planned efforts through teacher-education programmes to raise the level of consciousness of teachers regarding their roles, responsibility, accountability and their own value-development. This should be done by developing correct self-understanding in them regarding values. In the NCERT seminar on Moral Education, Dr. Prem pointed out that in the emerging conditions and needs of today, 'Man and his own self: The human person: The inner man' is one of the major value concepts. The three broad areas of action suggested by him consisted of (i) Working with the people, (ii) Looking inward and (iii) Broadening life's horizons.

Of these three, looking inward and understanding oneself is now increasingly being accepted and appreciated as a very important aspect of life and education. Since value oriented education is essentially an education for becoming and self-exceeding which means a transcendence from the lower to the higher level of existence, it is first of all necessary to master the technique and develop the habit of constantly watching one's own mental states and processes. Self-understanding has various aspects. One of the aspects is understanding one's own mental states, experiences, needs, impulses, motivation, interests, aptitudes, etc. Another aspect is the understanding of one's own responses and attitudes towards his roles and responsibilities, one's accountability and obligation towards social institutions.

There are various methods of self-understanding. Some of them are:

1. Knowing and accepting one's image from the feedback given by others, i.e. from the assessment of other people.
2. Knowing oneself through group thinking, group discussion and transaction analysis.
3. Maintaining diary to record one's mental states at various conditions, reflecting over it and assessing oneself at a later time.

4. Being trained in self-observation and self-analysis.
5. Himself analysing or getting analysed by others the dreams, fantesies, etc.
6. The practice of meditation and yoga.

**Yoga and Meditation Way**

Of these, meditation and yoga are psycho-physical practices very closely linked with the practices of some specific religions like Hinduism, Buddhism etc. Sometimes they are linked with religious obscurantism. Hence they may not be acceptable to the modern rational mind or to persons belonging to other religions. In this connection, we should keep in mind that there are many religious practices that are good for mental and moral health, development of character and personality. These practices need not necessarily be rejected simply because they are linked with a particular religion. We should keep our mind open and judge the effectiveness of these practices on the basis of experimental evidences.

Patanjali, the ancient Hindu *rishi* and the propounder of the yogic school of philosophy mentioned of yogic exercises. The meditation was developed and practised by the Buddhists and Jains in India, China and Japan through ages. In the present age, Swami Vivekananda, Swami Abhedananda, Sri Aurobindo etc. developed meditation and yogic exercise lessons. Rabindranath Tagore had the conception of yoga of a very different kind. It was not *Pratyahara* or withdrawal of the mind from the world of the senses. To him, yoga was the union of the individual self with the cosmic universe including all animate and inanimate objects and it was to take place through calm and detached sense perception. He said, "I will have the joy of salvation through the innumerable ties that I have with everything of the world." To him, it was a gradual expansion of the self by loving and identifying oneself with the outer world and then recreating the world in one's own mind. He wrote in one song "Come out of your ownself and you will get the whole world in you." Tagore was highly inspired by the famous Sloka of the Upanisada:

> *"Yastu Sarvani Bhutani Atmanyev Nupasyati*
> *Atmatmt Sarva Bhuteshu na tato Vijugupsate"*

He, who sees everything in himself and himself in everything is not isolated from anything.

Everyday, Tagore used to get up very early in the morning, sat silently and gazed with concentration towards the rising sun, the sun who is the revealers of every visible thing in the world. The sun who is the symbol of all light and all awakening. To Tagore knowing oneself and knowing the world were two sides of the same coin. In a poem he wrote, "This process of knowing myself will never be over, along with knowing myself, I shall be able to know you."

In Santiniketan, Tagore made arrangements for close contact with nature, participation in creative activities, corporate hard working life in the ashrama, serving people of the community and joining the Mandira-assembly every morning and evening and also on special occasions during the seasonal festivals. These were the regular programmes for reaching fullness of the personality through self-understanding, self-enhancement and self-actualisation. Discipline also has a very definite role in this process, but it was self-imposed discipline, the ultimate aim of which was self-enhancement. Rabindranath Tagore's conception of the 'Mandir', the place of '*Upasana*' was somewhat different from the conception of the traditional Hindu temple. The 'Mandir' in Santiniketan is a glass-hall built for the purpose of community *upasana*. There are plenty of doors, all wide open so that the participants can see the beauty of nature outside, the trees, the flowers, the shadows, the sky, the rising and the setting sun etc. The prayer song becomes one with the hymn of the universe. Tagore said of *Bodher Sadhana*—the practice of a higher form of sense-awareness, through which the union of the individual self with the cosmic universe is established. This is yoga in the Tagorean sense.

However, we should neither accept nor reject any of the practices we have discussed simply on its face-values. We should study the relative effectiveness of each of the procedures through systematic research and find out the merits and limitations of each of them. There are scientific, religious, metaphysical and poetic approaches to self-understanding, self-enhancement and self-actualisation. These approaches may be studied separately, or there may also be an integrated approach. The approaches should be studied, tested, experimented and evaluated. It is high time to realize that the conception of total education for the development of an integrated personality is being utterly neglected at the present age by laying too much emphasis on imparting of information and development of cognitive abilities, which is not primarily understanding-oriented but achievement-oriented. The education of today is producing a greedy consumerist society. This is not the goal of human race. This education does not lead to the recognition of the hierarchy of human needs and reaching to self-actualisation through the satisfaction of these needs. Education should also develop compassion and fellow-feeling, finer aesthetic sensibility, moral zeal and control over ones own egoistic impulses and finally to capability of feeling a sublime joy by re-establishing the lost harmony between the individual self and the larger world, the ultimate value of human life. The practice of self-understanding is only the first step in the achievement of these higher values in human life.

Colleges of education are the proper places for experiments in reach ideas and practices, because many of them have got the curricular, co-curricular and organizational infrastructure of such experimentation. While ideas of value, orientation and self-understanding can be incorporated in teaching the topic of educational philosophy, educational psychology, mental hygiene, etc. programmes for self-development may be arranged through co-curricular creative activities, group discussion on value problems, taking up case studies, developing value quiz, self-rating questionnaire and systematic observation on value development and change of values, self-enhancement through cultural and community programmes, sports, games and other forms of physical education, practice on meditation and concentration and so on. It is time to think of whole teacher-education programme as a value-conscious programme that will serve to raise the level of consciousness of teachers, students and their parents...in a word the consciousness of the whole society.

## REFERENCES

1. Norman C. Dowsett: *Psychology for Future Education.* Department of Educational Research and Levelopment, Sri Aurobindo Society, Pondicherry.
2. Amlan Datta: *The Third Movement,* Ananda Publishers Private Limited.
3. James, L. and Hendersoh: *The Undrilled Ego.*
4. *Report of the High Level Seminar on Moral Education* (Sinha, 1981).
5. *Report of the working group to review Teachers' Training Programme.* (In the light of the need for value orientation). Ministry of Education and Culture, Govt. of India (1983).
6. *Challenge of Education — A Policy and Perspective.* Ministry of Education (1986).

7. Report on "Value Orientation in Teacher Education". Meeting of Deans of Education (1986). South Indian University, Sponsored by NCERT, New Delhi, Department of Education, Andhra University.
8. K.M. Gupta: *Report on Training cum Research Project in Value Orientation*, Department of Teacher Education, Special Education and Extension Services (NCERT) 1988.
9. *Value Orientation* (Journal) VII. VIII, July 1988.

# 22

# Values in University Teaching

MADHULIKA PAUL AND V. K. GUPTA

*"The man of truth is he whose thought and word and deed all three are one.*
*Such men can earn nearness to God and attain Heavenly Bliss, for sure."*

This is a teacher's province to hold aloft the torch, to enlist at all times and all places that this nation of ours was founded on idealism and that whatever may be the prevailing tendencies of the times, our children shall learn to live "among the sun-lit peaks."

A teacher cannot be without values. If he lacks it, he will be like salt without its flavour. A teacher must touch the hearts of his students. Boys imbibe more from the teacher's own lives than they do from books. If teachers impart all the knowledge to their students but do not inculcate truth and purity among them then in a way they betray themselves.

Teachers have thus, to accept their responsibility of guiding their students keeping in view the existing malaise in the society. By entering to the teaching profession they, *ipso facto*, accept this obligation. As it is truly said—*'A guide has to be very careful about himself. He has to be on the right track himself, before he can bring others onto it.'*

The secret of teaching values is to inspire and kindle the quest among the students by means of one's own example of character and mastery of knowledge. It is by embodying values within ourselves that we can really radiate values to our students.

The main reason for degradation of teachers is their lust for money and lack of sacrifice for students. India, reputed in the ancient core as the custodian of the 'soul' is now becoming a nation without soul, thus joining the 'suicide gallop' of the West. Education, instead of helping the students to develop meaning and purpose of life, has placed them in a vicious circle. The common man is groaning under the weight of rampant corruption. We are in the grip of narrow sectarianism, regionalism and fanaticism. Thus a breakthrough programme is urgently needed. *'The ethos of the teachers needs to be changed from those of the merchants to those of the Gurus.'*

A teacher whose soul is wrinkled and whose heart is atrophied, who is deviod of energy and enthusiasm, capacity and character is a disgrace. A teacher must not regard himself as a mere wage-earner whose job begins at 10 a.m. and ends at 5 p.m. He is a spiritual alchemist charged with the sacred work of creating cultured citizens. The teacher has therefore to instruct, inspire and illumine. A teacher must be a committed man, committed to the future of man, to the future of humanity and to the future of his country and the world.

We, in our country look upon teachers as Gurus or as Acharyas. An '*Acharya*' is one whose '*achar*' or conduct is exemplary. He must be an example of '*sadachar*' or good conduct. He must inspire the pupils who are entrusted to his care with love of virtue and goodness.

In addition to this if a teacher himself does not possess learning, how can he impart it to others? *A lamp cannot put light into other lamps if it does not itself burn and sheds light.* The teacher who merely represents bookish knowledge mechanically can never teach anything and can never inspire and without proper inspiration, independent creature faculties can never develop.

Further, one cannot pour out from the vessel unless and until one has put into it, and if a teacher is a poor and shallow from within, if there is no sparkling wine in him he cannot quicken the mind or humanise the emotions of his students; if he is not a lighted candle himself, he will never be able to light up the flame in others.

Thus the need of the hour is that teacher has to transmit existing values of the society to the next generation. As such he is a defender of the *status quo*. He has also to be an agent of change for bringing about quick changes needed by society. As such he has to be revolutionary.

In addition to this a teacher should value tolerance and humanism. He should respect other's views and should value honest dissent. He should be able to give love, tolerance and understanding to his students.

He should know students individually and should be a true friend to students.

A teacher is not expected to be a walking encyclopaedia. He should, however, be a full man, educated and capable of educating in both breadth and depth. Further a teacher should try to divert the energy of his students towards constructive channels of work. *He can be a great catalytic agent for social change.*

As a physician cannot digest the food for his patient, he has to help their system to digest it. Similarly a teacher cannot make the lives of his students, he can only motivate them and help them to think for themselves.

*A Teacher should be a 'Trimurti' of Brahma, Vishnu and Mahesh.* As a creative thinker he is a Brahma, as a teacher and sustainer of knowledge he represents Vishnu and as a scholar who reads widely and deeply, who revels in swimming in the ocean of knowledge, finding pearls and rubies and making them accessible to his students, he represents Mahesh.

A teacher should be able to inspire in every student commitment to basic human values and to the welfare of his country and mankind. This requires special commitment to the welfare of the weak, the downtrodden and backward sections of the society. He should do his best to see that his students get committed to the service of the *Daridra Narayan.*

*Further a teacher has to be in a position to teach basic human values like truth, tolerance, justice, mutual respect, service, sacrifice, goodness, both by precept and by example.*

In the domain of *Physical Education*, the values that we ought to seek are those of health, strength, plasticity, grace and beauty. In the domain of *Emotional Education*, the values that we ought to seek would be those of harmony and friendliness, of courage and heroism, of endurance and perseverance and of resistible will to conquer the forces of ignorance, division and injustice.

In the domain of the *mental development*, the values that we ought to seek would be those of utmost impartiality and dispassionate search of the truth. The values pertaining to the *aesthetic development* would be those of the vision of the beauty and creative joy of the deepest possible aesthetic experience and expression. Values that we should seek in the *moral and spiritual* domain are those of sincerity, faithfulness, obedience gratitude, honesty, benevolence, generosity, cheerfulness and selflessness.

A teacher must no doubt teach certain subjects, but the purpose is not merely to impart knowledge and presents facts and figures in front of students. *He is expected to relate what he teaches, through process of formal and non-formal instructions on the wide objectives of education, viz. cultivation of spirit of independent enquiry and sensitiveness to moral obligations and good tastes.*

The teacher must ever be alert and watch out what may affect the future of humanity. The future is before him in the class-room; in the youth under his tutorage. His main concern would obviously be to strive to cultivate interests and skills of his students.

Now-a-days, good teachers have found a way out by earning, what is now called 'private coaching'. It is known that some teachers, use their position in their schools and colleges for increasing the popularity of their private coaching classes and their income. There is another category of teachers which aligns itself with party politics and gain good position and transfer to the places of their own choices. There are also teachers who exercise effective control over governmental machinery and party politics. In some places teachers seek elections to the parliament, state assemblies and other positions of importance. There are, of course noble teachers who do not regard their poverty as a barrier to performance of their duties and who have the strength within them to reject temptations for positions of power and monetary gains. These are the teacher most respected and remembered for their selfless character and for giving their best to the pupil.

## Conclusion

The teachers are destined to play a major role in shaping the destiny of the mankind. In view of the fact that this destiny stands today in a balance, fraught with dangerous possibilities of upheavals, catastrophies and cataclysm. We must pay central attention to the task of building up a large number of men and women teachers who can stand in the coming days as hero warriors and as teachers and pioneers dedicated to highest values, the promotion of which alone can ensure the survival and fulfilment of the human race. In this task, programmes of value-oriented education will play a notable role.

At the present era of science and technology, teacher should develop and enhance scientific approach in every walk of life. That is to filter out truth from the trash, to search relentless and not to be satisfied with anything but truth, not to be guided by propaganda, hypocrisy, superstitions and dogmatism etc. Further teacher should give due importance to economic values in life. They should be economic not only of money but of their time, energy and resources. Extravagance is to be avoided at all costs as it leads to dissatisfaction in the last.

Besides, social and moral values which plays a pivotal role in shaping ones character should be inculcated by teachers. Social values like co-operations, social-service, humility, broadmindedness, tolerance etc. and moral values like faith in supreme being, spirit of optimism etc are to be developed to save the country from social and emotional disintegration and to achieve the target of universal brotherhood and international understanding.

We expect the teachers to bring about the revolution, not merely a change in management of socio-economic affairs but a change in man; a revolution born of joy, not of sacrifice.

To conclude, I quote the words of Dr. Sarvapalli Radhakrishnan in which he has stressed the need for creation of human beings who possess high ideals on which depends the upliftment and the progress of the society:

> *"A civilization is not built with brick and mortar or steel and machinery. It is built with men, their quality and character."*

## REFERENCES

1. Santhanaraj, Stephen, *Approaches to Developing Managers: The Philips Experience, Developing Managers in Asia*, Edited by Tan Jing Hee & You Poh Seng, Addison-Wesley Publishing Company, Singapore.
2. Rao, T.V., *Readings in Human Resource Development*, Oxford and IBH Publishing Co. Pvt. Ltd., Bombay.
3. Prahallada, N.N., Contemporary Significance of Value Education, *University News*, Feb. 14th, 1994.
4. Mohanty, A.K. and Sahu, P.K., The Need for Organisational Dynamics for Attaining Managerial Excellence under the Changed Global Environment, *Indian Journal of Commerce*, Sept., 1995.
5. Lahiri, R.K., Organizational Dynamics and Managerial Excellence, *Indian Journal of Commerce,* Sept., 1995.

23

# Values in Higher Education

*A Sociological Appraisal*

RAJ SINGH AND M.L. SHARMA

## The Concept of Values

The term 'Values' may refer to interests, pleasures, likes, preferences, duties, moral obligations, desires, wants, needs, aversions and attractions and many other modalities of selective orientation (Pepper, 1958). Values, in other words, are found in the large and diverse universe of selective behaviour. Presumably sheer reflex behaviour does not manifest values or valuing: neither an involuntary eye blink or knee jerk nor any one of numerous bio-chemical processes in the human body constitutes value behaviour. However, it is very doubtful that anyone descriptive definition can be complete justice to the full range and diversity of recognizable value phenomena. One of the more widely accepted definitions in the social science literature considers values to be conceptions of the desirable influencing selective behaviour. In the broader view, anything good or bad is a value (Pepper, 1988) or a value is anything of interest to a human subject (Perry, 1954). In Western Sociology, values were often regarded as somehow "subjective" and were not included among the "hard facts" that were thought to be proper objects of study. Beginning perhaps with "The Polish Peasant in Europe and America (1918), the concept of values found increasing use, although the full influence of this study was not felt until the 1930s. By 1949, it could be said that a movement was under way "to come out in the open with an explicit presentation of values and full analysis of their moral presuppositions, deductions and consequences" (Mukerjee, 1949).

## Value Analysis

Values as empirical elements in human behaviour certainly arise out of human experience and hence may be affected by many conditions, including social conditions that affect experience. Values may, therefore, be analysed as dependent variables, subject to changes that are consequent to changes in population, technology, economic production, political organization, and so on. Once established, however, values also operate as independent variables channelling reactions to prior innovations and serving as a basis for further innovations.

Sociological thought generally attributes strategic importance to moral values in processes of institutionalisation and social control. Indeed, one important modern social theory holds that "moral standards constitute, as the focus of the evaluative aspect of the common culture, core of the stabilizing mechanisms of the system of social interaction" (Parsons, 1964). Besides, the extent to which individual value realization is compatible with social, cultural, and biological survival values requires much additional analysis. Likewise, oppositions and conflicts of value are present in all societies. Under conditions of rapid social change, special strains are placed upon value integration, when serious conflicts arise over basic values, it is doubtful that either suppression or compromise is effective in producing new integration as is the expansion of interests to rearrange and recenter value priorities (Allport, 1959).

## Objectives of Higher Education

Pandit Jawaharlal Nehru in his convocation address to the University of Allahabad in 1947, thus summed up the basic objectives of the university and its role in national life: "A university stands for humanism, for tolerance, for reason, for the adventure of ideas and for the search of truth. It stands for the onward march of human race towards even higher objectives. If the universities discharge their duties adequately then it is well with the nation and the people". These great words highlight in basic truth that universities have a crucial part to play in the life, welfare and strength of a nation. They can, however, fill this role only if they owe uncompromising loyalty to certain fundamental values of life. They are essentially a community of teachers and students where in someway, all learn from one another or at any rate, strive to do so. Their principal object is to deepen man's understanding of the universe and of himself in body, mind and to apply it in the service of mankind. They are the dwelling places of ideas and idealism and expect high standards of conduct and integrity from their members. Max Weber while discussing science as a vocation pointed that sun, however, is the truth of science, which alone seizes not upon illusions and shadows but upon the true being. Therefore, science contributes to the technology of controlling life by calculating external objects as well as man's activities. And it can contribute something that the green grocer cannot: methods of thinking, the tools and the training for thought. Science today is a 'vocation organised in special disciplines of higher learning in the service of self-clarification and knowledge of interrelated facts.'

**Dilemma of Higher Education**

To quote Sir Eric Ashby, Indian universities have failed to adapt themselves sufficiently to the vast and unique opportunities which surround them; they seem to have lost enthusiasm and initiative under the crushing problems which have beset them. With a few notable exceptions they remain examining bodies and their students naturally regard success in examinations as the sole end of an undergraduate career. As universities multiply in number, their academic standards-relative to those elsewhere do not improve. This failure of the university to meet the challenge of Indian society has many complex causes, however, exclusion of the whole of oriental learning and religion. There is a general feeling in India that the situation in higher education is unsatisfactory and even alarming in someways, that the average standards have been falling and that rapid expansion has resulted in lowering quality. The examination results, the reports of Public Service Commissions, the views of employers and the assessment of teachers themselves, the results of research done—all seem to support this conclusion. Besides, in many of the weaker colleges and universities, a majority of teachers teach mechanically and listlessly. The subjects in which they lecture do not often involve their intellectual passion.

The situation with regard to the students is no better. In the last couple of decades so much has been written about problems of student unrest, its numerous ugly manifestations and the causes responsible for it. Sociological explanation is likely to be mistaken for their justification. Urgent steps are, therefore, needed to curb these trends and to ensure that, whatever else education may or may not aim at doing, it should at least strive to enable young men and women to learn and practice civilized norms of behaviour and commit themselves honestly to social values of significance. It is also necessary to remember that the responsibility for the situation is not unilateral, it is not merely that of the students, or parents or teachers or state governments or the political parties but multilateral.

**Values Promoting Higher Education**

The education system should emphasize the development of fundamental social, moral and spiritual values at the universities level. It is, therefore, necessary that students energies are channelled into meaningful and challenging pursuits. This would be partly achieved through intensification of curricular programmes. But, that is not enough. It is also necessary to develop a rich and varied programme of co-curricular activities including yoga, meditation and science of living.

Professor S.C. Dube (1989) observed that for a country of India's cultural heterogeneity, social complexity, economic inequalities, unanimity in respect of all values is neither possible nor perhaps desirable. The area of personal belief has therefore to be omitted from this discussion. However, a consensus is needed regarding some premises and in respect of some core socio-political as well as academic values such as:

- In the knowledge industry, especially in the teaching profession, one has to acquire and also add to the fund of existing knowledge. For a teacher acquisition of knowledge alone would be a selfish and unproductive pursuit, if it is not followed up by the transmission function. Teaching is not to be viewed as a mechanical process. It is not enough to tell the students what one knows about a subject. Teaching involves an element of high creativity. Creativity thus emerges as a central value in the academic profession.
- Knowledge is important itself but at some stage one has to ask the question. Knowledge for what? Knowledge, thus, has to be socially relevant and useful. To invest a social purpose into education the teaching-learning process must aim at sharpening the problem solving capabilities of the learners.

Application orientation will have to be accepted as a value, if the ideal of creative teaching is accepted.

- The criterion of relevance necessarily brings us to a consideration of the irrelevance of some knowledge. Therefore, continuous renovation and innovation in the knowledge field, thus emerges as an important value. Good teachers can never rest on their oars, mentally they have always to be on the move.
- Institutions of higher learning today are symbols of indiscipline. Students indiscipline was followed by non-teaching staff indiscipline, and even teachers have joined forces with these indisciplined sectors. The picture presented here is grim but the hard truth needs to be told. This does not mean that the teacher is the only villain of the piece. Many others form part of the demolition squad. The teacher cannot divorce himself from his social milieu. He, like all other citizens, lives in a convoluted social order characterised by erosion of values distortion of social character, and institutional collapse. The situation is bleak but not without hope. There are individual examples of academic courage and there certainly exist islands of excellence in the arid zone that is the academic life of our country today. It is a cause for regret that these exceptions are not multiplying. The country faces a horrendous future unless we make a determined effort to cultivate excellence, develop trained competence, and produce a large number of young minds with problem solving capabilities. Therefore, devotion to academic pursuit emerges as another important value for progress.

## REFERENCES

Allport, G.W., (1959). Normative Compatibility in the Light of Social Science. In Abraham, H.M. (Ed.), *New knowledge in Human Values*, New York. Harper.

Dube, S.L., (1989). Professional Values. In "*Higher Education in India*" Amrik Singh and G.D. Sharma (Eds), Konark Publishes Pvt. Ltd.

Kothari, D.S., (1966). *Report of the Education Commission, 1964-66*. Ministry of Education, Government of India, New Delhi.

Mukerjee, R.K., (1949). *The Social Structure of Value*. London: Macmillan.

Parsons, T., (1964). *Social Structure and Personality*. New York: Free Press.

Pepper, S.C., (1958). *The Sources of Value*. Barkeley: University of California Press.

Perry, R.B., (1954). *Realms of Value: A Critique of Human Civilization;* Cambridge Mass: Harvard Univ. Press.

Roy, Girish, C., (1983). *Value Conflict in Study of Social Change in India*. S Chand and Company Ltd., New Delhi.

Weber, M., (1967). From Max Weber: *Essays in Sociology*. Routedge & Kegan Paul Ltd., London.

24

# Towards Value Based Management in University Education

A.K. PANDEY

## Backdrop

One of the greatest challenges of the 21st century world is concerned with the reorienting of educational system so as to promote, preserve and propagate basic human values. Education is said to be a man making process. Implicit in this process is the vision of man—his powers and potentials, his dreams and realisations and his aspirations and achievements. Education is to play an important role in actualisation of the vision of "man" projected by a society which provides education either through the formal or non-formal or both the arrangements. Recently both the formal and non-formal sectors of education have been confronted with the basic questions relating to quality of man to be shaped through their instrumentally. Traditionally speaking education was conceived as a process of acquiring knowledge and information. It involved a triadic interaction between the teacher, the learner and the subject matter. The concept of subject matter was confined mostly to the acquisition of knowledge in most of the cases. It is only very recently that in addition to promoting knowledge and skills, development and inculcation of values is also stressed as the prized goal of education.

In the Indian context, the concept of knowledge was strongly rooted in values and conduct. Thus, all education in the true sense of the term was aimed at achieving the goal of emanicipation or liberations of mankind. (Sa *Vidya Ya Vimuktay)* by implying a vision of liberated mind and soul for whom the entire world becomes a family (*Vasudhaive*

*Kutumbakam*). It may be seen that values were considered to be the foundation of all knowledge to be acquired by a person in order to behove the appellation of a human being.

## I

One of the constraints in organising education—formal or non-formal and in meeting their lofty goals has been the lack of clarity in our vision of a man. The various social sciences as also the sciences have not been able to contribute richly to the refinement of this vision. As a consequence thereof our universities, the colleges and the schools which are the principal exemplars of formal system of education have not been able to design courses and programmes of studies in the truly interdisciplinary perspectives culminating and converging into value-orientations.

The report of Kothari Commission which appeared in 1966 had made a clarion call on imparting a proper value frame at all levels of education. Even the NPE of 1985 and its POA (1986 and 1992) had made fervent plea for making our educational endeavour dearly and strongly value based. In the international context, through the processes of globalisation and the concept of global village concerns, the drive for a value based system of education has been launched in direct as well as indirect forms. The report of International Commission on Education prepared under the chairmanship of Jacques Delors which appeared under the caption 'Learning, the treasure within', has underlined the importance of the four pillars of a learning society. This according to the report was to become the dominant reality of the 21st century world. These pillars are *learning to know, learning to do, learning to live cooperatively and learning to be.* Needless to mention that the document is quite categorical in stressing that devoid of values no society or system could think of its continued sustenance or nurturance in the new millennium. It may be, therefore, readily perceived that there is global concern manifest with regard to the promotion and development of basic values, value-based programmes through education and its various instrumentalities. It will be in fitness of things if we first define the concept and meaning of the term value and value-based processes and systems with special reference to that of education in general and higher education sector with its administrative apparatus in particular.

**Value and Value Based Education—Defined**

A thing has value when it is perceived as good and desirable. Food, money and housing have value because they are perceived as good; and the desire to acquire them influences attitudes and behaviour. Not only material goods but also ideals and concepts are valuable, such as truth, honesty and justice.

Values are the bases of judging what attitudes and behaviour are correct and desirable and what are not. It is, therefore, of crucial importance that there be an appropriate framework as well as strategy for providing the context and operational guidelines for implementing a value managed programme.

Some generalized descriptive statements which explain the nature, import and effect of value based processes may be shown as follows:

Values are *complex entities* through which people show preferences for certain ways of living and conditions of existence. People may hold thousands of beliefs which combine to form attitude orientations toward responding to an object or set of circumstances in a certain way, and attitudes are the building-blocks of values. Self-concept and self-esteem are intimately tied to human values and people seek to maintain consistency between their values and behaviour, and their own perceptions of their true identity (Caduto, 1999).

An individual's *socialization* has a strong influence on how his or her values are formed, being derived from experiences in home, school, religion and government.

Some main *determiners of value formation* are a person's psychological development and the system of punishments and rewards that he or she grew up in.

Certain *values tend to be regarded more highly among various sectors* of a society: the sexes, socio-economic classes and age groups.

As people grow in their *capacity for complex, abstract thought, their morality also develops from being dependent on authority figures for moral direction to autonomy,* having a moral mind of their own.

It has been found in several studies that males tend to orient more toward external moral rules, particularly *concept of justice,* while women tend more toward a *morality of love, compassion and caring* in relationship with others.

Values are dynamic throughout life.

Social support is a crucial determiner of a person's commitment to values and modes of conduct.

Psychologically healthy people naturally orient towards positive growth values and behaviours. Depending upon whether their most basic needs are met, *people will move up the hierarchy of growth values*, from physiological to safety needs—then seeking love, esteem and self-actualisation. People tend towards self-actualisation, making full use of their own talents, potentials and capabilities (Abraham Maslow, 1954).

Thus, considerable expansion has been given to the meaning of the term 'value' which covers eight realms—morality, religion, art, science, economics, politics, law and custom. The main distinction of significance, which a system of values is consistently confronted in the development of a person and a society in all aspects, is three fold; *Intrinsic value* postulating good as an end in itself pursued for its own sake, '*instrumental*' value pursuing good as means of achievement of some purpose and '*technical*' value which relates to performance of one's allotted task by stressing good doing something excellently. It may be observed that it is the intrinsic value which should be the goal of a qualitative excellence of the individual and human institutions.

Hence, it may be stated that some values are viewed only in terms of practical utility, usefulness or of benefit or success-potential. Other values are there which keep on changing or developing according to societal needs of times. In contrast there are values which are deemed external, foundational or fundamental and, therefore, immutable and unalienable for the reason that they hold good some ideal of intrinsic value which is absolute as an end in itself for all times and in all places. Also values may be social, moral, legal or even constitutional. It may be seen that the concept of value is indeed deeply embedded in human thoughts and actions. On the one hand, there are the higher values which are related to absolute moral principles and are deemed ethically and socially binding on all human beings at all times and in all places. On the other hand, there are other values which can refer to personal belief of individual persons or the collective concepts of a community bound together by a sense of fellowship and cultural unity. (R.P. Dhokalia, 2001)

In this connection it will be pertinent to refer to the statement of Prof. Elizabeth Anderson (1993) who observed as:

> "When National choice is represented in terms of the maximization of value on preference satisfaction, and when intrinsic value and rational preferences are defined independent

> of expressive norms and contexts, we are tempted to think that the optimising behaviour of consumer in the market place sets the standard of rationality for all social life."

The one concept that is most universal is Value based Education (or in India's case, Value Education). The reason is obvious. The idea of value is universal and it applies to many things—some of which most cultures are likely to share. Value Education is more generic and consequently, aspects of religious, moral and social education can all fit under its roomy umbrella. Thus, *values* may be defined as the abstract qualities of high order governing principles relating to behaviour, conduct, accomplishment, success and excellence in any field of human endeavour—management, administration, control and regulative mechanisms. These values are usually reflected in the vision statements of an institution. It may be worthwhile to point out that all educational institutions—schools, colleges and universities are founded within the overarching framework of these visions or goals which are basically their value frames. In the insignia or the logo developed for a university or college, such a value statement hints at the possible goal or direction to be preferred while deciding the programmes, policies and the activities to be organized on the campus.

## Value Based Processes in a University System

Value based processes relate to the actual chores, programmes, methodologies and strategies adopted to achieve the pre-specified results. In this framework, the value based processes in the University system consist of the various academic programmes enforced on the campus, the teaching-learning activities promoted, the overall societal concerns emphasised and the various extra mural activities which are accentuated through the University calendar. In such processes there may be both explicit as well as implicit or hidden agenda being stressed by various vested groups which take the reins of the campus at one moment or the other.

The value based systems are those which are functional in terms of statutory and non-statutory structures created to realise the avowed goals of an institution. In the case of Universities these structures operate through various authorities statutorily created such as Board of Management (BOM)/Executive Council/Syndicate, Academic Councils, the University Court, the Planning Board, the Finance

Committees, the Faculty and the Departments of Studies. These systems are required to function in terms of certain formal stipulations which flow from and are derived from the Acts, Statutes and Ordinances of the University. The University system is envisioned as an autonomous body with inherent powers and mandates enjoined through the various enactments. Underlying all these structures and their regulative powers, there are value frames which inform and inspire the various decisions, policies and actions contemplated by the University in the best interests of its stake holders—the students, the community, the parent and the public.

From the foregoing attempt at defining the terms—values, value based processes and systems, it may be now somewhat easier to describe the basic principles and draw up the guidelines for having value based management of educational institutions specially at the tertiary level. In the following pages, therefore, a few guiding principles for value based University management will be indicated in the first instance.

II

## Guiding Principles for Value Based Management with Reference to University System

*he first guiding principle* of a University system is concerned with romoting excellence in areas of teaching, learning, research and dministration. A university has to strive hard to achieve and ensure excellence through its programmes and policies for which a very dynamic administrative setup will have to be created and established. The creation of such an administrative setup will largely depend on the capability of its leader—the Vice Chancellor and its team consisting of the Registrar, the Finance Officer, the Deans and other faculty members. It may be remembered that excellence is not a matter related to short lived pursuits of a day or a month. It is rather a long drawn pursuit requiring a longer continued time frame, concerted efforts, team spirit and formulation of a vision congruent with the ultimate goals and purposes for the realisation of which the university has been founded. In other words, excellence is a relatively long term goal which requires ceaseless efforts on the part of the leader of the team in particular and all other functionaries working in the university in general.

*The second principle* is related to equity, justice and empowerment. It implies and assumes a genuine concern for the socially disadvantaged and challenged sections of our society. It does not imply the governance of the system with populist mentality and slogans derived from considerations such as the caste, the creed and the regional and linguistic affiliations. The university system has, therefore, to work very hard to evolve such policies and programmes which will really ameliorate and remedy the social disadvantages suffered for long by the various pockets of our society.

This will also entail formulation of socially defensible set of rules and procedures which will take care of the interests and needs of the so called downtrodden and weaker sections of our society. In this perspective several remedial measures will have to be thought of and incentive schemes will have to be floated with a view to providing genuine help and assistance to those who are in need of it.

*The third principle* is derived from the second one. It is concerned with providing equality of opportunity to all the students who have suffered from disadvantages attributed to factors such as gender, caste, class and area—rural and urban etc. and to strive to reduce their effects to the minimum or below threshold level in operational terms. This will require designing of programmes, curricula and packages of activities and experiences which will benefit the various sections of students irrespective of their class, caste, creed or gender as the case may be. In other words, if a student who joins the university system with any of these social disadvantages and disabilities as enumerated above has to be enabled and empowered to benefit from the programme and courses of studies being offered, so as to have equality of educational opportunity.

With the advent of the 21st Century, massive changes are taking place in our socio-economic environment. New developments in science and technology, coupled with 'competition and media revolution' are making a deep impact on the education sector also. They are making new demands and posing fresh challenges to our established educational systems and practices.

More importantly, these changes require a reorientation of the educational system and channellisation of manpower in the right direction. In the reports of the various commissions and committees, the need and importance of the reorientation of the education has been emphasized and suggestions have been given for restructuring of the educational programmes in higher education system so as to provide suitable manpower for economic growth and sustainable development. This means that educational process is to be linked with production and employment. Reorientation of educational programmes thus needs to be undertaken in such a manner that it helps to produce self-reliant and self-development prone citizens. The thrust of this exercise should be to produce a human resource which is founded on long term perspectives and at the same time satisfies the fast changing needs and requirements of our society.

It may be mentioned that higher education in India is becoming increasingly challenging due to the rapid advances in technology. It may be seen that the need for higher education to keep pace with the increased awareness of importance of higher education for social, cultural and economic development has brought higher education to the fore front in the scenario of nation building programmes.

Education today is no more a one time certificate oriented activity, rather, it is a life long process. Upgradation of knowledge and skills have become inevitable not only for progress but also for survival of mankind. It is primarily the universities that unite all the additional functions associated with the advancement and transmission of knowledge—research, innovation, teaching and training and continuing education. To these one can add another function that has been growing in importance in recent years: international co-operation.

These functions can all contribute to sustainable development. As an autonomous centre for research and creation of knowledge, a university can address some of the developmental issues faced by a society. It educates the intellectual, political leaders, company heads administrators of tomorrow as well as many of the teachers. performing a social role, universities can use their autonomy in the service of debate on the great ethical and scientific issues facing the society of the future so as to serve as links with the rest of the education system by providing further learning opportunities for adults and acting as a centre for the study, enrichment and preservation of culture.

It is obvious, therefore, that a university is one of the main instruments for development and change. It has an important task of preparing qualified manpower to meet the emerging challenges of our society especially in the process of its development. While addressing the graduates of Allahabad University about fifty-five years ago, Pandit Jawaharlal Nehru had rightly stressed,

> "A University stands for humanism, for tolerance, for reason,

> for the adventure of ideas and for the search of truth, it stands for the onward march of the human race towards even higher objectives. If the Universities discharge their duties adequately, then it is well with the nation and the people."

Thus, universities function as the focal centres of higher education. With the accent on liberalization, modernization and internationalization, the role and functions of the university are undergoing rapid transformation. In addition to advancing knowledge through scholarship and research they have to produce trained manpower required for industry, agriculture, administration, economic sector, social services and other fast emerging new avenues in the world of work.

III

## Dynamics of Value Management for a University

When viewed in this backdrop, it may be readily perceived that the university systems and processes have to be organized on the basis of the aforementioned three principles with an eye on value management. The concept of value management is a new coinage so far as managerial practices are concerned. It involves the total area of operations in a typical environment of the systems. It deals with various management situations on the basis of a time frame. Thus, in a university context value management will imply the following four specific operations to be carried out in the top down and bottom up approaches to talking and handling the administrative problems and issues:

*Value Engineering* (VE) which requires administering the situations pertaining to student involvement, student activism and student achievements before or during the start of the academic calendar.

*Value Control* (VC) which involves active monitoring right from the stage of enrolment and admission to that of management of teaching-learning activities and research programmes.

*Value Analysis* (VA) which implies the detailed working out of the impacts and effects of teaching-learning designs and various research programmes undertaken by students and faculty members.

*Value Management* (VM) which stands for overall management with stress on values for which the university has been established.

Thus, value engineering is a key concept underlying university administration. It may be defined as 'the conscious and systemic application of a set of techniques that identify the needed functions, establish values for them, develop the alternatives to perform these functions at minimum cost with desired liability'. It hardly needs stating that the value management methodology can be applied to any area where we intend to be cost effective. In this context it may be indicated that cost is a common element in all management functions. A typical value engineering programme concentrates on cost-effectiveness, i.e. the return on investment and an early breakeven. For this what is considered to be important is to clearly define the functions and find out alternative approaches to accomplish these functions. These techniques can be applied to any area of university administration to enhance reliability, maintainability of performance, ease of handling etc. of various programmes and services being extended through its various wings.

IV

## Techniques of Value Management in the Context of Tertiary Level of Education

Although a number of techniques may be employed for effective value management and in order to ensure cost effectiveness and value improvement, here only a few viable ones are being mentioned. It may be remembered that the number of techniques of Value Management (VM) is not so important as its contribution to the improved academic ethos and the competence and expertise level of the system as a whole. These techniques are shown in a summary form in Box I.

**Box I**: Techniques of Value Management

- Getting information from best source.
- Performance auditing and appraisal at various points.
- Overcoming road blocks.
- Using currency sign on tolerance.
- Using good human relations.
- Goal setting and goal evaluation.

A brief description of these techniques of value management may be considered to be desirable in order to ensure competence, achievement and excellence through university level systems.

*Getting Information from Best Source*

The information in respect of the student performance, faculty contributions and administrative accountability constitutes a very significant stuff for quality improvement. These informations have to be elicited in the most authentic manner possible. The university system has to promote a culture of not only culling out the information from time to time but also identifying the best sources of doing so. For this purpose a viable data base with the help of a computer centre has to be generated and utilized when there is a need for doing so.

*Performance Auditing and Appraisal at Various Points*

Performance Auditing and Appraisal at various levels require setting specific criteria and norms of accomplishing results. In the university system this forms an integral part of the processes of admissions, examinations, faculty participation, work output of administrative staff and quality control measures. These activities when formalized, render the process of administration much more transparent and effective. Thus, for most of the processes pertaining to administration, standards are laid and appraised in terms of actual outputs. This system of work audit contributes to the promotion of healthy work culture also.

*Overcoming Road Blocks*

There are several types of impediments in the university system which block the ways of getting desired results. While some of these are visible, most of them remain invisible and unidentified. Thus, the apathy, indifference, incompetence and lack of commitment on the part of faculty both academic and administrative create major road blocks in the production of desired results so far as university management is concerned. These negative aspects have to be identified and dealt with immediately with the help of interactive and brain storming sessions, sensitivity training and informal discussions at various levels on a regular basis. For this faculty meeting on the weekly, fortnightly and monthly basis may be held with a view to sort out the immediate problems and their solutions.

### *Using Currency Sign on Tolerance*

Tolerance is a very important attribute which has to be cultivated by constant practice. This requires using various signs of tensions and tension resolutions in the day to day processes of administration. Sometimes the tolerance factor may be enhanced for a better management of the near at hand situations. Thus, for example if a lower division clerk does not produce the promised results, he/she has to be given time and exposed to well tried practices for effective handling of the various aspects of his/her job. This will require putting up a face on the part of the administrator which will allow for small errors and their rectification's. This procedure may be evolved with due regard to the courtesies in terms of subordinate-superordinate relationships of the administrative hierarchy.

### *Using Good Human Relations*

Administrative acumen requires setting up a management scenario where proper and adequate human relations in the institutional concerns will be assigned due weightage. These relations are multidimensional and they arise from the planks of teacher-student relations, student-student relations, teacher-administrator relations, administrator-administrator relations and so on. The foundation of good human relation is based on trust and the same has to be achieved through creating trust and goodwill. It has to be spontaneous and unhypocritical. It may be remembered that nothing is more contagious on the campus than the personal relation and goodwill with which one person deals with the other.

### *Goal Setting and Goal Evaluation*

Goal setting and goal evaluation are transactional skills which tend to raise the level of quality of results and accomplishments. Every member of the academic and administrative faculty has to be inducted into the art of formulating the specific task oriented goals and appraising the extent to which same have been realised. This requires preparing a flow chart of tasks and duties and their close execution and monitoring.

The description of these techniques as delineated here is purely illustrative and it should not be considered prescriptive by any stretch of imagination. A very dynamic, farsighted and flexible approach is called for in respect of the exercise of value management in the context of the university systems. It will be considered a great feat of management if the 'University vision' gets translated through its various formal and informal processes which appear in both short term and long term perspectives.

It may be rightly stressed that value management is a comparatively new field and has been developed as a result of rapid changes taking place in our socio-economic environment. To assess the presence of the extent of value management in universities, very few studies have been made. Specific researches are required to go into of ascertaining the existing level of value management and suggest steps to bring about a desired managerial ethos. The basic characteristics of a value based system, as discussed earlier, may be found in Indian Universities in varying degrees. Some of the new trends in this regard are perceptible through the introduction of value based courses and the concern for value management in university administration. It goes without saying that notwithstanding their linkages with the traditional model, universities have succeeded in making a similar, if not qualitatively different, higher education available to the millions of deprived and disadvantaged sections of the people at a low cost. Universities have to strive hard for maintaining a standard of 'learning' in the context of a relatively less restrained or less structured form of educational arrangements.

## REFERENCES


1. *Best Practices in Higher Education*, National Institute of Educational Planning and Administration, Delhi, 1999.
2. Delors Jacques, *Learning, the Treasure Within*, UNESCO, 1996.
3. Dhokalia, R.P., *Eternal Human Values and World Religions*, NCERT, Delhi, 2001
4. *Education for Affective Development*, UNESCO Principal Regional Office for Asia and the Pacific, Bangkok, 1992.
5. John W. Newstrom/Keith Davis, *Organisational Behaviour—Human Behaviour at Work*, Tata McGrow Hill Publishing Company, New Delhi, 1997.
6. Lomesh, S., *Value Management*, Sterling Publishers Pvt. Ltd., Delhi. 1997.
7. Micheal, J., Caduto, *A Guide on Environmental Values Education,* UNESCO, Division of Science, Technical and Environmental Education, 1985.
8. Moorhead and Griffin, *Organizational Behaviour*, Jaico, 1997.

25

# Value Education Based on Ethics in University Leadership with a Special Reference to the Indian Tradition

R.R. VERMA

## Introduction

The value of education is really the most powerful instruments of change and it provides a unique opportunity for real mutual cooperation in International terms. The outcome of modem age education, specially based on information technology, is witnessing a paradoxical phenomena. On the one hand, there is:

> Tremendous advancement of knowledge; and on the other, there is conspicuous degradation of human values.

Human beings make all attempts to know but no effort to become valuable person of the society. They value everything except values essential for humanity and its sustenance and development. In our country, i.e. India, the "Value Education" is believed to be as old as the human civilization. But with the passage of time, the value education got imparted on modernity. The need to study the issues systematically was felt only in the recent times. It was necessitated by the observance of identity crisis among the youth and subsequent evidence in support of the erosion of fundamental values of multicultural society that India has always been.

On the above theme, I have reviewed the value-studies as suggested in ancient Indian scripture "*Sa vidya ya vimuktaye*" which means —

"Education is meant for liberation". It is, therefore, implied that the ultimate questions and values in university leadership are aimed at providing 'freedom from bondage'. A man endeavours to achieve four goals during his lifetime. They are: (1) participation in the cosmic order in accordance with one's nature (*Dharma*), (2) Wealth (*Artha*), (3) Fulfilment of desire (*Kama*) and (iv) salvation (*Mokshha*). The last one has been set out as the supreme goal. Traversing on the path of religion and balancing the two, namely wealth (*Artha*) and desire (*Kama*) and acquiring salvation (*Mokshha*) is the ultimate aim of man's life. The foundation of this way of life is laid right from the student days. This is what the students of oriental countries like India have been following. However, with the advent of modern civilization and rapid industrialization specially based on information technology, the fundamental things have changed a lot. In the blind race for economic advancement and the desire to have more and more worldly objects and comforts of life, the ultimate aim of students has undergone a substantial transformation. They have become totally materialistic in their outlook. Today, the universities are providing education to the students not for salvation but for physical enjoyment of life.

**University Leadership and its Development**

The foremost ethical question about value education in universities and other institutions of higher learning are particularly concerned with the aim of advancing its purpose meaning and significance for the teachers, students and the general community. There should be spirit of dedication and the sense of purpose which should guide the activities of those who are functioning in the statutory bodies of the universities. The administrative wing of the university as well as the academic wing must work in a spirit of cooperation, understanding, and imagination. Mutual human concern must always be present on the university campus, in the classrooms, co-curricular activities and even in purely administrative matters. Lines of communication between different sections of the university community must always remain alive and should never be allowed to be blocked.

It is of considerable importance that university organization should set before the community at large the ideal of debate and dialogue, communication and exchange of ideas conducted freely, fearlessly and objectively in interpersonal communication. It is this pattern of free exchange of ideas that can go a long way in resolving conflicts and tensions.

We venture to express the hope that proposals which we are making in the following paragraphs will reshape the orientation of university education. It will lead to progress and desirable changes not only in the outlook of all constituents of university community, but also in the activities of the statutory bodies of the university and its administrative wing such as its Act, Statutes and Ordinances etc.

In an open atmosphere of free exchange of ideas, the leadership in the university will naturally seek to inculcate its own ethos in the minds of the teachers and students. It is this that will help and sustain the proper functioning of the university system. The leadership will endeavour to make such recommendations regarding the pattern of organizational setup of the universities and their functioning which would facilitate the implementation of their tasks and obligations.

**Key Values**

In the case of ideal leadership, actions speak louder than words, what the leaders do sets the ethical tone and creates the moral environment on the University campus. The leaders exemplify the spirit of dharma (duty). Consequently, they can truly inspire their subordinates, students and colleagues. They must cultivate the following qualities:

1. *Dana* : Charity, generosity and liberality
2. *Sila* : Moral character
3. *Pariccaga* : Sacrificing everything for the good of the people
4. *Ajjava* : Honesty, integrity and sincerity
5. *Maddava* : Kindness and gentleness
6. *Tapa* : Austerity, self-control and simple life
7. *Akkoda* : Freedom from hatred, ill-will and anger
8. *Avihimsa* : Non-violence and promoting peace
9. *Khanti* : Patience, forbearance, tolerance and understanding
10. *Avirodha* : Non-opposition, that is, ruling in harmony with his people.

The first condition of good leaders is that they should not have any craving or attachment to wealth and property, but should give it away for the welfare of the University. Besides possessing a high moral character, they must be prepared to give up all personal comfort in the interest of the university. They must be free from fear or favour in the discharge of their duties, must be sincere in their intentions and must not deceive the University in anyway. They must be kind and gentle in their speech, thought and action. Leading a simple life based on self-control and non-indulgence in a life of luxury are must. Freedom from hatred, ill-will, enmity and bearing no grudges make one a good leader. A good leader must promote peace by avoiding and preventing everything that involves violence and destruction of life. Patience, forbearance, tolerance, understanding and readiness to bear hardship and difficulties are again the hallmarks of good university leadership. Last but not the least is the working in harmony with the colleagues by not obstructing their efforts which would be conducive to the welfare of the university faculty, staff and students.

It is this type of university leadership which can succeed in creating the atmosphere of mutual trust and concern and thus enable realization of the goals of education. It is this kind of leadership that can rise above the ruinous struggle for power. In such an atmosphere the one who conquers oneself is more respected that than the one who conquers millions by military and economic ware fare. The avarice and greed do not invade their minds and compassion is the driving force of action. The faculty, staff and students would enjoy life in peace, harmony, and material contentment. They pay attention to the highest and noblest aim, i.e. the realization of Ultimate Truth and the Goals of University education so as properly equip students to meet the challenges of practical life.

The ancient centres of higher learnings in India such as Nalanda, Vikramshila, and Tachhashila sought to operationalise these ideals and effectively succeeded in attaining their objectives.

In our view true education and teachers must incorporate the spiritual dimension of human life. In ancient India we find countless examples of educational leaders who at periodic intervals retreated to the solitude of forests for spiritual resurgence. They moved from one seat of learning to another so as to spread their message through their words and deeds. They founded 'Sanghas', the institutions of learning and spirituality, where the learned ones came to live and practice the life of austerity. They not only guided pupils engaged in intellectual pursuits but also trained and prepared them to lead virtuous life.

The members of these seats of learning practiced renunciation of sensual pleasures and made effort to transcend the sense of ego by cultivating love for all sentient beings through universalization of their ownself. The Sanghas in a way exemplified the ideal order of society wherein a very high standard of conduct in all spheres of life was maintained. The essence of 'Dharma', i.e. universal friendship (*maitri*) and compassion (*karuna*) were the beacons of these organizations.

The Sanghas functioned as per the charter of obligations. It consisted of the obligations of self-restraint, uprightness, good deeds in act and word, pure means for livelihood, good conduct and of being always alert. Thus the ethical purity was not confined to mere form of external acts of the doer but rather to his/her mental purity. The individual not only had to refrain from ethically wrong actions, he had to make conscious efforts, to constantly train his mind to deter from forbearing ethically wrong ideas and desires. In the practical-experimental-university-laboratory of the Sanghas, there had to be perfect harmony between '*mansa, vacha, karmana*' i.e. the motivation, the word and the deed. The ethically right thought and right deed must spring forth from ethically right mind.

It was the responsibility of the enlightened Sangha (University) leaders to shape the life of Sangha along the right lines by increasingly orienting its members to lead moral life. The Sanghas showed their concern and love for ordinary man in six ways:

1. Restraining evil;
2. Exhorting to be good;
3. Loving, with kind thoughts;
4. Teaching what one had not heard;
5. Correcting and purifying what one had heard; and
6. Revealing the way of heaven.

In our view, the Sangha that is the University, the secular society and the State are interdependent. The condition of each affects the condition of others. The University education should aim at producing such educated persons who can create and sustain harmonious reciprocity between these three elements.

## Learning Subjects for the University

A few noteworthy points emerge from Great King Ashok's leadership of India, which can be considered as the desirable learning subjects for all Universities. They are:

1. Take refuse in the learning institution (*Buddham Sharanam Gacchami*),

2. Take refuse in the human values (*Dhammam Sharanam Gacchami*),
3. Take refuse in the spiritual order (*Sangham Sharanam Gacchami*),
4. Not only preach moral values but also practise and modify life accordingly,
5. Formulate and adopt policies and principles based on dhamma (moral values),
6. Constantly struggle for purity in public life and harmony in domestic affairs,
7. Discourage unethical conduct at all levels; promote and encourage ethical conduct,
8. Reiterate commitment to dharma (righteousness),
9. Be even-handed, impartial, objective and diligent, and fulfil the obligations to the Organization/Institution/State,
10. Ensure the welfare and happiness of human beings at large,
11. Establish personal contact with rank and file of co-workers and treat them alike,
12. Improve all types of services by adding the element of dhamma,
13. Utilize the resources of the organization, institution and the state to promote dhamma.

Acts, Statutes and Ordinances as well as Regulations of the university administration should be governed and implemented so as to incorporate the values and the ideas expressed above in 1 to 13.

**Concluding Remarks**

> There is no gift like the gift of dhamma
> No acquaintance like acquaintance with dhamma
> No distribution like distribution of dhamma
> No kinship like kinship through dhamma.

To conclude, I wish to say that in India the Great King Ashoka gave up a life of insatiable hedonism and embraced a life of tireless service—as a servant of his subjects. Countless kingdoms of great monarchs have suffered devastation, but the glorious emergence of the power of benevolence in Ashoka remains an imperishable asset to humanity. Ashoka's love for virtue and his devoted practice through personal example made him an incomparable leader. While mundane political empires on earth have proved ephemeral in existence, the spiritual empire that Ashoka attempted to establish has survived through ages in the history of mankind. Ashoka is perhaps the only example of a victorious conqueror at the Zenith of his power, still possessing the strength to continue his territorial conquests yet renouncing war and violence and turning to peace and non-violence. It is a matter of consolation and also of inspiration to think today that at least there was one great leader, well known in history, who had the courage, confidence, vision and will to provide an administration based entirely on genuine human values. We the administrators in the modern Universities may inculcate these values in our present university system so as to ensure a better future.

## REFERENCES


1. Radha Kumud Mookerjee, (1775). *Ashoka* (Third revised edition) Delhi: MacMillon.
2. *Journal of Human Values*, (2000). Sage Publication, New Delhi/Thousand Oaks, February, London.
3. *Ethics in Management* (1997). Oxford University Press, New Delhi.
4. *University News*, (2000). Association of Indian Universities, January, New Delhi.
5. *Ethics in Management* (1997): S.K. Chakraborty, Oxford University Press, New Delhi.

26

# Restructuring Teacher Education for Value Orientation

V. USHA SRI

## The Complex Reality

Man in his craving for material comfort and dominance over nature, has made life complicated for himself and others. Caught in the mess he has created, now he is frantically in search of a solution. Time, many say, has come to stop the mad race, to contemplate with a calm mind as to what he needs for real happiness and he must preserve for future generations. The crisis of values—even weakness of character and frustrations in life are considered to have been the outcome of a defective structure of education. It is argued that ignorance of worthy goals for life has clouded the minds of the youth. Concerned with the absence of a sound value system, the National Policy on Education, 1986 states—

> "The growing concern over the erosion of essential values and an increasing cynicism in society has brought to focus the need for readjustments in the curriculum in order to make education a forceful tool for the cultivation of social and moral values.
>
> In our culturally plural society, education should foster universal and eternal values oriented towards the unity and integration of our people. Such value education should help eliminate obscurantism, religious fanaticism, violence, superstition and fatalism.

> Apart from this combative role, value education has a profound positive content, based on our heritage, national goals and universal perceptions. It should lay primary emphasis on this aspect."

## Teacher Education at Cross Roads: Challenging Role for Teachers

The teacher is not a mere facilitator of knowledge and information; he has also to be a source of inspiration. Quite often, even now, in their formative stages, children consider the teacher a fountain head of wisdom and a model for shaping their lives. The International Commission on the Development of Education, established by UNESCO in its report in 1972 under the title 'Learning to be,' stated—

> "One of the essential tasks of educators at present is to change the mentalities and qualifications inherent in all professions; thus they should first be ready to rethink and change the criteria and basic situation of the teaching profession, in which the job of educating and stimulating students is steadily superceding that of simply giving instructions."

Further, the conditions of teachers' training would have to be so transformed so as to prepare 'educators' for different ages of educands, rather than making them into mere specialists in passing on predetermined knowledge according to given curricula. It has been emphasised that the teaching profession will best fulfil its future role only if its structure is adapted to the modern system of education.

Education Commission (1964-66) pointed that the "essence of a programme of teacher education is to 'quality' and in its absence, teacher education becomes not only a financial waste but source of overall deterioration in educational standards." Hence, for improving the quality of teacher education, the Commission offered many suggestions. One is to revise the curricula and programmes at all levels of teacher education in the light of the fundamental objectives of preparing teachers for their varied responsibilities in an evolving system. The teacher's philosophy and attitudes towards changing society and social issues can be shaped through a well-conceived teacher education programme.

In order to be models to generations of students, teachers have to acquire character and imbibe high principles of life. Since the teacher is perceived as the guiding light to drive away ignorance, "he or she is rightly looked upon as the creator of worthy personalities, the preserver of what is desirable, and the absolver of the evil." It is paramount that a teacher should adopt high values in personal life and profession. The high place accorded to the teacher in the community can be justified only if he/she holds fast to the higher goals and values in his/her own life.

The objectives of teacher education are many. Some of these put forth by the National Council of Teacher Education are:

1. Development of Gandhian Values.
2. Creating a self-image in which the teacher perceives her/his role as a change agent in society.
3. Developing the capacity to play her/his role not only as a leader of children but also that of a guide to the community.
4. Functioning as a liaison between the school and the community and employing suitable ways and means for integrating community life and resources with educational programmes.
5. Adopting a warm and positive attitude towards growing children and their academic, socio-emotional and personal problems, with skills to guide and counsel them.
6. Not only using but also helping in the preservation of environmental resources and protection of historical monuments and other symbols of cultural inheritance.
7. Developing an understanding of the objectives of school education in the Indian context and awareness of the role of school in achieving the goals of building up a democratic, secular and socialistic society.
8. Developing competence to teach on the basis of accepted principles of teaching and learning.
9. Developing understanding, interests, attitudes and skills which would enable the teacher to foster all-round growth and development of the children placed under her/his care.

The High Level Seminar held in Simla in 1981 on Value-oriented Education offered very pertinent recommendations. Relating to teachers and their training for value education it recommended that:

— All teachers in the schools should be regarded as teachers of value education and all subjects including physical education can be used for inculcation of the right values.

— There is a need for establishing a resource centre for literature on value-oriented education. Besides printed matter, this centre should also produce 35 mm films emphasising desirable values. An effective distribution system for making these materials available in all corners of the country should be developed.

— Special teacher-orientation programmes should be taken up at the State level to train teachers in the effective methods of development of values among students and teachers.

Following upon the seminar cited above, the Working Group to Review Teachers' Training Programme (in the light of the need for value-orientation) made the following recommendations:

- The curriculum relating to value education and to the study of Indian culture should be immediately implemented in all the teacher training institutions.
- Until the training institutions are remodelled on new lines as suggested in the report, as an interim measure, teachers' training institutions should offer the following three new papers as optional in place of any other three prescribed papers.

  Paper 1 : Philosophy, Education and Values;
  Paper 2 : Psychology, Education and Values;
  Paper 3 : India and Indian Values.

In addition, teachers' training institutions may be advised to incorporate in their total programme of teachers' education as many elements as possible from amongst all the various suggestions that have been made.

Simultaneously, efforts were sought to be initiated, without delay, into two streams of teacher training programmes:

1. Five-year teacher education programmes after Senior Secondary level, leading to master's degree in education; and

2. Two-year teacher education programme, three years after graduation. These programmes would be designed on the basis of the pedagogical ideas and value-oriented curricula suggested in the report.

A provision may also be made on an optional basis for the two-year teacher training programme in such a way that a teacher trainee could complete the full programme in two phases, the first phase being of one year duration and the second phase of not more than five year duration, during which the second year programme could be covered through summer courses or other short-term courses. Those who have completed the first year programme could be made eligible for appointment as teachers on probation.

Pioneering and pace-setting value-oriented institutions should be established, preferably one in each State, which should be utilised as centres for training teachers on the basis of the new ideas and values recommended in the report. In this context, it would be essential to avoid harking back to the mythology and metaphysics of the old religious systems of India. A few national institutions of teacher education should be designated and established, especially to educate the staff of the colleges of teacher education in value education in India.

An all India Public Examination for the evaluation of teacher trainees should be instituted, which would have novel features such as the combination of the written test with oral test and submission of a project report, all of which would have a special thrust towards the promotion of excellence, value-education and a sound acquaintance with India and Indian Values.

The Conference of Deans of Education and Chairmen, Boards of Studies in Education of Southern Universities in 1986 made certain far-reaching recommendations which are different from the Review Committee's recommendations. Some of the recommendations propose early action in respect of:

- Expeditious action to be taken up by the Deans, and Chairmen of the Boards of Studies to revise the B.Ed. and M.Ed. programmes in their respective universities for implementing Value Education at the earliest.
- Fully equipping at least one Department of Education in a University or a College of Education in every State with well

qualified and adequate staff and an enriched library together with cultural materials and other artefacts and equipment for successful organisation of value education programme. There is no need to start new pace-setting institutions.

- Instead of introducing additional courses of study in Philosophy, Psychology and Indian Culture or Freedom Struggle, the same material can be properly integrated with the existing course, and for this the Department of Culture, Government of India may be involved.
- The National Council for Teachers Education may be given statutory status and empowered to certify licensed teachers, recognise courses and qualifications and accredit teacher education institutions as per the norms developed and agreed to by professional/expert committees of the N.C.T.E.
- Case studies may be prepared of selected institutions where conscious attempts for value education have been made and have met with notable success.

## Role of the National Council of Educational Research and Training

The significance of value education to emerging India and the urgency for its propagation have been stressed at various conferences, seminars and workshops. As a follow-up action, the National Council of Educational Research and Training is undertaking several measures. In the area of teacher training, renewal of teacher education curricula both at the elementary and secondary levels has been taken up to incorporate value education components and the development of courses and text books. Resource material and handbooks for the use of teachers are being prepared.

The NCERT has also produced prototype instructional resource support material for the use of educational planners and administrators, teacher trainers, teachers, and students. These are in the form of reading materials, exemplar units, source books and audio-visual materials so that the States can develop their own materials or modify/adapt these to suit their specific needs and requirements. The Central Institute of Educational Technology has produced a wide range of educational technology materials—films, video programmes, charts, slides, and film strips pertaining to different areas of learning.

With regard to the teacher education programme, Advance Planning by NCERT includes: Organising short training programmes for the production of non-traditional instructional materials for State level functionaries working in SCERTs, and SIEs and leading Teacher Education Institutions etc.

## Developing Curriculum in Education

A carefully planned, effectively implemented and appropriately evaluated curriculum is essential to any level and any course in education. Teacher education has to undergo continuous reorientation in order to meet the dynamic conditions and growing demands faced by the teaching community. The Curriculum Development Committee adopted a systems-based approach first by obtaining the syllabi of B.Ed. and M.Ed. courses of various Colleges of Education and Departments of Education of Universities, reviewing the same and suggesting a modified curriculum. Regional Curriculum Development Centres have to monitor the implementation of this and evaluate the curriculum in action.

Value Education as a Paper does not find a place in the recommended curriculum in the above attempt. It has been relegated to the status of a mere unit in the Paper: Teacher and Education in Indian Society. Again, the sub-units are not properly balanced. The classification of Values is narrow; the hierarchy of Human Values is missing. Significance of Traditional and Modern Values, their sociological implications and value as the guiding lights in formulating the objectives of education, value crisis in the present society and the need for inculcating values and the teachers' role through a well-devised programme of education are not included. In the suggested modules of Core Papers for the M.Ed. level sub-units deal with the origin of values, discussion about the nature of values, absoluteness and relatively which aims at intellectual exercise. There is a mere suggestion that the students will examine the scope for the realisation of the values through education.

## Objectives of Teaching Values in Teachers Colleges

At the National Seminar on Inculcation of Ethical and Social Values in Education at the Ramakrishna Mission Vidyalaya in 1980, the following objectives were suggested.

It was envisaged that the training should help the teacher trainee to:

(a) acquire knowledge and understand the need for imparting; education in ethical and social values in secondary schools;
(b) realise their roles as spiritual guides in schools;
(c) pick out those aspects of the syllabi in their disciplines at secondary level, which may lend themselves for moral instruction;
(d) effectively involve the pupils in learning the values through curricular and co-curricular activities; and
(e) organise various activities for the pupils' involvement in learning the concepts of moral education.

**Methods and Techniques of Teaching Values**

The Department of Teacher Education, D.A.V. College, Dehradun, organised a 4-week All India Workshop on Methods and Techniques of Teaching Values. Apart from the traditional method of teaching, modern value clarifying approaches for value development were also discussed in detail. Critical incident sheet, value activity check list, value games, value voting, value continuum, incomplete value sentences, role playing, mediational counselling and fantasy exploration were also prepared and demonstrated. Four Value Kits for teaching Social, Scientific and National Values and Punctuality were prepared by the participants after analysing each value and defining it operationally. After an indepth discussion, the behavioural objectives, methodology, teaching-learning materials, teaching strategies, and evaluation scheme were finalised. General guidelines for using these kits were also formulated. The following are some of the recommendations which emerged out of the workshop:

- A separate Teacher Training University be established in every State wherein value education programmes should be made an integral part of the teacher training programme.
- The U.G.C. should take a lead in introducing value education programmes for teachers at the higher education level.
- Teacher orientation programmes should be taken up at the national, state, regional and district levels.

— Value education kits should be prepared for each important value and should be validated scientifically. These should be distributed free of cost and the teachers of colleges and universities should be encouraged to make use of these kits effectively.
— Detailed guidelines, uniform through the country, related to value teaching should be prepared and made available to teachers.

**Source Book on Education in Values**

Regional College of Education, Mysore involved a team of teachers, teacher educators, philosophers, sociologists and psychologists of education by organising a series of meetings and workshops to carry out the stagewise completion of the source book project: 'Education in Values—a Source Book'. This has been published by the NCERT.

**Ramakrishna Institute of Moral and Spiritual Education, Mysore**

The institution firmly believes that training of teachers is the most important need for effective value education. The B.Ed. course affiliated to the University of Mysore has been designated to provide value education in theory and practice. It has a compulsory course for the study of the major religions of the world and stress on the essential unity in all these religions so as to foster a sense of brotherhood of man and fatherhood of God. Due focus is given on the social problems that hinder moral education such as drug addiction, drinking, corruption, environmental pollution and decline in moral values. The students are given special training in preparation of suitable instructional materials. Daily routine of the course starts with a morning prayer and it includes many activities like meditation, yoga classes, *shramadan*, classroom lectures, independent studies, music and *bhajans*, sports and games. These activities promote desire for excellence, spirit of patriotism, sense of equality, dignity of labour and spiritual upliftment.

The Government of Karnataka deputes 200 teachers every year for a two-month Diploma course in Moral and Spiritual Education. In each of the four courses of two-month duration, the purpose is to enlarge the outlook of teachers and to stimulate them for thinking on different dimensions of moral and spiritual path to be followed. The training programme includes regular discourses and discussions on prominent world religions and their common universal teachings for the well-being and progress of mankind. India's cultural heritage, biographies of great men including scientists, and saints, philosophers and statesmen to provide inspiration to students form an integral part of the programme. Special lectures by guest speakers, film shows pertaining to social and moral values are included.

**Sri Sathya Sai Institute of Higher Learning**

In the Foundation Course of the B.Ed. Programme, students are exposed to an overall knowledge about our land and people, Indian culture and Constitution, world perspectives covering physical, commercial and geographical features, world's races, major religions of the world, literature and arts, landmarks in the study of science, spiritualism and science, nature of man, Indian and Western view points, transformation of man, self-fulfilment, national system of education, Sri Sathya Sai Model of Education, insights into the personal philosophy of life etc.

In addition to the foundation course, 'Education in Human Values' is another course of the B.Ed. programme. It introduces the trainees to the concept of values, need for value-based education, unity of mankind, values enshrined in the Indian Constitution, organisation of values under five core sectors of Truth, Righteous conduct, Peace, Love an Non-violence; methods and techniques of teaching human values in the schools and their evaluation. There are practical exercises as well.

**National Commission for Value Education**

The Indian Council of Philosophical Research organised a National Level Seminar on Value Education in 1992. They have recommended:

- — Immediate constitution of a non-governmental voluntary national commission for value education which will work out an indigenous system of education from what is available in the best of Indian and non-Indian traditions and to promote the cause of value education.
- — Establishment of a national centre for value education with fur separate wings: (1) educational and training wing,

(2) research wing, (3) extension wing, and (4) a co-operation and administrative wing to effect coordination between the functioning of the other three wings of the centre.

— The centre would work under the overall supervision and guidance of the commission which should be set up immediately.

— The Union Ministry of Human Resource Development, the UGC, the AIU, various Boards of Education at the State and national level, the Universities, the college development councils and schools should create special cells to promote value orientation in education and to monitor their implementation.

— Social service should be made meaningfully compulsory and should be a condition for awarding any degree or certificate in the field of education.

— All universities, colleges, schools and their faculty should show a commitment towards Gandhian, cultural, secular, national, scientific, and non-gender-bias values.

**Core Group on Value Orientation of Education**

The Planning Commission, in its Eighth Five Year Plan (1992-97), incorporated a statement about constituting a Core Group on Value Education in Education. The Core Group has representatives of the Union Ministry of Human Resource Development, National Council of Educational Research and Training, University Grants Commission, Association of Indian Universities and Navodaya Vidyalaya Samithi, and Eminent educationists with practical experience of working in pace-setting institutions and organisations, who have made significant contribution in developing concrete programmes of education in human values. The Core Group recommends establishment of a National Coordination Agency for promotion and coordination of efforts in value orientation of education.

The Core Group offered very pertinent recommendation about the role of the UGC in value orientation. It suggested that the UGC should:

— carry out in collaboration with NCERT, its Regional Colleges of Education, SIEs etc., a comparative study of the content of M.Ed., and B.Ed., programmes of various Universities and develop self-contained Foundation and Awareness courses as well as specific programmes relating to 'Education in Human Values' for new entrants to the teaching profession at the school stage. Some operational model courses, which have been worked out by universities and college after considerable experimentation should be used for making working models. The Universities need to be assisted for undertaking modules for enlisting teachers.

— suitably modify various components of the Academic Staff College designed for fresh teachers of the colleges to incorporate material relating to Indian culture and ethos. Role and Duty of Teaches, Spiritualism and Science, Youth Psychology and Learning, Great Teachers of the world, Secularism, Indian Constitution, Unity of India, Human Values and human excellence etc., should be projected.

— make available Audio-visual and printed materials to Academic Staff College which would be expected to introduce these as part of the orientation programmes in:

Component A : Awareness of linkages between society; environment, development and education.

Component B : Philosophy of Education stressing the inter-relation between society, Indian education system and pedagogy.

Component C : Subject upgradation.

Component D : Management and Personality Development in the context of society, environment and development of education.

### * Suggested Value Education Programme in Teacher Education

In the light of the above review of efforts to incorporate value education in teacher education, the need for a well-defined programme for adoption in Colleges of Education has become apparent. Mere appending of a unit on value education to the existing Core Papers would not do justice to this important subject. Hence, a Paper on Value Education should be introduced in the B.Ed. course. It should have both theoretical and practical aspects. Where non-semester pattern is followed, the Value Education Paper should have at least 12 units of Theory. The same syllabus can meaningfully be divided into two parts suitable to the institutions where semester pattern is in vogue.

**Value Education Paper : Objectives**

The teacher-trainees will be assisted through this paper to:

(i) understand the importance of values in human life and the necessity of value of education;
(ii) appreciate the basic principles of major religions of the world;
(iii) acquire the knowledge of the greatness of Indian culture and the significance of our national goals;
(iv) understand the relevance of the values advocated by great leaders;
(v) acquire the knowledge and values enshrined in Indian constitution; and
(vi) understand the methods of inculcating values and, in this context, the role of family, school and society.

**Syllabus for the Programme**

The syllabus will have 12 units with the following contents:

*Unit - I*

Values – Definition – Classification of Values – Value consciousness; Importance of Values.

*Unit - II*

Values emphasised in the Scriptures of Major Religions of the World : Vedas and Upanishads—The Bhagavad Geeta, The Quran and The Bible.

*Unit – III*

Values advocated by Kabir, Guru Nanak, Swami Vivekananda, Sri Ramakrishna Paramhansa, the Sufis and Sir Sarada Devi. The Gandhian values—Implications for education.

*Unit – IV*

India's common cultural heritage and ethos – Values enshrined in Indian Constitution – Removal of social barriers – Equality of the sexes – Inculcation of scientific temper – small family norm – protection of the environment.

*Unit – V*

Importance of Peace and Cooperation—National Integration and International Understanding—Universal brotherhood.

*Unit – VI*

Traditional and modern values—Absolute and Relative values—Value Conflict—Value Crisis—Need for Value Education—Science and Spirituality.

*Unit – VII*

Levels of development of the Affective Domain—Internalisation of Values—Kohlberg's stages of Moral Development.

*Unit – VIII*

Inculcation of Values—Role of Family, society, religious organisations, voluntary organisations—the impact of Mass media.

*Unit – IX*

Inculcation of values—curriculum of the school—school practices and traditions—impact of the Teachers—peer group.

*Unit – X*

Methods of teaching values—Direct and Indirect—Social Learning Model—Jurisprudential Inquiry Model—Critical Incident Approach and Integrated Atmospherical Approach—Value Clarification Approach.

*Unit – XI*

Assessment of Values—Observations, Cumulative Record, Anecdotal Record, Situational Tests—Value Scales, Projective Techniques.

*Unit – XII*

Analysis of Text books of secondary classes—treatment of values.

*** Practical Aspect of Value Education in Colleges of Education**

1. Morning assembly—prayers from different faiths—silent prayer-sayings of great persons—short speech by students on the life of great leaders, humanitarians, inventors—mass physical exercise.
2. Manual Labour—social service—youth for mass literacy.
3. Observation of days of importance—participation in cultural activities.
4. Review of articles in magazines, programmes in radio, T.V., films for depiction of values.
5. Preparation of album, conducting an exhibition on value theme.

*** Suggestion for Implementing Value Orientation in Teacher Education**

A. With its vast experience and resource, Ramakrishna Institute of Moral and Spiritual Education can serve as a Model Institution for inculcating value education to teacher educators through pre-service and in-service programmes. Short-term course for them can be organised.
B. The proposed National Commission can function with close contact with the RIMSE.
C. Such Colleges of Education, which are already following exemplary value education oriented programmes can serve as pace-setting Centres with well-equipped library, teaching media, and a well-maintained research wing in the field.
D. The Pace-setting institutions should (i) prepare reading material, (ii) prepare source books, instructional aids and

modules, (iii) evaluate, and (iv) standardise the same for use in different teacher-training institutes.

This would provide flexibility to make wise adaptations to regional language and literature. The SCERTs should take initiative in the conduct of such work under its guidance.

E. The orientation courses and refresher courses conducted by the Academic Staff Colleges should mould, their programmes to offer the teacher educators a sound basis in value education.

## REFERENCES

1. Chourasia, G. Teacher Education for the 21st Century, *Progressive Educational Herald,* Vol. 4 No. 2, 1990.
2. *Ethical and Social Values in Teacher Education* : Report of the Working Group, 27-29th August, 1980 at Sri Ramakrishna Vidyalaya, Coimbatore.
3. *Inculcation of Ethical and Social Values in Teacher Education* : Report of the Working Group N.C.E.R.T., 1982.
4. National Commission for Value Education, *University News*, Vol. xxx, No. 30, 1992.
5. *National Policy on Education*, 1986.
6. News Letter Vol. 7 No. 6 1992, Regional College of Education, Mysore.
7. *Report of the Core Group on Value Orientation of Education*, Planning Commission, Government of India, New Delhi, 1992.
8. *Report of the Curriculum Development Centre*—Education Vol. 1 (1989), Vol. 2 (1990) : U.G.C.
9. *Report of the Working Group to Review Teachers' Training Programme* (in the light of the need for Value Orientation), Ministry of Education and Cultural, Government of India, New Delhi, 1983.
10. *Resource Material*, Parts I and II : National Scheme of Inservice Training of School Teachers, N.C.E.R.T., 1987.
11. Ruhela, S.P. *Value Orientation of Teacher Education Curricula in India, Human Values and Education,* New Delhi : Sterling Publishers Private Limited, 1986.
12. Singh, R.P. *Teacher Education in India : An Appraisal, Progressive Educational Herald,* Vol. 6, No. I, 1991.
13. Techniques of Teacher Values, *University News*, Vol. xxvi, No. 33, 1988.
14. *Value Orientation to Education* : Report of the Conference of Deans of Education, N.C.E.R.T., 1986.

# SECTION III

## VALUES IN BUSINESS MANAGEMENT

27

# Managing Value Based Ethical Behaviour in Business and Governance

SHAILENDRA SINGH AND KUMUD SINGH

Society always sets certain norms, codes, and set of standards to regulate the behaviour of its members. These norms, codes or set of standards depict what is good or bad human behaviour and what constitutes sensible human existence. There are also set of standards, code of behaviour set by the society for managing, governing and doing business. These codes may be termed as codes of business/managerial ethics. Thus business ethics provide guidelines as to what is right or wrong in the work place and doing what is right. Nash (1994), while emphasizing study of business ethics stated that idea of ethical conduct in business is not so simple. People may argue that most if not all of the values that constitute ethical behaviour in business : honesty, fairness, respect for others, service, promise keeping, prudence, and trustworthiness are familiar part of most managers' socialization. However it is a sad story that these common sense values have experienced setback at work. Although we have accepted *Satyameva Jayate* as a part of our national emblem, our country has become the country of scams having earned distinction of Urea scam, Sugar scam, stock market scam, UTI scam, Hawala scam, Fodder scam, Telecommunication scam, Cricket Match Fixing scam, Tahelka scam and the most recent Punjab Public Service Commission Appointment scam just to name a few. Recognising our distinction in corruption, Transparency International, based on results of 12 surveys, has declared us one among top 20 most corrupt nations of the world (Transparency International, 2001).

Debating on values and anti-corruption measures cannot be overemphasized at this juncture when the society, organizations and individuals are bitten by corruption bug and experiencing crisis of values at its peak. Even our Late Prime Minister had admitted that only 15 paise out of one rupee reaches to beneficiary. Vittal (1999) pointed out that there are five key players to Indian corruption scene. These are the corrupt politician (*neta*), the corrupt bureaucrat (*babu*), corrupt business (*lala*), the corrupt NGOs (*jhola*) and finally the criminal (*dada*). There are five reasons why our system encourages corruption. These are: (*i*) scarcity of goods and services, (*ii*) lack of transparency, (*iii*) red tape and delay due to obsolete rules and procedure which are time consuming and encourage speed money, (*iv*) cushion of legal safety due to compassionate principle that everybody is innocent till proved guilty, and (*v*) finally, *biradari* or tribalism, where the corrupt public servants protect each other. The issue of roots and consequences of corruption and ways and means of dealing with them is very vast topic and is beyond the scope of this paper. To limit the scope of this paper under the presented backdrop, we propose to address following questions:

1. What are the underlying principles for acceptance of values?
2. How managerial transactions and ethical dilemmas can be understood within ethical and legal framework?
3. What are the ways to deal with ethical dilemmas and eroding values at work?

## Underlying Principles for Acceptance of Values

People use different criteria and underlying principles while making value base ethical choices. Here are four different underlying principles which are often used in decision making by managers:

1. Test of universality
2. Test of utilitarianism
3. Test of rights
4. Test of justice

*Test of Universality:* This criterion emphasizes that we should not do anything that we would not like in similar circumstances. Under the test a code will be considered ethically correct if it can be applied universally. This is a general principle that helps us evaluate all other values and provides a balance when people experience a conflict of values. For example. Would I like to be fired for whistle blowing? The answer is—No. Thus the action of firing for whistle blowing does not pass the test of universality, hence, it should be considered unethical behaviour within this framework.

*Test of Utilitarianism:* The objective of utilitarianism is to provide the greatest good for greatest number. This view dominates managerial decision making. It is in line with organizational goals of efficiency, productivity, and profitability. By maximizing profits, for example, a manager can assert that he is achieving the greatest good for greatest number by declaring dismissal of 10 per cent of his employees.

*Test of Rights:* This principle focuses on individual's basic rights. This puts responsibility on the managers to take decisions that do not violate fundamental rights of people affected by the decisions. Such rights include right to privacy, right of freedom of speech, right of association, and right of individual choice. Whistle blowers get protection under this criterion when they report malpractices of their organization to media or government agencies on the ground of freedom of speech.

*Test of Justice:* This test focuses on justice. This requires individuals to enforce or administer the rule fairly and impartially, so that there are equitable benefits and costs. Unions and staff associations typically support this view. It justifies paying people the same wage for a given job irrespective of performance differences.

Each of the four principles has pluses and minuses. The test of universality leads us to choose values as 'absolute standards' by invoking conscience. Universality will be judged by ethics of means and not on the basis of end justifies means. Only problem with this approach is that conscience is very subjective and we may end up having bewildering decisions by different people, each following their own conscience (Sekhar,1997). Utilitarianism promotes productivity and efficiency but it tends to ignore rights of some individuals, particularly those with minority representation in the organization. Use of rights as a criterion furthers the interest of people, and is consistent with freedom and privacy, but it can create overtly legalistic work environment which may ultimately hamper productivity and efficiency of the organization. Test of justice helps protect the interest of weaker and minority but may likely to reduce risk taking, productivity, and innovation by developing a culture of entitlements.

Managers are most comfortable in decision making while following utilitarian criterion. A lot of questionable decisions get justified when explained as being in the best interests of the organization and stockholders. It is also always opposed to universality criterion. Universality criterion poses relatively less problem. The real challenge arises when these decisions are put to scrutiny on other criteria such as justice and rights. Thus whatever criteria managers or administrators will be following, there will bound to be ambiguities and contradictions which they have to tolerate and live with. The political processes in organizations and society therefore determine as to which criteria will be followed by managers. The group or groups having more power will influence the choice of ethical principle.

Ethical principles are based on natural law which precede the codified law passed by various legislature. There may be many situations where codified law is not evolved, and therefore unethical behaviour does not get subsumed under illegal behaviour. Similarly, on certain issues codified law has its provisions which actually do not pass the criteria of ethical principles. If we want to classify any decision or behaviour of individual, group, or organization in two dimensional ethicality and legality framework in Fig. 27.1 emerges:

| Legality \ Ethicality | Unethical | Ethical |
|---|---|---|
| Illegal | Q1<br>Zone of Crime | Q3<br>Post-conventional<br>Conscience driven<br>Behaviour |
| Legal | Q2<br>Ethical Dilemma | Q4<br>Normative Behaviour |

**Fig. 27.1**: Behaviour in Ethical-Legal Framework

**The First Quadrant: The Zone of Crime**

Individuals, groups and organizations displaying behaviour which are unethical as well as illegal will amount to crime. Behaviour of managers as individuals or as agents of organizations falling in this zone will be treated as crime. We can have a long list of behaviour that can be classified in this quadrant. An illustrative list is provided below by way of example:

1. All kind of corrupt practices using official position for personal gains.
2. Corporate frauds.
3. Tax evasion.
4. Falsifying organizational records.
5. Submitting false statement to officials and media.
6. Making false assertions in reports to misguide stockholders.
7. Making false claim about product and services to cheat customers.
8. Not fulfilling contractual obligations.
9. Not paying to employees their due.

**The Second Quadrant: The Zone of Ethical Dilemmas**

This quadrant refers to the behaviour full of ethical dilemmas as behaviour classified here is legal but does not pass the test of ethical standards. Behaviour are considered legal as there is no explicit prohibition for that behaviour under any law of the land, but the same time treated as unethical when various tests of ethical standards are applied. People displaying such behaviour, though justify means with to achieve the end, experience considerable dissonance and will try to move towards normative behaviour represented in quadrant four. Managers dismissing their permanent employees may be considered legal but unethical. Similarly, trying to get promotion in the job by ingratiating the boss can be considered legal but unethical behaviour. Some more examples follows:

1. Non-cooperation with colleagues.
2. Obey to authority, however unethical and unfair it may be.
3. Breaking a promise for better returns.

4. Subcontracting jobs in order to avoid industrial relations problem.
5. Not providing employment to persons of a particular community.
6. Not working with full sincerity.

## The Third Quadrant: The Zone of Post-Conventional Conscience Driven Behaviour

Behaviour subsumed in this category are ethical but fail to pass the scrutiny of legality. This zone belongs to ethical law-breakers (Sekhar, 1997). Not that such people break the law in ordinary course of action. But on many occasions law is inconsistent with their personal values, their personal conscience forces them to violate law and behave on the dictates of conscience. Kohlberg (1981) describes a situation where a person did not have money to pay for medicine for his wife, and pharmacist will not give the medicine on credit. The wife is critical and will die if she does not get medicine on time, the person experiences value conflict between saving a life and the other of not stealing and breaking the law. Then he applies the test of universalisability. How would I behave if I were in the place of pharmacist? I would not have minded if someone would have broken into the shopunder similar condition. Thus decides to break law to save the life of wife. Kohlberg call this stage of moral development as post-conventional stage of moral development where persons develop their own set of ethical standards for judging right or wrong. Behaviours subsumed in this quadrant, though, ethical disturbs the fabric of social order, and erodes trust, thus are not condoned by law. These sets of behaviour also point out that current legal position is against the ethical standards, and put pressure on law makers to transform the law in line with current ethical thinking. Thus ethical law breakers although experience ethical dilemma, resolve their dissonance by preferring to break the law and accept punishment till the law does not change. A conscience driven employer may like to employ homosexuals in his organization even if this means violation of law of the land.

## The Fourth Quadrant: The Zone of Normative Behaviour

This quadrant includes those behaviours that are legal as well as ethical. This is the ideal situation individuals, organizations and society should aspire for. The bigger the area of this quadrant, the higher will be the effectiveness and health of organization. Similarly, smaller the area of quadrant one reflects soundness of organizational health.

Quadrant two and quadrant threc represent zone of ethical dilemmas and dissonance among decision makers. In order to manage values what we need to do is to suggest ways and means to reduce the quadrant one behaviour and promote and reinforce behaviour congruent to quadrant four. Ethical dilemma faced by decision makers need to be reduced by refining our legal system. The next section is devoted to exploring ways and means to deal with ethical dilemmas and eroding values.

## Towards Developing Value based Ethical Behaviour

In order to deal with ethical dilemmas and eroding values let us propose a three-dimensional framework having three agencies: Individual self, organization and the Third party to bring about change in behaviour of two targets (Individual self or organization) in preventive or curative ways. The term 'preventive' has been used in positive way suggesting protection and upholding of ethical behaviour:

| *Agency to Initiate Change* | *Target of Change* | | | |
|---|---|---|---|---|
| | *Individual Self* | | *Organization* | |
| | *Preventive* | *Curative* | *Preventive* | *Curative* |
| (Individual) Self | 1 | 4 | 7 | 10 |
| Organization | 2 | 5 | 8 | 11 |
| Third Party | 3 | 6 | 9 | 12 |

**Fig. 27.2:** Strategies for Developing Value based Ethical Behaviour

1. *Self Initiated Preventive Measures for Individual Self:* As mentioned in previous section experience of ethical dilemma generates a lot of dissonance in the individual and this dissonance is a painful psychological state. Person invariably wants to resolve this dissonance. Person makes deep introspection to his own values and behaviour, seeks counselling, approaches a mentor to clarify ones thoughts and feelings. Person can devote time to the study of business ethics literature to clarify ones values. Ones the individual gets guidelines, his dilemma may get resolved. Persons constantly

remain in touch with self, so that they are prepared to resolve dilemma in advance.

2. *Organization Initiated Preventive Measures for Individual Self:* Organization considers that preventive measures are better than cure, and thus tries introduce a series of policies and programmes which can maintain ethical values of high standards among its employees. The Josephson Institute of Ethics has proposed six ethical values which they call 'Six Pillars of Character' of individuals and organizations:

   (a) *Trustworthiness:* honesty, integrity, promise-keeping, loyalty.
   (b) *Respect:* autonomy, privacy, dignity, courtesy, tolerance, acceptance.
   (c) *Responsibility:* accountability, pursuit of excellence.
   (d) *Caring:* compassion, consideration, giving, sharing, kindness, loving.
   (e) *Justice and fairness:* procedural fairness, impartiality, consistency, equity, equality, due process.
   (f) *Civic virtue and citizenship:* law abiding, community service, protection of environment.

   Organizations need to set ethics programme which aims to develop and reinforce above mentioned values and such programme should be democratic in nature having support of all sections of employees. A checklist of guidelines provided by McNamara (2002) may be useful for organizations while developing code of ethics:

   1. Review any values which need to adhere to relevant laws and regulations.
   2. Review which values produce the top three or four traits of a highly ethical and successful product or service in your area.
   3. Identify values needed to address current issues in your workplace.
   4. Identify values needed, based on findings during strategic planning.
   5. Consider any top ethical values that might be prized by stakeholders.

6. Collect from the above steps, the top five to ten ethical values which are high priorities in your organization.
7. Compose your code of ethics; attempt to associate with each value, two example behaviours which reflect each value.
8. Include wording that indicates all employees are expected to conform to the values stated in the code of ethics.
9. Obtain review from key members of the organization.
10. Announce and distribute the new code of ethics (unless you are waiting to announce) it along with any new codes of conduct and associated policies and procedures.
11. Update the code at least once a year.

Organization can also start counselling and mentoring programmes where counsellors and mentors are available to employees for providing support and guidance in the moments of crisis and dilemmas. Persons provided with such support may most likely to behave within the zone Quadrant 4 and not fall in Q1, Q2 and Q3.

3. *Third Party Initiated Preventive Measures for Individual:* Sometime organizations don't initiate any change process itself but opens its gate for individuals and organizations to undertake the work of sensitising people within organization about ethical values. Starting various kinds of meditation programme accompanied with discourses on underlying philosophies by an NGO and a spiritual guru may be example in this category. Similarly, many activists visit organizations and interact with people and try to sensitize them to behave more ethically. NGOs, activists and spiritual *gurus* try to influence individuals to bring change in themselves. Socializing agents including parents, teachers, and community have responsibility to inculcate right behaviour and *samskaras* among the young so that they display ethical behaviour once they attain adulthood.
4. *Set-Initiated Curative Measures for Individual:* Many times persons slip into zone on illegal and unethical behaviour without much awareness. Once they realize that they have crossed the boundaries of legal and ethical behaviour, their conscience prick them and they start experiencing sense of guilt. They try to confess with near and dear and with

organizational superiors. They admit their mistakes and try to reform themselves. Similarly they actively seek counselling and mentoring, and devote their time in activities by way of *prayschita.* They try to work for community, do *shramdan,* or other form of service to compensate for their wrong doing and make *chitta shudhi.*

5. *Organization Initiated Curative Measures for Individuals:* Many times individuals cross the limits of ethical and legal behaviour. Organization detects the unethical behaviour, and initiates counselling process to cure the problem. Many organizations have regular ethics officer in place to attend such problems. If the violation is intentional and injures the interest of organization and community and does not get mended even after counselling, then the organizations have their regular disciplinary procedures to deal with such people. Vigilance Commission and police departments are also meant to deal with such behaviour. But organizations should use the help of law enforcing agencies only as a last resort once all other measures have failed.
6. *Third Party Initiated Curative Measures for Individuals:* Many NGOs and individuals serving as watchdogs of society are trying to cure the ills of society. They expose unethical and illegal behaviour of individuals. They try to invite attention of media to bring about change in such deviant people. Judicial pronouncements, social movement, and community pressure can be used to bring out curative changes in the behaviour of persons. In rural society still practices of boycotting: such as *Viradari bahar* (outcasting), *hukka pani band* (ban on sharing food, water and smoking), *jurmana* (fine) etc. are being used effectively for modifying behaviour unacceptable to the community.
7. *Individually Initiated Preventive Measures for Organizations:* There are individuals who are more sensitive to ethical standards than their employers are. Once they see any possibility of violation of somebody's rights they raise the issue with the organizations. They may be called conscience keepers of the organization. Such people are helpful for organizations as organizations are saved from experiencing a lot of embarrassment, hostility, litigation, and losses. Such people also

suggest to rule makers of the organizations to evolve and recast the rules in such a way that is just and equitable for one and all and people don't need to break the law in normal circumstances. For example, if organization is willing to get rid of a particular employee without any problem from employee's side, ethically oriented person will oppose this move. Many times these people threaten to take the role of whistle blowers to prevent unethical behaviour of organizations.

8. *Organizationally Initiated Preventive Measures for Organizations:* Organizations are well aware that following ethical standards are also in their business interest. Thus they initiate ethics programme to enforce ethical standards. McNamara's guidelines for initiating ethics programme in organizations holds true for this section also. Whether a decision is an ethical decision or not, need to be often clarified in corporate board room as well as in media. Managers may consider answering following questions to clear any ambiguity from their mind. If answers to these questions are clear yes then, then decision may be considered as ethical (Wallace & Pekel cited by McNamara, 2002).

   *Relevant Information Test*. Have I/we obtained as much information as possible to make an informed decision and action plan for this situation?
   *Involvement Test*. Have I/we involved all who have a right to have input and/or to be involved in making this decision and action plan?
   *Consequential Test*. Have I/we anticipated and attempted to accommodate for the consequences of this decision and action plan on any who are significantly affected by it?
   *Fairness Test.* If I/we were assigned to take the place of any one of the stakeholders in this situation, would I/we perceived this decision and action plan to be essentially fair, given all of the circumstances?
   *Enduring Values Test*. Do this decision and action plan uphold my/our priority enduring values that are relevant to this situation?
   *Universality Test*. Would I/we want this decision and action plan to become a universal law applicable to all similar situations, even to myself/ourselves?

*Light-of-Day Test*. How would I/we feel and be regarded by others (working associates, family, etc.) if the details of this decision and action plan were disclosed for all to know? Organizations also develop rules, regulations and personnel policies which are consistent with ethical standards and are not biased against any section or class of employees. Organizations also periodically broom the outdated and time consuming rules and regulations.

9. *Third Party Initiated Preventive Measures for Organizations:* Many NGOs and voluntary organizations having promotion of equity, justice and fair play and prevention of corruption as their objectives, prepare charters of behavioural norms and expect organizations to comply with stipulated norms in the charter and make voluntary disclosures regarding:
    1. Whether the organization is helping the community and how?
    2. Whether the organization is equal opportunity giving employer?
    3. Whether the organization is protecting the environment?
    4. Whether the organization is employing child labour?
    5. Whether the organization is following the policy of transparency?
    6. Whether the organization fulfils its promises?

    To avoid embarrassment of losing face before public and media or due to their own ethical compulsions organizations tend to comply to these charters. Initially complying to these charters seems to be pain in the neck, but gradually organizations learn to internalize these norms and values and then following those norms and values come naturally.

10. *Individually Initiated Curative Measures for Organizations:* Organizatinal members individually take on their employers if they feel that their employers are behaving unethically. Many times individuals who disclose unethical and illegal behaviour of their employers suffer personally, but the force of the conscience is so strong, that they cannot stop calling it fowl. Chief Vigilance Commissioner has already approached Chairman, Law Commission to enact Whistle Blower Act on line of Public Disclosure Act of UK (Vittal,1999) to protect the rights of whistle blowers.

11. *Organizationally Initiated Curative Measures for Organizations:* Curative measures are used when disease has set in. Organizations are bleeding because of corrupt and unethical practices used by employees as well as management disease of corruption and unethical behaviour is so deep that it has created rot. Organizations in both private and government sectors if want to deal with this rot, they have to undergo drastic surgery. Organizations should make stringent rules and regulations to deal habitual and intentional offenders. Of course these rules should be made available to the employees for their knowledge and understanding prior to implementation. In private sector organizations, once top management detects malpractice done by an officer, normally (s)he is asked to quit. Depending on the nature of misconduct and past performance employer either gives her/him simple discharge or dismissal with a stigma. It is public sector and government organizations where problem is complicated. Vittal (1999) has given certain guidelines to deal with corruption in this sector. His salient suggestions given below, may be considered as beginning point to start the operation:

1. On the line of Transparency International Survey, organizations may be surveyed and corruption perception index may be generated. Managers may be asked to reduce their score on corruption index by introducing perceptible changes. They operationalise what precisely they have done to reduce corruption.
2. Zero tolerance of corruption should be a principle not only from the demand side but from supply side also, meaning that by that both giving and receiving bribe are offence. Business organizations especially Chambers of Commerce, CII, ASSOCHAM, and FICCI should come together and sign antibribery convention and ensure that their members will not bribe.
3. Managers and public servants should declare their property annually.
4. Take speedy disciplinary action and punish the guilty.
5. Remove law and practices which are obsolete and require cumbersome and time consuming procedure.

6. Remove law and practices that promote corruption. For example, name of wilful defaulters must be disclosed to public and the banking secrecy practices should be stopped.
7. Enact Corrupt Public Servants (Forfeiture of Property Act).
8. Implement the Benami Transaction (Prohibition) Act and confiscate benami property.

12. *Third Party Initiated Curative Measures for Organizations:* Name of Anna Hajare, Khaimar will be written in golden words for upholding consumer rights movement and for fighting corruption respectively. Their effort was a third party effort to bring change in rotting system. Similarly, transporters of Delhi were not concerned with extent of pollution in Delhi; it is the Supreme Court of the country that took upon itself to re-establish cleaner and greener Delhi. Similarly, many voluntary organizations, and trade unions are raising issues to protect the interests of weaker sections and persuading or forcing organizations to behave more ethically.

The strategies for promoting value based ethical behaviour presented here clearly suggests that Q1 behaviour needs to be minimized. Normally this will be zone of counsellors, disciplinary authorities, vigilance professions and police. These authorities while promoting value based behaviour perform correctional function and represent all types of curative strategies. If overall social climate generated through culture, reinforcements, disciplining is positive, people are prevented from falling in that zone. Thus if parents and other socializing agents are discharging their responsibilities well by modelling trustworthy, kind, human, considerate, industrious behaviour, we shall have the largest population of Q4 behaviour. Generally, Q4 is the zone of normative behaviour which requires to be reinforced off and on, so that people repeatedly demonstrate ethically and legally sound behaviour. Ethical law breakers (Q3) give the message that law is inadequate. Thus they expect a curative change in organization systems, rule regulations and the law initiated by organization itself or by the third party. Behaviour falling in Q2 requires preventive measures initiated by individual, organization, or third party to make ethical norms more clear. Using Wallace and Pekel's (cited by McNamara, 2002) can also be handy to resolve ethical dilemmas.

## Conclusion

There is constant struggle for upholding value based ethical behaviour in organizations. We examined four criteria often used in decision making by managers: (*i*) Test of universality, (*ii*) Test of utilitarianism, (*iii*)Test of rights, and (*iv*) Test of justice. Using different criteria managers may arrive on different decisions as choice criteria is very subjective. When multiple individuals/groups are involved, the most powerful individuals/group choice of ethical principle or criteria is to be followed. Further the behaviour has been classified into a two dimensional framework forming four quadrants: Q1—Illegal and Unethical, Q2—Legal and Unethical, Q3—Illegal and ethical and Q4—Legal and Ethical. These zones were called zone of crime, zone of ethical dilemma, zone of ethical law breakers, and zone of normative behaviour respectively. A three dimensional framework has been proposed to manage and transform individuals and organizations value based behaviour in preventive and curative way.

**Transparency International Corruption Perceptions Index 2001**

| *Rank* | *Coutnry* | *2001 CPI Score* | *Surveys Used* | *Standard Deviation* | *High-Low Range* |
|---|---|---|---|---|---|
| 1 | 2 | 3 | 4 | 5 | 6 |
| 1 | Finland | 9.9 | 7 | 0.6 | 9.2-10.6 |
| 2 | Denmark | 9.5 | 7 | 0.7 | 8.8-10.6 |
| 3 | New Zealand | 9.4 | 7 | 0.6 | 8.6-10.2 |
| 4 | Iceland | 9.2 | 6 | 1.1 | 7.4-10.1 |
| 5 | Singapore | 9.2 | 12 | 0.5 | 8.5-9.9 |
| 6 | Sweden | 9.0 | 8 | 0.5 | 8.2-9.7 |
| 7 | Canada | 8.9 | 8 | 0.5 | 8.2-9.7 |
| 8 | Netherlands | 8.8 | 7 | 0.3 | 8.4-9.2 |
| 9 | Luxembourg | 8.7 | 6 | 0.5 | 8.1-9.5 |
| 10 | Norway | 8.6 | 7 | 0.8 | 7.4-9.6 |
| 11 | Australia | 8.5 | 9 | 0.9 | 6.8-9.4 |
| 12 | Switzerland | 8.4 | 7 | 0.5 | 7.4-9.2 |
| 13 | United Kingdom | 8.3 | 9 | 0.5 | 7.4-8.8 |
| 14 | Hong Kong | 7.9 | 11 | 0.5 | 7.2-8.7 |
| 15 | Austria | 7.8 | 7 | 0.5 | 7.2-8.7 |
| 16 | Israel | 7.6 | 8 | 0.3 | 7.3-8.1 |

(*Contd.*)

| 1 | 2 | 3 | 4 | 5 | 6 |
|---|---|---|---|---|---|
| 17 | USA | 7.6 | 11 | 0.7 | 6.1-9.0 |
| 18 | Chile | 7.5 | 9 | 0.6 | 6.5-8.5 |
| 19 | Ireland | 7.5 | 7 | 0.3 | 6.8-7.9 |
| 20 | Germany | 7.4 | 8 | 0.8 | 5.8-8.6 |
| 21 | Japan | 7.1 | 11 | 0.9 | 5.6-8.4 |
| 22 | Spain | 7.0 | 8 | 0.7 | 5.8-8.1 |
| 23 | France | 6.7 | 8 | 0.8 | 5.6-7.8 |
| 24 | Belgium | 6.6 | 7 | 0.7 | 5.7-7.6 |
| 25 | Portugal | 6.3 | 8 | 0.8 | 5.3-7.4 |
| 26 | Botswana | 6.0 | 3 | 0.5 | 5.6-6.6 |
| 27 | Taiwan | 5.9 | 11 | 1.0 | 4.6-7.3 |
| 28 | Estonia | 5.6 | 5 | 0.3 | 5.0-6.0 |
| 29 | Italy | 5.5 | 9 | 1.0 | 4.0-6.9 |
| 30 | Namibia | 5.4 | 3 | 1.4 | 3.8-6.7 |
| 31 | Hungary | 5.3 | 10 | 0.8 | 4.0-6.2 |
| 32 | Trinidad & Tobago | 5.3 | 3 | 1.5 | 3.8-6.9 |
| 33 | Tunisia | 5.3 | 3 | 1.3 | 3.8-6.5 |
| 34 | Slovenia | 5.2 | 7 | 1.0 | 4.1-7.1 |
| 35 | Uruguay | 5.1 | 4 | 0.7 | 4.4-5.8 |
| 36 | Malaysia | 5.0 | 11 | 0.7 | 3.8-5.9 |
| 37 | Jordan | 4.9 | 4 | 0.8 | 3.8-5.7 |
| 38 | Lithuania | 4.8 | 5 | 1.5 | 3.8-7.5 |
| 39 | South Africa | 4.8 | 10 | 0.7 | 3.8-5.6 |
| 40 | Costa Rica | 4.5 | 5 | 0.7 | 3.7-5.6 |
| 41 | Mauritius | 4.5 | 5 | 0.7 | 3.9-5.6 |
| 42 | Greece | 4.2 | 8 | 0.6 | 3.6-5.6 |
| 43 | South Korea | 4.2 | 11 | 0.7 | 3.4-5.6 |
| 44 | Peru | 4.1 | 6 | 1.1 | 2.0-5.3 |
| 45 | Poland | 4.1 | 10 | 0.9 | 2.9-5.6 |
| 46 | Brazil | 4.0 | 9 | 0.3 | 3.5-4.5 |
| 47 | Bulgaria | 3.9 | 6 | 0.6 | 3.2-5.0 |
| 48 | Croatia | 3.9 | 3 | 0.6 | 3.4-4.6 |
| 49 | Czech Republic | 3.9 | 10 | 0.9 | 2.6-5.6 |
| 50 | Colombia | 3.8 | 9 | 0.6 | 3.0-4.5 |
| 51 | Mexico | 3.7 | 9 | 0.6 | 2.5-5.0 |
| 52 | Panama | 3.7 | 3 | 0.4 | 3.1-4.0 |
| 53 | Slovak Republic | 3.7 | 7 | 0.9 | 2.1-4.9 |
| 54 | Egypt | 3.6 | 7 | 1.5 | 1.2-6.2 |
| 55 | El Salvador | 3.6 | 5 | 0.9 | 2.0-4.3 |

*Contd.*

| 1 | 2 | 3 | 4 | 5 | 6 |
|---|---|---|---|---|---|
| 56 | Turkey | 3.6 | 9 | 0.8 | 2.0-4.5 |
| 57 | Argentina | 3.5 | 9 | 0.6 | 2.9-4.4 |
| 58 | China | 3.5 | 10 | 0.4 | 2.7-3.9 |
| 59 | Ghana | 3.4 | 3 | 0.5 | 2.9-3.8 |
| 60 | Latvia | 3.4 | 3 | 1.2 | 2.0-4.3 |
| 61 | Malawi | 3.2 | 3 | 1.0 | 2.0-3.9 |
| 62 | Thailand | 3.2 | 12 | 0.9 | 0.6-4.0 |
| 63 | Dominican Rep. | 3.1 | 3 | 0.9 | 2.0-3.9 |
| 64 | Moldova | 3.1 | 3 | 0.9 | 2.1-3.8 |
| 65 | Guatemala | 2.9 | 4 | 0.9 | 2.0-4.2 |
| 66 | Philippines | 2.9 | 11 | 0.9 | 1.6-4.8 |
| 67 | Senegal | 2.9 | 3 | 0.8 | 2.2-3.8 |
| 68 | Zimbabwe | 2.9 | 6 | 1.1 | 1.6-4.7 |
| 69 | Romania | 2.8 | 5 | 0.5 | 2.0-3.4 |
| 70 | Venezuela | 2.8 | 9 | 0.4 | 2.0-3.6 |
| 71 | Honduras | 2.7 | 3 | 1.1 | 2.0-4.0 |
| 72 | India | 2.7 | 12 | 0.5 | 2.1-3.8 |
| 73 | Kazakistan | 2.7 | 3 | 1.3 | 1.8-4.3 |
| 74 | Uzbekistan | 2.7 | 3 | 1.1 | 2.0-4.0 |
| 75 | Vietnam | 2.6 | 7 | 0.7 | 1.5-3.8 |
| 76 | Zambia | 2.6 | 3 | 0.5 | 2.0-3.0 |
| 77 | Cote d'lvoire | 2.4 | 3 | 1.0 | 1.5-3.6 |
| 78 | Nicaragua | 2.4 | 3 | 0.8 | 1.9-3.4 |
| 79 | Ecuador | 2.3 | 6 | 0.3 | 1.8-2.6 |
| 80 | Pakistan | 2.3 | 3 | 1.7 | 0.8-4.2 |
| 81 | Russia | 2.3 | 10 | 1.2 | 0.3-4.2 |
| 82 | Tanzania | 2.2 | 3 | 0.6 | 1.6-2.9 |
| 83 | Ukraine | 2.1 | 6 | 1.1 | 1.0-4.3 |
| 84 | Azerbaijan | 2.0 | 3 | 0.2 | 1.8-2.2 |
| 85 | Bolivia | 2.0 | 5 | 0.6 | 1.5-3.0 |
| 86 | Cameroon | 2.0 | 3 | 0.8 | 1.2-2.9 |
| 87 | Kenya | 2.0 | 4 | 0.7 | 0.9-2.6 |
| 88 | Indonesia | 1.9 | 12 | 0.8 | 0.2-3.1 |
| 89 | Uganda | 1.9 | 3 | 0.6 | 1.3-2.4 |
| 90 | Nigeria | 1.0 | 4 | 0.9 | -0.1-2.0 |
| 91 | Bangladesh | 0.4 | 3 | 2.9 | -1.7-3.8 |

***Explanatory Notes***

*A more detailed description of the CPI methodology is available at www.transparency.org or www.gwdg.de/-uwvwf2001html*

**CPI 2001 Score** relates to perceptions of the degree of corruption as seen by business people, academics and risk analysts, and ranges between 10 (highly clean) and 0 (highly corrupt).

**Surveys Used** refers to the number of surveys that assessed a country's performance. A total of 14 surveys were used, and at least three surveys were required for a country to be included in the CPI.

**Standard Deviation** indicates differences in the values of the sources: the greater the standard deviation, the greater the differences of perceptions of a country among the sources.

**High-Low Range** provides the highest and lowest values of the sources. Since each individual source has its own scaling system, scores are standardised around a common mean for the subset of countries featuring in the individual survey. As a result, it is possible in rare cases that the highest value exceeds 10.0 and the lowest can be lower than 0.0. Only the aggregate final country scores are restricted to the reported range between 0 and 10.

### *Note on the Bangladesh Score*

Data for this country in 2001 was available from only three independent survey sources, and each of these yielded very different results. While the composite score is 0.4, the range of individual survey results is from -1.7 to +3.8. This is a greater range than for any other country. 71 stresses, therefore, that this result needs to be viewed with caution.

## REFERENCES

Kohlberg, L. (1981). *Essays in Moral Development*, Vol. I. New York: Harper & Row.

McNamara, C. (2002). *Complete Guide to Ethics in Management: An ethics toolkit for managers*. www.inapnp.orglibrary ethics ethxgde.htm

Nash, L.L. (1994). Why business ethics now? In John Drummond and Bill Bain (Eds.), *Managing Business Ethics*. Oxford: Butterworth-Heineman.

Sekhar, R.C. (1997). Ethical choices in business. New Delhi: Response.

Transparency International (2001) *Transparency International Corruption Perception Index* 2001. Berlin Germany: Transparency International Secretariat.

Vittal, N. (1999). *Applying zero tolerance to corruption*, www.cvc.nic.in/vscvc/note.html

# 28

# Values and Managerial Excellence in the Changing Business Environment

SWAMI PRASAD AND SHALINI NIGAM

## Introduction

Values are socially defined desires and goals that are internalised through the process of conditioning, learning and socialisation. In other words, values are goals set for achievement and they motivate, define and shape one's all activities — cognitive, affective and conative.

In the modern industrialized environment, serious erosion of moral values in all respects of life and the crises of values is experienced. We are witnessing tremendous value crisis throughout the world today. As the vitality of human belief in value is dying out in every land, the new generation has started to pooh pooh the unique epics and institutions giving place to erosion of spiritual and moral values in mind. As a result, the mind of man has been laciniated in to small frictions and fragments which makes the value content of human life a diminishing factor in modern times.

However, the picture appears to be slightly different in India. No doubt industrialization and technological development have hurted values of our people, but it is very little as compared to other western countries. Some other factors that have contributed to the value crises in India can be personal greed, meanness, selfishness, indifference to other's interests, laziness etc. Moreover, whatever may be the reason of present value crises, there is no gain saying the fact that the weakening of moral values in our life is creating serious social and ethical conflict. Thus, on one hand the declining moral standards in personal, behavioural and social life and the national ideological commitment to the values of democracy, socialism, secularism and modernization on the other hand have constituted the need and importance of value orientation in every sphere of our life including business management and the managerial excellence.

**Value of Business Managers**

Values of business managers can be understood by analysing their expected role and actual role performed by them. In India, managerial role is believed to be what it should be. It is felt that it is only the practising manager who knows to some extent the difference between the expected role and actual role. Even in Western countries many management thinkers have observed that there is difference between the both.

However, some of the important values, i.e. main perceptions regarding the expected role of business manager are as under:

1. *Entrepreneurial Values*: Refer to how managers take initiative towards work and environment. It includes efficiency orientation and pro-activity.
2. *Intellectual Values*: Refer to how managers think and use analytical reasoning. It include logical thought, conceptualization and diagnostic use of concepts.
3. *Interpersonal Values*: Refer to how managers interact with people. It include self-confidence, development of others, use of unilateral power, use of socialized power, use of oral communications, positive regard, group managing power, persuasion of others and upholding the image and reputation of others.
4. *Social Emotional Values*: Refer to the ego development and maturation of managers. It includes self-control, spontaneity, perceptual objectivity, stamina and adaptability.

Besides above managerial values or skills of a manager, there are some other attributes which contribute to the excellence of business managers. These are:

* *Experience based learning*—which includes experience, reflection, lessons and their application.

* *Personal growth and effectiveness plan*—which helps managers to strive for and effectiveness rather than just being busy in a mass of activities. It includes planning and organising, implementation of plans, evaluation of plans and learning from experiences.
* *Organizational socialization*—which enables the managers to learn value system, norms and the required behaviour pattern of the society.

Values held by managers, play a very important role in development of himself, the organization and the environment inside and outside the organisation in following manners:

1. Values have strong influence on organizational culture and climate.
2. Values help the management in determination of corporate strategy.
3. Values lead to action and decision making capacity.
4. Values decide perception of the organisation as impersonal, paternalistic, formal, informal, hostile etc.
5. Values are intrinsic part of the life and behaviour.
6. Managerial values determine the quality of work value and the strong work values lead to acceptance of challenges, serving others, prestige, status, creativity and the independence.

## Changing Business Environment and Managerial Excellence

Change is the law of nature and it is believed that organisation is not a static establishment. Hence, due to changes in environment, technology and socio-economic conditions here is always a corresponding change in the organisation. The rapid socio-economic changes and the growing complexities of the business environment have necessitated the organisational changes in continuing basis and at faster rate. It is felt that in the ever changing and complex business environment our managerial task is quite challenging. Today, a manager has to learn new skills, carry the staff along and shoulder the burden of responsibility. The success of business hinges on how efficiently the manager perform his job and thus, our business management style, philosophy, efforts and values are bound to change.

The economic, social and political outlook of India in last twenty years has tremendously changed due to restructuring of economy as well as science, technology, business, trade, industry etc. Recently, the New Economic Policy declared by the Government of India has changed the entire scenario of our trade, industry, business and related services also. The move towards privatisation, liberalisation and globalisation in context with the recent GATT Agreement has led to a New World Trade Order. All these changes have opened the doors of wide business opportunities. These new opportunities abound as a result of delisensing, opening of the previously controlled sectors and expansion in the global market. Meanwhile, competitive intensity also increases daily with imports, new domestic competition, and entry and expansions of multinationals. In this situation Indian trade and industry has no alternative but to get ready to meet progressively with the international competition. Therefore, it is necessary for our Indian management to take a fresh look at their respective business as to what they ought to do and how best to do it.

In the present highly competitive environment it is very much essential for our business managers to maintain their values and should develop new management thoughts and practices. Innovation, speed, service and quality are watchwords of the decade in order to attain dramatic improvements in performance of a business.

It is apparent that the present changing environment on one hand has created a number of business opportunities on the other it has hurted values of our business managers. Today, there seems a gap between the expected role and actual role performed by them especially in public sector undertakings in India. Some of the main attributes which contribute the fall in values of controlled sectors and expansion in the global market. Meanwhile, competitive intensity also forces the persons of one organisation to establish contact with the persons from other organizations, wishing subordinates on the shop floor level wishing higher authorities on wedding anniversaries and visiting sick employees etc. These duties are very much important in managerial life which contribute to good human relations.

## Problem Generating Factors

- Managers do not perform liaison role properly and do not play their leadership roles effectively. They do not take interest in giving directions, appraising performance, taking feedback, correcting mistakes, giving suggestions to the subordinates and determining rewards, punishment etc. in an appropriate manner.

- They do not collect required information from adequate channel. They use to take all information including unrelated ones from their personal contacts which they have developed.
- They do not follow proper communication pattern which creates frustration and dissatisfaction amongst subordinates ultimately leading to strikes, lockouts, bandh etc.
- Managers use to delegate their own powers to the subordinates which leads to managerial ineffectiveness.
- Managers do not take active part in negotiation with internal agents like union leaders, supervisors, subordinates, and colleagues and external agents like business parties, potential clients, Government agencies' representative etc.
- It is also felt that managers are involuntarily responding to pressures and crisis situation. With increasing indiscipline in the working class, with use of strike tactics, power breakdown, rising prices, tax hits, uncertainty in material supplies, energy crisis, delay etc. managers are becoming more and more involved.

**Remedial Measures**

The managers today are encircled with the circular path which is moving with the process of change. In fact the changes of the present time are so fast that the managers are unable to catch their breath in time. Thus, the values of our business managers are falling continuously.

In order to achieve success in the liberalised and globalise scenario of India, managers are to take advantage of the current situation. They are to build effective organisation structure, train motivated and committed staff and take sound decisions. But, these action will need to develop and a vision which may be considered a central theme of the total business development process. A vision may include various important aspects like values, philosophy, policies, commercial, rational, financial performance, direction priorities etc. In these days of complex economic scenario and cut throat competition the managers are required to prepare for a quantum jump. It is, therefore, suggested that:

1. In order to ensure company growth, efficient product planning, good quality of product, efficient marketing methods, effective

pricing policies, advertisement, adequate profit margin, conflict resolution, self-analysis and others appraisal, our managers should maintain their values and should develop their knowledge, skill, competence etc.

2. Our business managers should give more emphasis on strategic management based on common sense and current needs.
3. They should follow some systems of thought. In addition to the general education they must acquire specialised knowledge and experience in the field of specific operations.
4. Our managers should acquire technical skill, a wide perception and understanding to the business environment.
5. Managers should acquire and develop some basic qualities in them. These are: (a) physical qualities, (b) mental qualities, (c) moral qualities, (d) specialised knowledge, (e) value based general education, (f) skill, (g) initiative, (h) motivation, (i) flexibility and (j) courage.
6. Our managers must touch and influence the lifestyle of subordinates, make them aware of their potential, show the way towards better accomplishment, reduce obstacles and cause employees to achieve goals, provide effectiveness to human efforts etc.
7. Managers should initiate interaction and interrelationship at all level of management mainly to extract the best out of any individual.
8. It is for the management to initiate management development programmes and to appraise them from time to time. The techniques of management development are two dimensional viz. On the job techniques and off the job techniques. On the job techniques mainly include coaching, job rotation, understudy, multiple management etc. and off the job techniques are case study, incident method, role playing, in basket exercises, business games, sensitivity training, simulation, grid training, conferences, lectures etc. These techniques contribute to the managerial effectiveness and excellence to great extent.
9. Our management education pattern should also be reviewed and should be value based so that our new managers may be able to possess value oriented managerial capabilities, skill, competence etc.

10. In the changing environment our organisational structure should be realized and job enrichment, human resource development and participative management system should be adopted. This will be the natural step towards enhancing organizational effectiveness.

## Conclusion

From the above description it is clear that the need for values of business managers and managerial excellence is enormous in the present changing business environment. Today, the job of manager is to anticipate this change and to turn it into new opportunity. Fundamentals of business also need change towards flexibility, team work, speed to market and quality management in the new environment. Therefore, the introduction of a system like KAIZEN will be of great help today. KAIZEN is a Japanese management concept which means continuous improvement. It implies non-stop improvements leading to zero management.

## REFERENCES


1. Santhanaraj, Stephen, *Approaches to Developing Managers: The Philips Experience, Developing Managers in Asia*, Tan Jing Hee & You Poh Seng (Eds), Addison-Wesley Publishing Company, Singapore.
2. Rao, T.V., *Readings in Human Resource Development*, Oxford and IBH Publishing Co. Pvt. Ltd., Bombay.
3. Prahallada, N.N., Contemporary Significance of Value Education, *University News*, Feb. 14th, 1994.
4. Mohanty, A.K. and Sadhu, P.K., The Need For Organisational Dynamics For Attaining Managerial Excellence Under the Changed Global Environment, *India Journal of Commerce*, Sept., 1995.
5. Lahiri, R.K., Organizational Dynamics and Managerial Excellence, *India Journal of Commerce*, Sept., 1995.

29

# Values for Business Managers

V.K. GUPTA AND MADHULIKA PAUL

---

An organisation succeeds or fails mainly due to the quality of its Management. A sleeping company becomes vibrant with a change of managerial team. The growth and development of a country also depends on to a considerable extent on the quality of its administrators. Rapid economic progress of the USA, Japan and West Germany has been because of the competence of the people who manage in these countries.

A professional manager is one who has undergone systematic training and experience and who utilises available tools with a scientific outlook and a sense of direction. Merely possession of an academic degree or diploma cannot make a manager an effective executive. People with formal education and training will have to prove their competence through good performance in terms of productivity, social dedication and sense of personal responsibility.

The word "ethics" is derived from the Greek word "ethos" which means character. Ethics is the discipline which deals with values relating to human conduct. From the standpoint of management, ethics may be defined as the standards governing the usual conduct of the members of the management. Ethics or values provide a basis for determining what is right or wrong, good or bad in terms of a given situation.

Ethics does not rest on feelings of approval or disapproval but is based on hard core realities of the present world. It may, for example, be unpleasant to fire a man but ethics may demand just this. Principles, not feelings give us ethics.

Business ethics relates to the behaviour of businessmen. It is concerned primarily with the relationship of business goals and techniques to human welfare. It studies the impact of business actions on the society as a whole. It is concerned with obligations which a person accepts when he becomes a part of the business world. It requires businessmen to be honest with themselves as well as with the society. It contains rules of conduct which businessmen should observe while dealing with others. However, there are certain cases which can be described as unethical. Few of them are given below—

- Keeping two sets of books to evade taxes,
- Using company property for personal use,
- Bribing public officials to obtain undue favours,
- Revealing confidential information or trade secrets,
- Overlooking safety violations to get the job done,
- Using false claims in advertisements,
- Understanding educational qualifications to get a low level job, and
- Artificially inflating profits to get re-elected as Directors.

Ethical considerations are as important in management as in any other occupation. In the field of morality, personal life is not separate from business life.

The social dimensions of business ethics cannot be overlooked because many problems arise from the relationship of business to the broader society. Ethical considerations are significant for managers due to the following reasons:

1. For every individual job is the centre of life. Unless job values are in harmony with the rest of life, he cannot be a happy and healthy person.
2. Modern society is an industrial society. Therefore, business values become the values of the society as a whole.
3. A business executive must take into consideration the moral and social considerations because these are the real motivating factors.
4. When an organisation fails to behave in avoidance with the social expectations, it may lose not only its image and market share but its very right of existence.
5. Today, a business manager is *expected to serve as a trustee of various social groups*. As the trustee he must observe the ethical values of the society.

**Ethical Influences on Business**

| *Functions* | *Ethics* |
|---|---|
| Marketing | Treatment of customer complaints |
| Advertising | Truth of claims |
| Location | Impact on community and environment |
| Production | Pollution treatment claims |
| Transportation | Safety regulation compliance |
| Administration | Concern for social values |
| Finance | Profits to re-compensate investors safeguarding assets |
| Personnel | Meeting promises to pay fair treatment in hiring, promotion, dismissal and pensions |
| Purchasing | Avoid hoarding |
| Information | Credibility validity |

As an organisation is an conglomeration of individuals, its values are the collective values of its members. That is why a conflict may arise between the values of the organisation and those of the individuals.

Further, the objectives of an organisation influences the values of its members. A business is an economic institution and it must be profitable. Many times, managers may be forced to compromise their personal ethical values in order to achieve organisational goals. But the goal may be tempered by many values. Leadership, integrity, knowledge and skills, survival are some of them. All these factors change the goals of an organisation and consequently expected behaviour from its members.

Another important factor which affects business ethics is work and career. Work refers to the job and the tasks or responsibilities associated with it. Career, on the other hand, represents a series of jobs or positions. Each work has its own values and persons performing the work follow these values, e.g. sales people may have different values than engineers. Thus, work and career creates special values that give unity, cohesion and meaning to persons and groups.

One more factor which affects the values in an organization is the role played by superiors. Most people succumb to pressure from superiors in doing things that they may consider unethical otherwise.

For example a secretary may tell a visitor that the boss is out when he is actually in because her boss has told her to do so. Many a times an employee may sign false documents due to pressure from the boss.

## Code of Conduct for Professional Managers

A professional manager is primarily responsible to his organisation. He is thereafter responsible to the following six stakeholders of his Organisation:

1. Investors,
2. Employees
3. Suppliers
4. Customers
5. Government
6. Community.

(*a*) As regards to ORGANISATION, a professional manager should:

1. Act both with loyalty and honesty in carrying out the lawful policy and instructions of his organisation and not undermine its image or reputation.
2. Plan, establish and review objectives, which are compatible with the codes of practice of other professionals in the enterprise and will help to meet the enterprise's overall objectives and, by his own work and through leadership and coordination direct all available efforts towards the success of an enterprise.
3. Provide a working climate in which innovation exchange of ideas are encouraged.
4. Fully respect the confidentiality of information which comes to him in the course of his duties, and not to use confidential information for personal gain or in a manner which may be detrimental to the organisation for which he works or has worked,
5. Pay proper regard to the safety and protection plant, material and processes committed to his charge.
6. In his contacts and dealing with other people, demonstrate his personal integrity and humanity and when called upon to give an opinion gives an opinion that is objective and reliable.

(*b*) As regards the INVERSTORS in his organisation, a professional manager should:

1. Ensure that surplus generated in the operations of the company is divided fairly among investors, employees and for further growth opportunities.
2. Ensure that the investors are given fairly accurate financial and other important operating information periodically.

(c) As regards the EMPLOYEES, a professional manager should:

1. Set an example for his subordinates through his own work capability and performance, through his leadership and by taking account of the needs and problems of his subordinates.
2 Train people in such a way so that they can discharge their duties properly and effectively.
3. Pay proper regards to the safety and well beings of the personnel for whom he is responsible.

(*d*) As regards the CUSTOMERS and SUPPLIERS, a professional manager should:

1. Ensure that the terms of all contracts and terms of business be stated clearly and unambiguously.
2. Operate an organisation's policy or require one to be established, which excludes corrupt practices, with regard to the giving or receiving of gifts or benefits and not to tolerate any activity which could lead malaise and unfair trade practices.

(*e*) As regards GOVERNMENT, a professional manager should:

Conform to the national interest as expressed in Government policy.

(*f*) As regards the COMMUNITY, a professional manager should:

1. Make the most effective use of all natural resources employed.
2. Be ready to give professional assistance in community affairs.

To conclude we can say that value is a conviction that a person holds about a specific mode of conduct and the importance which he attaches to his convictions. Values are dynamic because people seek, test and change values. Managerial ethos is concerned with the character and values of managers as a professional group. A true manager has to be an institutional builder. He has to be a value shaper not simply a manipulator of rewards. His values should be diffused throughout the organisation right from top to the bottom. Business flourishes only when the leader who has inhuming desire for excellence stimulates the employees to share the same spirit of devotion and dedication to achieve the desired targets.

## REFERENCES


1. Gupta, B.C., 1992, *Contemporary Management*, Ashish Publishing.
2. Heejing Tan & Seng Poh Vou: 1986, *Developing in Asia*, Addision-Wesley Publishing Company.
3. Humbke John, 1973, *The Experienced Manager*, McGraw-Hill Book Company (UK) Limited.
4. Rao, V.T., 1991, *Readings in Human Resource Development*, Mohan Primlani For Oxford & IBH Publishing Ltd.
5. IGNOU Notes.

# 30

# Role of Business Managers

SHALINI NIGAM, SWAMI PRASAD AND PUNEET MATHUR

---

Jawaharlal Nehru was once asked why he did not dispense with the corrupt people around him. His answer was that he would love to do so but for the fact that it is only they who work hard and get things done! It is obvious that corrupt people have a strong motivation of money and power. The question follows why honest people lag behind in output. Can honest men and women be also made similar or even better achievers?

An answer to this question forms the underlying theme of the discussion. It is a commonly accepted fact that a crisis of values that has lately gripped Indian society has led to a reassessment of the nation's social, moral, ethical and professional structure. The sharp fall in standards all around, the callous disregard of the common man's interests, the increasing hypocrisy have progressively caused a deterioration that may be described as alarming. The fabric of Indian society is degenerating. The race all round is for the plums of office, the accumulation of wealth by all possible means, a few of them fair out most of them foul, unethical, and even illegal. Morals, ethical values, performance of duty, regard and consideration for fellow men, sympathy and compassion seem to have gone with the wind and are among the major casualties of the post-independence period.

Certain pertinent posers are now being put by the conscientious section of the elite in Indian society. We have become slaves of unethical practices. Have we not lost our bearings? Are we not treading the path of ruin by disregarding the basic concepts and values so hopefully defined by the leaders of the past generations and set as goals for the Indian people? Centuries of slavery debased us until our saviours, the

Saints, Sufis like Kabir, Nanak, Tulsidas and many others, emerged on the scene and by personal example and precept, showed us the right path. Mahatma Gandhi in more recent times highlighted 'Ahimsa' and good moral conduct. A country where Jainism, Buddhism and other religions thrived and showed the path of virtue and renunciation, today materialism holds sway and dominates our thinking, our actions, our planning and programmes, our very being and the ends justify the means. In fact nobody bothers about the ethics of the means and methods adopted by those who corner the gains of the progress, social and economic, at the cost of the mute, long-suffering but very patient masses. The malaise afflicting the Indian people has permeated to all sections of society, especially the young and the middle aged people.

A closer examination reveals that the degeneration has started from the roots; whether the young are merely following in the footsteps of their elders, or whether they themselves are the products of a degenerated decaying society is another matter.

Let us begin with the younger generation. They disrespect their elders. They ignore the laws and their morals are decaying. They riot in the streets inflamed by wild nations. Indian Saints and Sages, and in the recent times our national leaders and statesmen, like Mahatma Gandhi, Dr. S. Radhakrishnan, and Jawaharlal Nehru, have all spoken of the "crisis of character". But the tragedy is that such talk and the realization of reality and promises are soon forgotten. The nation is back to square one as the phrase goes. Corruption continues merrily as if nothing else matters. Acquisition of wealth in various forms, including cash, gold, land property and fancy consumer goods, seems to have become the be-all and end-all of one's existence, almost one's religion.

At present the attention is focused on defending the unjust and social criminals simply because they can pay fat-fees. A judge raised an interesting question recently. How many rich people have been sent to the gallous for murders and other serious offences?

The innocent and honest poor people get punished because they get caught and cannot afford to engage experienced lawyers who have high contacts with the judges. Most people suffer in silent at the hands of exploiters, murderers, greedy doctors, lawyers and members of other professions.

With exceptions here and there, we tend to forget Dr. Radhakrishnan's dictum that civilizations are not built with brick and mortar, steel and machinery. They are built with men and women, their quality and character. The "crisis of character" has often attracted the attention of Committees and Commissions, but perhaps more reported on such matters as character building and educational reforms gather dust on the shelves of Central and State Government secretariats than any other. The fact is that few people at the top are interested in such matters as inculcation of high values and character building. Moreover, with what face can they talk if high values and honesty when every day they betray dishonesty, unbecoming greed and love of materialism?

Take the case of the report submitted by Sri Prakash Committee on character building; its recommendations were later endorsed by the Kothari Commission (and accepted by the Central Government). The task entrusted to Shri Prakash Committee was a familiar one; to report on the need for moral and religious education in educational institutions. The Committee strongly urged deliberate inculcation of moral and spiritual values from the earliest years of life. No concrete steps have so far been taken to follow up the suggestions.

The tasks for professionals were clearly outlined in a declaration made by the First National Convention on "Professions for the People". Although little follow-up action has been taken, the convention made several valid points. It expressed concern for, and commitment to, the vast masses of the people whose pathological problems, disabilities and injustices do not receive the consideration they deserve. There is urgent need for the intellectual community to arrest the escalating anti-constitutional values, and to radicalise the ethics, methodologies and delivery systems to the deprived millions of the weaker sections of humanity.

Three major challenges have been listed. First, the obligation to strive for excellence in all spheres, and to provide reasonably competent services to the needy. Second, to ensure that the code of ethics and professional conduct is strictly enforces. Thirdly, there is a need to develop structures and strategies in order to make accessible professional services even to the ordinary men who may, on account of social and economic disabilities, not be in a position to pay for them.

If the senior members of each profession devote a part of their time, talents and resources to inculcate professional values among their juniors and ensure high standards of conduct, India would be transformed into healthy society free from the decaying trends that threaten to cripple it for all times.

Every organisational man or woman is aware, in theory at least, about the existence of a code of ethics, which should be applicable both at the personal and company levels. In many cases, they also subscribe to the code of ethics which is enjoined upon them by the dictates of the profession to which they belong.

What has happened in reality is that, over a period of time, the ramifications of the code have disappeared somewhere along the proverbial grey area, even though no such area is supposed to exist in the matter of ethical behaviour. What is good for the individual is not necessarily good for the organisation to which he or she belongs, and *vice versa*.

There still are a few corporations left in the country which have developed an uncompromising equation between personal and company ethics. Their executives are an example of probity to the business community and the decision-makers in the corridors of power, even though they are an embarrassment to the sections of our bureaucracy.

A foreign journalist, who was based in India for a number of years came to this country on a short assignment from his new base in Jakarta, Indonesia. Comparing his experiences in the two countries, he told his friend, "Very little ever get done in Indonesia. Comparatively, India is heavenly and this is because of your well-organised corruption". As his friends discovered, he was not making a facetious remark.

His justification was that if impoverished Third World governments cannot afford to remunerate their employees decently, there should be an implicit understanding that citizens wanting to get their jobs done should some how make up the differential in wages. But many questions still remain to be answered: for example, is there a line to be drawn somewhere and secondly, what happens if such practices in a system like ours become institutionalised?

Going by several recent accounts of scandals which have rocked even the highest corporate citadels in countries like Japan and the United States, the response of some business writers would appear to be: Let the market forces decide. Those who have an experience of working in Japan, however, say that what would amount to a scandal in the West or elsewhere would be "structural" of "institutional" adjustment that would help grease the wheels of the nation's economic machine.

Again, where does one draw the line? Even a top Indian industrialist, who is chairman of a large business group, said recently, "there should develop a benign partnership between the Government and the industry dedicated to serve the national interest and protect and enhance the well-being of our people". He held out the practice in Japan as a model for this country.

Is there no place for personal well-being? Many of our people would ask, pointing to differences in the psyche of people in various climes as well as their national and historical perspectives. An Indian expert in human resource development, after a study tour of Japan, discovered wide variations in the priorities of individuals which, he said, were reflected at the corporate level. An Indian's priorities were: self, family, organisation, society and nation, where as to a Japanese they were more or less in reverse: nation, organisation, society, family and self.

The issue is by no means easy to resolve and there would appear to be no ideal set of priorities, whether in India or anywhere else. It is for this reason that this area of management has started to receive attention, both in corporate boardrooms and in management schools and other teaching institutions.

As has happened in the United States, some Indian teaching institutions have decided to install chairs in business ethics, based on considerations of individual morality and organisational social responsibility.

There are institutions in India which have traditionally had a bad name, both before and after independence. Business is one of them, police another. Petty bureaucracy in control of the essential services is not far behind. It is easy to justify lack of ethical behaviour and practice by pointing our finger to other countries, but there are fundamental differences. First, unethical conduct, as is manifested in the widespread corruption in our system, does not influence the daily lives of people in the better-run systems as it does in India. Secondly, it does not hinder the normal pursuit of people's daily lives. Most importantly, it is a measure of the authority and power to harm others. For example, a senior executive in an organisation, through his unethical behaviour and actions, can inflict greater harm than, say, a petty worker or a clerk. The same is true at the bureaucratic and political management levels, lest our quest for the "lowly" scapegoats continues to be endless.

We now focus our attention to the role of Business Managers. In the words of Peter F. Drucker, "Management is a social function and embedded in a culture a society a tradition of values, customs and beliefs, and in governmental and political systems. Management is and should be culture conditioned; but in turn, management and managers shape culture and society. The managers of the various institutions, have to take social responsibility, have to think through the values, the beliefs, the commitments of their society and have to assume leadership responsibility beyond the discharge of the specific and limited mission of their institutions."

Because our society is rapidly becoming a society of organizations, all institutions, including business, will have to hold themselves accountable for the quality of life and will have to make fulfilment of basic social values and beliefs.

Management is fast becoming the central resource of the developed countries and the basic need of the developing ones. From being the specific concern of business, i.e. the economic institution of society, management and managers are becoming the distinctive organs of developed society. What management is and what management will do will, therefore and properly become increasingly a matter of public concern rather than a matter for experts, management will increasingly be concerned as much with the expression of basic beliefs and values as with the accomplishment of measurable results. It will increasingly stand for the quality of life of a society as much as for its standard of living. In modern society there is no other leadership group but managers. If the managers of our major institutions, and especially of business, do not take responsibility for the common good, no one else can or will. Government is no longer capable, as political theories will have it, of being the "Sovereign" and the "guardian of the common good", in a pluralistic society of organisations. In the words of Peter F. Drucker, "Countless sermons have been preached and printed on the ethics of business or the ethics of the businessman. Most have nothing to do with business and little to do with ethics."

One main topic is everyday honesty. Businessmen, we are told solemnly, should not cheat, steal, lie, bribe or take bribes. But nor should anyone else. Men and women do not acquire exemption from ordinary rules of personal behaviour because of their work or job. Nor, however, do they cease to be human beings when appointed vice-president, city manager or college dean. And there has always been a number of people who cheat, steal, lie, bribe, or take bribes. The problem is one of moral values and moral education, of the individual, of the family, of the school. But there neither is a separate ethics of business, nor is one needed.

Having realised that there is hardly any separate ethics of business than the one applicable to every other group, the next step is to identify the various constituents of ethics and morality, the set of values to be cherished and inculcated and which have degenerated over the years. Next comes the question of identification of desired code of conduct, the extent of its violation and the steps required to be taken to modify the course contents, methodology of the teaching, etc. to ensure that the universities produce well qualified well morally sound professionals.

Developed or underdeveloped countries both have witnessed the phenomenon of financial frauds, and scandals bringing to light unethical business practices. The orange country derivatives scandal in the 1980s which exposed corrupt inside traders from big companies like GEC etc. The Junk bond Nichael Milken Scandal which exposed illegal amassing of funds which led to ultimately Milken being hit with a ninety-eight count federal indictment charging him with securities fraud and market manipulation in 1987. The very recent Nick Leeson fraud which almost brought the Baring Bank to closure and rendering it bankrupt. But recently in the past few months, the politician-businessmen nexus has come to light, in South Korea where the 'choebls' or corporate giants have admitted to giving funds to a former Prime Minister. The companies whose CEO's charged with fraud include Daewoo Corporation, Samsung Electronics, Goldstar Electronics etc. live in very highly developed countries like Japan and Italy, scandals have exposed various unethical practices.

Coming back to our home territory India we have been witnessing various scandals and scams in the Bombay stock exchange and more recent the MS Shoes Scandal involving lagging of shoes and insider trading by the company's managing director.

As business is increasingly stained by such unethical practices, a recent survey 'ETHICS ENIGMA' by the Business Today group throws light on the level of ethical practices as seen by the business managers at the strategic level. The survey reveals that a majority of the managers feel that current level of business ethics have declined of late in India. A majority of the managers feel that liberalisation is going to bring in a new moral school of thought. Does it mean that the free the economy becomes the better the values we are going to have? Does it mean restrictions breed unethical practices? Well not really Singapore said to be a free but disciplined economy did see the Nick Leeson Scandal this year how pane coming to factor responsible for poor corporate ethics the managers spell out licence permit era, poor law enforcement, high taxes, and dearth of competition and lack of work culture. All the above factors are no doubt important but the lack of work cultures and a code of conduct is really startling. The need is to look at this factor very closely as an individual is groomed by his work culture. In the aforementioned survey Multi-National Corporations feel that it is possible to succeed in corporate India without breaking the moral values. 99 per cent managers of the survey point their fingers at politicians for degeneration of ethical standards. However all the managers feel that it is possible to stay legally clean and still break the corporate code of conduct.

In our opinion ethics and morality derive heavily from religion. Unless identification of these values is done it will be difficult to proceed further and discuss some remedial action. The moral side of all major religions are similar, rather identical, some of the major constituents of morality or ethics can be summarised as under:

- Honesty
- Truthfulness
- Justice
- Duty
- Loyalty
- Ahimsa

We can now proceed to identify the set of values which have degenerated over the years:

1. *Undue importance to materialism and accumulation of wealth, by any means; fair or foul*: The growing materialistic attitude of the society as a whole and greed for wealth has brought us to a point where we are no longer able to sustain ourselves by what we earn in a moral way but want to ask for more. The vicious circle of wants and their fulfilment has no end and hence controls need to be put when one looks for more wealth. This would mean that a business manager must not look for unattainable goals and should see that wealth is accumulated only after equitable distribution takes place between all the factors of productions.
2. *Sense of duty*: Every individual must cherish and engender in himself a deep sense of duty, which can be towards the very important parts of the society and which form the basic framework of the society. Sense of duty may be of various categories as:
   — Duty towards the nation
   — Duty towards the organisation

— Duty towards the family
— Duty towards one's neighbourhood
— Duty towards oneself
— Duty towards God.

Japanese people call it as Giril. Giril constitutes of

— Sense of duty
— Sense of justice
— Mutual trust and regard
— Sense of beauty
— Sense of honesty and fair play
— Dedication and commitment to work
— Sense of temperance

If it were true that education can mould societies, it would be necessary to restructure our education drastically to take care of moral and spiritual values. As someone put it, even if there were no God, it would be necessary to invent one. Fear of God can rightly be said to be the panacea for all the evils of society and institutions. If fatherhood of God and brotherhood of mankind becomes universally acceptable, all the problems melt away. If the other man is a brother, who would steal him, cheat him, hurt him, and the like.

Coming back to the question posed in the beginning, we are now in a position to answer the same. To recapitulate, the corrupt people are taught moral and spiritual values, or rather our new education system produces honest people, they would not need the acquisition of wealth as a motivating force or remarkable achievement. In that case, the motivating force would be fear of God, sense of duty, sense of righteousness, compassion for fellow-men, and other virtues. They would be guided by such lofty ideals as doing '*Karma*' or duty without aspirations, the essence of Gita. All the strife that is rampant in India and the world at large would disappear within no time. This would be advent of another '*Satyuga*'.

Since people don't live by bread alone, recourse has inevitably been found in extra-ethical activities which got translated from the individual to the company or corporate level. This kind of transference of convenience, as students of organisational behaviour know, has not contributed much to the respectability of corporations since the base of ethics has always remained in individual propriety. Values are socially defined desires and goals that are internationalized through the process of conditioning, learning and socialisation. In other words, values are goals set for achievement and they motivate, define and colour one's all activities—cognitive, affective and conative.

In the modern industrialized environment, serious erosion of moral values in all respects of life and the crises of values is experienced. We are witnessing tremendous value crises throughout the world today. As the vitality of human belief in value is dying out in every land, the new generation has started to pooh pooh the unique epics and institutions giving place to erosion of spiritual and moral values in mind. As a result, the mind of man his been laciniated into small frictions and fragments which makes the value content of human life a diminishing factor in modern times.

31

# Values for Business Managers:

## *An Integrated Approach*

D.N. KAPOOR AND NIRAJ GUPTA

Today, the world is in the process of becoming a true open system under which most things will be related and inter-dependent. The artificial political and geographical boundaries to markets are getting demolished. All industrialised societies, even the developing ones including India, have recognised the opportunities of going global.

Ever since independence, Indian industry and business operated and grew in a highly protected environment and has now been thrown, open by the recent on going liberalisation and the economic reforms of the government. It has set in motion a number of changes to which Indian companies and Business Managers are required to respond efficiently.

It is a matter of fact that can easily be witnessed by the practices of Indian Managers, in the yester years, of importing managerial and technological skills along with the value systems from other countries which have no roots here. Moreover, the ignorance of systematic and profound philosophical foundations of Indian value-system has resulted in a skill-strong, values weak orientation, which has acted to the detriment of efficient organizational functioning with the blind imitation of western patterns and styles and creating a problem in facing the challenges posed by the recent changes.

The role of managers, in the present Indian context, is to transform the society into a vibrant and dynamic one wedded to growth and development. What is needed most, therefore, is social productivity and spiritual enlightenment through the integration of orientation of values in management education with their actual practice in the corporate world.

## Values—An Overview

Value is a conviction that a person holds about a specific mode of conduct and the importance which he attaches to his convictions. A value represents prune evaluation of moral and social good. From the managerial standpoint values may be defined as the standards governing the usual conduct of the members of management. They provide a basis for determining right or wrong action in terms of a situation. Value system represents prioritizing of individual values in relation to their relative importance. In other words, we all have a set of values which are identified by the assignment of relative importance to various values say freedom, pleasure, self-respect, honesty, obedience, equality and so forth.

Personal values are imbibed from parents, teachers, elders, friends, colleagues. As an individual grows and starts playing different types of roles in various capacities, values are adapted and refined in the light of new knowledge and experiences gained from the literature, media and different sections of the community. In business organisations, the founder-entrepreneur or Chief Executive Officer, in this regard, has an important role to play, the fragrance of which lasts long in the operational history of the organisation concerned.

The following are some of the main features of values:

- They stem from personal beliefs, opinions and standards.
- They have dynamism and therefore they change from person to person and organisation to organisation.
- They recognise the importance of desired action.
- They possess conceptuality.
- They are the basis for the management philosophy of an organisation or manager.
- They serve as the means as well as the end state.
- They require synthesis of several disciplines.
- They do not rest on feelings but principles for approval or disapproval of an action.

## Values—The Role of Managers

In the present corporate structure where the ownership has been divorced from management, a manager has to deal with peers, subordinates, owners, customers and society as a whole playing vivid roles of Figurehead, Leader, Liaison, Monitor, Spokesman and Disseminator. This wide variety of managerial roles give a multi-dimensional effect to the roles to be played by values in the performance of his activities. Some of them are:

(i) Job, being the centre of life, requires its values to be harmonised with the personal values of concerned managers, for, a happy and healthy performance of his job.

(ii) The decisions to be taken by the managers should be in conformity with values of those receiving the impact of the said decisions.

(iii) Organisational values should be followed in doing the right thing because it is right, irrespective of any one's personal interest.

(iv) Value based management tends to present new and higher standards with the spirit of self to social development without any legal pressure.

(v) Failure of an organisation to react according to social expectations, spoils its image and share in the market.

(vi) Managers ought to come forward to be the leaders of the society by presenting social norms and examples by providing eco and health friendly products and services.

(vii) Managers, as trustees, must observe the public interest otherwise the public may protest by demanding restrictive laws and regulations or through boycotting them.

Managers, while practicing management and performing their respective jobs in their concerned organisations for the attainment of their organisational objectives via satisfying their personal interests or the other way round (this is again subject to their personal values), are expected to give due consideration to their ethical roles as has been explained earlier. But there is a wide gap between the expectations and the real practice.

In the present environment prevailing in India, managers, like most of us, are becoming more and more rationalistic, materialistic and individualistic concerned only with personal gains and profits. Today concept of socialistic pattern of society is evaporating day by day because the interest of Indian managers and leaders for the social well being is now subject to diminishing returns. Therefore, the so called social welfare activities are also inspired by the personal gains, monetary or otherwise, which one could get probably in long run.

More recent research studies in this direction suggest a hierarchy of levels, which is capable of explaining the set of values. Indian managers perceive the problem of disparate values in the organisation. There are different levels of personal values which hold good for various levels of managers in India, senior or junior, young or old.

*Level I—Reactive*: The one who react to basic physiological needs, being unaware of the human element.

*Level II—Tribalistic*: The one who is highly dependent on the authorities and traditions.

*Level III—Egocentrism*: The one who believes in individualism with aggressive and selfish attitudes.

*Level IV—Conformative* : The one who thrust one's own values on others, having different set of values.

*Level V—Manipulative* : The one who indulges oneself in manipulating people and facts for getting success, money and recognition.

*Level VI—Sociocentric* : The one who wants to get along rather than leading others with a room for manipulation, materialism and conformity.

*Level VII—Existential* : The one who tolerates the ambiguity of people and values and expect to do the same. He also believes in arbitrary use of authority.

Most people in today's organisations operate between the above mentioned levels, however, the managers in Indian organisations am mostly operating at 5th, 6th and 7th level. Such operations give rise to various problems within and/or outside the organisations. Poor industrial relations, high labour turnover, poor work culture, public distrust and protest against the organisation, unefficient functioning of the organisation are some of the important ones.

We all live in India, and managers too, having a culturally plural society. Therefore, the discussion on the problem of dis-values or on the remedial measures for the revival and restoration of values etc. may not attract so much attention in any country as in case of India. It is really a serious matter to be discussed by us, who have a deep rooted structure of values in the Indian culture and society along with a wealth of didactic material and rich repertoire of myths, legends, epics and religious lore. We had solid philosophical and psychological messages of vedantic spiritualism along with a lot of literary heritage guiding us for purity of mind, public welfare, tolerance, devotion, dedication, selflessness etc.

What has happened to the practice of all this in Indian organisation can well be understood from the contrast of the occupational values of Indian managers (Set A) with the guidelines of Indian system (Set B).

CONTRASTING VALUES

| | *Set A* | *Set B* |
|---|---|---|
| 1. | Freedom from supervisions/subordination | Self-discipline |
| 2. | Adventurous experiences/challenges for reducing monotony of job and for personal gain | Facing challenges for social and national development |
| 3. | Leisure welcomed | Sacrifice, fear of pleasure |
| 4. | Emotion, intuition and instinct | Rational, cause and effect relationship |
| 5. | Job security | Social security |
| 6. | Development of all-round personality | Feelings of nationality |
| 7. | Control over others | Self-control and self-restraint |
| 8. | Aggression | Tolerance |
| 9. | Mobility (switching over the organisation) | Devotion and dedication |
| 10. | Handsome pay-packets | Selflessness |
| 11. | Concealment and manipulation | Transparency and purity of mind. |

## Value Education—The Need of the Hour

There is an apparently growing opinion among management academicians and practitioners that formal orientation of value education, focusing the elements of traditional Indian culture and philosophy, can provide an alternative approach to effective management *vis-à-vis* the rationalistic-materialistic-individualistic approach characterising western management concepts and practices. In this regard the lesson can be learnt from Japan who had demonstrated its own mode of such development and growth with the help of its traditional culture and values.

It is noteworthy at this stage that few institutions in India including IIM Calcutta and T.A. Pai Institute of Management have taken the initiative in the guidance of Prof. S.K. Chakroborthy and Prof. R.C. Shekhar for the introduction of optional/compulsory courses on ethics in business management. However, a lot is yet required to be done.

Therefore, at this juncture, for the restoration of the Indian Value System in business management by changing the outlook of the present and future managers of India an integrated approach in management education can be suggested which should incorporate both the learning and practicing aspects of values.

With regards to the learning aspect there is a misconception that the intellectual substance of Indian Value System is averse to progress and prosperity. Rather, it emphasises entrepreneurship, continuity, patience and innovative attitude which are second-to-none for their application in modern Indian work situation and can present Indian managers model ones. Some examples, quotations, messages, from the treasure of Indian culture and literature can be cited here for supporting various values of Indian Value System:

* The idea contained in "*Karamanneya Wadhika Raste Maa Faleshu Kadacanah*" conveys the message of work is worship, selflessness, self-confidence.
* The concept of "*Nishkam Karma*" teaches us to work hard with indifference to personal rewards.
* The clue of social protection and welfare is strongly given by the concept of "*Yogakhemam Whamyaham*".
* The theory of '*Karma*', i.e. "As you sow, so shall you reap" is nothing but a guidance for us to do the right things in right manner with a sense of bringing in effectiveness and efficiency in the functioning of the organisation.
* *Ayam Nij Paroveti Gandana Laghuchetsam Udarcaritanam Tu Vasudaiv Kutumbakam* places impetes on the responsiveness to the social needs and "Subordination of individual interest with general interest", one of the fourteen principles of management given by Henry Ford.
* "GYAN-YOGA" of "GITA" lays its stress for developing excellence through "ATMA-VIKAS", i.e. Self-exaltation and self-actualisation.
* Importance of principle, of Espirit-de-corps and the social service is well explained in Uphnishada:

  "*Sarve Bhavantu Sukhinah Sarve Santu Niramayah, Sarve Bhdrani Pashyantu, Ma Kasdut Dukh Bhag Bhavet.*

* The concept of "*Swadharma*" in its essence, refers to full realization of ones own duty with "*Swadharme Nidhanam Shreyam Pardharmo Bhayawaha*".

Likewise, a lot many lessons can also be given with due interpretation for imbibing the Indian manager's with creative thinking, self-respect, feeling of nationality and integrity, commitment and confidence, equity and justice, team-spirit, sacrifices and service motives, common good etc.

There is a need for the Indian identity to assert itself when the ethical climate of India is being disparaged by western concepts and approaches. What is required at present is the "Indianness" of the management of Indian organisations. However, mere imparting the value education of managers will be an unbalanced approach as excerpted by most of the management practitioners.

Value education will be of no use unless the managers learn to use it in real life situations and try to innovate the feasible ethical paths for the economic and social well being of the organisation and society both. Therefore, neither the ethical pennissivenes nor self-righteousness is feasible because—

- Values do not prescribe any formula for contemporary achievement of economic and social objectives of the organisation.
- A mix of values is required for the selection of best out of numerous alternatives having different costs and benefits.

Hence, the learning aspect of values should also be integrated with its practicing side so that it can really prove socially useful. This, however, can be a ticklish task to perform, but not impossible. There are certain tasks which, managers, irrespective of their capacity, have to perform (except a few). They are:

- Establishing objectives
- Developing alternatives
- Evaluation of alternatives
- Selection of the best alternative
- Implementation
- Feedback and control

While performing each of them, managers have to keep the values in mind and are required to translate them into practice. For this purpose, the following three main upcoming concepts with regards to values, at global level, can be practiced.

- Pragmatism
- Moderation
- Contextuality

*Pragmatism* means simply that we must truly be practical, problem-solving change agents when we engineer our environment for learning conscious of constraints, systematic in approach and mindful that every programme must be oriented to specific results. In this the managers sometimes may not influence or change the ultimate solution to the problem but try to make it more useful and better. Therefore, in practicing the concept the manager should go for a mid path between ethical absolutism and ethical expediency. *Example*: If to be selfless or profit indifferent is difficult for the managers then they can adopt a mid path of profit with maximum social well being.

*Moderation* means an activity of the manager in which he will have to moderate the

- Values and interests of different groups within the organisation.
- Values and interests of the organisation with the outside parties.

The essence of the concept is that in any commercial endeavour all parties related to it must gain and prosper, i.e. the act of balancing gains of various parties.

*Contextuality* means that the values should not be considered as a product or formula rather a process in which its application is subject to the requirement because sometimes it seems to rest on reciprocity. Therefore, the useful instruments of Indian psychology alone would not suffice unless used contextually.

To sum up, business schools must become more sensitive towards this issue for ensuring that the future managers coming out of them are well tuned to the Indian culture and values. Teaching of management is not a science or technology but a practice based on a number of disciplines. Hence, B-Schools should incorporate an integrated approach to value education based on Indian Value System. So that they can produce business leaders of the future and not just managers. Leaders who are intellectually alert, socially involved and committed to the general pursuit of excellence.

**REFERENCES**


1. Chakroborthy, S.K., (1991). *Management by Values*, Oxford University Press.
2. Chakroborthy, S.K., (1995). *Ethics in Management*, Oxford University Press.
3. Giri, V.P., (1992). *Manager's Outlook : A Quest for Indian Model*, International Seminar on Management, Udaipur (1992).
4. Gupta, C.B. : *Contemporary Management, Ashish Publishing House.*
5. Kosambi, D.D., (1964). *The Culture and Civilisations of Ancient India.*
6. Monappa, Arun, (1987). "The Ethical Attitude of Indian Manager", AIMA.
7. Nandy, Ashish, (1983). *Intimate Enemy - The Loss and Recovery of Self Under Colonialism*, Oxford University Press.
8. Sekhar, R.C., (1995). Ethics and the Indian Manager, *Economic and Political Weekly,* (Nov.).
9. Stark, Andrew, (1993). What is the matter with Business Ethics, *Harward Business Review*, May-June.

# 32

# Managerial Value System in Internationalised Business Environment

A.K. SATSANGI AND S.P. KAUSHIK

## Introduction

Present business environment is heading towards openness, transparency, competitiveness, quality consciousness etc. A specific value system in business managers is required for working in such environment. It is tile value system that helps in adjusting an individual in a particular environment in absence of a specific managerial acumen, the organisation may face adverse situation in business operation specially in international business. It is now very difficult to have watertight compartment regarding domestic and international business environment due to speedy pace of information regarding consumer needs, quality perceived and price of the product. What is demanded in USA market today could be demanded in India tomorrow. In common parlance value is associated with the innate nature of an individual to perceive a tiling in a particular manner. Importance of management values can be summed-up as follows:

- The values possessed by an executive have strong influence on organisational climate.
- These are important determinants in selecting a particular corporate strategy.
- Values decide nature of actions and shape of decisions.
- Values are intrinsic part of life and behaviour of an executive.

- Values decide perception of organisation as well as of an executive as impersonal, paternalistic, formal, informal, hostile, friendly etc.

Values held by an executive are an intrinsic part of his life and thought. These are transmitted to him through his parents, teachers and other significant persons in his environment who in turn, acquired their values in similar fashion. Due to this nature, values come closer to personality. Indeed, they are part of it. They become lasting convictions that are held by an executive, accompanying the mode of conduct and the importance of the convictions to the persons.

**Values Based Classification of Business Executives**

Evidences can be collected from several literature available on managerial values and value system and its impact on business operations. Much has been written on values, on classification of values, types of values, and its contribution to culture, profession etc. Business executives can also be categorised in the following categories on the basis of value system possessed by an executive. This classification is based on typology presented by C. Kluckholn and A. Shills in 1961 (Table 32.1).

1. *The Theoretical Executive* : He is interested in the truth, systematic ordering of knowledge, cognitive approach, looking for identities and difference, empirical, critical and rational. He is an intellectual, scientist or philosopher.
2. *The Economic Executive* : His interest lies in practical influences, in the production, marketing, consumption of goods, use of economic resources and accumulation of tangible wealth.
3. *The Aesthetic Executive* : He is interested in artistic aspects, creativity and harmony of values. He views experiences in terms of grace symmetry, harmony etc.
4. *The Social Executive* : He demonstrates the feeling of love and affection towards people. He is kind, sympathetic and unselfish. He puts love, at the top of all human relationship and his approach is humane.

**Table 32.1:** Value Based Classfication of Business Executives

| *Theoretical* | *Economic* | *Aesthetic* | *Social* | *Political* | *Religious* |
|---|---|---|---|---|---|
| Interested in<br>• Truth<br>• Systematic ordering of knowledge<br>• Cognitive approach<br>• Looking for identities and differences<br>• Imperical<br>• Critical<br>• Rational | Interested in<br>• Usefulness<br>• Production<br>• Marketing<br>• Consumption<br>• Use of economic resources<br>• Accumulation of wealth | Interested in<br>• Artistic aspect<br>• Creativeness<br>• Harmony of value<br>• Experience in terms of<br>• Grace<br>• Symmetry<br>• Harmony | • Loving<br>• Kind<br>• Sympathetic<br>• Unselfish<br>• Humane | • Power Oriented<br>• Influencing<br>• Belief in<br>• Personal power<br>• Recognition<br>• Competition | • Belief in<br>• Unity<br>• Relation of individual to Universe<br>• Satisfying Value<br>• Experience |

5. *The Political Executive* : He is characterised as power oriented in area of functions. He believes in role of competition in life, power as the most universal motive. These beliefs drive him to search personal power, influence and recognition.
6. *The Religious Executive*: His mental structure is directed to the creation of the highest and absolutely satisfying value experiences.

The dominant value is unity. He believes in relation of individual to the universe.

A questionnaire relating to above classification was administered by Renato Taguin of Harward Business School in 1965. The following average value profile was resulted:

| *Value* | *Score* | *% Score* |
|---|---|---|
| Economic | 45 | 18.75 |
| Theoretical | 44 | 18.33 |
| Political | 44 | 18.33 |
| Religious | 39 | 16.25 |
| Aesthetic | 35 | 14.58 |
| Social | 33 | 13.76 |
| | 240 | 100 |

## Managerial Value System and International Business

International business is a special situation of national marketing. Relationship between value system of an executive and Internationalised Business Environment can be understood as given in Table 32.2.

The following qualities are observed in a successful international marketing system:

1. *Quality Product*: Now-a-days standard quality products are demanded in international market. In global market demand of product is elastic in nature. The product having standard quality can create an element of monopoly in international market and can maximise total profit.
2. *Cost Effectiveness*: The cost of product refers to sum of all costs incurred in launching that product in international market. From international point of view only such products can stay

**Table 32.2:** Relationship between Values and Internationalised Business Environment

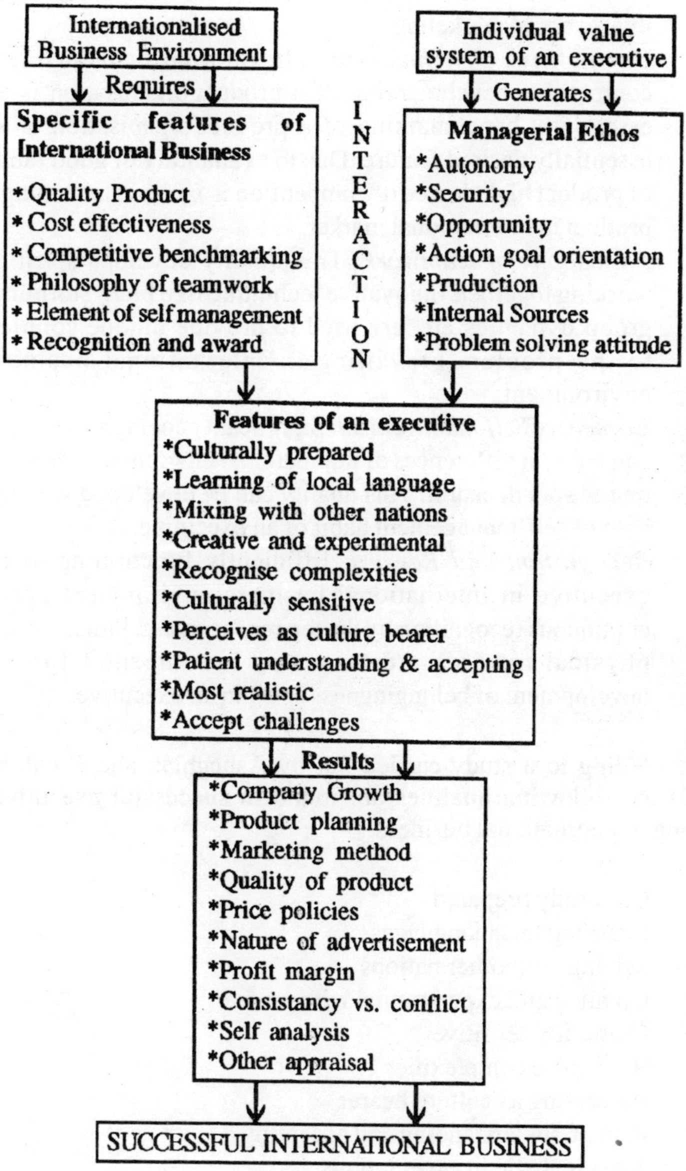

in the market which are comparatively cheaper. Therefore, production at minimum cost is an essential factor for international marketing.

3. *Competitive Benchmarking*: In international business competitive benchmarking of a product/organisation is an essentially benchmarking of a product/organisation is an essentially desired feature. Due to availability of good range of product high degree of competition is faced in launching a product in international market.
4. *Philosophy of teamwork*: This quality develops spirit of working together. Innovative technique like brain storming, group dynamics etc. are used to provide unique solution to the problem prevailing in international business environment.
5. *Element of Self-management*: Significant geographical, social and cultural differences of international environment demand on the spot decision. This quality can be developed with the help of self-management habit of an executive.
6. *Recognition and Reward*: Efficiently functioning of an executive in international business environment needs continuous recognition by the top management. Financial and physical rewards are also very instrumental for the development of belongingness spirit in an executive.

According to a study carried out by Asheghian and Ebrahimi (1990) the following qualities are found in successful executives working in international business:

- Culturally prepared
- Learning local languages
- Mixing with other nations
- Creative and experimental without fear
- Culturally sensitive
- Recognize complexities
- Perceiving as culture bearer
- Patient, understanding and accepting
- Most realistic in expectations
- Accept the challenges

Generation of the above stated qualities in an executive working in international area is very essential. Inculcation of these qualities in an executive depends on his value system. An executive having particular value system can generate the qualities very efficiently. This value system matures into the following managerial ethos in an executive:

- Autonomy
- Equity
- Security
- Opportunity
- Action goal orientation
- Proaction
- Internal resources
- Problem solving attitude

When an executive having above managerial ethos interacts with international business environment he influences the following areas:

1. Company growth
2. Product Planning
3. Marketing Method
4. Quality of Product
5. Price Policies
6. Nature of Advertisement
7. Profit Margin
8. Consistency *vs* Conflict
9. Self-Analysis
10. Others' Appraisal.

Achievement of the above stated features in international business area can be ensured by the value system held by an executive. If such type of efforts are made to preserve and channelise, an organisation can get success in international business environment.

**Conclusion**

The changing scenario of international business environment recognises individual's importance in business management. Secondly, it has also broaden the scope of complexity of international market. Therefore more efficient executives are required to operate a business successfully in international market.

Since the nature of value system of an individual is static, an effort can be made to channelise creative functioning required for international business environment. To the opinion of the researchers following efforts can be made to maximise the output of an individual operating in international business ambience with the under mentioned specific set of values.

- Provide as much as possible freedom to the executives for taking decisions related to his problems in his area of operation.
- Try to provide him equity in form of justice and rewards related to his performance.
- The top management should try to provide emotional as well as economic security to an executive as much as possible.
- Enough opportunities should be given for career advancement of executives working in international marketing.
- Organisers should develop an atmosphere to optimise all resources functioning together.

By adopting such measures the management can make efforts to streamline the value system of his executives. But whenever issues of internationalised business environment arise, we have to think in terms of internationalised managerial value system.

## REFERENCES

1. C. Kluckholn and A. Shills, (1961). *Value and Value Orientations in Theory of Action*, Harvard University Press.
2. Renato Taguin, V., (1965). *Value Classification and the Relationship of Managers and Scientists*, Advanced Management Programme, Harward Business Schools.
3. Asheghian, P. and Ebrahimi, B., *International Business*, Harper and Row, New York, pp. 283-84.

33

# Relational Values of Managers

*A Key to Successful Training and Development Programme*

PRAVIN SAXENA AND SWAMI PRASAD

## Introduction

Training is a major manpower management function. It is a part of management development and also a form of organisational development. It is an organised,.instructional process for improving employee's skill, knowledge, behaviour, work habits and attitude towards the requirement of job and organisation. It is also a teaching and learning activity carried on for the primary purpose of helping members of an organisation to acquire and apply the above qualities. The most effective managers are those who can best develop the human resources of an organisation for the purpose of' achieving organisational goals and objectives through training and development.

Training and development is basically aimed at improving one's productive capacity for the betterment of both the trainee and the organisation of which he is a member. It is believed and is quite justified that training especially behaviour oriented training can accomplish the goal of the organisation.

Where training fails the main reason, to a large extent, is attributed towards good "match" between the trainee's personality structure and demands of the situations in which he is going to perform. The failure in achieving is intended behavioural change need not lie in the training programme or the trainer. More often then not the resultant failure could be attributed to the assessment of human nature which means that we tend to look at people as infinitely malleable, infinitely capable of changing their behaviour and of being changed by a just few hours of training.

## Significance of Values on Training and Development

The fact is that human beings tend to develop a system of core values, viz. relational, temporal, humanistic and activity centred over a whole life and these values have a direct impact on their behavioural patterns. In this connection Peter F. Drucker rightly pointed out that training and development cannot succeed if its aim is to dramatically alter personalities or values. Any attempt to completely restructure or to modify someone's personality or change his value system nearly always fails because most of us have deeply rooted system of values which are resistant to change over a short period of time. Thus, among other things the value orientation upon which personality structure is based have a great impact on the acquisition of knowledge and skills and use of such skills and knowledge in organisational setting. Therefore, an understanding of the structure and content of the relational values, which appears to have far reaching impact upon behaviour, is of paramount importance for both the trainee and the trainer.

## Significance of Relational Values on Training and Development

Relational value is considered to be one of the most important values that human being contribute in varying degrees and every culture in every sphere of human activity. Man to man relationship play a vital role in bringing about the desired results. A large amount of human interaction takes place in both organisational process and managerial actions.

Human relationship is considered to be an important aspect of communication, group behaviour, adaptation, goal setting, leadership behaviour, co-ordination and conflict resolution. Thus, the nature and content of relational values has an important influence on organisation effectiveness.

Management development is a process in which both the top management and employees believe. It needs guidance of able and skilful leaders who are looked upon with respect and who are able to coach, guide and assist others in becoming competent. Apart from sound selection procedure manpower planning and performance evaluation, management development involves planned learning experience, i.e. on the job training such as courses, seminars, workshops etc.

The success and failure of training and development programmes largely depends upon two factors, viz. the individual and the environment in which he is functioning.

An individual's thoughts and actions are facilitated and influenced by the basic value orientations. Among these, the relational value orientation is considered to be a major factor in the success or failure of a training and development programme. In absence of a relational element no behavioural training and development programme can achieve success. It is the person to person relationship that creates a suitable bond between the trainee and the trainer, manager and the supervisor, supervisor and subordinate, manager/supervisor and peer. It is felt that the productivity and performance will suffer if this linkage is fragile. Hence, it is truly said that for getting the work done the relational value should be present in the management because management is not just getting work done through people but working with people, by people, and for people.

Another attribute to the success or failure of training and development is considered to be the environment in which the individual is functioning. The environment is mainly centred around the organisation of which the individual is a member.

An organisation is mainly concerned with strategies and policies, structures and relationship. It is only the relationship that links strategies and structure and makes an organisation a viable entity.

## Significance of Relational Values of Managers on Training and Development

Manager's participation in the training and development process brings in specific content, expertise: knowledge and skills often peculiar to the organisation for which they work. Managers can offer practical applications of this expertise to actual on the job situations. They are also up-to-date on the latest procedures and techniques. The contribution of managers in the training and development programme gives the effort enhanced credibility making it easier to solicit both their future participation as well as course attendance by their subordinates.

Managers exposure to the training function provides them a clear understanding of its benefits and pitfalls and a greater sensitivity to what training can and cannot do in upgrading the organisation staff.

It is worthwhile to mention here that the training programme can upgrade the organisational staff only when the manager understand his prime responsibility to nurture and maintain relationship with the organisation staff. The form and nature of the relationship that a manager has with other members, viz. supervisors, subordinate and other staff during a training and development programme of the organisation indicates the extent to which they could work together in achieving both organisational and personal goals. Managers can offer application of this expertise for a successful on the job training programme.

On the job training, a most effective means of training, is a continuous learning and coaching process which requires much time and resources for paying long term dividends to the organisation. A continuous on the job training programme includes, first of all complete and thorough basic training. This must be followed by close observation to spot any weak points in the trainee's performance and to correct errors in performance before work is impaired. It is not sufficient to tell a man how to do a job or to show him how to do it and then leave him to his own devices or to the assistance of the fellow colleagues,

In order to ensure efficient and effective performance by the trainee during on the job training programme, it is must that there exists good relationship between the trainee and the trainer.

## Conclusion

In nutshell, it can be said that whatever kind of training an individual gets, if his dominant value orientation in the relational area does not exist with that of his peers, supervisors and subordinates, there is bound to be friction. Trainer should understand both the individual and the organisational environment in which they are functioning.

Developing persons is not a matter of making persons become something. It is a matter of fact of creating an organisational environment where conflicting and contradictory value system are identified so that there can be alignment among individuals and the organisational environment.

It is easier said than done to change one's value system over a short period of time. Yet, training programme can be designed to play a role in changing values in the long run. In the short run what we can do is to find matching situations where individuals feel comfortable. It would not be suitable to make an attempt to put square pegs into the round holes.

## REFERENCES

1. Fiedler, Fred. E., (1976). *The Leadership Game: Matching the Man to the Situation*, Organisational Dynamics.
2. Druker, Peter F., (1974). *Management: Tasks, Responsibilities and Practices*, New York, Harper and Row.
3. Rao, Subba P. and Rao, V.S.P., *Personnel/Human Resource Management*, Konark Publishers Pvt. Ltd., Delhi.
4. Farb, Howard Silver, *Utilising Managers as Training Resources.*
5. *Human Resource Planning* (MS 23) IGNOU, New Delhi.
6. *Times of India*, October 25, 1995.

34

# Values in Management and the Labour in the Perspectives of Globalisation

I.C. AWASTHI

## Introduction

The new economic policy has brought about fundamental change in the Indian industry and business. The major component of new economic policy is globalisation—linking the Indian economy organically with the world economy. A series of measures have been taken to ensure 'level field' to the domestic and international competitors. The basic premise of reforms is to bring about efficiency in resource utilisation, increasing degree of openness, changing structure of incentives and institutions, which aims to reduce the role of state and rely on market forces. This process is associated with other reforms, viz., trade, commercial, deregulation and financial reforms. It is argued that the higher rate of economic growth can be achieved through allowing foreign competition in the domestic market, and this will increase competitiveness on the one hand and reduce costs and boost exports on the other. The policy measures also include free flow of direct foreign investment, technology, management, and skills. Fast industrial restructuring has brought about many beneficial consequences to business. The joint ventures, collaborations, strategic alliance, mergers, acquisitions, takeovers are taking place fast in a bid to make industries more competitive and efficient.

Technological changes have thus profound impact across enterprises and industries in terms of work organization, employment, skill profile, management, industrial relations and labour standards.

Organisations are, therefore, under the constant pressure for increased productivity, quality and profitability against the background of shifting business perspectives, globalisation and ever-increasing competition. These pressures are altering organization options not merely how to manage current business but looking beyond it through focusing on key skills, core competencies and flexibility to meet new challenges and circumstances posed by the external environment. In this milieu, the importance of stakeholders is becoming more widely accepted. In a complex yet exciting environment, organizations are developing and resorting to solution-oriented approach combining wide range of analytical, diagnostic tools and qualitative approach to meet the objectives. The core of organisational success remains with its improved knowledge and understanding the business environment and anticipate future trends. In a bid to bring efficiency, the organisations have resorted to shed their labour. This process has obvious implications to labour market process. Indeed market is becoming powerful instrument for guiding future stakes and improving the efficiency of resources. But then there are obvious limitations to this approach particularly to those who have little or no access to market. A large segment of population is marginalised, socially and economically excluded and therefore it would be imperative to empower them through protective social security.

Provision of employment is the most powerful instrument to provide social security. In this background it is argued here that how the value in management assumes critical role to protect the interests of vulnerable lot.

## Employment Structure

Employment generation has been one of the principal concerns of development planning in the country. However, growth of employment has generally slowered than the growth of labour force and as a result, backlogs of unemployment continued to rise over time. While the annual growth of gross domestic product (GDP) grew over time, the employment did not increase correspondingly. Most of the GDP growth was thus derived from productivity growth rather than increase in employment. As a result, employment elasticity of GDP growth declined. The decline in employment elasticity in respect of GDP has declined more sharpely in recent periods. In 1977-78 to 1983, the elasticity was estimated to be 0.53, which declined to 0.41 in 1983 to

1993-94. This has further decelerated to about 0.15 in 1993-94 to 1999-2000 (Planning Commission, Task Force Committee, 2001). The annual growth of employment has also declined from 2.43 per cent (UPSS) in 1988-94 to about 0.98 per cent in 1999-2000. Agriculture, being the largest employing sector, did not show any increase in employment. Employment elasticity in manufacturing, electricity; trade, finance, real estate, insurance and business services declined. Community and personal services saw steep decline. Almost all sectors of economy had a deceleration trend in employment elasticity except in construction and transport and storage. Unemployment rate increased from about 1.90 per cent of labour force to about 2.23 per cent (UPSS) and by CDS it increased from 6.03 to 7.32 per cent during 1993-94 and 1999-2000. Also, there has been distinct shift away of workforce from self-employment and wage employment to casual employment. Casualisation process is more conspicuous in the rural areas. Organised sector employment has been declining and that of unorganised sector employment increasing. Organised sector workers (7-8 per cent) are protected by comprehensive legislation and labour standards whereas an overwhelming majority of workers (92-93 per cent) in the unorganised sector are not covered by social security measures. The structural changes in employment raise some relevant questions. As the evidence goes, the problem of creation of employment opportunities is getting resolved in someway through the enterprise of the job seekers. In most cases, however, casual work is being accepted under duress. This has resulted in irregular employment of the casual workers, depression of wage rates relative to the official minimum wages and deskilling of workers. There is another aspect of the above issue. If employment has been literally casual, i.e. irregular for without significant association with industries and providing low incomes, the group of persons depending on casual employment would have no opportunities in their lives for acquiring skills for further development (Ramanujam and Awasthi, 1995). The available evidence indicates that about 44 per cent workforce is illiterate and about 23 per cent is educated up to primary level. The marketable skills among workforce are dismally low. The skilled percentage among rural female is 6 per cent, rural male 10 per cent and in urban female it is about 20 per cent (Planning Commission, Task Force Committee, 2001). At the policy plane such situation raise issues of one kind. Overall unorganised or informal sector employment is rising and there is evidence to show that organised sector will not be able to absorb growing labour force particularly in the context of current industrial restructuring environment. The sources of future employment growth are likely to be the small manufacturing enterprises, rural non-farm activities and urban informal sector and services (Papola, 1993). The policy measures for generating productive employment in the organised and unorganised sectors calls for different approaches.

## Industrial Restructuring and its Impacts

The new economic policy initiated also poses a variety of challenges to the economy. These challenges are improving productivity, enhancing competitiveness and efficiency through work reorganisation, skill development and technical progress. The most important challenge is immediate job losses as a result of restructuring. Rapid changes in technology and knowledge have profound impact on industrial restructuring. It is widely believed that restructuring would promote productivity and efficiency. Of course, this has to be accompanied by other measures of improvements such as reorganisation of production, improved human resource management and other labour market policies. One of the implications of restructuring process is large redundancy and unemployment particularly in the short run. However, in the long run, it is argued that positive gain in employment would occur though increased productivity and more investment and through greater forward and backward linkages. There are evidences across the countries that in the short run such restructuring have an adverse impact in terms of unemployment particularly among poor and disadvantaged classes.

Restructuring and revamping of industries led to adoption of new technologies and rationalisation. This process of restructuring accompanied by redundancies and closure of sick industries. This provided management a greater flexibility to redeploy workers, adopt different production strategies and management styles. This process of reforms has obvious impact on labour relation. Curtailment of public expenditure along with exit policy led the displacement of labour by capital in the inefficient units both in the public and private sector. The impact of restructuring created substantial unemployment particularly to those who are either unskilled or having low level of skills. To cope with the redundancies, government has constituted National Renewal Fund (NRF) in 1992 to protect the interests of redundant workers. NRF was basically setup to assist sick central public sector enterprises to reduce their workforce under voluntary retirement scheme (VRS). This fund was primarily established to assist redundant workers in terms of separation benefits and provide them training and redeployment. The objectives of NRF has been to provide compensation to the workers rendered surplus, providing retraining and redeployment, promoting area employment generation schemes and setting up of insurance fund for income guarantee. The performance of NRF, however, has been quite disappointing. There were 1,28,384 workers who opted voluntary retirement during 1992-99. About 52,177 workers were given counselling, 35,899 workers were retrained and only 11,360 workers could be redeployed. It is quite surprising that out of Rs. 2,262 crores allocated, about Rs 1,800 crores (90 per cent) was incurred on assistance to VRS and less than 10 per cent was spent on training and retraining. There are, however, number of issues for successful redeployment. For instance, what is the duration of retraining for redeployment in self-employment? What are the skills area needed (say traditional or emerging)? What are the initial level of education and training profile of retrenched workers? How to make employment sustainable? What are the levels of productivity and income? Whether income support during training is sufficient? Whether training infrastructure support is adequate and relevant? What should be the role of different actors (viz. Government, NGO and private sector)?

Employment has been one of the core issues in rationalisation process in the different industry groups as evident from the micro-level studies. It has been observed that the Indian industries have been undergoing fundamental changes since 80's with regard to the nature of employment (Davala, 1995). The eight case studies conducted in tea plantation, jute industry, coal industry, ports and docks, engineering, power sector and chemical and pharmaceutical have amply shown that there has been perceptible decline in employment with the growth of industries. In the tea plantation (West Bengal), permanent labour has declined overtime and casual labour increased. In the jute industry also employment has declined to the extent of 20 per cent (employer's estimate) to 45-50 per cent (labourer's estimates). Casual employment has been increasing 5-10 per cent annually replacing regular workers. In ports and docks, permanent employment has been on the decline but certain activities have witnessed increase in contract labour. In engineering industry (Andhra Pradesh and West Bengal), employment has increased in small and medium enterprises and not in large ones. Increased ancillarisation process has created large causal and contract labour with decline in permanent employment. Power generation industry (Andhra Pradesh) employs a large number of contract and causal labour particularly in construction activities. Being a highly capital-intensive industry, it is also placing greater reliance on contract labour in some of the regular operations. In chemicals and pharmaceuticals (Maharashtra), more than one-fourth employment constitutes contract workers. Coal industry, however, seem to be exception to the general trends of employment observed in other industries. But employment does not seem to have increased either with the growth of industry.

The process of declining employment in large industries seems to have gained further momentum with the reforms process. It is also evident that small enterprises have been undergoing with greater strains and becoming vulnerable due to increasing competition. The large industries are resorting to decentralised production system with increasing ancillarisation. This has created the flexibility in terms of casualisation; contract jobs with fall in regular and permanent jobs. In any case public sector employment is likely to increase and so also in the case of organised private sector employment. One can, therefore, visualise that the major part of employment is likely to take place in the unorganised sector. The unorganised sector is unprotected with insecure employment, absence of social security and deterioration of labour standards.

The macro and micro evidences amply suggest that the industrial restructuring has resulted in job losses and increased the vulnerability of those who are unskilled or have low level of skills. This would have serious implications to the polity in the long run. The role of state is therefore inevitable to protect the interests of the poor.

## Institutions and the Values

As most of the employment is likely to be generated in small and decentralised segment in the unorganised sector, the enabling strategies has, therefore, to focus on small-scale unit development. The policy measures require active labour market policies which include improving labour market information system through effective monitoring, area regeneration, investment in training and retraining, emphasis in vocational and technical skill training and redeployment of retrenched workers. The proactive role of NGOs and state becomes critical. It is not simply the involvement of institutions but the inculcation of values in the management of development programmes, which ultimately will empower the poor.

### *(i) Role of Community and NGOs for Affirming Values*

Role of community and NGOs in the form of participation in developmental activities can be most effective in promoting productive employment and affirming a sustainable value system. NGOs have come closer for their mutuality and complementation to the state efforts. NGOs concentrate their activities for community development and economic well-being of the poor. They are regarded as most sensitive partners of development, more conscious and result-oriented. NGOs are also seen as the facilitators for the acquisition of knowledge, attitude and skills. All this has enabled them to be more responsive to the needs of people and have become major actors of development. Since they work with people at grassroots levels and hence have the ability to feel the pulse of the people. They have flexibility in their operations and can be educator to the Government about the needs of people. They can be better skill trainers for self-employment. There exists a wealth of possibilities for NGOs to bring about social and economic well-being through generation and dissemination of relevant knowledge, purposive training in skill and entrepreneurship development.

A variety of efforts have been made to promote unorganised sector employment through programme approach and through project approach in some of the countries (ILO, 1994). Programme approach has broad scope and cover large area whereas project approach has a specific location with limited duration. Much of the interventions to promote employment in this sector have been through project approach. The emphasis has been given through supply side intervention mainly credit, training etc. For instance, in Africa a number of projects have been in operation and many of them being assisted by the ILO. In Indonesia and Bangladesh, NGOs have sought to assist micro enterprises. In India, SJSRY, PMRY, IRDP have been in operation to promote employment through micro-enterprise development. Similarly, in rural areas number of programmes has been started. Notable among them are Grameen Bank of Bangladesh, PRODEM in the Dominican Republic and KUPPEDES in Indonesia. However, the focus of Grameen Bank and KUPPEDES has been in the rural area. In India, Self-employment Women's Organisation (SEWA) has been instrumental in promoting women's welfare through variety of employment and income generating schemes. SEWAs experience with self-employed women is most innovative. SEWA organised women's unions to struggle against exploitation and discrimination meted to them. SEWAs entry to development activities like SEWA Bank, Mahila Trust, and cooperatives like textile rags workers, block printing workers, cane and bamboo workers, paper picker workers, handloom workers, cleaning workers, dairying and milk workers are noteworthy. A large number of NGOs have come up on the scene to supplement the development efforts of the state. Yet not many are directly involved in promoting employment.

### *(ii) The Role of State*

Market can indeed provide important signals to the allocation of resources and thereby bring about improvement in the efficiency of resources. But the role of state even in the market economy cannot be undermined particularly in the spheres of social sector and providing social security to the poor and disadvantaged sections of society. In the fast globalisation age, those who are poor, unskilled or having low skills are most vulnerable groups. The state then becomes the lone ranger to safeguard the interests of these groups through variety of protective measures. Good governance is the major issue of the political economy. The politicians, the bureaucracy, the society and the media have important role to play for the enhancement of the poor's entitlements.

## REFERENCES

Davala, Sarath (ed.) (1995), *Employment and Unionisation in Indian Industry,* Friedrich Ebert Stiftung, New Delhi.

ILO (1995), *The Urban Informal Sector in Asia: Policies and Strategies,* RAS/90/M11/FRG, Geneva.

Papola, T.S. (1993), *Employment in South Asian Countries: Trends, Prospects and Issues,* Paper prepared for Fifth Meeting of Asian Employment Planners, Bangkok, November 29-30 (mimeo).

Planning Commission, Government of India (2001), *Report of Task Force on Employment Opportunities.*

Ramanujam, M.S. and Awasthi I.C., (1995), Integrated Approach to Rural and Urban Employment Planning, *Manpower* Journal, Vol. xxx, No. 4, January-March.

35

# Whither 'Humane' Governance?

*Searching for Values in Public Administration in India*

P. RAGHU RAM

## Introduction

This paper examines the role and significance of values in providing good governance to the people. It deals with the role of values in public administration. It discusses at length the existing state of affairs where our politico-administrative institutions have degenerated due to corruption, lack of integrity and character, which is an indication of drift in values. It examines the interaction between the value premises and the governance. It focuses on achieving better administration through proper value management because positive values constitute the essence of a good human being—whether it be a leader or a citizen. Finally, it proposes some steps to improve/correct/strengthen the situation so that effective, accountable and transparent governance is made possible.

SMART (Simple, Moral, Accountable, Responsive, Transparent) governance is the buzz word these days. I.T.- Savvy Chief Ministers and administrators have been strongly arguing for application of electronic governance to make the political system more effective. Without getting drowned in these plethora of formulations, one needs to examine what role can value system play in improving the administration? This is because the 'managers of the State' are after all human beings with their attendant trials and tribulations. Why there is a general perception that the moral fibre of our society is getting degenerated, breeding corrupt machinery and corrupt ways of life? Is there anything amiss in our society? What safeguards can be employed to improve the state of affairs? Firstly, what went wrong with our system? Secondly, what can be done to improve it? These are some of issues pertinent to this paper.

Corruption in public life begins with the corruption in the electoral process. The use of money and muscle power to capture political power and the brazen resort to any means to get power are the noteworthy trends in our public life, which are responsible for violation of citizen's rights. Rule of Law and also of public norms and morality in India. This is a deep-rooted problem which should be addressed lest the situation shall become worse. Participatory, citizen-friendly administration is the 'in' thing in modern times (HRD, 2001). However, situation hasn't been changed drastically, still the fruits of development aren't reaching the needy persons. The task of the administration is to make the fruits of development reach the poor efficiently and effectively. Self-preservation, it is said, is the essence of human nature. However, self-aggrandizement has become the defining feature of our political class. It is rare to find persons of character and integrity in our public life. Institutional reform may be a good idea to usher in good governance for the people of India. However, there is every need for attitudinal changes and behavioural transformation among the people based on certain value premises that can guarantee good governance. It is ultimately the human beings who operate these institutions. We need to introspect whether the humans have failed the system or *vice-versa.* An idea leads to action, that action leads to concrete result which may be good or bad. Good ideas flow from a positive attitude, which ultimately gets decided by one's value preferences or choices. Thus, values have a crucial role to play in any individual, group, society or nation.

## Values—Their Meaning, Scope and Extent in Human Progress

Let's examine what we mean by values and how they are shaped, how they can be nurtured for better governance. Values form the basis of human behaviour, they constitute an important dimension of social phenomenon. The study of values of societies or groups can provide a clue to understand how these societies or groups develop and transform themselves (Joseph La Palombara, 1963). How values are shaped and altered is a cardinal aspect of any discussion on development or change in any society. Individual's values are largely shaped by his upbringing, schooling and his/her socio-economic milieu. There can be variations in the value set-up of individuals within a group because of variations in their socialization process, exposure, schooling, association with others etc. The heterogeneous character of value framework indicates that values and ethics are not just designed for good times, but also to present bad times. They are like the laws of the land which you need more to protect the people from bad. Ethical choices reflect objectivity between right and wrong. Opinion may vary from culture to culture but values such as fairness, justice, integrity and commitment are universal and eternal. Ethics and justice involve (a) empathy, (b) fairness, (c) compassion for the marginalized, and (d) the larger interest of society.

A society becomes good or bad based on the ethical values of individuals and what give society its strength is its ethical values. Lack of instruction in ethics to young minds is a serious matter of concern. Ethics are usually left to be addressed by parents, however, young people are not being trained properly in values. Morals and ethics are logical, sensible principles of good conduct that we need for a peaceful society. Normally, greed, fear and pressure affect one's own ethical behaviour and this results in wide ranging conflicts of interests in me society. This poses problems to correct analysis of social behaviour and its value premises.

Marxist writers opine that value framework of any politico-administrative system is essentially linked with production processes and larger socio-economic context. If economic interest of individual differs, their value framework will differ. Marx said that all values, ideologies, culture—they are by-product or the super structure which emanate from the mode of production in the economy (Elster, 1990). As values get crystallized in a society, they transform themselves into structured institutions through which they get articulated. In the social pyramid these institutions range from the family at the base to the state at the top. The study of the behaviour of the institutions is an important way of understanding and strengthening them. In the developing countries, where the political institutions are not well developed, the administrative structures have come to play a dominating role. The research studies which throw light on the value framework of the administrative institutions are scanty.

Max Weber assumed that the public institutions can be value-neutral. Can any institution be value-neutral in a heterogeneous and developing society? There are two issues here: one, whether our administrative institutions reflect the dominant values prevalent in the society if so, how can they be transformed ? What values we need to imbibe to make the delivery of public goods and services more effective? Secondly, how important are values in providing better governance to the people. If a society undergoes transition, its value system also changes. Feudal societies get transformed into capitalist ones. Their whole work ethic, values and preferences change due to change in production processes. Thus the debate on the role of values is closely related with the level of economic development and the phase of social transformation. It is indeed very complex to define what constitute a 'value'. Values of an individual may differ from the values of a group, which may be different from the wider public and it goes on like that. 'Values' is a moral concept which implies that no one should harm others' interests. Values stand for honesty, integrity, uprightness, and positive attitude. This list is endless. However, there has to be a broad value framework for any society essentially for two purposes (a) to harmonise the interests of various sections within society and (b) to become torch bearer in a society's progress and development.

## Thinking Through Values—Civil Society, State and the Value FrameWork

No society can progress in the absence of a broad value framework. Concept of nationality and the feeling of national unity are the core values which the citizens imbibe to work for a great and prosperous nation. Notion of a common mother land, hard work for natural progress. These values need to be inculcated in the young minds. We also witness wide-spread oppression, socio-economic inequality, exploitation at different levels of our society. The values of compassion, fraternity, empathy, identifying oneself with human suffering— all these values are necessary to bring about social transformation, where everyone is treated with dignity in an equal and fair manner (Sethi, H., 1988). Equal, humane and just social order becomes a reality only when the value premises and attitudes of all stakeholders in the society undergo a change.

Why violence is resorted to, to resolve the conflicts in the society? Is this because of absence of values of trust, amity and mutual love? We witness communal riots and communal situation periodically. Hostility among the wide ranging conflicts of interests in the society. This poses problems to correct analysis of social behaviour and its value premises.

Communities breed hatred, which ultimately leads to carnage. This will make one lose one's human essence. Illiteracy, ignorance, lack of economic development, nature of the political regime and the social backwardness may be responsible to sustain communalism (Chandra Pipan, 1991). Peaceful co-existence among the individuals, groups and nations is a virtue which is hard to come by. Interestingly, people in highly developed societies are turning towards spiritualism for solace and mental peace. The art of living lectures by yogic gurus is the latest trend now-a-days. The point is that how much technological and material advancement one may achieve, he/she has to fall back upon some positive values only to lead a successful and peaceful life.

If we like to transform the social structures and relationships towards a humane and fair direction, the question of values becomes central. Attitudinal change is necessary in the society (a) to prevent the evils like sati, bride burning and child labour, and (b) to build a sense of trust, friendship and harmony among groups and individuals. How do we bring these changes? There can be different ways of doing it. The role of the state in the society is to work towards achieving the socio-economic well-being of the citizens. Civil society refers to a space where the state and society has an interface, where they come to interact with each other. Vibrant civil society institutions and vigilant citizenry will make the state functionaries more accountable. However, some of the civil society institutions and practices may themselves be undemocratic. For example: caste system (Chandoke, N.,1991). Then the task of building a humane and just society become more complex. The value based education, inculcating the social responsibilities becomes relevant in this context.

Value premises of individuals if they are Good, will lead to a healthy social development. The point is that one's values can be shaped and imparted through conscious training, motivation and some institutional safeguards. Otherwise, any society bereft of a moral framework will degenerate into a backward one. State, civil society and values premises have an organic interconnection. This is because we have to narrow down our focus on individuals, their behaviour, feelings, morality and opinions only in the ultimate analysis. It is the humans who can wreck or work for better systems. It is an established premise that most of our institutions of state and civil society need to be transformed based on fairness and equality. How do we do it unless we orient motivate/gear up the humans towards this task? Thus, the dissemination of positive values, value education is very significant starting from the family to school of offices and to wider society.

**Governance and Values: The Interconnection**

Our Constitution speaks volumes about the values and ideals, which we, Indians should cherish. Our Preamble envisages a society with important in-built values which are necessary for its growth and prosperity. Justice, equality, freedom, dignity and fraternity—these are the values, which the Constitution had set out for us to achieve (Shukla, V.N., 2002). But these ideals remain an empty pipe dream even after five decades of independence. What is wrong with us, and our institutions? Have we become moribund, have we failed as a nation? (Palkhiwala, N.A., 1989) Why do we lack probity in public life? Whether the society as a whole is corrupt or is it the few who are responsible for this mess? These questions need to be squarely answered. We need to examine the behavioural/psychological aspect of our public institutions. Value-based politics, ethics in business and in other professions of life—these words are confined to academia only in modern times. Religion without morality is contemptuous, politics without values are dangerous, as the saying goes.

We need to do an anatomy of corruption in India. What makes one corrupt both morally and monetarily? That person's value framework needs to be urgently attended to. Man's unending quest for power, prestige and wealth is a universal phenomenon. But this trend can be checked through value-based education and some institutional safeguards. Why do our public policies fail? Is it due to their faulty design or faulty implementation or due to both? Why our institutions of governance are ineffective and unresponsive? It is the constitutional duty of the functionaries of the State to deliver the goods and attend to the pressing problems of the people. Despite this, situation is not so encouraging on the ground. These questions need to be thought over seriously to drive home the importance of values in governance in India (Kothari, R., 1988) and social sensitivity are very much required to make the government work effectively. Positive values should promote governance to make it humane and citizen friendly.

However, the large scale inefficiency, rigid hierarchical structures, authoritarianism, suspicion, absence of team-work, breakdown of co-ordination, centralization of decision-making are some of the typical characteristics of the bureaucracy in India. Public functionaries are still guided by feudal and patriarchal values, whereas they are supposed to be "modern" (Haksar, N., 1993). Modern institutions of representative democracy are transplanted in a feudal social hierarchy with its primordial value framework. This contradiction leads to tensions and crises in our society. Value system keeps changing in consonance with the change in our production processes. Our institutions should be in tune with these trends.

Any administrative system cannot be separated from its larger socio-economic system. It reflects the value premises prevalent in the wider society. The administrative machinery gets influenced by the dominant values and choices in the society. Administrative machinery has to become an instrument of social progress and economic development. Rather, it has become an instrument of maintaining the *status quo*, resisting any positive change. The value premises and the mindset of our bureaucratic class are still influenced by primordial (caste, class, region and religious) considerations. This has been the paradox of India's political economy. Indian society is still under the grip of the feudal value framework. Indian Constitution avowed itself towards achieving the socialistic pattern of society. Indian State is engaged in the task of promoting capitalist mode of production. This complex mix of values, choices and goals is leading to tensions within our politico-economic system (Rao, R.S., 1995).

What are the value premises of the members of the bureaucracy, where from they imbibe their values? This can be gauged from the behavioural trends of the bureaucracy. Lack of social purpose, commitment and elitist bias among the bureaucrats makes the development programmes a failure. The rural bureaucracy in particular is depersonalised which is manifested in the indifference and hostile attitude towards the target groups of the government programmes. There has been an escapist tendency manifesting itself in widespread buck-passing. It is rare that accountability for implementing a programme is fixed and much less enforced. A fixed percentage to various functionaries in the delivery of development benefits is an open secret (Haragopal, G., 1995). The pilferages in all facets of administration have got institutionalized. This will defeat the very purpose of development programmes.

The environment in which they operate largely shapes the bureaucracies. The socio-economic environment can stimulate or strangulate the administration. The performance of the bureaucratic agencies is no match to the promises they generate. As a result, credibility of these agencies and their capability to perform the developmental role is increasingly being eroded. However, people are turning articulate, they have become conscious of the development programmes, so the lethargic and indifferent bureaucracy is feeling the heat now. The administrative system lacks a culture of accountability. It is now facing pressures from the public (Kohli, A., 1991), which Atul Kohli describes as the 'crisis of governability' in India. Rajni Kothari describes this as a crisis of values in Indian society.

The structural infirmities of the administration can be corrected, if the behavioural pattern is adequately geared to the tasks of the administration. The value framework of the bureaucracy again decides this pattern.

How do we make the governance responsive and citizen-friendly? Firstly, by building some institutional checks and balances, secondly, by simplifying the rules and procedures. Finally, by bringing positive attitudinal changes in those who govern. Values framework, and the ethical practices of the individuals are crucial in shaping their public behaviour which in turn affects their functioning as public servants (Ramesh K. Arora, 1991). One needs to establish a link between governance and values—Values of duty, integrity.

## Values in Public Administration: The Rhetoric and the Reality

Bureaucracy is supposed to be value-neutral, legal-rational and objective. The administrative agencies are meant for serving the people, the poor in particular. However, the difference between the rhetoric and reality may be glaring. Mahatma Gandhi said that there are seven deadly sins : wealth without work; pleasure without conscience; knowledge without character; commerce (business) without morality; science without humanity; religion without sacrifice; and politics without principles. We find it depressing that the democratic deficit is growing in our society. The latest U.N. Human Development report talks of his deficit. Despite that ours is the electoral democracy, where elections are held regularly, our democracy lacks legitimacy (The Hindu, July 2002). This is because of lack of effective institutions that can translate electoral promises into concrete policy outcomes.

The approach of 'Reinventing Government' put forth by David Osborn and Ted Gaebler has greatly influenced the debate on the elements of good governance. This concept is understood to be the manner in which power is exercised in the management of a country's economic and social resources for development. The World Bank identified three distinct aspects in the conceptualisation of 'good governance': (a) The form of political regime, (b) The processes by which authority is exercised in the management of social and economic resources. The capacity of governments to design, formulate and implement policies for people's welfare. We need to do an introspection of our own institutions in the light of above conceptualisation (HDR, 2001).

E-governance is considered as an important tool of good governance. The use of information technology in government will improve the capacity of the government to respond more effectively to the needs of people. The new technologies will facilitate better interface between people and government and more transparency in its operations.

The year 2001 is declared by the Government of India as the year of E-governance. Good governance includes a host of factors which include transparent, efficient and responsive governance, with probity in public life and people's participation. It also means building social capacities with ethical approach to the human concerns (Prasad, V.S., 2001).

Indian administration is designed on Weberian premises of legal-rational authority. However, this Weberian form is found to be incongruent in Indian context. For example the security of service is seen as a cause for inefficiency. Heirarchial ordering of relationships may not be well-suited to the working of partnership-based network organizations of modern times. Procedure orientation of Weberian form conflicts with the result orientation and need for social sensitibility of the system (UPA, Jan-March, 1999).

## Achieving Humane Governance Through Value Management

Till now we have discussed various infirmities associated with our politico-administrative system. Corruption and criminality deeply afflict this system. We have also underlined the need for imbibing the values of integrity and character among our citizens. Through improving our public morality and individual probity alone, we can improve the functioning of our public institutions. An attempt is made in this section to address the question of applying some correctives to our system, by emphasizing on inculcating positive values both among the powers-that-be and the citizenry.

The Vohra Committee Report vividly documents criminalisation of politics, the nexus between bureaucrats, politicians and the criminals. Judiciary and the Election Commission have been pro-active in reviving the electoral process from the cesspool of muscle power and money power. If the public policies, legislations are drafted and implemented according to wishes of the dominant elite in the society, this will have an adverse effect on the other sections of population. The situation can be redressed through a multi-pronged approach:

(a) By nurturing and disseminating positive values of morality, honesty, uprightness, discipline and social commitment both in private and public lives of citizens.
(b) By bringing attitudinal/behavioural changes among the political-class, members of bureaucracy and other functionaries. This can be done through vigilant public through their organizations and the grassroots movement. Right to information becomes a key factor in achieving transparency in governance.
(c) Finally, by bringing about institutional reforms at different levels. This is because welfarian legal-rational authority will help in containing human arbitrariness and also the whims and fancies of senior officials. Legal, judicial reforms, reforms in police and administration and electoral reforms will create necessary institutional safeguards and conditions for better governance.

The rural bureaucratic behaviour is largely characterised by absence of concern for the poor. Added to it, obsession with self-development, superficial understanding of the magnitude of the problems leads to negative disposition harming the purpose of public policies. The structural infirmities and the bureaucratic dispositions have not been in consonance with the goals of development. In fact, it is both the inner processes and the larger socio-economic system and its political processes that determine the nature and character of any, administrative agency. Paul Appleby opined that the mismatch between development needs and bureaucratic dispositions result in policy failures (Appleby, P., 1963).

The political dimension of administration is significant. Despite that bureaucrats can influence the policy making and the policy outcomes, they are directed by political masters who are the elected representatives. Political manipulation of bureaucracy for selfish party interests shall defeat the public purpose (Chaturvedi, T.N., 1990). The administrative behaviour is also influenced by culture. Good governance is a value-laden process. Transparency, accountability, competition and efficiency are all processes and values. The neo-liberal view consider the social capital—the collection of norms, beliefs attitudes and practices that govern relationships between an individual and groups in a society — as very important to reduce the transaction costs of governance (Mathur, K., 1996). However, administrative corruption is also sustained by the kind of social relationships that characterize society.

Right to information is the key to make the governance accountable. However, everyone pays lip service to this demand. Freedom of Information Bill, 2000 is under active consideration of parliament since one year (Prasad, V.S., 2001). Many drives for administrative action can be traced to cultural roots. Many problems in policy implementation are traced to attitudes. Good governance after all requires good human beings. Democratic governance is an important requirement of good governance despite its limitations. The legitimacy and credibility of the state are very important to enable it to play the 'mobilisation role' for good governance (Sen, A., 2000). State, civil society and market have to play their assigned role in a balanced manner.

The thrust of development administration is towards professionalism and behavioural change in the bureaucracy (Mathur, K., 1998). However, bureaucrats often collide with the local ruling groups in taking decisions. The networks of bureaucracy are often described as rent-making or rent-seeking (Bardan, P., 1985). Mutuality of interest has been the guiding principle between the politicians and bureaucrats (Bhambri, 1998). Government's initiatives may fail in the absence of a supportive environment. Without effective political control and social accountability, the bureaucracy will use its autonomy for its self-aggrandizement as well as for promoting the predatory forces in the society.

Despite these limitations and ills of bureaucracy, this important organ of the government can still help promote the social purpose we need to apply some correctives to our politico-administrative system. An overhaul of the system is necessary to make it more responsive and effective.

**Conclusion**

This paper made a modest attempt to identify various issues concerning the role of values in bringing about better governance. Giving more autonomy to the bureaucracy and strengthening its capacities are the first steps to be taken. However, this is not enough, supportive measures such as popular consent for the public policies, legitimacy for mobilizing resources for future investments are equally necessary. This can be achieved through democratic processes such as grassroots movements, debate and dialogue among the informed citizenry. To sum up, this chapter began with clarifying the meaning of the terms 'value' and 'governance'. Values are certain ideals of conduct in social life. Secondly, it explored the interconnection between the two. Thirdly, it dealt with the widening gap between the promise and performance of those who govern. Finally, it focused on how best the correctives can be applied in the system through proper value management. Let us conclude by saying that the organic relationship between the values, bureaucracy and the wider society need to be understood thoroughly before we proceed with any suggestive measures for improvement.

## REFERENCES

1. Bardan, P., *Political Economy of Development,* OUP, Delhi.
2. Bhambari, C.P., Of a Self serving. Partisan Bureaucracy, *Pioneer*, 23 Sep. 1998.
3. Chandra, Bipan (1995). *Communalism in Modern India,* Oxford University Press.
4. Chandoke, Neera (1991). *State and Civil Society,* Sage Publication.
5. Chaturvedi, T.N., (1990). Inaugural Paper, in Bureaucracy, Development & Change, Pant & Gupta (ed.) Segment Books.
6. Elster, John (1990). *Making Sense of Marx,* Clarendon Press, London.
7. Haragopal, G., (1997). *Political Economy of Human Rights*, Himalaya Publication Company, Bombay.
8. *Human Development Reports* (2001 & 2002), U.N.D.P. Programme, New York.
9. Haksar, N., (1993). *Demystification of Law for Women,* Lancer International, Delhi.
10. Kothari, Rajni (1988). *State Against Democracy,* Ajanta Publication.
11. Kohli, Atul (1991). *Democracy & Discontent*, Princeton University Press.
12. Lapalomara, J, (1963). *Bureaucracy and Political Development*, Princeton University Press.

13. Mathur, Kuldeep (1996). *Development Policy and Administration*, Sage Publication.
14. Palkhiwala, N.A., (1989). *We the People*, Manohar, Delhi.
15. Prasad, V.S., (2001). Keynote address at the NEPASI Conference on Governance for Development Issues and Strategies at IGNOU on 24-25 August.
16. Shukla V.N., (2002). *Constitution of India,* Eastern Book Company, Lucknow.
17. Rao, R.S., (1995). *Towards Understanding Semi-Colonial, Semi-Feudal Society*, Perspectives, Hyderabad.
18. Mathur, K., (1999), Strengthening Bureaucracy, *ICSS Review*, Jan.-June 1999 Vol. 1 (1).

36

# Values in Public Services

MARINA R. PINTO

*God, Give us Men!*

*God, give us men! A time like this demands*
*Strong minds, great hearts, true faith and ready hands;*
*Men whom the lust of office does not kill;*
*Men whom the spoils of office cannot buy;*
*Men who possess opinions and a will;*
*Men who have honour; men who will not lie;*

—Josiah Gilbert, Holland

Indeed! In the world of today, we need such men in public service! Particularly so in developing countries such as India. The need is imminent, given administration's structural disharmonies, incompatibilities and incompetences; the tension area of politician-administrator relationships, the conflict area of generalist *versus* the technocrat administrator and the defective operating culture of administration.

Public service is generally viewed as a high and noble calling. It is service in the cause of the nation and there can be no service higher than that of the sovereign state. At the time of Independence, the unique value of public service was recognised and appreciated and young men responded in a big way to the call of the state. Today, public service is equated with not virtues of dedication and selfless service but with evils of corruption, nepotism, power and money. One is reminded of the ancient Greek city-state where a citizen found fulfilment only in the service of the state. It was the city-state or polis which made the 'good life' possible. His self-fulfilment and his contribution to public life in the polis were two sides of the same coin. Today's world is a cry from the situation that obtained at one time in history. Not that one can re-create such a world gone by, but one can certainly revive the spirit of those times and the values that motivated men to action.

## Importance of Values

Values are the driving force of human behaviour. In fact, what man does can be explained in terms of his value structure. Values help determine one's norms, standards and goals. They enable one to select the means to realise chosen goals or ends of action. Hence, values regulate human behaviour. Values may be explicit or implicit; they may be held by an individual or a group. In any case, they constitute a code or a standard which provides a yardstick to approve or disapprove human action.

Values are often confused with facts. This is because, often in our experience, they overlap. For instance, a bracelet is an object, i.e. a fact having value because it was a gift from someone special, or because it was made of gold or may be because it was a piece of antique jewellery. But in itself, in essence, it is value neutral. It is the owner who, knowing its worth has imbued it with a certain amount of value. Value lies in the mind of the value-holder and is, therefore, subjective. Value is a function of the individual mind, of one's conscious thinking.

Value is something other than motive, want or need. It has been described as a concept of the desirable with motivating force. Kluckhohn has defined a value as "a conception, explicit or implicit, distinctive of an individual or characteristic of a group of the desirable which influences the selection from available modes, means and ends of action."[1] A better way of looking at values would be as "phenomenological entities intermediate between motives and attitudes". Christopher Hodgkinson has coupled this definition with a diagrammatic presentation of the concept as given in Fig. 36.1.[2]

In sum, values are important because they prompt human behaviour. However, they lie in the mind and are interconnected with motives and attitudes. Hence, to examine values is no easy task. One has primarily to probe into the fields of sociology and ethics as much as government and politics if one has to get a grip on values in public service.

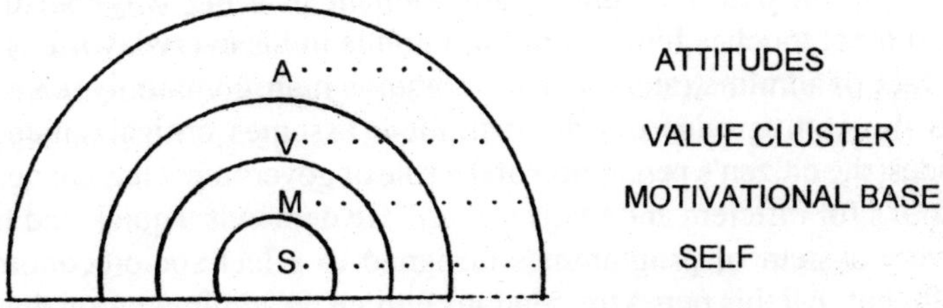


**Fig. 36.1:** Interface of Self and World

## Public Service in a Welfare State

The credibility and capability of a given polity largely depends on the quality of the public service, both in matters of policy-making and policy-implementation. At one time, administration was generally viewed as an activity mainly concerned with functional rationality. It was divorced from politics and was regarded as being value-neutral. Besides, the role of the state itself was highly restricted and limited. With the accepted ideology of individualism in the political field, accompanied with the economic doctrine of *laissez faire*, the best state was the one that did the least. The state, very much like a policeman, performed limited regulatory functions.

The world wars effected a sea-change in political thinking. Warfare paved the way for welfare. In fact, welfarism was now the state's major concern, thanks to the aftermath of the industrial revolution seen in human degradation, poverty and misery. The word wars only precipitated the concern for human welfare. Soon the state took on a positive role of being not just a social service state but a welfare state. One hearts of the state that goes beyond welfare thinking. It is the Redistributive State or Equity State wherein emphasis is placed on the attainment of freedom, justice, equality or even dignity and fulfilment. Goals of this nature emphasise public service and necessarily bring in question of values, norms and ethics. Also, in such a state, politics-administration dichotomy is no longer emphasised; emphasis now seems to be on the area of fusion of the two. Administrators are now frequently described as political administrators. They are deeply involved in policy analysis, policy studies and policy sciences.

The welfare state poses difficulties, not only in matters of goal formation but also more critically in the area of goal-implementation.

The common man encounters government in a big way, because government touches him at a million points in his everyday life. The interface of administrators with the common man, commonly referred to as the cutting edge of administration, assumes critical salience. Besides, the citizen's perception of the role of government has changed. He looks for efficient and ready service. He demands a quick and fair delivery system of programmes designed to effect socio-economic upliftment. All this puts a tremendous burden on administration that is often ill-equipped to deliver the goals.

Burgeoning state activity means expanding bureaucracy, growing public sector and complex inter-mingling of public and private sectors. Civil servants get more directly involved in complex relationships with citizen bodies, be they organised or not. Such activities call for "practical judgement" and "negotiating skills" as expressed by the Fulton Report. It also calls for professional knowledge and expertise. Above all, it calls for a service orientation and a sense of commitment and devotion to the common cause. Given the widening and deepening area of governmental operations, administrative behaviour and the values that inform it, becomes all important.

## India—A Historical Perspective

If one were to take a peep into India's early history, one would discern a paternalistic administration. Whether it was benevolent or not, depended on the king. Administrators were at the beck and call of the ruler who was often king, military chief and priest rolled in one. Administration was personalised, and reflected the head of state's interests and concerns. It was not public service but royal service with administrators as an extension of the royal household.

The British continued the paternalistic tradition, but with a difference. The basic foundation of their administrative machinery was the Indian Civil Service, significantly described by Lloyd George as the 'steel frame'. The ICS implanted in India, the tradition of anonymity, impartiality, neutrality and loyalty. In fact, "the whole structure of the raj celebrated generalist control and continuity, not specialist expertise and innovation".[3] The ICS men were servants of the imperial power. They had a special relationship of trust with that power and, due to constraints of time and distance, has to be given considerable autonomy and discretion to decide and act on the spot. Though government did take up medical and sanitary operations and such like activities, yet their main preoccupation related to law and order administration, revenue and tax collection and safeguarding the legally recognised rights of the people.

After Independence, administration could no longer be primarily regulatory. With a determined bid to effect a social revolution through the instrumentality of the state, and a commitment to welfare state ideology to be worked out through the mechanics of a democratic, parliamentary, federal and political system, administration found itself in an unenviable position.

India consciously and deliberately opted for development administration as its principal tool to effect a total re-organisation of its society's values, institutions and performance-patterns with reference to the goals of nation-building and socio-economic and technological progress. Administration had to be change oriented, action bound and goal conscious. It had to be imbued with a sense of urgency, dedication and commitment to work. All this had to be accomplished in the changed political environment where the administrators were not the rulers, functioning as the strong arm of the British Raj, but servants of the people.

## India Today

But the administrative machinery today, is still a legacy and replica of the British system. The IAS continues in the foot-steps of the ICS. Though the context, tasks and role have changed, the service continues to conform to the Weberian rational model. The generalist still reigns supreme, the formal colonial structure continues and the established habits, prejudices and interests remain elitist in character. David Potter's painstaking research has led him to the conclusion that "the ICS had gone, but the central feature of their tradition lived on in the 1980s."[4]

It has to be realised and recognised that development administration upholds values of industrialisation and modernisation. It is administration for rapid change envisaged through programmes for action. Therefore, the administrative structure, work techniques and procedures, personnel policies and practices, and above all, interaction with citizens—all must be attuned to the goals and processes of such national development.

In making a society 'modern' in the totality of this term, the political and permanent executives have lead roles to play. As far as our bureaucracy goes, marginal or peripheral adjustments—structural, functional and procedural—have been effected rather than fundamental changes in the Weberian system. An administrator in modern India could find it difficult to be 'aseptic' to politics, for often his political involvement would be dictated by his being the principal initiator of change: Being conditioned to Weberian thinking, he may not find it easy to be "analytical as a thinker, creative and dynamic as a goal setter; pragmatic as a planner and innovative as a programmer".[5] Hence, the whole focus must be on the man, the individual bureaucrat and how to change him. Since, his behaviour pattern is dictated by the values he upholds, it is necessary to examine these value clusters.

## INDIAN BUREAUCRACY AND ITS VALUE ORIENTATIONS

To understand values in public service, which can be equated with bureaucratic values, one must begin by a consideration of bureaucratic culture as values are rooted in culture. This, in turn, necessitates a close examination of societal, political and administrative cultures because of linkages between them and their contribution to the formation of value clusters. Diagrammatically, this could be represented thus:[6]

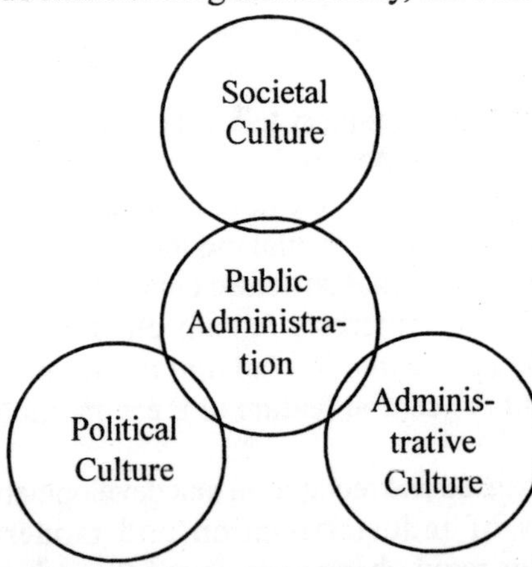


**Fig. 36.2**: Factors Contributing to Value Clusters

While general societal value orientation will affect an administrator's behaviour in specific situations, he could be affected by political or administrative culture.

## Societal Values

Indian bureaucracy is a sub-system of the general societal system. Its culture is part of the total culture of society. Bureaucratic culture reflects, in varying measures, general social values, for a civil servant is essentially a creature of his society. Put differently, administration cannot be plucked out from the tissue of culture in which it is embedded as a member of the wide societal system, a bureaucratic will reflect, the spirit and ethos of that society. His actions are bound to be the manifestation of his cultural moorings. Value orientations of the society, to which he belongs, will affect or influence his behaviour.

Indian society is largely Hindu, feudal and traditional. Social bonds of caste, religion, community and language are very strong. An individual cares more for his group identity and has greater respect for customs and tradition rather than for low and reason. Typical traditional social values could be described as ascriptive, particularistic and diffused to use Riggsian terminology.

At the same time, Indian society is in the throes of change. This continuous process of fundamental change also described as a churning process, penetrates into the social, economic, cultural and psychological basis of society. The result is a heterogeneous blend where the old and the new orders co-exist. Administration reflects this character of society, because though enmeshed in a traditional culture, it is undoubtedly cross-influenced by these currents of change.

Indian societal values, therefore, are indicative of a modernising, traditional culture. Industrialisation, urbanisation, education and parliamentary democracy have affected Indian societal value system. While ascriptive status is valued and upheld, values that emanate from a democratic, socialist, welfare state also find a place in the value cluster. All this makes for a degree of ambivalence and is reflected in the societal value cluster than affects administrative behaviour.

## Political Values

A consideration of political culture is necessary because it throws up another value constellation which affects public service. Political values are important because administration functions in a political milieu and administration cannot be 'aseptic' to political happenings. Hence, they do carry political values in their mental baggage.

According to Lucian Pye, "In essence, the political culture consists of the system of empirical beliefs, expressly symbols and values which define the situation in which political action takes place".[7] Almond and Verba, express the same idea when they define political culture as the political system "internalised in the cognitions, feelings and evaluations of its population."[8]

Political culture throws up the dominant value of democracy. Democracy is to be viewed not only as a responsible and responsive government, but in terms of its underlying morality. Democratic morality upholds the dignity and worth of the individual. For man, the ultimate measure of all human values is man himself. This is the individualistic foundation of democratic morality. Coupled with this idea and flowing from it, is the equalitarian component of democratic morality, namely, that all men have worth deserving social recognition. Together, these ideas would uphold free and equal opportunities for fullest personal development. Thirdly, democratic morality underlines participation in the governmental processes. This calls for freedoms which are ensured through constitutional guarantees.

Since democratic values centre round the individual, both as a person and as a member of a collectivity, the concept of public interest or the common good assumes critical salience. The administrator, though in public service, is yet uncertain of the ramifications of this phrase. With no "cohesive public" with "consensual value patterns", public good is difficult to define. Moreover, administrators functioning as a vital component of the democratic system, have not fully imbibed democratic values. This could partly be explained by the fact that a bureaucracy structured on Weberian lines has a built-in bias against democracy. After all, it enshrines the principle of inequality because of senior-subordinate relationships, negates liberty because it nurtures conformism and rigid adherence to set patterns and procedures, and belies fraternity as a neocasteism creeps into it.

Thus, there are inherent contradictions in bureaucracy and democracy. The conflict in their value clusters is neatly summed up by Pai Panandikar and S. Kshirsagar. According to them, "The essential values of bureaucracy and hierarchy, status, secrecy, specialisation, rules and an unflinching obedience to authority. In contrast, democracy is built round almost diametrically opposite values of egalitarianism, non-hierarchy, open discussion and above all, dissent. The guiding principle of bureaucracy is rationality, which in essence, means efficiency. The guiding principle of democracy is popular will."[9]

India is committed to development through democracy. This puts a colossal burden on administrators, who now have to imbibe democratic and developmental values as well. To speed up development, they need technical knowledge; requisite training and managerial skills. Democratic values would necessarily imply client-oriented behavioural pattern. Administrators need qualities of head and heart, a basic understanding of fellow-men, and a realisation that their performance cannot be delinked from citizen cooperation and participation.

## Administrative Values

These are institutional values reflective of administrative culture. The Indian bureaucrat sees himself as part of a Weberian construct. He is attuned to an administrative system that is authoritarian, rigid, neutral and impartial. In his world of papers, files, rules and regulations, he adheres to Weberian principles and upholds a Weberian value system. His organisational values would include impersonality, neutrality, secrecy, efficiency, status, rule-orientation and commitment to public good. Additionally, the colonial past has brought in attitudes of haughtiness and arrogance among the higher civil servants. In public service, along with 'hard values' mentioned earlier, an administrator must imbibe 'soft values' like pity, compassion and consideration for man, especially when an administrator directly interacts with the public.

## Personal Values

One must not leave out of the reckoning the personal or private value cluster of the administrator. A personal value constellation or a private code of conduct would include ethical values rooted in religion or the subconscious or would just reflect the discipline of the mind. Here one would find values related to self, like the desire to satisfy one's needs and those related to the family. The personal values cluster would be as important as any other values listed earlier. There is the possibility of intra-value conflicts as much as inter-value conflicts.

It is not always easy to resolve value conflicts. McGregor has posed the dilemma in an arresting way. He queries, "Will he marry the job if this involves shirking his responsibilities as a husband and father? ... will he accept and support decisions and policies made by others which, at least occasionally are in conflict with his conceptions of fair and just treatment of his fellow human beings"?[10] Difficulties arise because man does not act as a rational being all the time. Through experimental research, behavioural scientists have proved that the emotional self in man is as real as his rational self and together they constitute the real man. Man often acts on the basis of "non-logical thought processes". Value conflict according to Bernard could result in "...paralysis of action, accompanied by emotional tension and ending in a sense of frustration, blockade, uncertainty or in loss of decisiveness and lack of confidence."[11]

In trying to resolve conflicts, an administrator may adhere to one value constellation and ignore or violate another. If he persistently upholds one cluster, he may even destroy the others. For instance, a corrupt administrator may soon develop a lax conscience and stoop to even greater forms of corruption, thus killing many values.

To resolve value conflicts, one may act subconsciously, in terms of a system of priorities or develop a priority among value clusters or codes of conduct or be morally creative. The last is the most significant, though difficult. It is "a process of inculcating points of view, fundamental attitudes, loyalties to the organisation or co-operative system, and to the system of objective authority, that will result in subordinating individual interest and the minor dictates of personal codes to the good of the co-operative whole."[12]

In public service, an administrator needs to develop a sort of "ethical pluralism" that will enable him to take the proper action in a specific situation. Conflict resolution has to be "worked out" and calls for ability, imagination, innovation and above all courage.

## Professionalism: Its Underlying Values

A good way to examine values in public service is to put the spot-light on professionalism. This will show the civil servant as a professional in action and indicate how he handles and projects his value system.

Public services of yesteryears cannot copy with the administrative imperatives of tomorrow. The compulsive position of the modern state compels public services "to marry ideological philosophy with administrative idiom, to transform policies into programmes and to function as a feed back for suggesting not merely what is rational but also what is feasible."[13] Administrators require conceptual, technical and human relations skills which are born of knowledge and experience; in short they must acquire professionalism.

Professionalism in public administration could be understood by adopting the functionalist model, advocated by Bernard Barber and Talcott Parsons. This model stresses the functional value of professional activity and lists four essential attributes. These are: (1) a high degree of generalised and specialised knowledge; (2) Behaviour and management through a code of ethics; (3) Primary orientation to public service or community interest; and (4) A system of rewards. Let us examine each of them.

Professionalism, first and foremost, denotes specialism. The Fulton Committee Report (1968) commented on the professionalism of specialised cadres in the Civil Service, like doctors and engineers and recommended that these professionals be given more responsible positions and accordingly be trained in administration. It also indicated that the generalist administrators "must acquire the basic concepts and knowledge whether social, economic, industrial or financial relevant to his area of administration and appropriate to his level of responsibility."

In India, the Administrative Reforms Commission adopted the line of thinking of the Fulton Committee and emphasised specialisation.

The Study Team on the Machinery of the Government of India and its Procedures of Work stated, "Policy position in departments and ministries dealing with science and technical matters or with functions of highly specialised character should include persons having relevant specialised experience or expertise".[14] The Report on Personnel Administration preferred to distinguish between functional and non-functional services to be manned by suitably qualified staff.

The 'specialist *vs.* generalist' debate is an unfortunate development in the Indian context. It is indeed a sterile debate. It is not as if one would seek specialists at the cost of the generalist. Each is as important as the other. One could speak of the specialism of a generalist where his speciality lies in method rather than in subject matter. Moreover, as a professional administrator, the generalist must develop a 'scientific temper'. He must understand and appreciate the core content of projects and programmes, so that the technical aspects of the job are not lost on him. All this is possible through training courses that provide grounding in social and behavioural sciences and also literacy in fields of science and technology. In a complementary fashion, specialists need administrative training, for at higher levels functions become more generalised and acquire a greater administrative dimension.

The critical need is to break the barrier or artificial wall between generalists and specialists and develop the new type of administrators who are experts in the humanistic approach and in the professional use of diverse and expert knowledge and experience. To acquire appropriate specialisms is an undisputed value for an administrator.

Every profession develops its professional code of ethics. Such a code presupposes the prevalence of an inherent sense of pride and strong in-group feelings, a wide sharing of a common set of values, a confidence that the profession has a capacity for self-regulation to ensure technical proficiency, moral integrity, discipline and a fair amount of autonomy.

The British high professional standards have commanded world-wide admiration. Despite the fact that it is not easy to have a code of ethics to help resolve conflict situations especially since a civil servant is saddled with multiple responsibilities to the Minister, administration, Parliament and community, yet the established code of ethics (estacode) upholds undivided allegiance to the state, avoidance of the use of public office for private gain, personal honesty, integrity, neutrality and impartiality. America, in the early 1950s, drafted a Code of Ethical Proprieties as a supplement to the Administrative Procedures Code. India has yet to evolve such a code.

In India, standards of integrity in public services have registered a steady decline. The cancer of corruption has eaten into the vitals of the body politic and the services are not exempt from it. Civil servants are expected to carry out activities with great honesty and probity. To ensure this, government has conduct rules, restrictive laws and disciplinary measures. However, these have their limitations. Some are sketchy and vague and could conflict with Fundamental Rights. The machinery to examine serious charges of corruption at the initial stages is faulty and inadequate. Political interference has had a disastrous effect on discipline. What compounds the situation is the vitiated work environment and the exasperating work ethos.

Even if one were to argue that civil servants only reflect a general social malaise, there is no denying the fact that they are very special persons; they are torchbearers who have to set the pace for others by themselves adhering to high moral standards. They must be social moralists in action, living up to Appleby's dictum that "responsible government is ethical government".

In public service, ethical problems arise from conflicts in value clusters. Will one adhere to a personal code which upholds obligations to self, family and friends? This could clash with the public interest or professional obligations. Ticklish questions that arise are: One should do *right*, but who defines it and for whom? And to what end? One should be *honest*, but how and to what extent? One should do one's *duty*, but towards whom and what?

Primary orientation to public interest raises issues of what is the public interest and who defines it. The ruling politician and the bureaucrat claim to serve the public. But their perception of the common good and the means to realise it may not coincide. One is reminded of what R.P. Noronha once said quite sarcastically: "When the politician speaks of democracy, he has in mind the greatest good of the greatest number of his supporters. Public spiritedness refers to that section of the public which has voted for him. Dedication means dedication to himself. And patriotism—well your guess is as good as mine."[15]

It must not be forgotten that because a civil servant has to work in close liaison with the political executive and is accountable through him to the public, his perception of the common good may simply coincide with that of the minister. This can have dangerous implications and far reaching consequences. The civil servant may end up becoming a slave of his political boss. He may be tolerant of political meddlesomeness; he may permit blatant manipulation of routine administrative operations. He may dent a policy to accommodate a minister and be at pains to defend it in the administration or by the public. In the process, he will have resolved the conflict in values by compromising with his ethical and institutional values.

The essence of democratic polity is equality before the law and equal protection of the law. In concrete terms, this means adhering to rules and regulations, guidelines and work procedures. The bureaucrat may find himself in an embarrassing position when he is pressurised by his superior, perhaps in collusion with his political boss, to break procedures or violate rules resulting in forsaking public interest for personal or partisan ends. In such a situation, the administrator, who tries to conduct himself according to his organisational code of conduct, may find his very survival at stake. Unfortunately, a large number of administrators are afraid of standing up for their principles and easily succumb to political or other pressures. C.D. Deshmukh opined that there are few officers who "have been men enough to resist these pressures" and most have learned to become "courtiers and to fight shy of accepting personal responsibility for decisions".[16] Commissions of Inquiry have also testified to this fact. For instance according to the Shah Commission of Inquiry, "Even the cream of the talent of the country in the administrative field often collapse at the slightest pressure".[17]

However, there are examples of civil servants who have had the strength of character to stand by their convictions and steadfastly serve the public interest. In early times, we have the case of N.B. Benarjee who, in 1950, resigned because, among other things, he could not adjust to the "altered administrative ethic". N. Bakshi, in his resignation letter of March 16, 1959 stated "my spirit was not in harmony with the official environment of my life".[18] More recently, we have the fine examples of P.S. Appu and B.B. Vohra.

Unfortunately, it is common to see administrators resolve dilemmas by making personal gain their supreme value. They can hardly resist the temptation to take "a share of grease money and enter the charmed circle of friends of rulers".[19] In the typology given by J.K. Ray in *Administrators in a Mixed Polity*, the majority of Indian administrators are either detractors or accommodators. Others have described them as being pliant and suppliant rather than defiant. It is a said commentary on erosion of basic values.

Civil servants are expected to be committed to the public good in accordance with the basic philosophy of the Constitution. Such a commitment does not negate the doctrine of neutrality. For neutrality does not mean indifference or lack of emotional involvement in one's task. It implies deep involvement in policy politics and not party politics. Unfortunately, in the Indian context, the terms commitment and neutrality were viewed as opposites and a plea was made in the late 60s for a committed Civil Servant. This commitment was to the ruling party's ideology and meant over-politicisation to the extent of wearing a party label. Though a civil servant as a charge-agent cannot be totally apolitical, it does not mean that he gets sucked into the vortex of politics.

Since a civil servant must be a committed man, commitment must be clearly defined. It means acceptance through intellectual conviction of certain social and economic values which may or may not have emergėd in society but are uphold by the Constitution. It does not relate to the programme of a political party or the views of an individual.

While traditionalists religiously uphold neutrality and seek a civil servant whose only commitment is to discipline and hard work in the public interest, there are others who could be described as innovators. They would want changes in the system, such as placing in "crucial positions" the bureaucrats who will come and go with the party. Others have suggested inducting outside experts in administration whom the minister may like and who would be solely responsible to him. It could even be a kind of a mini secretariat for the minister, duration of which will coincide with his tenure. These aides should function as "the brain of the Minister and the eye of the Master" forming a linkage between administration and policy. India should examine this issue in the light of the experiences of other democracies and find a system that facilitates an administrator's primary orientation to public interest.

As for the last attribute of professionalism, i.e., a system of rewards, there is much that can be said on the subject. Suffice it to say that rewards on the job relate to a good system of promotion which combines judiciously the principles of merit and seniority. If civil servants must be true to their calling and not stoop to bribery and corruption there must be a foolproof system of rewards and punishments. Happily, the Fourth Pay Commission has hiked pay scales and it is hoped that the removal of major grouses will have a tonic effect on the services. However, the highest reward is a sense of fulfilment of reaching out in humble service to the common man even at a personal cost.

## Conclusion

An examination of professionalism in public service has pin-pointed the values of knowledge, code of conduct, service orientation and intrinsic reward which flows from the realisation of "the sanctity of public office as a public trust". Given various value clusters which often compete and at times clash, an administrator must find his own ways to sort things out. He may decide after careful thought, or just act on the spur of the moment. To help him in this difficult task, he needs education and training and the backing of professional or service associations.

A word needs to be said about training. Its importance has always been recognised in India right from the time of Independence. The Administrative Reforms Commission appreciated the need for not only functional specialisation but fine tuning of administrators for development tasks. It rightly focuses on development-oriented values, attitudes and motivation which an administrator could imbibe through training. Some of the recommendations of the ARC, like the establishment of a separate Department of Personnel and Ombudsman type institutions of Lokpal and Lokayukta and performance budgeting have been implemented.

Change in the work ethos, acquisition of requisite managerial skills and inculcation of right values can be effected through training.

Reorientation of bureaucracy must be in terms of capabilities needed for a wide range of new functions in the field of development and economic management. But our training programmes leave much to be desired in terms of structure and content. Top bureaucrats frown on training. The lower ones could not be careless. Trainees feel training is a waste because they go back to an indifferent administrative environment and feel even more frustrated and demoralised.

It would be a good idea to have not rule-oriented but task-oriented training programmes. This means bringing together personnel whose rank, grade and service affiliation may vary, but who are, nevertheless, involved in a given task. Such training would have greater credibility and relevance to the job situation.

Research is important. It being the knowledge base for training, training institutions must have research wings manned by scholars and academicians who could undertake in-depth analysis of specific problems, case studies, work methods and approaches.

Above all, attitudinal training is a must. Since a successful administrator must empathise with those he serves, he must be 'conscienticised'. This up to a point, is possible through training. However, much of the success rate in this costly venture depends on the right inputs like careful selection and training of the trainers themselves.

While administrators must have in-service training, periodical refresher courses and sabbatical leave for further education, they do need the backing of professional or service organisations or associations. If an administrator is to take a principled stand and uphold values and norms of his profession, he needs the certainty and assurance that he does not fight his battles alone.

While administrative responsibilities are stressed, the accompanying element of accountability is often ignored. Accountability and responsibility go together. Accountability implies holding public officials responsible for their lapses. Public Servants may not do what the law requires them to do for reasons, such as ignorance, indifferent or corrupt influence; or they may be guilty of waste and damage; or a duty may be undertaken beyond what the law and custom oblige or empower. The difficulty lies in enforcing accountability. This is because of composite decision-making, diffused responsibility and frequent transfers. Nevertheless, an administrator must be made aware of this dimension of his work. He is accountable to the public *via* the minister and parliament.

I would like to conclude with a summary of a beautiful essay entitled: "The Administrator" by Robert M. Hutchins. An administrator in public service must develop the qualities of courage, fortitude, justice and prudence or practical wisdom by practising them. Though these virtues may be separated for purposes of analysis, they are one in practice. The administrator cannot exercise prudence without courage, which is the habit of taking responsibility; fortitude, which is the habit of bearing the consequences; and justice, which is the habit of giving equal treatment to equals.

The administrator is a man who decides. If he fails to decide he is not an administrator but an office-holder. As an administrator, the strain on his character is great. If he is afraid of anybody or anything, he is lost. If he cannot stand criticism, including slander and libel, he is lost. If he cannot give equal treatment to equals he is lost. The administrator today needs this combination of practical and philosophical wisdom with the moral qualities necessary to sustain it to discharge his duties well. Hutchins concludes by saying, "The rewards of the administrator may not be public memorials, religious rites and a pleasant journey to the Islands of the Blest. For those things he should care not at all. His satisfaction will come, even if he fails, from having seen and attempted one of the most difficult works of the mind and one of the most challenging human tasks."

## REFERENCES

1. Talcott Parsons and Edward A. Shils, (1962). *Towards a General Theory of Action,* New York, Harper, p. 395.
2. Hodgkinson Christopher, (1978). *Towards a Philosophy of Administration*, Oxford, Blackwell, p. 109.
3. David C. Potter, (1986). *India's Political Administrations 1919-1983,* Oxford, Clarendon Press, p. 34.
4. *Ibid*, p. 245.
5. Bata K. Dey, (1978). *Bureaucracy, Development and Public Management in India,* New Delhi, Uppal, p. 25.
6. B. Guy Peters, (1984). *The Politics of Bureaucracy*, New York, Longman, (2nd edition), p. 39.
7. L.W. Pye and Sydney Verba, (1968). *Political Culture and Political Development,* Princeton, Princeton University Press, p. 7.
8. G. Almond and Sydney Verba, *The Civil Culture,* Princeton, Princeton University Press, p. 1.

9. V.A. Pai Panandikar and S.S. Kshirsagar, (1978). *Bureaucracy and Development Administration,* New Delhi, Scientific Policy Research, p. 157.
10. Douglas McGregor and Warner G. Benis, (1967). *The Professional Manager,* New York, McGraw Hill, p. 51.
11. C.I. Bernard, (1947). *The Functions of the Executive*, Cambridge, Mass, Harvard University Press, p. 264.
12. *Ibid.*, p. 279.
13. Bata K. Dey, *op. cit.*, p. 31.
14. India, Administrative Reforms Commission, (1968). *Report on Machinery of the Government of India and its Procedures of Work,* p. 103.
15. R.P. Noronha, (1976). *A Tale Told by an Idiot*, New Delhi, Vikas, pp. 72-73.
16. C.D. Deshmukh, (1974). *The Course of My Life,* New Delhi, Orient Longman, p. 105.
17. Shah Commission of Inquiry, (1978). *Interim Report II,* New Delhi, Government of India Press, p. 142.
18. Kewal L. Panjabi (ed.), (1965). *The Civil Servant in India,* by ex-Indian Civil Servants, Bombay, Bharatiya Vidya Bhawan, p. 211.
19. A.K. Chatterjee, (1984). "Tinkering with the Rule of Law" in R.B. Jain (ed.), *Public Service in a Democratic Context*, New Delhi, IIPA, pp. 23-24.

# 37

# HR-Management: A Holistic Value-based Approach

B.P. SINGH, A.K. SINGH AND K.K. GOEL

## Introduction

Mahatama Buddha, while passing through forests, without uttering a single word, could create an environment and could manage the nature of the beasts where they were bound to leave their violent habit and those beasts started licking the holy feet of the Revered Buddha and they behaved like tamed animals by waving their tales.

Chaitanya Maha Prabhu, when started *Kirtana* (singing in concert of the adventures of Lord Krishana or Rama) in forests and started dancing with his followers, there they created such an environment where the beasts also had to join them and even the lions started dancing.

These were the holy souls who could get things done through beasts even without preaching or giving any type of direction to those living beings.the beasts had to join them and had to act as these souls were doing.

Today, the world has become a village every type of information can be received only at a click of mouse. The executives are more qualified in comparison to the past and more and more facilities are provided for the work force. But every manager is tense and finds himself unable in getting the things done through subordinates.

This is only due to the fact that the present galaxy of managers has not understood the real meaning of the Management of Human Resource. **The meaning of Human Resource Management is the Management of the Nature of Human Being.**

If a manager is competent and intelligent enough to read and understand the nature of the person to be managed then he can very easily manage it and would be able to get the things done through that human being. But this capability can only be achieved when that manager is having the ability of reading and understanding his own nature first. A person who could not visualize and interpret the nature of his/her own it would not be possible for him/her to be in control master of understanding and interpreting the nature of others. A person who is able to elevate himself/herself above the worldly moorings can only read and understand the nature of his/her own and the nature of other people. It is only when such a state of elevation is reached that a person can remote control the nature of others, and such a person would be the most successful manager.

Such a type of capability can be attained only through sterling and stable values. Since the nature is driven by such values, its only a person of *Saatvika* (virtuous or pure) nature who can earn and acquire such type of ability of mastering the nature of his/her own and the nature of others. This *Saatvikata* is directly attached and effected by the values in life and is potent enough to shower boundless happiness and peace all around.

The present materialism is unable to provide real happiness either to people or to organizations or to societies, or to countries, which have given their exclusive attention towards materialism to the neglect of values.

Only values can decorate our life, add fragrance to it and open the doors of every type of success for us. Every person, who strives for success, happiness and real peace in his private and organizational lives would have to nurture and follow the values.

Senior Vice President, Reliance Industries, while unfolding the secrets of success stated that 'Trust and Relationship' are two key 'Values' for success of Reliance Group. He also told that Reliance Group has earmarked on 'spiritual journey in business' by introducing Self Managing Leadership course. (Mathew, 2000)

Nohria (2000), Chairman, Crompton Greaves Limited, and President of All India Management Association, opined that spirituality is to give happiness to others, so also the purpose of business is to satisfy others, that is, shareholders, customers and even employees.

Nagarjuna Group of Companies in Hyderabad, India, since its inception, this Group's mission has been to serve society through industry. Its founder, K.V.K. Raju, believed that if an industry is to prosper, it has to seek to create wealth for society. K.V.K. practiced the concept of trusteeship propounded by Mahatma Gandhi. Trusteeship as expressed by Gandhi ji, means 'having faith and confidence in a process of taking responsibility for assets and social values, and administering their rightful and creative usage for the benefit of others- now, and in coming generations'. (Bader, 1995)

A news in a leading daily News Paper 'The Times of India' under the heading "At Infosys, drivers, electricians are millionaires" Nandan Nilekani, Managing Director of the Infosys company declares "We are in the knowledge industry which has an Ethos of sharing wealth amongst its employees."

The statements of these Top-level executives unfold the secrets of success of their industries. Besides these, different studies have been made and their conclusions confirm that the values in business are the really strong foundation for the growth and sustainability of the business organization. "A careful study of successful business enterprises and organizations that have survived over the long term and whose products and services have become a household name, demonstrates that they have been based on the foundation of a sound philosophy of business, with some core values and code of ethics that has enabled them to win the trust and confidence of customers, employees and the general public. Some such studies have demonstrated beyond doubt that good ethics and sound values are the basis of good business".

Infosys Chairman N.R. Narayana Murthy, has improved his ranking in Asia's top-50 "influential communicators" (Hong Kong-based Asia Week magazine said in its recent survey titled "People Mover") and he has been placed on 27th rank by the surveying organization. Terming Infosys chief as "India's ethical software king", Asia Week said "Murthy keeps one message high on his agenda: Do business ethically and legally." (The Tribune)

Swami Ranganathananda (1996) felt that before political independence of our nation we had observed values to guide our actions but after independence, we have almost forsaken all values. He feels that it is our good fortune that since the last few years our nation has become aware of this fall from value-oriented attitudes and actions and started discussing how to bring back values to our society.

Mohammed Galib Hussain conducted a research study on 271 middle level executives and has suggested that if the organizations decide to improve upon the existing organizational culture, deepening of love, biophilis, freedom and liberation should the main thrust of their HRD policies. As the study has shown that managers have transcendental experience, the organizations would do well to adopt **yoga system** of *Patanjali* for improving their transcendental experience. However, self-actualization needs of the executives should not be ignored and therefore, all the existing practices for providing self-actualization need should be continued till self-transcendence becomes the vibrating culture of the organizations. (Hussain, 1996).

Singh (1998) conducted a research study to measure the satisfaction level among employees including highly paid executives of various public and private sector organizations covering 125 respondents from organizations scattered over 26 cities from 12 states covering all regions of India. The low satisfaction level proved that satisfaction is independent of the material wealth that an organization can give to an individual as the respondents were highly paid executives. Thus the study concluded that satisfaction lies in the mind of a person or is dependent upon the values of a person.

Thus, if the Indian values are followed, the managers will be able to experience the real happiness and peace. Indian philosophy has always emphasized the point that the real happiness can be realized only through self-actualization. If we want to add fragrance to our own and organizational life we will have to strive for values and if we pull out the values; if individuals or organizations follow certain principles then the same become the ideals and guidelines for others.

At the time of recruitment of personnel, we should strive to recruit only the *Saatvika* persons. If we are able to ensure the exclusive recruitment of such persons in the organization and are able to observe and practice the following guidelines we would be in a position to develop self managed team and that will require minimum attention of the manager to get the organization move to new heights:

1. Specific parameters need to be built into our test modules meant for written and oral tests bearing the values of life.
2. The stable and sterling value parameters need to be built into the pre induction training module so as to bring out and sharpen the latent inherent spiritual dimensions of one's personality.
3. Organizational structure and design needs a holistic approach in terms of developing suitable levels of hierarchies of management, creating a proper and suitable balance between centralization and decentralization, delegation of authority, empowerment, accountability. Directing as a managerial

function must focus on the need for achievement and need for recognition, an enabling and facilitating leadership style, and a communication flow in all the directions based on trust, openness and transparency.

As and when the above mentioned functions and activities get into full play in the organizational setting, it would generate a positively anchored organizational climate imbued with *Atma Prabandhahb* (Self Management) where much of the dysfunctional activities indulged in by some of the negative elements in an organizational setting shall diminish in a phased manner. A self managed group would effect lot of savings in the use of non human resources, and generate job satisfaction and productivity resulting in benefit to both the humans at work and to the organization. But such an organizational climate would be created only when right from top to bottom every one in the organization is committed to the kind of organizational philosophy and culture sketched out above.

No credible research study could be found out which studied the impact of moral values on the managerial efficiency and effectiveness in the present day materialistic business world.

**Hypotheses**

The basic hypothesis of the present study is that the managers with high moral values can work more efficiently and effectively even in the present day environment and can earn real happiness and peace for themselves and growth and prosperity for the organization for which they work. Some of the specific hypotheses listed for the present study are as follows:

1. There is very high impact of high moral values on managerial efficiency and effectiveness.
2. The impact of high moral values on managerial efficiency and effectiveness is very frequent.

**Research Design and Methodology**

The sample was drawn from selected organizations located in 134 cities across India spread over 22 states.

Business and other organizations representing a wide range of activities such as manufacturing, mining, banking, construction, services such as transport, finance, judiciary, education, income-tax, healthcare, communication etc. were covered. Top and middle level executives selected from 153 organizations constitute the sample. The primary data was collected since the eve of the 20th century till the morning of the 21st century.

In all 313 executives responded. The responses of these executives were obtained in four age groups as given here below:

No. of Respondents in Age Groups

| *Age group* | *No. of Respondents* |
|---|---|
| 18-25 | 034 |
| 26-40 | 105 |
| 41-55 | 135 |
| Above 55 | 039 |
| Total | 313 |

Perceptions of the people cannot be measured precisely hence non-parametric statistical test namely Chi-square has been used for analyzing and interpreting the data generated through structured questionnaire and personal interviews. Chi-square test has been used to test whether there is significant difference of opinion between the respondents belonging to different age groups. The scale index (mean, percentages and weighted mean) has been calculated to find out the average score on five-point scale to make the analysis objective. Weighted mean was calculated by giving weights to 'very high', 'high', 'moderate', 'low' and 'very low' as 5, 4, 3, 2, and 1 respectively in case of perceived importance and 5, 4, 3, 2, 1 to 'Always', 'usually', 'sometimes', 'rarely' and 'never' respectively in case of application/realization.

An analysis of the impact of high moral values on managerial efficiency and effectiveness has been made in this paper. The executives of selected organizations in India were asked to give their opinion on two questions through a structured questionnaire on a five point likert scale.

In all fifteen factors as given here below were studied to find out their impact on managerial efficiency and effectiveness of managers with high moral values:

1. Sustainability of growth and development of company
2. Discharging duties efficiently and effectively
3. Quality decision-making skills
4. Increasing the wealth of shareholders
5. Effective control
6. Quantum of work done
7. Mental satisfaction of executive
8. Mental satisfaction of shareholder
9. Mental satisfaction of board of directors
10. Minimizing tensions at work place
11. Effective leadership
12. Individual development
13. Group development
14. Creating positive attitude
15. Getting things done through others

The respondents were asked the following two questions to mark the degree of impact and frequency of impact of high moral values on managerial efficiency and effectiveness.

*First Question Was*: How much impact they think of high moral values on the different factors related to managerial efficiency and effectiveness?

*Second Question Was*: How often they experience this impact of high moral values on managerial efficiency and effectiveness?

To ascertain the degree of impact of high moral values they were asked to mark their valuation, either 'very high', 'high', 'moderate', 'low' or 'very low'. To know the frequency of impact they were given the five choices viz. 'Always', 'usually', 'sometimes', 'rarely' or 'never'. Chi-square, percentages and weighted mean were calculated. Weighted mean was calculated by giving weights to very high, high, moderate, low and very low as 5, 4, 3, 2, and 1 respectively. To know the degree of impact weights of 5, 4, 3, 2, 1 were assigned to 'Always', 'usually', 'sometimes', 'rarely' and 'never' respectively.

## Analysis of Data

*Quantum of Impact of Moral Values on Managerial Efficiency and Effectiveness*

On analyzing the opinion expressed by the Executives through questionnaire, age group wise, rank tables have been prepared by calculating weighted mean for fifteen factors related to managerial efficiency and effectiveness. Table 37.1 exhibits the most effected factors.

**Table 37.1:** Most Affected Factors

| *Rank* | *Age 18-25* | *26-40* | *41-55* | *Above 55* |
|---|---|---|---|---|
| 1. | Creating positive attitude | Creating positive attitude | Discharging duties efficiently | Discharging duties efficiently |
| 2. | Individual development | Sustainability of growth, dev. of company | Creating positive attitude | Effective leadership |
| 3. | Quality decision Making skills | Discharging duties efficiently | Sustainability of growth, dev. of company | Effective control |
| 4. | Discharging duties efficiently | Quality decision making skills | Mental satisfaction of executive | Quality decision making skills |

Data shows that there is very high impact of high moral values on managerial efficiency and effectiveness. Hence the hypothesis that there is very high impact of high moral values on managerial efficiency and effectiveness is accepted.

It is clear that if an executive is of high moral values then he/she can discharge duties very efficiently and effectively as there is very high impact of moral values on this factor. The executives have felt this impact with the increasing rate with their increase in age. Moral values have helped very much in 'creating positive attitude' as per the views of the executives of less than 55 years of age. But the executives of more than 55 years of age have felt that the impact of high moral values has been more on the effectiveness of 'Leadership and Control'. 'Quality decision-making skills' have also been highly affected by moral values as per the views of the executives falling in the age groups of 18-25, 26-40 and above 55 years. The rank of 'Quality decision making skills' by the age group of 41-55 has been found out as fifth which clarified that when the executives are value based and can elevate themselves above self interests then the quality decision making skills will positively improve. Moral values highly effect the 'sustainability of growth and development of the organization' as per the views expressed by the executives falling in the age groups of 26-40 and 41-55. The young executives have also felt very high impact of moral values on Individual development.

So it is very clear from the above analysis that even in the modem age a very high impact of moral values is there on the factors related to managerial efficiency and effectiveness.

**Table 37.2:** Least Affected Factors

| *Rank* | *Age 18-25* | *26-40* | *41-55* | *Above 55* |
|---|---|---|---|---|
| 12. | Mental satisfaction of shareholder | Quantum of work done | Mental satisfaction of B. of directors | Minimizing tension at work place |
| 13. | Increasing wealth of share-holders | Getting things done through others | Mental satisfaction of shareholders | Getting things done through others |
| 14. | Mental satisfaction of B.of directors | Increasing wealth of share-holders | Increasing wealth of share holders | Mental satisfaction of shareholders |
| 15. | Quantum of work done | Mental satisfaction of shareholders | Getting things done through others | Increasing wealth of share-holders |

On going through Table 37.2 it seems that shareholders remain only interested in increasing their wealth and they are least bothered/ concerned about moral values of managers of their organizations. It is evident that moral values have least impact on 'Increase in wealth of shareholders' as per the views of the executives of every age group. Moral values do not help much in 'getting things done through others' as per the views expressed by the three age groups of the executives viz. 26-40, 41-55 and above 55 years. 'Quantum of work done' has also been least affected by the moral values as expressed by the executives falling in the age group of 18-40 years of age. 'Mental satisfaction of board of directors' has been least affected by moral values as per the opinions of the executives of 18-25 and 41-55 years of age. The old generation of executives has felt that moral values have not helped in minimizing tensions at work place.

Computed values of Chi-square for all the fifteen factors have been shown in Table 37.3 given here below:

The following three factors were found significantly associated with age:

- Creating positive attitude.
- Sustainability of growth and development of Company.
- Quantum of work done.

**Table 37.3:** Chi-Square Results of Factors (Quantum of impact of high moral values)

| *Sr. No.* | *Factor* | *Computed value of Chi-square* |
|---|---|---|
| 1. | Creating positive attitude | 13.02* |
| 2. | Individual development | 5.12 |
| 3. | Quality decision making skills | 6.64 |
| 4. | Discharging duties efficiently | 11.88 |
| 5. | Effective control | 15.95 |
| 6. | Sustainability of growth, development of Company | 23.54* |
| 7. | Mental satisfaction of executive | 13.75 |
| 8. | Minimizing tensions at work place | 19.13 |
| 9. | Group development | 11.72 |
| 10. | Effective leadership | 15.95 |
| 11. | Getting things done through others | 9.02 |
| 12. | Mental satisfaction of shareholders | 17.32 |
| 13. | Increasing wealth of shareholders | 12.46 |
| 14. | Mental satisfaction of B. of Directors | 14.12 |
| 15. | Quantum of work done | 20.87* |

* Significant difference of opinion

### *Frequency of Impact of Moral Values on Managerial Efficiency and Effectiveness*

It was also found out that the impact of high moral values on managerial efficiency and effectiveness is very frequent too. Hence the hypothesis that there is very frequent impact of high moral values on managerial efficiency and effectiveness was accepted.

After going through the following Table 37.4 it is clear that following factors were most frequently affected by high moral values.

**Table 37.4:** Most Frequently Affected Factors

| *Rank* | *Age 18-25* | *26-40* | *41 - 55* | *Above 55* |
|---|---|---|---|---|
| 1. | Creating . positive attitude | Creating positive attitude | Discharging duties efficiently | Discharging duties efficiently |
| 2. | Discharging duties efficiently | Discharging duties efficiently | Creating positive attitude | Mental satisfaction of executive |
| 3. | Effective control | Individual development | Sustainability of growth & development of Company | Effective leadership |
| 4. | Effective leadership | Sustainability of growth & dev of Company | Quality decision making skills | Effective control |

The data in the table also unveiled that one of the factors i.e. 'Discharging duties efficiently and effectively' was most frequently affected as per the opinion of every age group of the executives. An executive of sound morals has its own impression and is able to create and develop a good environment where the duties can be discharged efficiently and effectively.

Executives upto the age of 55 years opined (the executives of the age group of above 55 have given fifth rank to this factor) that high moral values helped very frequently i.e. almost 'Always' in 'creating positive attitude'. 'Effectiveness of Control and Leadership' has also been affected by moral values very frequently as per the opinions of the youngest and oldest executives. 'Sustainability of growth and development of company' has been affected most frequently according to the views of the executives falling in the age group of 26-55 years.

**Table 37.5:** Least Frequently Affected Factors

| *Rank* | *Age 18-25* | *26-40* | *41-55* | *Above 55* |
|---|---|---|---|---|
| 12. | Quantum of work done | Mental satisfaction of board of directors | Min. tensions at work place | Group development |
| 13. | Getting things done | Getting things done | Getting things done | Getting things done |
| 14. | Increasing wealth of shareholders | Increasing wealth of shareholders | Increasing wealth of shareholders | Mental satisfaction of shareholders |
| 15. | Mental satisfaction of shareholders | Mental satisfaction of shareholders | Mental satisfaction of shareholders | Increasing wealth of shareholders |

Factors that were found least frequently affected by high moral values of managers were 'increasing wealth of shareholders' and 'mental satisfaction of shareholders' as per the opinions expressed by the executives of every age group. It has also been felt by most of the executives that moral values have rare impact in 'getting the things done through others'. 'Quantum of work done', 'Mental satisfaction of board of directors', 'Minimizing tensions at work place' and 'Group development' also have rare impact of high moral values as per the views of the executives falling in the age groups of 18-25, 26-40, 41-55 and above 55 respectively.

For analyzing the significantly associated factors with age the following table presents the computed values of Chi-square at 5 per cent level of significance.

**Table 37.6:** Chi-Square Results of Factors (Frequency of impact of high moral values)

| *Sr. No.* | *Factor* | *Computed value of Chi-square* |
|---|---|---|
| 1. | Creating positive attitude | 21.53* |
| 2. | Individual development | 11.28 |
| 3. | Quality decision making skills | 20.79* |
| 4. | Discharging duties efficiently | 28.01 * |
| 5. | Effective control | 10.70 |
| 6. | Sustainability of growth, dev. of Company | 25.17* |
| 7. | Mental satisfaction of executive | 14.73 |
| 8. | Minimizing tensions at work place | 15.99 |
| 9. | Group development | 23.54* |
| 10. | Effective leadership | 10.70 |
| 11. | Getting things done through others | 18.59 |
| 12. | Mental satisfaction of shareholders | 13.58 |
| 13. | Increasing wealth of shareholders | 17.61 |
| 14. | Mental satisfaction of B. of Directors | 16.55 |
| 15. | Quantum of work done | 41.67* |

* Significantly associated factors

After having compared the computed and table values of Chi-square the following **six factors were found significantly related to age:**

- Creating positive attitude
- Quality decision-making skills
- Discharging duties efficiently and effectively

* Sustainability of growth and development of company
* Group development
* Quantum of work done

The data in the comparative table showed that 'Creating positive attitude', 'Discharging duties efficiently and effectively', 'Quality decision-making skills' have very much and very frequent impact of high moral values as per the opinions of the executives of all the age groups. The executives upto the age of 55 years have expressed that 'Sustainability of growth and development of the company' also has very high and very frequent impact of high moral values. The executives of higher than this age have felt the degree and frequency of impact of high moral values at a little lower rate as the rank for degree and frequency of impact have been 11 and 10 respectively. For these executives high moral values are important for 'Effective leadership' and 'mental satisfaction'. It appears that though the importance of high moral values has been accepted by most of the executives but the impact of high moral values has been perceived differently. The younger executives feel the impact in individual related factors like 'Creating positive attitude' and 'Individual development'. Middle-aged executives significantly see the importance of high moral values for 'Sustainability of growth and development of the company'. Executives aged above 55 years of age have felt high moral values important for 'effective leadership and control' in the organization.

As per the views of the executives of every age group shareholders seem to be satisfied only when their wealth is increased and are they least concerned with the moral values of the executives. It is also evident from the data that 'Increasing wealth of shareholders', 'Mental satisfaction of shareholders', 'Getting things done through others' and 'Mental satisfaction of board of directors' have the least and rare impact of high moral values as per the views of the executives of every age group. Probably the low perceived impact of high moral values on the external agents (shareholders and board of directors) to whom the executives are accountable is responsible for the differing ranking of high impact of moral values given by the executives in different age groups. Executives above 55 years of age think them important from the point of view of 'Effective leadership and Control' while younger executives think factors like 'Positive attitude' and 'Individual development' more important. The ranking of younger executives is influenced by their own priorities of personal growth at this age.

## Conclusions

Age group wise analysis of the views of the executives of selected organizations in India was made to know the quantum of impact and frequency of impact of high moral values on managerial efficiency and effectiveness. The findings that emerged may be summarized as follows:

High moral values had very high impact on the factors related to managerial efficiency and effectiveness.

Executives of all the age groups viewed that moral values had very high impact and very frequent impact on the factors viz. Creating positive attitude, Discharging duties efficiently and effectively and Quality decision making skills.

The managers in search of sustainable growth and development of their companies must become the persons of high moral values because these have very high and frequent impact on this factor as per the views of the executives up to the age of 55 years. Executives above 55 years of age found a greater role of higher moral values for effective leadership and control as compared to younger executives.

Effective leadership and mental satisfaction by the executives will be achieved through moral values in their organizational life, opined by the senior executives (more than 55 years of age).

In comparison to other factors the following factors have the least and rare impact of high moral values on managerial efficiency and effectiveness:

(a) Increasing wealth of shareholders.
(b) Mental satisfaction of shareholders.
(c) Mental satisfaction of Board of directors.
(d) Getting things done through others.

## Recommendations

We visualize a new global civil society based on human values that puts people at the centre of all concerns. In the third millennium the ultimate objective of mankind has to be brought to the centre stage by putting people at the centre of all thoughts and creating a value based management environment.

Only those people who have internal commitment can actually become successful managers as well as leaders.

At the time of procurement of work force the Saatvika persons should only be allowed.

The managers seeking for real. growth and development of organizations, consistent profit for the years to come, happiness and peace for their own and the organizational life, successful career as manager must nurture and follow high moral values as these have very high and frequent impact on the efficiency and effectiveness of managers.

## REFERENCES

Bader, (1995) G. Gandhi on Trusteeship: A Transforming Ethic; *World Business Academy Perspectives*, December 1995.

Hussain, M.G. (1996) "*Personal Values, Personality and Managerial Behaviour: A study based on selected organizations*" Unpublished Ph. D Thesis, submitted to the University of Madras.

Narayana, (1992) *Responsible Leadership in the Gita*: Foundation for Integral Management: Bombay.

Singh, Ajay Kumar (1998) "Management" Pranjana: *The Journal of Management Awareness*, Vol. I, No. 1.

Swami Ranganathananda (1996) *Practical Vedanta and the Science of Values*: Advaita Asharam, Calcutta, February 2.

Mathew (2002) *Values for a Better World*: Prajapita Brahama Kumaris Ishwariya Vishwavidyalaya, Mount Abu, Rajasthan.

Swami Vivekananada, (1987) *Vedanta: Voice of Freedom*; Advaita Ashrama, Calcutta.

Nandan Nilkani, Managing Director of Infosys in "The Times of India".

Noharia (2000) Chairman, Crompton Greaves Limited in All India Management Association's Meeting.

Narayana Murthy, Chairman, Infosys, "People Mover" Hong Kong based *Asia Week Magazine*.

# 38

# Ethics in Advertising

AMISH AMEYA

## Introduction

To start with, let's have a look at what the Kenneth Blanchard and Norman Vincent Peale say in their book, THE POWER OF ETHICAL MANAGEMENT about the concept of ethics in the business context. The authors have articulated what has been called the three way ethical check. The ethical check questions are as follows:

- Is it legal? Will it be violating either civil or company policy?
- Is it balanced? Is it fair to all concerned in the short term as well as in long term? Does it promote win-win relationship?
- How will it make me feel about myself? Will it make me proud? Would I feel good if my decision was published in the newspaper? Would I feel good if my family knew about it?

These ethical check questions provide a good reference point to decide on ethical issues, which arise in the contemporary Indian management. The authors have also provided the following five principles of ethical power for organisations:

- **Purpose:** The mission of our organisation is communicated from the top. Our organisation is guided by the values, hopes and a vision that helps us to determine what is acceptable and unacceptable behaviour.

- **Pride:** We feel proud of ourselves and of our organisation. We know that when we feel this way, we can resist temptations to behave unethically.
- **Patience:** We believe that holding to our ethical values will lead us to success in the long term. This involves maintaining a balance between obtaining results and caring how we achieve these results.
- **Persistence:** We have commitment to live by ethical principles. We are committed to our commitment. We make sure our actions are consistent with our purpose.
- **Perspective:** Our managers and employees take time to pause and reflect, take stock of where we are, evaluate where we are going and determine how we are going to get there.

Experience of excellent companies and visionary companies shows that in the ultimate analysis values do matter, ethics does matter. In their book, "In Search of Excellence" by Peters and Waterman, the authors pointed out how one of the characteristics of excellent companies was "hands on value driven". While the managements are hands on and decide on day-to-day matters, they have also not forgotten their values. Similarly in their book, "Built To Last", Jeremy Porrass and James Collins pointed out that ultimately the visionary companies, the companies which lasted much longer 50 to 100 years compared to the normal lifetime of 15-20 years of the standard companies, one main characteristic was their core values which irretrievably linked with their company practices and procedures. In other words, the long-term basis for success appears to be internalization of ethical values and ensuring that these are woven irretrievably into the company policies and practices.

## Advertising—Communicating the Communication

"*Remember, a good ad gives you a nice feeling. It excites you. Its like a good piece of composition. After all, you are the consumer.*"

Yes, this is the power of advertising. The importance of advertising is "steadily on the increase in modem society." That observation, made by a reputed council a quarter century ago as part of an overview of the state of communications, is even more true now.

Just as the media of social communication themselves have enormous influence everywhere, so advertising, using media as its vehicle, is a pervasive, powerful force shaping attitudes and behaviour in today's world.

Role and responsibilities of media have always been addressed in a fundamentally positive manner, viewing the media as "gifts of God" which, in accordance with his providential design, bring people together and "help them to cooperate with his plan for their salvation."

In doing so, it has been stressed the responsibility of media to contribute to the authentic, integral development of persons and to foster the well being of society. "The information provided by the media is at the service of the common good. Society has a right to information based on truth, freedom, justice and solidarity."

It is in this spirit that the society should enter into dialogue with communicators. At the same time, it also calls for the attention to moral principles and norms relevant to social communications, as to other forms of human endeavour, while criticizing policies and practices that offend against these standards.

I wish to call attention to positive contributions that advertising can and does make; to note ethical and moral problems that advertising can and does raise; to point to moral principles that apply to this field; and, finally, to suggest certain steps for the consideration of those professionally involved in advertising, as well as for others in the private sector, and for public officials.

Our reason for addressing these matters is simple. In today's society, advertising has a profound impact on how people understand life, the world and themselves, especially in regard to their values and their ways of choosing and behaving.

The field of advertising is extremely broad and diverse. In general terms, of course, an advertisement is simply a public notice meant to convey information and invite patronage or some other response. As that suggests, advertising has two basic purposes: to inform and to persuade, and—while these purposes are distinguishable—both very often are simultaneously present.

Advertising is not the same as marketing (the complex of commercial functions involved in transferring goods from producers and consumers) or public relations (the systematic effort to create a favourable public impression or 'image' of some person, group, or entity). In many cases, though, it is a technique or instrument employed by one or both of these.

Advertising can be very simple—a local, even a 'neighbourhood' phenomenon—or it can be very complex, involving sophisticated research and multimedia campaigns that span the globe. It differs according to its intended audience, so that, for example, advertising aimed at children raises some technical and moral issues significantly different from those raised by advertising aimed at competent adults.

Not only are many different media and techniques employed in advertising; advertising itself is of several different kinds: commercial advertising for products and services; public service advertising on behalf of various institutions, programs, and causes; and—a phenomenon of growing importance today—political advertising in the interests of parties and candidates. Making allowance for the differences among the different kinds and methods of advertising, we intend what follows to be applicable to them all.

It's always argumentative with the assertion that advertising simply mirrors the attitudes and values of the surrounding culture. No doubt advertising, like the media of social communications in general, does act as a mirror. But, also like media in general, it is a mirror that helps shape the reality it reflects, and sometimes it presents a distorted image of reality.

Advertisers are selective about the values and attitudes to be fostered and encouraged, promoting some while ignoring others. This selectivity gives the lie to the notion that advertising does no more than reflect the surrounding culture. For example, the absence from advertising of certain racial and ethnic groups in some multi-racial or multi-ethnic societies can help to create problems of image and identity, especially among those neglected, and the almost inevitable impression in commercial advertising that an abundance of possessions leads to happiness and fulfilment can be both misleading and frustrating.

Advertising also has an indirect but powerful impact on society through its influence on media. Many publications and broadcasting operations depend on advertising revenue for survival. This often is true of religious media as well as commercial media. For their part, advertisers naturally seek to reach audiences; and the media, striving to deliver audiences to advertisers, must shape their content so to attract audiences of the size and demographic composition sought. This economic dependency of media and the power it confers upon advertisers carries with it serious responsibilities for both.

## The Benefits of Advertising

Enormous human and material resources are devoted to advertising. Advertising is everywhere in today's world, so that, as somebody remarked, "No one now can escape the influence of advertising." Even people who are not themselves exposed to particular forms of advertising confront a society, a culture—other people—affected for good or ill by advertising messages and techniques of every sort.

Some critics view this state of affairs in unrelieved negative terms. They condemn advertising as a waste of time, talent and money—an essentially parasitic activity. In this view, not only does advertising have no value of its own, but also, its influence is entirely harmful and corrupting for individuals and society.

However, I do not agree with this. There is truth to the criticisms, and we shall make criticisms of our own. But advertising also has significant potential for good, and sometimes it is realized. Here are some of the ways that happens.

### *(a) Economic Benefits of Advertising*

Advertising can play an important role in the process by which an economic system guided by moral norms and responsive to the common good contributes to human development. It is a necessary part of the functioning of modem market economies, which today either exist or are emerging in many parts of the world and which—provided they conform to moral standards based upon integral human development and the common good—currently seem to be "the most efficient instrument for utilizing resources and effectively responding to needs" of a socio-economic kind.

In such a system, advertising can be a useful tool for sustaining honest and ethically responsible competition that contributes to economic growth in the service of authentic human development. The growth of a person's productive capacity, and also on the ever-widening network of relationships and exchanges between persons and social groups, can become a wholesome and efficacious instrument for reciprocal help among people.

Advertising does this, among other ways, by informing people about the availability of rationally desirable new products and services and improvements in existing ones, helping them to make informed, prudent consumer decisions, contributing to efficiency and the lowering of prices, and stimulating economic progress through the expansion of business and trade.

All of these can contribute to the creation of new jobs, higher incomes and a more decent and humane way of life for all. It also helps pay for publications, programming and productions—that bring information, entertainment and inspiration to people around the world.

### *(b) Benefits of Political Advertising*

Valuing the democratic system in as much as it ensures the participation of citizens in making political choices, guarantees to the governed the possibility both of electing and holding accountable those who govern them, and of replacing them through peaceful means when appropriate..

Political advertising can make a contribution to democracy analogous to its contribution to economic well being in a market system guided by moral norms. As free and responsible media in a democratic system help to counteract tendencies toward the monopolization of power on the part of oligarchies and special interests, so political advertising can make its contribution by informing people about the ideas and policy proposals of parties and candidates, including new candidates not previously known to the public.

### *(c) Cultural Benefits of Advertising*

Because of the impact advertising has on media that depend on it for revenue, advertisers have an opportunity to exert a positive influence on decisions about media content. This they do by supporting material of excellent intellectual, aesthetic and moral quality presented with the public interest in view, and particularly by encouraging and making possible media presentations which are oriented to minorities whose needs might otherwise go unserved.

Moreover, advertising can itself contribute to the betterment of society by uplifting and inspiring people and motivating them to act in ways that benefit themselves and others. Advertising can brighten lives simply by being witty, tasteful and entertaining. Some advertisements are instances of popular art, with a vivacity and elan all their own.

*(d) Moral and Religious Benefits of Advertising*

In many cases, too, benevolent social institutions, including those of a religious nature, use advertising to communicate their messages—messages of faith, of patriotism, of tolerance, compassion and neighbourly service, of charity toward the needy, messages concerning health and education, constructive and helpful messages that educate and motivate people in a variety of beneficial ways.

**The Harm Done by Advertising**

There is nothing intrinsically good or intrinsically evil about advertising. It is a tool, an instrument: it can be used well, and it can be used badly. If it can have, and sometimes does have, beneficial results such as those just described, it also can, and often does, have a negative, harmful impact on individuals and society.

*Communio et Progressio* contains this summary statement of the problem: "If harmful or utterly useless goods are touted to the public, if false assertions are made about goods for sale, if less than admirable human tendencies are exploited, those responsible for such advertising harm society and forfeit their good name and credibility. More than this, unremitting pressure to buy articles of luxury can arouse false wants that hurt both individuals and families by making them ignore what they really need. And those forms of advertising which, without shame, exploit the sexual instincts simply to make money or which seek to penetrate into the subconscious recesses of the mind in a way that threatens the freedom of the individual... must be shunned."

*(a) Economic Harms of Advertising*

Advertising can betray its role as a source of information by misrepresentation and by withholding relevant facts. Sometimes, too, the information function of media can be subverted by advertisers' pressure upon publications or programs not to treat of questions that might prove embarrassing or inconvenient.

More often, though, advertising is used not simply to inform but to persuade and motivate—to convince people to act in certain ways: buy certain products or services, patronize certain institutions, and the like. This is where particular abuses can occur.

The practice of "brand"-related advertising can raise serious problems. Often there are only negligible differences among similar products of different brands, and advertising may attempt to move people to act on the basis of irrational motives ("brand loyalty," status, fashion, "sex appeal," etc.) instead of presenting differences in product quality and price as bases for rational choice.

Advertising also can be, and often is, a tool of the "phenomenon of consumerism," in which it is not wrong to want to live better; what is wrong is a style of life which is presumed to be better when it is directed toward having rather than 'being', and which wants to have more, not in order to be more but in order to spend life in enjoyment as an end in itself. Sometimes advertisers speak of it as part of their task to "create" needs for products and services—that is, to cause people to feel and act upon cravings for items and services they do not need. "If ... a direct appeal is made to his instincts—while ignoring in various ways the reality of the person as intelligent and free—then consumer attitudes and life-styles can be created which are objectively improper and often damaging to his physical and spiritual health."

This is a serious abuse, an affront to human dignity and the common good when it occurs in affluent societies. But the abuse is still more grave when consumerist attitudes and values are transmitted by communications media and advertising to developing countries, where they exacerbate socio-economic problems and harm the poor. It is true that a judicious use of advertising can stimulate developing countries to improve their standard of living. But serious harm can be done them if advertising and commercial pressure become so irresponsible that communities seeking to rise from poverty to a reasonable standard of living are persuaded to seek this progress by satisfying wants that have been artificially created. The result of this is that they waste their resources and neglect their real needs, and genuine development falls behind.

Similarly, the task of countries attempting to develop types of market economies that serve human needs and interests after decades under centralized, state-controlled systems is made more difficult by advertising that promotes consumerist attitudes and values offensive to human dignity and the common good. The problem is particularly acute when, as often happens, the dignity and welfare of society's poorer and weaker members are at stake. It is necessary always to bear in mind that there are "goods which by their very nature cannot and must not be bought or sold" and to avoid "an idolatry of the market" that, aided and abetted by advertising, ignores this crucial fact.

### *(b) Harms of Political Advertising*

Political advertising can support and assist the working of the democratic process, but it also can obstruct it. This happens when, for example, the costs of advertising limit political competition to wealthy candidates or groups, or require that office-seekers compromise their integrity and independence by over-dependence on special interests for funds.

Such obstruction of the democratic process also happens when, instead of being a vehicle for honest expositions of candidates' views and records, political advertising seeks to distort the views and records of opponents and unjustly attacks their reputations. It happens when advertising appeals more to people's emotions and base instincts—to selfishness, bias and hostility toward others, to racial and ethnic prejudice and the like—rather than to a reasoned sense of justice and the good of all.

### *(c) Cultural Harms of Advertising*

Advertising also can have a corrupting influence upon culture and cultural values. We have spoken of the economic harm that can be done to developing nations by advertising that fosters consumerism and destructive patterns of consumption. Consider also the cultural injury done to these nations and their peoples by advertising whose content and methods, reflecting those prevalent in the first world, are at war with sound traditional values in indigenous cultures. Today this kind of "domination and manipulation" via media rightly is "a concern of developing nations in relation to developed ones," as well as a "concern of minorities within particular nations."

The indirect but powerful influence exerted by advertising upon the media of social communications that depend on revenues from this source points to another sort of cultural concern. In the competition to attract ever larger audiences and deliver them to advertisers, communicators can find themselves tempted—in fact pressured, subtly or not so subtly—to set aside high artistic and moral standards and lapse into superficiality, tawdriness and moral squalor.

Communicators also can find themselves tempted to ignore the educational and social needs of certain segments of the audience—the very young, the very old, the poor—who do not match the demographic patterns (age, education, income, habits of buying and consuming, etc.) of the kinds of audiences advertisers want to reach. In this way the tone and indeed the level of moral responsibility of the communications media in general are lowered.

All too often, advertising contributes to the invidious stereotyping of particular groups that places them at a disadvantage in relation to others. This often is true of the way advertising treats women; and the exploitation of women, both in and by advertising, is a frequent, deplorable abuse. "How often are they treated not as persons with an inviolable dignity but as objects whose purpose is to satisfy others' appetite for pleasure or for power? How often is the role of woman as wife and mother undervalued or even ridiculed? How often is the role of women in business or professional life depicted as a masculine caricature, a denial of the specific gifts of feminine insight, compassion, and understanding, which so greatly contribute to the civilization of love".

### *(d) Moral and Religious Harms of Advertising*

Advertising can be tasteful and in conformity with high moral standards, and occasionally even morally uplifting, but it also can be vulgar and morally degrading. Frequently it deliberately appeals to such motives as envy, status seeking and lust. Today, too, some advertisers consciously seek to shock and titillate by exploiting content of a morbid, perverse, pornographic nature.

What this Pontifical Council said several years ago about pornography and violence in the media is no less true of certain forms of advertising: As reflections of the dark side of human nature marred by sin, pornography and the exaltation of violence are age-old realities of the human condition. In the past quarter century, however, they have taken on new dimensions and have become serious social problems. At a time of widespread and unfortunate confusion about moral norms, the communications media have made pornography and violence accessible to a vastly expanded audience, including young people and even children, and a problem, which at one time was confined mainly to wealthy countries, has now begun, via the communications media, to corrupt moral values in developing nations.

We note, too, certain special problems relating to advertising that treats of religion or pertains to specific issues with a moral dimension. In cases of the first sort, commercial advertisers sometimes include religious themes or use religious images or personages to sell products. It is possible to do this in tasteful, acceptable ways, but the practice is obnoxious and offensive when it involves exploiting religion or treating it flippantly.

In cases of the second sort, advertising sometimes is used to promote products and inculcate attitudes and forms of behaviour contrary to moral norms. That is the case, for instance, with the advertising of contraceptives, abortifacients and products harmful to health, and with government-sponsored advertising campaigns for artificial birth control, so-called "safe sex", and similar practices.

**Some Ethical and Moral Principles**

If the media is to be correctly employed, it is essential that all who use them know the principles of the moral order and apply them faithfully in this domain. The moral order to which this refers is the order of the law of human nature, binding upon all because it is "written on their hearts" (*Rom* 2:15) and embodies the imperatives of authentic human fulfilment.

In this context, the media of social communications have two options, and only two. Either they help human persons to grow in their understanding and practice of what is true and good, or they are destructive forces in conflict with human well-being. That is entirely true of advertising.

Against this background, then, we point to this fundamental principle for people engaged in advertising: advertisers—that is, those who commission, prepare or disseminate advertising—are morally responsible for what they seek to move people to do; and this is a responsibility also shared by publishers, broadcasting executives, and others in the communications world, as well as by those who give commercial or political endorsements, to the extent that they are involved in the advertising process.

If an instance of advertising seeks to move people to choose and act rationally in morally good ways that are of true benefit to themselves and others, persons involved in it do what is morally good; if it seeks to move people to do evil deeds that are self-destructive and destructive of authentic community, they do evil.

This applies also to the means and the techniques of advertising: it is morally wrong to use manipulative, exploitative, corrupt and corrupting methods of persuasion and motivation. In this regard, we note special problems associated with so-called indirect advertising that attempts to move people to act in certain ways—for example, purchase particular products—without their being fully aware that they are being swayed.

The techniques involved here include showing certain products or forms of behaviour in superficially glamorous settings associated with superficially glamorous people; in extreme cases, it may even involve the use of subliminal messages.

Within this very general framework, we can identify several moral principles that are particularly relevant to advertising. We shall speak briefly of three: truthfulness, the dignity of the human person, and social responsibility.

### *(a) Truthfulness in Advertising*

Even today, some advertising is simply and deliberately untrue. Generally speaking, though, the problem of truth in advertising is somewhat more subtle: it is not that advertising says what is overtly false, but that it can distort the truth by implying things that are not so or withholding relevant facts. At both the individual and social levels, truth and freedom are inseparable; without truth as the basis, starting point and criterion of discernment, judgment, choice and action, there can be no authentic exercise of freedom.

To be sure, advertising, like other forms of expression, has its own conventions and forms of stylisation, and these must be taken into account when discussing truthfulness. People take for granted some rhetorical and symbolic exaggeration in advertising; within the limits of recognized and accepted practice, this can be allowable.

But it is a fundamental principle that advertising may not deliberately seek to deceive, whether it does that by what it says, by what it implies, or by what it fails to say. "The proper exercise of the right to information demands that the content of what is communicated be true and, within the limits set by justice and charity, complete. ... Included here is the obligation to avoid any manipulation of truth for any reason."

### *(b) The Dignity of the Human Person*

There is an "imperative requirement" that advertising "respect the human person, his right duty to make a responsible choice, his interior freedom; all these goods would be violated if man's lower inclinations were to be exploited, or his capacity to reflect and decide compromised."

These abuses are not merely hypothetical possibilities but realities in much advertising today. Advertising can violate the dignity of the human person both through its content—what is advertised, the manner in which it is advertised—and through the impact it seeks to make upon its audience. We have spoken already of such things as appeals to lust, vanity, envy and greed, and of techniques that manipulate and exploit human weakness. In such circumstances, advertisements readily become "vehicles of a deformed outlook on life, on the family, on religion and on morality—an outlook that does not respect the true dignity and destiny of the human person."

This problem is especially acute where particularly vulnerable groups or classes of persons are concerned: children and young people, the elderly, the poor, and the culturally disadvantaged.

Much advertising directed at children apparently tries to exploit their credulity and suggestibility, in the hope that they will put pressure on their parents to buy products of no real benefit to them. Advertising like this offends against the dignity and rights of both children and parents; it intrudes upon the parent-child relationship and seeks to manipulate it to its own base ends. Also, some of the comparatively little advertising directed specifically to the elderly or culturally disadvantaged seems designed to play upon their fears so as to persuade them to allocate some of their limited resources to goods or services of dubious value.

### *(c) Advertising and Social Responsibility*

Social responsibility is such a broad concept that we can note here only a few of the many issues and concerns relevant under this heading to the question of advertising.

The ecological issue is one. Advertising that fosters a lavish life style which wastes resources and despoils the environment offends against important ecological concerns. "In his desire to have and to enjoy rather than to be and grow, man consumes the resources of the earth and his own life in an excessive and disordered way.... Man thinks that he can make arbitrary use of the earth, subjecting it without restraint to his will, as though it did not have its own requisites and a prior God-given purpose, which man can indeed develop but must not betray."

As this suggests, something more fundamental is at issue here: authentic and integral human development. Advertising that reduces human progress to acquiring material goods and cultivating a lavish life style expresses a false, destructive vision of the human person harmful to individuals and society alike.

When people fail to practice "a rigorous respect for the moral, cultural and spiritual requirements, based on the dignity of the person and on the proper identity of each community, beginning with the family and religious societies," then even material abundance and the conveniences that technology makes available "will prove unsatisfying and in the end contemptible." Advertisers, like people engaged in other forms of social communication, have a serious duty to express and foster an authentic vision of human development in its material, cultural and spiritual dimensions. Communication that meets this standard is, among other things, a true expression of solidarity. Indeed, the two things—communication and solidarity—are inseparable, because, solidarity is "a consequence of genuine and right communication and the free circulation of ideas that further knowledge and respect for others."

## Conclusion: Some Steps to Take

The indispensable guarantors of ethically correct behaviour by the advertising industry are the well formed and responsible consciences of advertising professionals themselves: consciences sensitive to their duty not merely to serve the interests of those who commission and finance their work but also to respect and uphold the rights and interests of their audiences and to serve the common good.

Many women and men professionally engaged in advertising do have sensitive consciences, high ethical standards and a strong sense of responsibility. But even for them external pressures—from the clients who commission their work as well as from the competitive internal dynamics of their profession—can create powerful inducements to unethical behaviour. That underlines the need for external structures and systems to support and encourage responsible practice in advertising and to discourage the irresponsible.

Voluntary ethical codes are one such source of support. These already exist in a number of places. Welcome as they are, though, they are only as effective as the willingness of advertisers to comply strictly with them. "It is up to the directors and managers of the media which carry advertising to make known to the public, to subscribe to and to apply the codes of professional ethics which already have been opportunely established so as to have the cooperation of the public in making these codes still better and in enforcing their observance."

We emphasize the importance of public involvement. Representatives of the public should participate in the formulation, application and periodic updating of ethical codes. The public representatives should include ethicists and church people, as well as representatives of consumer groups. Individuals do well to organize themselves into such groups in order to protect their interests in relation to commercial interests.

Public authorities also have a role to play. On the one hand, government should not seek to control and dictate policy to the advertising industry, any more than to other sectors of the communications media. On the other hand, the regulation of advertising content and practice, already existing in many places, can and should extend beyond banning false advertising, narrowly defined. "By promulgating laws and overseeing their application, public authorities should ensure that public morality and social progress are not gravely endangered through misuse of the media."

For example, government regulations should address such questions as the quantity of advertising, especially in broadcast media, as well as the content of advertising directed at groups particularly vulnerable to exploitation, such as children and old people. Political advertising also seems an appropriate area for regulation: how much may be spent, how and from whom may money for advertising be raised, etc.

The media of news and information should make it a point to keep the public informed about the world of advertising. Considering advertising's social impact, it is appropriate that media regularly review and critique the performance of advertisers, just as they do other groups whose activities have a significant influence on society.

In light of this insight, it is important that media education regarding the role of advertising in today's world should seek to prepare people to be informed and alert in their approach to advertising as to other forms of communication and can give rise to a certain passivity among users, making them less than vigilant consumers of what is said or shown. Users should practice moderation and discipline in their approach to the mass media.

In the final analysis, however, where freedom of speech and communication exists, it is largely up to advertisers themselves to ensure ethically responsible practices in their profession. Besides avoiding abuses, advertisers should also undertake to repair the harm sometimes done by advertising, insofar as that is possible: for example, by publishing corrective notices, compensating injured parties, increasing the quantity of public service advertising, and the like. This question of preparations is a matter of legitimate involvement not only by industry self-regulatory bodies and public interest groups, but also by public authorities.

Where unethical practices have become widespread and entrenched, conscientious advertisers may be called upon to make significant personal sacrifices to correct them. But people who want to do what is morally right must always be ready to suffer loss and personal injury rather than to do what is wrong.

Advertising is an important element in today's society, especially in the functioning of a market economy, which is becoming more and more widespread. Moreover, for the reasons and in the ways sketched here, we believe advertising can, and often does, play a constructive role in economic growth, in the exchange of information and ideas, and in the fostering of solidarity among individuals and groups. Yet it also can do, and often does, grave harm to individuals and to the common good.

In light of these reflections, therefore, we call upon advertising professionals and upon all those involved in the process of commissioning and disseminating advertising to eliminate its socially harmful aspects and observe high ethical standards in regard to truthfulness, human dignity and social responsibility. In this way, they will make a special and significant contribution to human progress and to the common good.

# Index

Abhedananda 187
Abuse of Prescriptions by Patients 106
Academic Councils 206
Academic Staff Colleges 152
Acharya Mahapragya 157
Acquisition of Wealth 273
Administrative Procedures Code 336
Administrative Reforms Commission 335
Administrative Wing 216
*Advaita Vedanta* 54
Advertising 359
  Benefits of 362–63
  Cultural Harms of 366
  Ethics in 358
  Harms of 364
  Moral and Religious Benefits of 364
  Moral and Religious Harms of 367
  Social Responsibility 370
  Truthfulness in 369
Aesthetic Values 20, 152
Agriculture-Based Rural Society 183
AIDS 8
Allahabad University 209
Ancient Hindu Attitude 56
Anekant Theory 5
Annamaya, Acceptance of 27
Anti-National Movement 154
Aparigraha 9, 28
Appleby, Paul 321
Appu, P.S. 338
Ashby, Eric 198
Association of Indian Universities (AIU) 232
Astronomy 59
*Atma Prabandhahb* (Self Management) 347
*Atmavadi* (Spiritualistic) 53
Audio-Visual Materials 228
Authentic Concern 179
Autonomy Stage 18
Ayurveda 59

Bakshi, N. 338
Benami Transaction (Prohibition) Act 254
Benarjee, N.B. 338
Blower, Whistle 252
Bodher Sadhana 188
Brahmacarya 7
British Rule 183
Broad Areas of the Value System 19
Broadmindedness 195
Buddhist 4, 93
Bull, Norman J. 70
Bureaucracy 319, 330
Business Today Group 278

Casual Employment 308
Casualisation Process 306
Celibacy (*Brahmacharya*) 28
Central Institute of Educational Technology 228
Centralization of Decision-Making 318
Centres of Continuing Education 72
Chaitanya Maha Prabhu 343
Chakroborthy, S.K. 286
Chambers of Commerce 253
Character Building 70, 120
Chief Vigilance Commissioner 252
Chinese Culture 22
Chi-Square 349, 354

Christ, Jesus 135
Citizen-Friendly Administration 313
Clark, Donald 179
Classroom Performance 173
Cleanliness 29
Closed Value System 92
Code of Conduct for Professional Managers 269
Cognitive
 Development 16, 157
 Dissonance 180
Colleges of Teacher Education 160, 163
Collins, James 359
Communalism 316
Compassion and Fellow-Feeling 189
Conformists 149
Confucian Moral Tradition 22
Consciousness 45
Consequential Test 251
Constitution of India 122
Consumer Behaviour Theory 86
Consumerism 52
Contentment (Santosh) 29
Contextuality 289
Corrupt Public Servants (Forfeiture of Property Act) 254
Corruption 273, 320
Cosmopolitan Criteria 12
Cricket Match Fixing 241
Criminality 320
Cultural Diffusion 151
Cultural
 Heterogeneity 199
 Value 152
Curriculum Development Committee 228

D.A.V. College 229
Decision Making Process 109
Declaration on Global Ethics 42, 49
Degradation of Teachers 192
Democratic Governance 322
Democratic Morality 332
Demographical Problems 8
Department of Culture 227
Deshmukh, C.D. 337
Development of
 Human Goodness 39
 Peace 40
Dewey, John 123, 156
*Dharma* 23, 55
Dhokalia, R.P., 201 205
Dignity of the Human Person 369
Dignity to Life 120
District Institutes of Education and Training 160, 163
Divisiveness 117
Doctrine of
 Anekanta 27
 Nishkamkarma 17
Dogmatism 38
Dowsett, Norman C. 182
Drucker, Peter F. 276–77, 300
Dube, S.C. 199
Durent, W. 153

Eastern Spirituality 49
Ecological
 Balance 71
 Problems 13
Economic
 Barbarism 39
 Equality 9
 Inequalities 199
 Values 152
Education Commission 223
Educational Research 175
Effective Leadership and Control 355
Egalitarianism 67
 Values of 332
Egoism 38
E-Governance 320
Einstein 66
Election Commission 321
Elizabeth Anderson 205
Emotional Education 193
Employment Elasticity 306
Enduring Values Test 251
English-Medium Schools 58
Entrepreneurial Values 260
Equity State 327
Erikson, Erik 177, 181
Erosion of Spiritual and Moral Values 259
Ethical
 Decision 110

  Principles 244, 368
  Value 44, 48, 101
Ethics Litmus Test 89
Evidence Act 83
Existentialism 164
Extension Services 72
Extra-Ethical Activities 280

Fairness Test 251
Feynman, Richard 45
FICCI 253
Finance Committees 206
Fodder Scam 241
Forbearance 218
Foreign Colonizers 53
Fraternity 67
Freedom from Bondage 216
Freedom of Information Bill 322
Free-Sex 8
Fulton Committee Report 335
Functioning of the University System 217
Fundamental Consensus 31
Fundamental Rights 336
Fundamental Values of Multicultural Society 215

Gandhi, Indira 118, 127, 156
Gandhi, Mahatma 119, 120, 273
  Non-Movements of 94
  Value System of 30
GATT Agreement 262
Gautama Buddha 143
Gender Empowerment Measures (GEMs) 91
Gender Values 101
Geometry 59
George, Lloyd 328
Ghosh, Aurobindo 63
Global Ethics 49
Global Unity 40
Globalisation 31, 88, 101
Goal Evaluation 213
Goals of University Education 218
Governance and Values 317
Grameen Bank of Bangladesh 311
Gun Powder, Discovery of 38
Guna Theory 22
Guru Nanak 273

Harmonious Character 56
Harmony
  Balancing of 27, 54
  Concept of 27
Hawala Scam 241
Hedonism 165
Higher Education and Values 128
Hindus to Christianity – Conversion 58
Hitopdesa 71
Hodgkinson, Christopher 326
Holistic (Intuitive) Values 23, 26
Human Capital School 97
Human Consciousness 21
Human Development Report 91
Human Relations 213
Human Sentiments 19
Human Spirituality 21
Humanism 197
Hutchins, Robert M. 341

Ice-Age 116
ILO 310–11
Indian Civil Service 328
Individual Development 355
Individualism 37, 149–50
Industrial Restructuring 307
Industrialization 151, 183
Inequality 101
Innovators 150
In-Service Education 73, 79, 180
INSET Programmes 80
Institutes of Advance Study in Education 160, 163
Insurgency Struggles 94
Intellectual Distinction 175
Intellectual Values 151, 260
Interiorization 15
International Business 294
International Commission on Education 203
Internationalised Managerial Value System 298
Interpersonal Values 260
Intra Professional Relationships 106

IRDP 311
Islamic Invasion 57

Jajmani Idea 57
Jnanapeeth Awardee 66

Kabir 273
Kanal, S.P. 45
Kartaveeryarjuna 146
Karuna (Compassion) 4
Kautilya's Arthashastra 57, 89
Kayotsarga 158
Keynes, J.M. 87
Kinder Garden Stage 68
Kluckholn, C. 292
Kohlberg 17, 246
Kothari Commission 170, 203, 274
Krishnamurthy, J. 63
Kshirsagar, S. 332

Laing, R.D. 43
Learning of Values 16
Learning Subjects for the University 219
Liberalisation 31, 210
Liberating Force 32
Liberty 67
Lokayukta 340
Lokpal 340
Lord Mahavira 167

*Mahabharata* 57, 135
Mahavira 4
Mahila Trust 311
Management Concept, Japanese 265
Management of Social and Economic Resources 320
Managerial
  Effectiveness 264
  Ethos 271
  Excellence 259, 261
  Value System 294
Mariner's Compass 38
Market-Driven Development 94
Marshall, Alfred 96
Marx, Karl 62, 96
Marxist Identification 25
Maslow, Abraham 181, 205
Material
  Progress 59
  Success 149
Materialism 149
Materialistic View 36
Measurement of Attitudes 180
Meditation (*Tapa*) 29, 187
Militant Struggles of the Naxalites 94
Mill, J.S. 96, 165
Mind-Brain System 46
Mini Transformation 95
Missionary Schools 58
Modernity, Advent of 183
Modernization 59, 154, 210
Mohammed Galib Hussain 345
Moral Development, Post-Conventional Stage of 246
Moral Judgement 16
Moral Principles 368
Moral Values 151
Muslim Invasion 53
Mutual Aggression, Rivalries for 39

Narayana Murthy, N.R. 345
National Commission for Value Education 231
National Commission on Teachers 58
National Council for Teachers Education 224, 228
National Council of Educational Research and Training 66, 186, 230, 232
National Institute for Educational Research 127
National Policy on Education 125, 160, 203, 222
National Renewal Fund 307
Nationalism 88
Nationalism, Japanese Believe in 89
Navodaya Vidyalaya Samithi 232
Nehru, Jawaharlal 81, 209, 272
New Economic Policy 262
New Education Policy 143
New World Trade Order 262
NGO 249–50, 311
Nichael Milken Scandal 278
Niti Sataka 71

Non-Aryan 93
Non-Dual Frame of Reference 49
Non-Orthodox Stream 93
Non-Possession 8
Non-Stealing (*Asteya*) 28
 Precept of 6
 Principle of 6
Non-Violence 6–8, 28, 127
 Culture of 31
Normative Economics 101
Noronha, R.P. 337
Nose-Grinding Activity 176

Obscurantism 222
OPEC Nations 98
Orthodox Societies 92, 140

Panandikar, Pai 332
Patanjali 187
 Yoga System of 346
Pay Commission 339
Performance Auditing 212
Phenomenology 164
Piaget 16
Pick-Pocketing 138
Planning Board 206
Planning Commission 232, 306
Polish Peasant 196
Political Advertising, Harms of 366
Political Transformations 95
Political Values 20
Porrass, Jeremy 359
Positive Attitude 355
Positivism 164
Post-Modern Debate 166
Poverty Alleviation 95
Powers of Discrimination 138
Practical Humanitarianism 38
Practical-Experimental-University-Laboratory 219
Pragmatism 289
Pre-Adolescent 69
Preksha Meditation 158
Pre-Moral Stage 18
Pre-Service Courses 79
Prevention of Evil Habits 71
Non-Violence, Principle of 4, 6
Principles in Clinical Dental Ethics 107
Privatization 31
Professional Morality 67
Pro-Service Education 180
Pro-Service Training 175
Psychodynamics of the Mind-Brain System 42
Psycho-Ontological Qualities 134
Public Administration, Values in 319
Public Disclosure Act 252
Public Service Commissions 198
Punjab Public Service Commission Appointment Scam 241
Puttappa, K.V. 66
Pye, Lucian 332

Quality of Care 104
Quantum of Work Done 351
Queen Amritamati 144

Radhakrishnan Commission Report 143
Radhakrishnan, S. 53, 195, 273
Ramakrishna Institute of Moral and Spiritual Education 236
Ramakrishna Mission Vidyalaya 228
Ranganathananda 45, 345
Rational (Pragmatic) Values 23
Rational Attitude 60
Rational Expectation 101
Rational Holistic (Rational-Scientific) Values 25–26
Rational Spiritual (Secularised Religious) Values 26
Rational Thinking 86
Rationalism 26
Real Life-Situations 70
Realization of the Spirit 37
Redistributive State 327
Regional Curriculum Development 228
Relational Values of Managers 299
Relevant Information Test 251
Religious
 Fanaticism 222
 Value 152
Reorientation of Educational Programmes 209
Report on Personnel Administration 335

Restructuring Teacher Education 222
Revolution of Values 132
Riggsian Terminology 331
Right to Information 322, 360
Ritualists 150
Rogers, Carl 181
Rural Bureaucratic Behaviour 321
Russell, Bertrand 39

Saatvika Persons 346
Santiniketan 188
Satyagraha 6
Satyavidya 59
Scientific Temperament 59, 67
Scientific/Secular Values 19
Secularism 36–37
Self-Actualization 346
Self-Awareness 29, 32
Self-Culture 119
Self-Development 124
Self-Discipline 154–55
Self-Education 64
    Tools of 80
Self-Employment Women's Organisation 311
Self-Enhancement 188
Self-Evaluation Techniques 74–75
Self-Identity 178
Self-Improvement 119
Self-Knowledge 46
Self-Mortification 166
Self-Understanding, Methods of 186
Service Education and Training 162
Set-Initiated Curative Measures for Individual 249
Sex-Lust 153
Shah Commission 337
Shekhar, R.C. 286
Shills, A. 292
Shri Prakash Committee 274
Significance of Relational Values 300–01
Significance of Values on Training and Development 300
Simple, Moral, Accountable, Responsive, Transparent (SMART) 312
Singh, R.P. 19
Slavery 272
Smith, Adam 88, 96
Social Character, Distortion of 200
Social Complexity 199
Social Contractualism 165
Social Emotional Values 260
Social Respectability 39
Social Value 44
Social Welfare 86, 101
Socio-Economic Environment 208, 214
Socio-Political Organisational 12
Socrates 63, 135, 166
Spiritual (Other Worldly) Values 25
Spiritual Evolution 47
Spiritual Guru 249
Spiritual Resurgence 218
Spiritual Values 20, 44, 151
Spiritualistic (*Atmavadi*) 27
Spirituality 3
Sri Aurobindo 27, 54, 60–62, 187
Sri Prakash Committee 274
Sri Ramakrishna's 54
Sri Sathya Sai Institute of Higher Learning 231
Statesman Awards for Rural Reporting 182
Statutes and Ordinances of the University 207
Stock Market Scam 241
Students Indiscipline 200
Suares, Carlo 29
Sugar Scam 241
*Svabhavavadi* (Materialistic) 53
*Svadharma* 61–62
Synthetic-Humanistic-Spiritualistic Attitude 61

T.A. Pai Institute of Management 286
Tagore, Rabindranath 61–62, 185, 187
Tahelka Scam 241
Taittiriya Upanisad 135
TBINSET 73, 80
Teacher Education Programme 223
Teacher Effectiveness 162
Teacher Training University 229
Teaching-Learning Process 176, 181
Technique of Syadvad 27
Technological Changes 304
Telecommunication Scam 241
Terminal Values 19

Third World Governments 275
Tolerance 218
Tradition and Modernity 59
Transparency International 241
Trends in Value Education 118, 130
Typologies of Values 167

UN Human Development Report 319
Understanding of Development 90
Understanding Values 30
UNESCO 127, 170
Union Ministry of Human Resource Development 232
United Nations Development Programme (UNDP) 91–92
Universal Belief Systems 19
Universal Consciousness 49
Universal Man 62
Universality Test 251
University Court 206
University Education 144–45
University Grants Commission 229, 232
University Teachers Problems 149
University Vision 214
Upgradation of Knowledge 209
Urbanization 151
Urea Scam 241
USA 91, 291
UTI Scam 241
Utilitarianism 165

Value Added Theory 143
Value Affirmation 21
Value Analysis 210
Value Based
  Classification of Business Execu-tives 292
  Education 204, 206
  Ethical Behaviour 241, 247
  Management 202, 284
  Management, Principles for 207
  Politics 317
  Processes 206
Value Clarification Approach 15
Value Climate 142
Value Control 210
Value Crisis 121, 133
Value Education 41, 100, 122, 157, 194, 215, 286
  Contents of 35
  Practical Aspect of 236
Value Engineering 210
Value Formation 15
Value Judgement 16, 86
Value Kits for Teaching 229
Value Management 210–11, 214
  Humane Governance Through 320
  Techniques of 211
Value of 'Brahmacarya' 8
Value of Business Managers 260
Value Realization 4, 133–34
Value System 25, 28
  in Business Management 287
  Nature of 48
Varna System 93
Varnasrama Dharma 60
Vedantic Spiritualism 285
Vedic Brahminical Values 93
Viable Methodologies 184
Vigilance Commission 250
Vision of Truth 12
Vivekananda 58, 61–62, 127, 143, 187
Vohra Committee Report 321
Voluntary Retirement Scheme (VRS) 308

Waking State of Mind 45
Weberian Rational Model 329
Welfare Economics 87
Westernization 59
White-Collar Job 59
Wilkins, Maurice H. 42
Woodroffe, Sir John 58
World Bank 97, 99
Worshipping the God 29

Yashodhara Charita 144
Yoga 187
Yogic Asanas 158
Yugadharma 61

Zoroastrianism Scripture 65
Zone of
  Counsellors 254
  Crime 245
  Ethical Dilemmas 245
  Normative Behaviour 246
  Post-Conventional Conscience 246